IES OF
ESSMENT
...iversity Library

To look forward, it is necessary to look back and learn. History is more than just facts about the past; it is a narrative told from a particular perspective. A proverb from Africa, "Until lions have their own historians, tales of the hunt shall always glorify the hunter," captures this best. Most of the scholarship about psychological assessment comes from very specific nationalities and cultures, which does not truly reflect the diversity and breadth of histories pertaining to the field. Covering 50 countries, this collection gives voice to those that have previously been under represented and sometimes marginalized. This book not only describes important moments in psychological assessment from around the globe, but also equips readers with the tools to map the future of psychological assessment across nations. It advocates for a more globally inclusive science of assessment that holds promise for enhancing creativity and innovation in the field.

SUMAYA LAHER is Professor of Psychology and the Head of Department of Psychology at the University of the Witwatersrand, South Africa. She serves as founding Editor of the *African Journal of Psychological Assessment*, and Associate Editor of the *South African Journal of Psychology* and editorial board member for the *International Journal of Testing*.

EDUCATIONAL AND PSYCHOLOGICAL TESTING IN A GLOBAL CONTEXT

EDITOR

Neal Schmitt, *Michigan State University*

The Educational and Psychological Testing in a Global Context series features advanced theory, research, and practice in the areas of international testing and assessment in psychology, education, counseling, organizational behavior, human resource management and all related disciplines. It aims to explore, in great depth, the national and cultural idiosyncrasies of test use and how they affect the psychometric quality of assessments and the decisions made on the basis of measures. Our hope is to contribute to the quality of measurement and to facilitate the work of professionals who must use practices or measures with which they may be unfamiliar or adapt familiar measures to a local context.

Published titles:

Dragoş Iliescu, *Adapting Tests in Linguistic and Cultural Contexts*, 2017

John C. Scott, Dave Bartram and Douglas H. Reynolds (eds.), *International Applications of Web-Based Testing: Challenges and Opportunities*, 2017

William H. Schmidt et al., *Schooling Across the Globe: What We Have Learned from 60 Years of Mathematics and Science International Assessments*, 2018

Maria Elena Oliveri and Cathy Wendler, *Higher Education Admission Practices: An International Perspective*, 2020

David Wells, *Assessing Measurement Invariance for Applied Researchers*, 2021

Sumaya Laher, *International Histories of Psychological Assessment*, 2022

INTERNATIONAL HISTORIES OF PSYCHOLOGICAL ASSESSMENT

EDITED BY

SUMAYA LAHER

University of the Witwatersrand

CAMBRIDGE
UNIVERSITY PRESS

University Printing House, Cambridge CB2 8BS, United Kingdom

One Liberty Plaza, 20th Floor, New York, NY 10006, USA

477 Williamstown Road, Port Melbourne, VIC 3207, Australia

314–321, 3rd Floor, Plot 3, Splendor Forum, Jasola District Centre, New Delhi – 110025, India

103 Penang Road, #05–06/07, Visioncrest Commercial, Singapore 238467

Cambridge University Press is part of the University of Cambridge.

It furthers the University's mission by disseminating knowledge in the pursuit of education, learning, and research at the highest international levels of excellence.

www.cambridge.org
Information on this title: www.cambridge.org/9781108485005
DOI: 10.1017/9781108755078

© Cambridge University Press 2022

First published 2022

A catalogue record for this publication is available from the British Library.

Library of Congress Cataloging-in-Publication Data
NAMES: Laher, Sumaya, editor.
TITLE: International histories of psychological assessment / edited by Sumaya Laher, University of the Witwatersrand.
DESCRIPTION: Cambridge, United Kingdom ; New York, NY : Cambridge University Press, 2021. | SERIES: Educational and psychological testing in a global context | Includes bibliographical references and index.
IDENTIFIERS: LCCN 2021029079 (print) | LCCN 2021029080 (ebook) | ISBN 9781108485005 (hardback) | ISBN 9781108755078 (epub)
SUBJECTS: LCSH: Psychodiagnostics. | Psychometrics–Cross-cultural studies. | BISAC: PSYCHOLOGY / Personality
CLASSIFICATION: LCC RC469 .I54 2021 (print) | LCC RC469 (ebook) | DDC 616.89/075–dc23
LC record available at https://lccn.loc.gov/2021029079
LC ebook record available at https://lccn.loc.gov/2021029080

ISBN 978-1-108-48500-5 Hardback
ISBN 978-1-108-71910-0 Paperback

Contents

v

Tables

Contributors

Editor

Sumaya Laher, Department of Psychology, University of the
Witwatersrand, South Africa

Section Editors

Africa: Sumaya Laher, Department of Psychology, University of the
Witwatersrand, South Africa

Americas: Kurt F. Geisinger, Buros Center for Testing, University of
Nebraska–Lincoln, United States of America

Arab-Levant: Pia A. Zeinoun, Psychological Assessment Center and
Psychiatry Department, American University of Beirut, Lebanon

Asia: Yiqun Gan, School of Psychological and Cognitive Sciences, Peking
University, China

Europe: Dragoş Iliescu, Psychology Department, University of Bucharest,
Romania

Oceania: Peter Macqueen, Griffith University & Compass Consulting,
Australia

Contributing Authors

Adote Anum
University of Ghana, Ghana

Suresh Arumugam
Defence Institute of Psychological Research, India

Dave Bartram
University of Kent, United Kingdom

Janet F. Carlson
University of Nebraska–Lincoln, United States of America

Regis Chireshe
Zimbabwe Council for Higher Education, Zimbabwe

Jan Corstjens
Ghent University, Belgium

Karma El Hassan
American University of Beirut, Lebanon

Melem L. Fangwi
University of Buea, Cameroon

Yiqun Gan
School of Psychological and Cognitive Sciences, Peking University, China

Kurt F. Geisinger
University of Nebraska–Lincoln, United States of America

Fei Huang
Central China Normal University, China

Dragoş Iliescu
University of Bucharest, Romania

Andrei Ion
University of Bucharest, Romania

Sumaya Laher
University of the Witwatersrand, South Africa

Michael Canute Lambert
University of North Carolina, United States of America

Jonas W. B. Lang
Ghent University, Belgium

Ivan M. H. Lee
Singapore Psychological Society, Singapore

José Livia
Federico Villarreal National University, Peru

Peter Macqueen
Griffith University & Compass Consulting, Australia

Krunoslav Matešić
University of Zagreb, Croatia

Asangha N. Muki
University of South Carolina, United States of America

Sverre L. Nielsen
University of Bergen, Norway

Kayi Ntinda
University of Botswana, Botswana

John O'Gorman
Griffith University, Australia

Seth Oppong
University of Botswana

Kwaku Oppong Asante
University of Ghana, Ghana

Jaime Pereña Brand
National Distance Education University, Spain

Janelle N. Robinson
John Jay College of Criminal Justice, United States of America

Asoke Kumar Saha
Jagannath University, Bangladesh

Marion K. Schulmeyer
Universidad Privada de Santa Cruz de la Sierra, Bolivia

Robert Serpell
University of Zambia and University of the Witwatersrand, South Africa

Ross St George
Massey University, Australia

Suresh Sundaram
Rajiv Gandhi National Institute of Youth Development, India

Fatemeh S. Tarighat
University of Tabriz, Iran

Therese M. S. Tchombe
University of Buea, Cameroon

Eugenia V. Vinet
Universidad de La Frontera, Chile

Solange Muglia Wechsler
Pontifical Catholic University of Campinas, Brazil

Lambert S. Wirdze
University of Buea, Cameroon

Ndzetar E. Wirmum
University of Buea, Cameroon

Mostafa Zarean
University of Tabriz, Iran

Pia A. Zeinoun
American University of Beirut, Lebanon

Mingjie Zhou
Central China Normal University

N. Sheereen Zulkefly
University of Putra Malaysia

Series Editor's Foreword

In the last several decades, globalization has influenced the lives of all people. Business and education, as well as scientific disciplines, have all experienced the need to understand and work with people whose political, social, cultural, and linguistic origins are often very different. This has been true of psychology, education, and other social science disciplines. These developments also have important implications for the development and use of measures of human individual differences. Business and educational institutions using tests and institutions interested in certifying or accrediting test users have all experienced the challenges and opportunities generated by increased globalization.

Recognizing the need for the education of psychometricians and users of tests, Jean Cardinet spearheaded the formation of the International Test Commission (ITC) in the late 1960s and early 1970s. It was formally established in 1978. Current members include scholars and institutions from most of the European and North American countries as well as some countries in the Middle and Far East, Africa, and South America.

The major goals of the ITC are the exchange of information among members and furthering cooperation on problems related to the construction, distribution, and use of psychological measures and diagnostic tools. To accomplish these goals, the ITC has initiated a number of educational activities. The ITC has also developed and published guidelines on quality control in scoring; test analysis and reporting of test scores; adapting tests for use in various linguistic and cultural contexts; test use in general; and computer-based and internet-delivered testing; as well as a test taker's guide to technology-based testing. The ITC publishes the peer-reviewed journal *International Journal of Testing*, which seeks to publish papers of interest to a cross-disciplinary international audience in the area of testing and measurement. In 2016, the ITC led the effort to produce the *International Handbook of Testing and Assessment*.

In 2013, the ITC proposed to Cambridge University Press a series of books on issues related to the development and use of tests. The goal of the series is to advance theory, research, and practice in the areas of international testing and assessment in psychology, education, counseling, organizational behavior, human resource management, and related disciplines. This series seeks to explore topics in more depth than was possible in the *Handbook* or in any single volume. The series will explore the national and cultural idiosyncrasies of test use and how they affect the psychometric quality of assessments and the decisions made on the basis of those measures. As such, we hope the series will contribute to the quality of measurement, but that it will also facilitate the work of professionals who must use practices or measures with which they may be unfamiliar or adapt familiar measures to a local context. We have asked both ITC members and other scholars familiar with a topic, and who are also familiar with the global situation related to various topics, to be the editors and contributors to individual volumes.

We are especially pleased to see this series develop and are confident that the books in the series will contribute to the effectiveness of testing and assessment throughout the world. Since the initiation of the series, we have hoped to produce a volume on the history of testing in various parts of the world. With the publication of this volume, we have realized that goal. It was a monumental effort and, thanks to the perseverance and vision of Sumaya Laher, I believe it is a really significant contribution to our understanding of how testing technology and practice have developed in various parts of the world. Most history "buffs" credit the Chinese civil service exams begun around 200 BCE as the first high-stakes examinations. These tests were discontinued in 1905 just as the rest of the world was beginning to develop and use standardized measures of human characteristics. This book details the efforts of scientists in various countries to develop tests and assessments during the twentieth century and the beginning of the twenty-first century. There are certainly commonalities across these efforts, but there have also been many unique approaches to testing embedded in local cultures as well. This book should be helpful to those scientists and practitioners who seek to understand differences in testing across countries and cultures, to adapt their practices to those cultures when appropriate and desired, and to benefit from the new ideas extant in various parts of our planet. It is our hope that this volume will contribute to the efforts of the ITC to promote good testing practices worldwide.

We hope to publish a book at least biennially and encourage scholars who might be interested in developing a book proposal that addresses assessment in an international context to talk with the series editor, the ITC president, or other ITC leaders.

Neal Schmitt

CHAPTER 1

Histories of Psychological Assessment
An Introduction

Sumaya Laher, Yiqun Gan, Kurt F. Geisinger, Dragoș Iliescu,
Peter Macqueen, and Pia A. Zeinoun

1.1 Introduction

History is described as a factual account of the past.[1] Yet it is clear that history is more than just facts, it is a narrative told from a particular point of view. This is evident from Hermann Ebbinghaus, when he wrote that "Psychology *has a long past, yet its real* history *is short.*" Ebbinghaus's quote reflects a status quo in psychology at present where mainstream psychology adopts the view that it developed primarily in the nineteenth century in the laboratories of Wilhelm Wundt. The field is attributed to having originated primarily in the Global North.

A famous proverb from Africa, *Until lions have their own historians, tales of the hunt shall always glorify the hunter*, captures this best in that the current historical narratives pertaining to psychology and psychological assessment are written by individuals from very specific nationalities and cultures and do not adequately capture the diversity and breadth present in the myriad of histories relating to psychological assessment. While the need to capture the histories of psychological assessment in one volume is evident and necessary, this becomes even more important in the context of globalization. Hence the assumption of the universal applicability of psychological assessment techniques characteristic of mainstream psychology must be debunked. This book, by virtue of focusing on the international histories of psychological assessment, highlights contributions from other spaces – nations in particular – that have traditionally been marginalized.

---

[1] We would like to acknowledge Prof. James Kagaari of Kyambogo University, Uganda and Prof. Grace Kibanja of Makerere University, Uganda for contributing the information in this introduction on assessment in East Africa. Also, Prof. Emeritus John O'Gorman of Griffith University, Australia and Dr. Ross St. George of Massey University, New Zealand for their assistance in preparing the introduction on Oceania.

Internationally there is evidence to suggest that assessment has always been used. By way of example, in ancient China, emperors would test workers to determine who had potential to serve as scholars and advisers using the imperial examination system (see Chapter 13). In Persia now Iran, Al-Razi (Rhazes) conducted the first assessments for mental health and wrote *Al-Hawi* in the tenth century (see Chapter 11). Around the same time there was work in philosophy and physiology from the University of Sankore in Timbuktu showing that the early precursors of scientific psychology were likely to have been studied at the university (see Chapter 4). These are just a few examples from the many that are presented in this book on the international histories of assessment.

1.2   Overview of the Book

This book brings together chapters focusing on the history of psychological assessment in particular countries across regions from all the continents. Chapters are not just narrative accounts of the development of psychological assessment in a particular country or region. Authors were asked to situate the chapters somewhere between narrative and historiography. Hence the chapters assume a more critical stance in reporting the history of psychological assessment that recognizes that history is never fact and always represents the subjective position of the author. Authors have drawn from existing sources and research but have simultaneously explored the social positionings of such research. We hope that this allows for a richer and perhaps even more interesting account of the international history of psychological assessment.

It is not a coincidence that the book begins with the chapters from Africa. Empirical evidence identifies Africa as the cradle of humankind. The earliest evidence of human existence has been found in the fossils located in East and South Africa. Further, there is evidence from East Africa as well as North Africa that speaks to sophisticated civilizations and kingdoms existing in Africa at least 200,000 years ago. However, the earliest known recorded histories from the continent are from ancient Egypt and later from Nubia, the Sahel, the Maghreb, and the Horn of Africa. Hence the African chapters are presented first in this volume followed by those from the Arab Levant, Europe, Asia, Oceania, and concluding with chapters from the Americas. We will now briefly discuss the contributions of each region.

1.3   Africa

There are 54 countries in Africa as we know it today. However, at a point pre the desertification of the Sahara there were at least 10,000 kingdoms on the continent. The continent has always been rich in terms of mineral and agricultural resources and had a number of wealthy dynasties that were core to trading between Europe and Asia over the years. Following the desertification of the Sahara, countries in North Africa became more intertwined with the Middle East and southern Europe. Countries to the south of the Sahara are commonly referred to as sub-Saharan Africa and this constitutes majority of the continent (46 of the 54 countries; O'Collins & Burns, 2007; Wilburn, 2008). Hence the African region focuses on the areas of sub-Saharan Africa while North Africa is discussed under the Arab Levant region.

According to the 2019 revision of the World Population Prospects, the population of sub-Saharan Africa was 1,038,627,178 in 2018. Primarily due to the Bantu migrations, which originated around West Central Africa possibly Cameroon through to Central and East Africa and into Southern Africa, the region shares a linguistic commonality but consists of a diverse mix of cultures and traditions across the regions and countries. While there is evidence of sophisticated kingdoms in sub-Saharan African over the years, we were unable to locate evidence of formal assessment processes akin to psychological assessment as it may have been practiced in ancient China.

Across the regions, the modern history of psychological assessment as we know it mirrors that of Europe and was primarily introduced in some way with the colonization of countries. Except for the Ethiopians, Haitians, and Liberians, Africans and people of African descent were living under some form of European colonial domination by the end of the nineteenth century. The principal powers involved in this modern day colonization of Africa were Britain, France, the Netherlands, Germany, Portugal, and Italy. However, by 1939 it was evident that France had colonized much of the Horn or west of Africa while Britain had colonized the east and southern parts (O'Collins & Burns, 2007; Nsamenang, 2007). Central Africa was split between France and Britain as indicated in Chapter 3.

Chapter 2 provides a history of assessment in South Africa, Botswana, Zimbabwe, and Zambia. All four countries evidence a history of colonialism that has impacted in different ways on the history of psychological assessment in these countries. The chapter gives a critical examination of the development of psychological assessment during and after colonialism arguing for a need to have assessments that are more relevant to the context. With the exception of Zambia, the three other countries rely on etic tests or local adaptations of etic tests. Zambia has been particularly innovative in developing emic tests using indigenous knowledge, for example, the Panga Munthu Test – a version of the Draw-a-Person test that requires children to make human figures out of clay (a material more familiar to local children). The innovations used across the countries in the region to ensure unbiased testing in multicultural populations are discussed.

Chapter 3 provides a brief history of psychological assessment in Central Africa, identifying types of psychological tests in use in Central Africa as well as the issues and problems that arise when making use of such psychological tests at both national and local levels. It is evident from the chapter that psychological assessments are largely used in educational settings and have yet to become more widely used across other areas. The chapter provides interesting suggestions for new possibilities for educational improvements in global and local contexts with regards to assessment technologies and practices, inclusion, educational psychology, and educational policy.

Oppong, Oppong Asante, and Anum describe the West African history of psychological assessment focusing on developments in Ghana, Nigeria, Liberia and Sierra Leone in Chapter 4. The chapter identifies Ghana as among the dominant players for psychological assessment in the region arguing that the origins of psychology in Ghana may be traced as far back as the establishment of the University of Sankore, Timbuktu (989 CE) through to the establishment of Basel Seminary in 1898, and more recently to the Department of Psychology at the University of Ghana. Nigeria's history of assessment may be traced back to the Islamic scholars in the northern part of Nigeria in the early fourteenth century. Modern day testing in Nigeria commenced in 1955 when organized and formal guidance and counseling services became available. To date Nigeria boasts the most psychology departments in the region. The chapter attributes the slow development of psychology and assessment in Liberia and Sierra Leone to the protracted civil war and the 2014 Ebola outbreak, which strongly impacted the mental health of both countries. The authors call for further development of assessment across the region identifying a need for indigenous measures and test adaptations as well as a need to share and disseminate assessment knowledge across the region.

The eastern region of Africa is not represented in the book but has also had interesting developments with regards to psychological assessment since the countries obtained independence from colonialism. Kagaari and Kibanja (personal communication) have argued that psychological assessment in East Africa is still in its infancy stages. In this ethnically diverse region, the practice of psychological assessment has been limited by cultural, political, and economic factors. The clash between ethical principles and cultural beliefs in the region limits the practice of assessment along with the politicization of psychological assessment leading to stigmatization of practice. Further, the lack of indigenous psychological assessment tools that are culturally sensitive is a core concern. There is also a huge variance in the region with regards to the pace at which psychological assessment is growing and being utilized across countries varying in political and cultural landscape. For instance, due to past wars and internal conflicts within Uganda, Rwanda, and South Sudan, psychological assessment is more broadly inclined to clinical assessment than other forms of assessment. Tanzania, South Sudan, and Uganda have over 50 ethnic groups, yet Rwanda and Burundi have a maximum of four. This implies that influence of language diversity during practice is more significant in the former countries than in the latter ones. Also, lack of vibrant legal entities to regulate practice amidst cultural diversity, psychology illiteracy, and political quagmire within countries has influenced the acceptance and use of psychological testing within the region.

It is evident that, except for a few countries across Africa, psychological assessment as it is practiced today is still in its infancy. In a number of countries war, internal conflicts, and economic and health challenges have ensured a very slow development of the field. In many countries in Africa psychological assessment is used on a broad scale in educational settings with a much lesser focus on assessment in other areas like clinical or organizational settings. This is in part due to the lack of trained individuals as well as the scarcity of accessible tests. International tests are too expensive and there are very few facilities that can assist with translating or adapting international tests or developing local tests. Despite these challenges it is evident from the chapters that assessments are being used and there is value to using them.

1.4 The Arab Regions

In line with the spirit of this book, encapsulated by the earlier quote from Ebbinghaus, psychology and psychological assessment in the Arab region has a very long past, but only a short history.

The Arab region, sometimes referred to as the "Arab world" is a loose term used to describe groups of countries spread across the African and Asian continents. The "inclusion" criterion of what constitutes an Arab country is often drawn along geopolitical, social, linguistic, and economic lines. Usually, the term "Arab countries" subsume the 22 countries that belong to the Arab League, with about 420 million people spread across countries that share Arabic as one of their official languages, but that are incredibly diverse. Narrower groupings have been more meaningful in terms of describing countries that are more homogeneous culturally, linguistically, and geopolitically, even though this does not necessarily include all countries in the Arab League. For this book, we group countries into those of the Arab Levant (Lebanon, Syria, Jordan, and Occupied Palestine), the Arab Gulf (Kingdom of Saudi Arabia, United Arab Emirates [UAE], Bahrain, Kuwait, Oman, Qatar, and sometimes Iraq is included), and North Africa (Algeria, Morocco, Tunisia, Libya, Egypt, and Sudan).

Psychology in the Arab region has its roots in early Arab scholars who wrote about the *nafs* (akin to the Greek *psyche*) – a concept that maps onto the self today. Under the umbrella of religion, philosophy, and medicine, the writings of Avicenna (Ibn Sina), Ibn Tufail, and many others were translated to Greek and Roman and transferred to Europe during the Dark Ages (Ahmed, 1992; Soueif & Ahmed, 2001).

The beginning of modern psychology in most Arab countries began around the 1940s when Arab psychologists, especially from Egypt and Lebanon, attempted to model the French and the Anglo-American psychological approaches in research, teaching, and practice. Egypt is often credited as leading the way in psychology, followed by Lebanon and Saudi Arabia – countries that are key players in their respective regions of North Africa, the Levant, and the Gulf. These countries were among the first to establish psychology departments, outpatient and inpatient mental health services, legislations regarding mental health parity, and professional regulation (Baker, 2012). They were also among the highest producers of academic research (Okasha & Karam, 1998), with more recent data still showing that almost 80% of research output across the Arab region between 2009 and 2019 was produced by Egypt, Saudi Arabia, Lebanon, Tunisia, and the UAE (Zeinoun et al., 2020). When it comes to psychological assessment in particular Egyptian psychologists and psychiatrists have translated tests from English to Arabic – initially aptitude and projective tests, and later tests of personality, psychopathology and self/social constructs (Baker, 2012).

To better understand the modern history of psychological assessment in the region, it is important to situate this history into a broader context. The field of psychology in the Arab region has witnessed many ebbs and flows in its overall development, which led to differential evolution across various countries throughout the last two centuries. First, the colonial history and recent wars in the region have left a diverse influence of British, French, and American schools of thoughts, which have led to different psychological traditions across countries. For example, in the 1980s many Lebanese psychologists used projective techniques owing to their educational and training background in French universities that were primarily psycho-dynamically oriented. In contrast, the British influence in Egypt saw many psychologists in the early 1900s gaining their education in the United Kingdom, and returning to Egypt to establish labs and engage in the then popular psychometric research and test standardization (Baker, 2012).

These influences meant that early work on psychological testing relied on importing psychological tests from the United Kingdom, United States, and France, and only recently has there been more effort to produce indigenous tests (e.g., Abdel-Khalek, 1998; Zeinoun, 2017). Arab countries are strongly influenced by the work of Islamic scholars in the ninth century who wrote about psychological concepts. In the past few decades, psychologists have attempted to blend Islamic concepts and spirituality into their understanding, measurement, and treatment of psychological phenomena (Keshavarzi et al., 2020).

Further, the various wars and political instabilities in the region were consequential to the field. Many countries with weakened states had poor infrastructure needed to fund, educate, and elevate the science of psychology, while at the same time many of these countries needed applied psychology to alleviate trauma and psychological distress. As a result, psychological services in countries like Lebanon and Palestine rely heavily on local and international non-governmental organizations (NGOs and INGOs). These organizations have contributed to improving psychometric tools in their research and services, but these are often from an etic perspective.

Nations in the region have also varied in the rate of their development. While countries like Egypt have shown a steady development of psychology across the years, some Gulf countries like the UAE, which was founded in 1971, show an exponential development and on various levels have surpassed other countries in terms of psychological services. For example, in the decades between 1966 and 1985, Egypt produced an average of 2.4 psychology-related articles per year, while the UAE did not produce any. However, two decades later, the UAE had surpassed Egypt in the rate of annual publications (Jaalouk et al., 2012).

Finally, despite the many linguistic and cultural commonalities across the Arab countries, they are also ornate with diversity across and within countries. Some argue that the terms "Arabic language" or "Arab culture" are not as homogeneous as they imply and that psychology needs to cater to both the commonalities between the countries as well as to local particularisms using a glocal approach (Daouk-Öyry et al., 2016). Case in point is the Arabic language that exists in multiple variations (e.g., Classical Arabic, Modern Standard Arabic), in addition to spoken vernaculars that can be almost unintelligible across distant countries. When adapting tests from a source language to "Arabic," there is an assumption that Arabic is one static, homogeneous language, and that an Arabic scale in Morocco would function just as well in Jordan – an assumption that is debated by many authors (see Daouk-Öyry et al., 2016).

This book includes one chapter from this region (Chapter 5), namely the Arab Levant (Lebanon, Syria, Palestine, Jordan). The Levant has long been at the center of cultural, social, and geopolitical changes in the region, which have been central in shaping the development of psychological practice and science in the region. The region has been at the cross section of multiple foreign influences (French, British, US, Arab), all of which have impacted academia. This resulted not only in multiple ideologies and schools of psychological thought that remain until today but also in a trilingual academic system that further deepens the disconnect among psychologists and test-takers in the region. Additionally, the Levant's experience of occupation, trauma, diaspora, and political instability has led to an increased need and interest in mental health services and displaced populations, and hence the measurement of related constructs. More recently, with increased funding for research on such populations, non-Arab researchers have gained a renewed interest in the region, which has led the way to increased collaborative efforts in the development of psychometric tools. The chapter begins with a general overview of psychological assessment in the region, followed by discussion on how test development and clinical testing have been impacted by the political and social fabric of the region. The chapter places a particular focus on the challenges and opportunities that lay ahead, in terms of research and practice in clinical, educational, and industrial/organizational practice.

1.5   Europe

The European section comprises five chapters that among them cover the geographical distribution of Europe almost completely. The chapters focus on: The United Kingdom, Northern Europe (Scandinavia), Western Europe (mainly Germany and France), Spain and Portugal, and Eastern Europe. These chapters offer a lucid account of the evolution of testing during the twentieth century and its current state, for the most prolific contributor to the invention and development of modern psychological testing: Europe. The other prolific contributor, North America (the United States and Canada) is much more homogenous in terms of language, culture, and consistency of trends across both time and geographical areas in comparison to Europe.

Given that Europe is so diverse, with so many cultural and linguistic differences, and has during the time span covered experienced two world wars, the accounts given in this section about the evolution of tests and testing in its different areas are equally diverse. These accounts show the large English influence in Western and Northern Europe, and the equally strong German influence in Central, Eastern, and Southeastern Europe, during the early years. They demonstrate clearly how dominant philosophical stances and trends in general science have shaped the zeitgeist and with it the emergence of testing. They also show how the emergence of testing and its diverse and promising incipient evolution in Eastern Europe was curtailed after World War II by the USSR. Finally, the chapters illustrate in what radical manners ideology can impact testing – especially if it is sanctioned by a totalitarian state, as was the case for Eastern Europe.

Chapter 9, focusing on the United Kingdom, tracks the developments of assessment originating with Darwin and Galton to the development of occupational testing (together with such innovations as Assessment Centers) and finally to the advent of Britain as an important producer of internationally used tests. The historical description of eugenics in the chapter shows that ideology has pushed psychology in general and testing especially in morally reprehensible directions not only in totalitarian regimes but also in democratic countries. At the same time, methodological advances that were made at that time have influenced psychology and assessment as well as other fields. The correlation coefficient and linear regression among others are creations of that time. The United Kingdom has also pioneered the use of psychological testing in work and organizational psychology, with such innovations as the development of Assessment Centers during World War II. During these years the

United Kingdom created its reputation as a "net contributor" to the worldwide repertoire of assessment instruments, with British companies such as SHL being in the forefront of occupational testing worldwide.

Western Europe is as dominant a player in the development of modern testing as the United Kingdom. In Chapter 7 Lang and Corstens discuss the contributions of Germany and France starting with Wundt's psychological laboratory in Leipzig and Binet's work on intelligence testing. The scholars that were trained there (among others, James McKeen Cattell and Charles Spearman) progressed to influence assessment in the United Kingdom and the United States. Other Germany laboratories like those run by Ebbinghaus, Münsterberg, Lipmann, and Stern spearheaded several breakthroughs in the first half of the twentieth century. The chapter also discusses assessment in the Netherlands, mainly focused on the work of de Groot and his interests in educational psychology. This important and influential work culminated with the founding of CITO (Centraal Instituut voor Toetsontwikkeling, National Institute for Educational Measurement) in 1968. Dutch psychometrics has since remained at the forefront and has been highly influential in the domain of measurement methodology and statistical methods over the past 30 years.

In Chapter 6 Nielsen and Bartram discuss the history of assessment in the Nordic countries focusing on Denmark, Norway, and Sweden. Scandinavian psychology was influenced from the very early days by all three centers that were at the forefront of modern-day psychological assessment: the Anglo-American, the French, and the German models. Contacts with France were strong with the Binet scale, for example, being adopted so quickly in Norway that it was used in Bergen in the same year as it was published in Paris, 1908. Links with Germany were also great, focused mainly on the work of William Stern. The US connection was focused on the work of Hugo Münster and has remained strong to date, especially in Norway. Psychology exploded in the Nordic countries, particularly in Norway after World War II due to the need to rebuild infrastructure and to effectively select and counsel individuals toward careers. Hence organizational psychology – and the heavy assessment-oriented stream that is part of it – has grown in Scandinavia into a separate field. Scandinavian countries today are closely linked to the European Federation of Psychologists' Associations (EFPA) and the International Test Commission (ITC) and are fully participant in the European assessment community.

The two Iberic countries, Spain and Portugal, share much in the history of psychology and of psychological assessment as discussed in Chapter 8.

The first laboratory of psychology was founded in 1914 by Achúcarro and Lafora and was inspired by the work of Binet in Paris. Later, through the work of Mira y López and Germain, modern psychological testing began to flourish in Spain. The post-World War II period was marked by a slow but steady development of tests as well as test adaptations of acknowledged international psychological measures. Since then, there has been a consistent development of indigenous measures. Much of this evolution is connected to the work of the Spanish test publisher, TEA Ediciones, that provided Spanish test authors the opportunity to publish and distribute their work. One of the particularities of Iberic psychological assessment is that the educational background of many of the scholars that contributed and still contribute to the field is diverse – philosophy, education, medicine, psychiatry, and psychology – allowing for inspiration from many philosophical schools of thought to inspire Spanish psychometrics.

Chapter 10 on Eastern Europe focuses primarily on Romania and the former Yugoslavian space, but also reflects on evolutions in Poland, Czechoslovakia, and Hungary and the very fast development of psychological testing in all these countries. Eastern Europe was struggling at the beginning of the twentieth century with challenges quite different from those of the rest of Europe. The dismantling of the Austro-Hungarian Empire at the beginning of this century led to the creation of the sovereign states of Yugoslavia, Czechoslovakia, Hungary, Greater Poland, and modern-day Ukraine (Galicia). The slow ascent of psychological science, heavily influenced by Germany and in part by France, was allowed to take place for only two decades before it was cut off abruptly by the communist regime imposed by Soviet Russia. In all these countries, psychology in general and assessment especially were for 50 years under the complete influence of communist ideology, with testing surviving mainly in industrial settings and connected to school psychology and career counseling. After the fall of the Iron Curtain, all these countries very quickly connected back to the international developments in psychometrics, and have developed to the current stage in which they have a modest indigenous production of tests but continue to rely heavily on adapted measures.

A few themes are pervasive throughout the entire European section. First, the region must be acknowledged for the wealth of ideas that helped shape the emergence of modern psychological assessment. Second, the power of ideology in influencing science must be acknowledged – misguided or otherwise. Tests have always been part of practical applications in society and were therefore quickly and heavily influenced by the dominant ideas of an age and a cultural space whether it be the eugenics movement in the United Kingdom, the ideology of the fascist regime in Germany, or the ideology of the communist totalitarian states in Russia and Russian-dominated Eastern Europe. Third, the conditions of scientific freedom that allowed for assessment to flourish and quickly recover lost ground are promising and suggest a resiliency to the field that will ensure its longevity. Fourth, we draw attention to the accelerated process of internationalization that can be observed in all European countries beginning with the 1990s. This is observable not only in the countries of Eastern Europe, that had to cover much lost ground in those years, but also in Spain, the Nordic countries, Germany, and so on. This is likely part of the accelerated process of internationalization that is visible in the assessment world internationally, but Europe is a very active participant in this process.

1.6   Asia

The Asian segment of the book is comprehensive in its coverage exploring the historical developments linked to psychological assessment in East, Southeast, and Central Asia. The Asian section comprises four chapters, which among them cover the 18 countries in Asia. There are both similarities and differences among the reviewed Asian regions and countries. Due to similar historical, social, and cultural factors, modern psychology as a scientific field is still underdeveloped in Asia compared with developed countries. Although Asian psychology has a unique past, compared with developed countries, the use of psychological assessment is relatively limited. These countries also share a culture of collectivism, where people depend on each other and accept traditional norms (Kim et al., 2001).

With the economic development of Asian countries, society has paid increasing attention to psychological tests and its application fields have been expanding. In the beginning, Asian countries depended heavily on importing Western psychological assessments (Cheung, 2004). However, due to cultural differences between Asia and the West, it was necessary to develop culturally sensitive and appropriate tools with adequate psychometric characteristics. Asian countries have made great efforts concerning the cross-cultural effectiveness of psychological assessment, committed to the cultural adaptation and development of instruments, and have achieved considerable progress (Byrne et al., 2009). Colleges and universities began offering psychometric courses and actively trained professionals. There has been a significant increase in the number of researchers and practitioners working on the development and use of psychological tests. Researchers in these countries have introduced traditional and modern psychometric theories from Western countries, such as classical test theory, generalizability theory, and item response theory, among others. They have adopted the strategy of gradually developing and compiling local tests from revising Western instruments, which has achieved satisfactory results during past decades.

With the development of psychological measurement teaching and research, psychological tests have been applied in many practical departments such as pilot selection, athlete selection, mental illness diagnosis, and children with intellectual disability. The consciousness of science serving society has been strengthened and the application in practice fields has been expanded. The upsurge of compiling and using scales in psychology has risen in recent decades. In major Asian countries psychological tests have gradually permeated into the medical, educational, and business organizations, as well as into personnel and judicial departments, and many other application fields, generating a significant impact on society. Education is the earliest and most important application field of psychometrics. Applications in other industries, such as human resources and psychological counseling, have rapidly developed and become increasingly prosperous. In public service and private sector organizations, psychological assessment and testing are growing as essential tools used in their work, which can be attributed to the high level of professionalism of trained psychologists contributing as scientists and practitioners (Cheung et al., 2003).

Chapter 11 is the first of four chapters in this book on the Asian region. It reviews the contribution to the expansion of psychological assessment in Central Asia. The authors examine the historical trends in psychological assessment in Central Asia making reference to early forms of assessment in Persia before discussing the contemporary assessment of psychological assessment starting in the 1950s and 1960s in countries like Iran and Pakistan. The chapter provides a good contextualization of the conflict in the region, which has impacted on the assessment and progression of psychology and psychological assessment. Chapter 12 introduces the history of psychological assessment in Southern Asia. The chapter narrates the history of psychological assessment both in ancient and modern times highlighting how assessment is done in various settings in India, Sri Lanka, Bangladesh, Nepal, and Bhutan and the authors point out that a number of industrial organizations and government bodies are increasingly using tests imported from the West. Further that psychological assessments are receiving greater acceptance in these communities.

Chapter 13 examines the development of psychological assessment in East Asia, including China, Japan, and South Korea. The ancient history of assessment in the region is reviewed, followed by modern developments starting in 1915. The chapter identifies the last 30 years as a period of intense developments in psychological assessments in the region and provides discussion on the generation of indigenous (emic) tests with a focus on the Cross-Cultural Personality Assessment Inventory (CPAI). The chapter calls for a more systematic and standardized approach to test development as well as the need to promote the practice and application of assessment. Chapter 14 highlights the developmental status of psychological testing in Malaysia and Singapore and describe the observable growth in the number of researchers and research studies in the field of psychology typically on the usage of psychological testing in recent years signifying the growth of the profession in these countries.

Psychologists in Asia still face many challenges in testing and assessment. These challenges include localization of psychological measurement, lack of qualified professionals, translation problems, high cost of standardized testing, big data protection, and copyright infringement in test use, among others. Looking ahead, Asia will actively develop new opportunities for test developers, users, and psychological researchers to create a prosperous future.

1.7   Oceania

The written history of psychological testing and assessment in Oceania begins in the late nineteenth century with the establishment of universities in Australia and Aotearoa/New Zealand that followed British models and taught philosophy and mental science within the British empiricist tradition (Buchanan, 2012; Haig & Marie, 2012). The findings of British and later American psychometricians were accepted as immediately applicable to the people of Australia and New Zealand because, as English-speaking Anglo-Celts, they shared a culture with the people of North America and Britain. To well into the twentieth century there was little if any innovation by Australian or New Zealand researchers or practitioners who reworked ideas rather than, for the most part, developed new ones based in the experience of their own countries. Although there were significant, if not large, indigenous populations in both countries, the study of cultural differences came quite late and was pursued at the edges rather than in the mainstream of research. Psychology and psychometrics were assumed to be universal in their reach and the ready assumption was that what worked or found to be so in the United Kingdom or the United States (the Anglosphere) would apply in Australia and New Zealand. The assumption was in time extended uncritically to the peoples of Papua New Guinea and Fiji and to the Pacific islands without deliberate recognition of cultural difference (St. George, 1987; Stewart, 2012).

A need for selection and classification, first in education and then in public administration, powered the application of testing, as decisions were made about how best to use scarce resources. Vocational and educational guidance were practiced in Australia and New Zealand in the interests of nation building and subsequently in island nations within their spheres of influence. In both countries, the Carnegie Foundation, an American philanthropic organization, provided an important stimulus to educational and psychological testing through grants for the establishment of Councils for Educational Research, and these still play a role in test development and distribution. World War II had a major impact on testing in Australia, although much less so in New Zealand, with psychological testing being used effectively in raising an army for service overseas. The successes stimulated the commercial use of testing. Mining and aviation widely promoted in the Pacific islands were industries that required skilled labor and testing found a ready market.

The hey-days of testing in Oceania were the 1960s into the 1970s, after which interest began to wane. There were a number of reasons for this. Paradigm shifts within the parent disciplines of psychology and education led to focus on the self and eschewed comparisons with others. The rise of clinical psychology saw testing isolated to neuropsychological interventions. Although the anti-testing movement was less marked in Australasia that in the United States the concerns were certainly felt. Changes in public administration that favored decentralized services made large scale testing redundant, although recent advances in technology have fostered emerging methodologies such as game-based assessment. Online testing, however, is regarded as a mixed blessing, with the increased use of "blind testing" in work settings. On the positive side, interest in cultural differences increased and with it an interest in how well-being was understood from world views beyond the Anglosphere. This was coupled with a growing assertion by indigenous people in all islands of Oceania of their rights and a recognition among the dominant culture of the wrongs done in the past as a result of colonization and the social planning that followed in its wake.

The history of testing and assessment in Chapter 5 on Oceania is thus a history of testing and assessment in Australia, in New Zealand, and in the islands that in the twentieth century fell into the sphere of influence of those two countries. The chapter seeks to briefly sketch the development of testing and assessment, its successes, and its limitations.

1.8   The Americas

History as told in the Caribbean and the Americas indicates that groups and individuals such as the Vikings, Christopher Columbus, Ferdinand Magellan, and Amerigo Vespucci "discovered" these new continents and the islands surrounding them. In truth, indigenous peoples filled these lands for centuries if not millennia before their "discovery" (Locks et al., 2013). The stories of colonization whether in the United States, Canada, the Caribbean, or any of the countries in Central and South America are traumatic for the peoples who had first claims to the lands of their ancestors. Settlers often enslaved, murdered, and drove residents off their lands, forcing them to settle in other locations. In many cases even today the original inhabitants of the Americas continue to face many varieties of discrimination.

The early settlers mostly came from Europe: Spain, Italy, Portugal, Great Britain, Holland, and France. They spoke many languages. They came voluntarily, unlike many of those who came involuntarily from Africa and to a lesser extent China. Immigrants from Spain, Portugal, and Italy dominated Latin America. The Caribbean Islands may represent the greatest diversity of immigrants with the various islands even today speaking Dutch, English, French, and Spanish alongside the indigenous languages depending upon the countries from which the settlers came (Locks et al., 2013).

As these societies matured, these peoples often stressed education as a path to advance personally and societally. This path was, of course, most true of the wealthier countries: The United States, Canada, Mexico, Brazil, and Argentina among others. Public education – new in the late 1800s in Europe – began in many of the countries of North, Central, and South America. Citizens founded universities in the first half of the twentieth century with numerous universities beginning to teach psychology, which often emerged from departments of Philosophy or Education. Testing was one of the foundational components of psychology and testing impacted society in a powerful manner. The beginnings of testing in North America came from the Europeans: Wundt, Galton, and Binet. A variety of North American and Latin American scholars did their graduate work in Europe and brought their knowledge and intellectual traditions when they came back to the Americas. Many of these scholars translated tests and attempted to validate and use them in the New World (Cohen & Swerdlik, 2018).

The chapter on the history of testing in North America suggests that although separate countries, the development of both Canadian and US psychology and psychological testing is highly unified. For many years the American Psychological Association (APA) was also the primary association for Canada's psychologists, and many Canadians have taken the lead in some subareas of psychology, such as the history of psychology. The United States is now perhaps the center of test development around the world, as many US tests are adapted and translated for other countries and cultures. In Chapter 18 Carlson and Geisinger trace how early US psychologists both trained in and borrowed primarily from German, French, and British psychological researchers.

Chapter 16 tracks the varying patterns of test development across Brazil, Bolivia, Chile, and Peru. One approach that those authors found was that most countries followed one of two paths: either an emphasis upon assessments based upon psychoanalytic theory or adapting measures developed in other countries, mostly from English. The history as described in Chapter 16 show how test adaptations have matured from straight word-for-word translations to culturally and linguistically appropriate assessments well suited for use in each of the four countries.

The Caribbean countries are small and highly varied in language and cultural influences as indicated in Chapter 17. Their unique psychology has been a blend of indigenous psychology with the influences of the settlers who came from the "old world." These countries are in the early stages of test development and are doing so while seeking a Caribbean-centric theory of psychology.

Hence the origin of modern testing in the Americas has its roots in Europe. The United States has established itself as the largest publisher and distributor of tests worldwide with many countries including those across the Americas using these tests as they are or adapting them. What must be noted is the progress in South America and the Caribbean with developing their own country- and culture-specific measures. This diversity of tools can only serve to benefit the discipline by expanding on dominant Western approaches to assessment.

1.9   Conclusion

Internationally there is evidence to suggest that assessment has always been used. The chapters in the book present evidence from early cultures in the eighth and tenth centuries where practices that would be classified today as assessment were used. However, as indicated across the chapters, the modern-day history of assessment across the regions is traced back to Wundt's experimental psychology in Germany, Darwin and his cousin Galton in the United Kingdom, and Catell in the United States. Whether in early dynasties or more recently, assessment has always been used to meet a need in society to distinguish a group of people from another for a particular reason. In ancient societies it was used to determine who gets which jobs (particularly for more senior positions), who gets educated, how to treat people with ailments, and so on. In the latter part of the nineteenth century and early in the twentieth century, it was no different. Psychometrics and psychological assessment were closely tied to eugenics – the dominant paradigm of thought in the West at the time.

As explained in Chapter 9, Galton set out to demonstrate that intelligence was heritable and people not of European lineage were genetically predisposed to be less intelligent. While eugenics was discredited particularly post the world wars, the work that started during this time with measurement and methods in psychometrics has persisted. Psychometrics and psychological assessment offered much to science since the turn of the twentieth century and the work on psychological assessments has continued in earnest primarily in Europe and North America as well as in the French, Dutch, German, and British colonies as evident in the chapters in this book. While this has been beneficial in many ways, it has also been very limiting in that most of what we know and practice today is rooted within this paradigm. Across the chapters from South America through to Asia, the Levant, and Africa, it is evident that this one-size-fits-all approach was not ideal, more so as these countries face significant challenges ranging from political instability and war through to economic and health challenges. Oftentimes these countries experience challenges with regards to literacy and language proficiency as well as access to resources. Most importantly the epistemological and ontological positions adopted for etic instruments did not always fit other contexts outside of America and Europe. As indicated in the chapters, the twenty-first century has seen the voice of cross-cultural psychology becoming more vocal, raising these challenges and discussing ways to mitigate this within the current assessment landscape. This has resulted in other ways of knowledge and practice with regards to psychological assessment that brings a much-needed plurality to the field.

Given this, it is our hope that this collection of histories will not only serve to describe and store important moments across spaces for the world history of psychological assessment but that it will also provide a lens with which to map the future of psychological assessment across nations. In an era of globalization, glocal approaches to psychological assessment are increasingly necessary. This volume has the potential to open channels for communication and research collaboration across the Global North and Global South, ultimately leading to development and progress of the field of psychological assessment that is more inclusive.

REFERENCES

Abdel-Khalek, A. M. (1998). The development and validation of the Arabic Obsessive Compulsive Scale. *European Journal of Psychological Assessment,* *14*(2), 146–158.

Ahmed, R. A. (1992). Psychology in the Arab countries. In U. P. Gielen, L. L. Adler, & N. A. Milgram (eds.), *Psychology in international perspective: 50 years of the International Council of Psychologists* (pp. 127–150). Amsterdam: Swets & Zeitlinger.

Baker, D. B. (2012). *The Oxford handbook of the history of psychology: Global perspectives.* Oxford: Oxford University Press.

Byrne, B. M., Oakland, T., Leong, F. T. L., van de Vijver, F. J. R., Hambleton, R. K., Cheung, F. M., & Bartram, D. (2009). A critical analysis of cross-cultural research and testing practices: Implications for improved education and training in psychology. *Training and Education in Professional Psychology,* *3*(2), 94–105.

Buchanan, R. (2012). "Australia." In D. B. Baker (ed.), *Oxford handbook of the history of psychology* (pp. 18–33). Oxford: Oxford University Press.

Cheung, F. M. (2004). Use of Western and indigenously developed personality tests in Asia. *Applied Psychology, 53*(2), 173–191.

Cheung, F. M., Leong, F. T., & Ben-Porath, Y. S. (2003). Psychological assessment in Asia: introduction to the special section. *Psychological Assessment, 15* (3), 243–247.

Cohen, R. J., Swerdlik, M. E., & Sturman, E. D. (2018). *Psychological testing and assessment: An introduction to tests and measurement* (9th ed.). New York: McGraw-Hill.

Daouk-Öyry, L., Zeinoaun, P., Choueiri, L., & Van de Vijver, F. (2016). Integrating global and local perspectives in psycholexical studies: A GloCal approach. *Journal of Research in Personality, 62,* 19–28. https://doi:dx.doi .org/10.1016/j.jrp.2016.02.008

Haig, B. D., & Marie, D. (2012). New Zealand. In D. B. Baker (ed.), *The Oxford handbook of the history of psychology: Global perspectives* (pp. 1–32). Oxford: Oxford University Press.

Jaalouk, D., Okasha, A., Salamoun, M. M., & Karam, E. G. (2012). Mental health research in the Arab world. *Social Psychiatry and Psychiatric Epidemiology, 47*(11), 1727–1731.

Keshavarzi, H., Khan, F., Ali, B., & Awaad, R. (2020). *Applying Islamic principles to clinical mental health care: Introducing traditional Islamically integrated psychotherapy.* London: Routledge.

Kim, B. S., Yang, P. H., Atkinson, D. R., Wolfe, M. M., & Hong, S. (2001). Cultural value similarities and differences among Asian American ethnic groups. *Cultural Diversity and Ethnic Minority Psychology, 7*(4), 343.

Locks, C., Mergel, S., Roseman, P., Spike, T. & Lasseter, M. (2013). History in the making: A history of the people of the United States of America to 1877. *History Open Textbooks.* 1, https://oer.galileo.usg.edu/history-textbooks/1

O'Collins, R. & Burns, J. M. (2007). *A history of sub-Saharan Africa.* Cambridge: Cambridge University Press.

Okasha, A., & Karam, E. (1998). Mental health services and research in the Arab world. *Acta Psychiatrica Scandinavica, 98*(5), 406–413.

Soueif, M. I., & Ahmed, R. A. 2001. Psychology in the Arab world: Past, present, and future. *International Journal of Group Tensions, 30*(3), 211–240.

Stewart, L. 2012. Commentary on cultural diversity across the Pacific: The dominance of western theory, models, research and practice in psychology. *Journal of Pacific Rim Psychology, 6*(1), 27–31.

St. George, R. 1987. Psychology in New Zealand: A history and commentary. In G. H. Blowers & A. M. Turtle (eds.), *Psychology moving East: The status of Western psychology in Asia and Oceania* (pp. 325–344). Sydney: Sydney University Press.

The United Nations Department of Economic and Social Affairs. World Population Prospects 2019. https://population.un.org/wpp/

Wilbirn, K. 2008. Review of the book "A History of Sub-Saharan Africa," *African Studies Review, 51*(2), 164–165.

Zeinoun, P., Akl, E. A., Maalouf, F. T., & Meho, L. I. 2020. The Arab region's contribution to global mental health research (2009–2018): A bibliometric analysis. *Frontiers in Psychiatry, 11*, 182.

Zeinoun, P., Daouk-Öyry, L., Choueiri, L., & Van de Vijver, F. 2017. A mixed-methods study of personality conceptions in the Levant: Jordan, Lebanon, Syria, and the West Bank. *Journal of Personality and Social Psychology, 113*(3), 453–465.

CHAPTER 2

Psychological Assessment in Southern Africa

Sumaya Laher, Robert Serpell, Kayi Ntinda, and Regis Chireshe

2.1 Introduction

As with any part of the globe, defining the boundaries of a region is fluid depending on whether one ascribes to geographical, geopolitical, or other indicators. For the purposes of this chapter we have defined the Southern African region as consisting of the following countries: South Africa, Botswana, Namibia, Angola, Lesotho, Eswatini, Mozambique, Malawi, Zimbabwe, and Zambia. These countries have different indigenous language dialects but all the dialects with the exception of the Khoi dialects in South Africa have roots in the Bantu or Nguni languages.[1] With the exception of Angola and Mozambique, which have a history of Portuguese colonization, and Namibia, which was briefly colonized by Germany, all the other countries share a history of British colonialism. English is therefore also a dominant language in these societies but not the home language of the majority of the populations (Thompson, 2001).

The history of Southern Africa as a geographical subregion over the past century has been characterized by extensive intercontinental and intracontinental human migration, political turbulence, and rapid social and economic change. The demographic profile of the African region is overwhelmingly young, with about two fifths of its population in the 0–14 age bracket and nearly one fifth (19%) in the 15–24 age bracket. The proportion of the population of sub-Saharan Africa residing in rural areas declined from 85% in 1960 to 59% in 2019, with marked variations across nations: 33% in South Africa, 30% in Botswana, 68% in Zimbabwe, and 56% in Zambia (World Bank, 2019). Prior to the mining industries launched by European immigrants in the late nineteenth century, the vast majority of people were engaged in rural subsistence

---

[1] South Africa also has an indigenous language, Afrikaans, which developed as an amalgamation of the multitude of languages spoken in the country following the arrival of different groups of people during the various colonization stages.

(agricultural and pastoral) economies. Industrialization fostered urbanization and economic inequalities, dominated by European immigrants and powered by modern science and technology (Feinstein, 2005).

The region has been home to various African kingdoms (Mapungubwe, Great Zimbabwe, and Mutapa among others) prior to colonization that traded with other nations across Africa as well as with the Arab, Asian, and European traders. While these kingdoms were sophisticated with social and leadership structures, there appears to be no evidence to indicate forms of assessment being used in these societies. Psychological assessment in the way it is currently understood emerged in the region in the nineteenth century at around the same time as in the West. Given the intimate relationship between these countries and Britain, it is not surprising when historical works reflecting on psychology in these regions describe its development as akin to that in the West. A rapid search of both academic and gray literature indicates that while psychology as a discipline is active in all the countries, it has been most active in South Africa, Botswana, Zimbabwe, and Zambia. This is particularly true for psychological assessment. Hence this chapter focuses more on these countries.

In the chapter to follow a brief critical history of psychological assessment is provided for South Africa, Botswana, Zimbabwe, and Zambia. This is followed by some reflection on future developments for assessment in the region.

2.2   Psychological Assessment in South Africa

South Africa is the southernmost country in Africa and is home to over 58 million people. The nation differs from others in sub-Saharan Africa in its demographic profile that includes a substantial minority (about 20%) of citizens with European or Asian ethnic heritage (Statistics South Africa, 2020). Prior to colonization the country was home to indigenous Khoi and San tribes in the West and Bantu and Nguni tribes in the East. The arrival of Portuguese (thirteenth century) and Dutch (seventeenth century) sailors followed by the British (eighteenth century) and the introduction of slaves from the East has ensured that the South African population is diverse in language and culture (Giliomee & Mbenga, 2007). The country has 11 official languages but English is the primary language of trade and teaching. The history of psychology as we know it in South Africa follows the international trajectory as South Africa prior to the advent of apartheid (1948–1994) had strong European ties emanating from its position as first a Dutch and then a British colony. The developments in psychology were strongly associated with the politics of the time with Claassen (1997) arguing that developments in psychological assessment in South Africa were intertwined with the country's political, economic, and social history.

Psychological assessment in South Africa was initially evident from 1915 when intelligence tests were used with black[2] children to demonstrate the inferiority of the native intellect (see Laher & Cockcroft, 2014). In the late 1930s and 1940s psychological assessment moved to the organizational field. It became evident that there was a class of poor unskilled and semi-skilled white workers who needed employment. To address this, vocational education and assessment was introduced at schools and unskilled white workers of rural origin were assessed for job competencies. Military personnel were also screened. There was also a need to assess individuals in the fast growing mining industry. Hence the National Institute of Personnel Research (NIPR) was formed and focused on the African worker's aptitude for industrial work (Laher & Cockcroft, 2014).

The NIPR was innovative in developing procedures such as the silent-film technique that used mime to convey test instructions and in introducing adaptability testing to the country. These were attempts at fairer and more equitable means of testing for black workers with higher potential (Seedat & Mackenzie, 2008, 81). While the development of new assessment techniques and the adaptation of international tests such as the Wechsler–Bellevue Intelligence Scales were praiseworthy achievements for the NIPR, there remained an underlying racist agenda, as evidenced in Biesheuvel's writing about the African worker:

> On the other hand, he (the African) makes up for his lack of speed by his liking of repetitive action, ... Africans may, therefore, prove far more tolerant to the monotony of machine operative work than Europeans. By transforming such works into mildly satisfying experiences, they may retain efficiency where the European becomes restless and frustrated (Biesheuvel 1952, cited in Seedat & Mackenzie, 2008).

In a similar vein to the NIPR, the Institute for Psychological and Edumetric Research (IPER) was developed at the same time to oversee measures for education and clinical practice (Foxcroft & Davies, 2008). These early developments of assessment in education and industry

---

[2] Under apartheid the SA population was classified as follows: black (indigenous African inhabitants), Indian (people of Indo-Pak ancestry), white (those of European ancestry), and colored (those of mixed race ancestry often including Malays). Asians could be classified as colored or white. This categorization persists today even though there are calls for this to change.

legitimized the discipline of psychology as a useful field within South Africa, but they served an egregious end (whether intentionally or unintentionally), in laying the foundations and justification for separate development based on race known as apartheid (Seedat & Mackenzie, 2008).

This racist agenda was prevalent throughout the 1950s, 1960s, and 1970s in South Africa where psychology and psychological assessment in particular were used to justify the government's apartheid policies. Tests of intellectual ability and personality were consistently normed on white standardization samples and used, without apology, with black individuals to demonstrate the inferiority of the black intellect (Bohmke & Tlali, 2008). Internationally sanctions were imposed against South Africa during this time and this had a direct impact on psychological assessment. Since there was no access to international tests, units like the NIPR and the IPER began developing tests locally like the High School Personality Questionnaire, the South African Personality Questionnaire, and the Jung Personality Questionnaire. However, these were still primarily developed for and normed on the white population, resulting in a bias against individuals with less exposure to Western culture. Also in the 1970s and early 1980s the researchers at the NIPR conducted pioneering work in the field of computerized testing developing the PSI Test and Siegmund systems, as well as research on the Austrian-based Vienna Testing System (Tredoux, 2013).

In the 1980s and 1990s, the NIPR and IPER were combined and formed part of the assessment division at the Human Sciences Research Council (HSRC). The growing realization of the unfairness of local measures inspired South African researchers to develop measures such as the General Scholastic Aptitude Test and the Ability, Processing of Information, and Learning Battery (APIL-B) – measures that could be applied to more than one cultural group (Foxcroft & Davies, 2008). The APIL-B was innovative in being the first learning potential battery developed for use with South Africans (Taylor, 2013). The Senior South African Scales-Revised (SSAIS-R), a test of intellectual ability in children, was standardized for English-speaking and Afrikaans-speaking white, colored, and Indian South African children but not for the majority of indigenous African children (Laher & Cockcroft, 2013a).

Following the release of Nelson Mandela from prison in 1990 and the advent of democracy in 1994, sanctions were lifted and imported tests were once again available in South Africa. However, tremendous distrust existed in the country about psychological assessments given the prominent role it played in legitimizing apartheid so much so that the trade unions campaigned for a ban of psychometric testing for employment purposes (see Laher & Cockcroft, 2014). Ultimately the Employment Equity Act 55 of 1998 (Section 8) was passed that states that psychological testing and assessment of an employee is prohibited unless the test or assessment is reliable, valid, unbiased, and can be applied fairly to all employees.

During the early 1990s and the transition period of the country, research in the field of psychological assessment in South Africa declined, but did not halt altogether. The Differential Aptitude Tests were developed and the Wechsler Adult Intelligence Scale, Third Edition (WAIS-III) was adapted and standardized by the HSRC for all South African race groups. The Learning Potential Computerised Adaptive Test (LPCAT), a computer-based test of learning potential that is still in use today, was developed. The LPCAT is based on the premise that individuals from disadvantaged backgrounds tend to underperform on traditional cognitive tests, and that nonverbal, figural items are less biased than verbal items. These advancements marked a change in values in the field of psychological assessment, as attempts were made to develop tests that were appropriate for and unbiased toward the diverse South African population.

From 2004 onwards, local research in psychological assessment appeared to gain some momentum. Several high-quality and useful textbooks have been published (e.g., Foxcroft & Roodt, 2013; Kaliski, 2006; Laher & Cockcroft, 2013b; Moerdyk, 2009), and local research on assessment is featuring more prominently in South African and international conferences and journals. The availability of tests imported from other typically Western countries led to the formation of private testing companies some of whom operate across Africa as premiere suppliers of tests for the continent.

Twenty years into democracy, there are signs of the development of a vibrant field. Psychologists specializing in assessment are actively contributing toward equity and redress by considering how to accommodate diversity in terms of language, educational background, and socioeconomic status when developing and conducting psychological tests. To date one of the only truly locally developed tests in the country is the South African Personality Inventory (SAPI). However, considerable work has been done on adapting tests. Hence the WAIS-IV and the 16PF5 have been adapted. Some work is proceeding on translating tests into indigenous African languages like Zulu and Xhosa. There is also research considering the use of assessments in context using more qualitative methods (see Bemath, 2020; Laher & Cockcroft, 2017).

The Psychometrics Committee at the Professional Board for Psychology at the Health Professions Council of South Africa (HPCSA) oversees the classification of tests as either psychological or not. The use of psychological tests is classified as a psychological act and may only be used by psychologists or psychometrists who are registered with the HPCSA as such and thereby licensed to practice in the country (Health Professions Act 1974). Recently the Assessment Standards South Africa (ASSA: see www.assa.co.za) was launched to assist with quality control of assessments in South Africa. ASSA aims to assist in implementing a robust, best-practice, and technology-enabled process that could be used to review people assessment instruments and tests. Further, based on the experience in other countries, the voluntary submission of assessment instruments for objective evaluation and reviews will raise the general standard and awareness of using quality tests (Jivan, Bischof & Laher, 2020).

2.3   Psychological Assessment in Botswana

Botswana is bordered by South Africa, Namibia, Zambia, and Zimbabwe. Botswana has a population of approximately 2.5 million people (UNDP, 2019). English and Setswana constitute its official languages. Botswana has a stable, market-driven economy and equally high economic growth rate. Plattner and Moagi-Gulubane (2010) assert that psychology is still at infancy stage of development in Botswana. There has generally been reluctance to seek psychological services by Batswana due to stigmatization of mental illness (Pheko et al., 2013). Research evidence also suggests that irrespective of the level of education and social status, Batswana continue to seek psychological help from traditional healers (Stockton et al., 2010).

Shortly after independence in 1966, initial counseling services were developed specifically to address the need for career guidance to support the demands of the rapidly growing economy. Beginning in the 1980s, this expanded into the development of more comprehensive guidance and counseling program in schools and subsequently a university program to train teachers to provide these services. However, the use of psychological assessment services in Botswana has a very brief history starting from the late 1980s. In the main, such services are available in the private rather than public schools (Mpofu et al., 2005). In Botswana psychological assessment services were initially provided in the private sector by psychologists because of the high number of people infected and affected by HIV and AIDS (UNAIDS, 2007). Subsequently, in the late 1990s, educational and psychometric assessment were also conducted in the private sector to measure academic achievement (i.e., mastery of knowledge or skills), diagnose learning problems and/or aptitudes, and select candidates for higher academic programs (Ntinda, 2012; Phelps, 2007).

The Botswana Association of Psychologists (BAPSY) was formed in 2005 and legalized as a society by the Department of Labour and Home Affairs in 2007. The Association strives to distribute knowledge and thought within the society to improve the credibility and acceptance of psychology as a field and profession that can contribute to solutions of the country's problems (Plattner & Moagi-Gulubane, 2010). The Botswana Health Professions Council (BHPC) has the authority to register psychologists but only clinical psychologists can be registered by this regulatory body. However, plans are underway to amend the BHPC act so as to register other specialist psychologists such as health and counseling in the country (Plattner & Moagi-Gulubane, 2010).

Clinical psychologists run private practice clinics where they conduct assessment and provide counseling services to children and adult clients in Botswana. Most of these psychologists have been trained in Western countries and therefore tests commonly used with children and youth tend to be those imported from the West. For example, Wechsler Intelligence Scales for Children, Draw A Person Test, Stanford-Binet Intelligence Scales, and the Wechsler Adult Intelligence Scales were identified among others by Oakland (2009) as most commonly used tests with children and youth in 64 identified developed and developing countries of which Botswana was one. There is still need for psychologists who specialize in assessment to assist in guidance and counseling services, establish intervention methods, evaluate progress, screen for special needs, diagnose disabling disorders, help place individuals in jobs or programs, and assist in determining whether individuals should be accredited, admitted/ employed, retained, or promoted in the Botswana public sector (Mpofu et al., 2015).

Significant shortages of trained manpower constrain the availability of such services in the public sector (Mpofu et al., 2005; Mpofu et al., 2009). This is despite the recognition by the Botswana government of the importance of psychological assessment to support student learning (Mpofu, Oakland et al., 2014; Ntinda, 2019). As in many other countries, psychological assessment services to support learners and particularly counseling in Botswana have developed alongside this process of transition from traditional agriculture to a more industrialized state. As this transition included social and cultural changes, the need for career, school, and mental health professionals emerged.

The University of Botswana introduced a psychology degree program in 2004 to overcome the problem of lack of trained personnel in the provision of these essential services, which was tailored to provide the graduates with skills that would enable them to work as professionals under supervision. This initiative was necessitated by the observation that many counseling services in the country were offered by persons with no specialized training in psychology (Pheko et al., 2013). However, students are still trained primarily on instruments imported from the West and there is little training on skills that will equip students to develop assessments locally.

In the 1990s the need for comprehensive counseling and guidance services was reflected in national government planning documents (Ministry of Education, 1994), and in this way became a part of the overall national development plan (Stockton et al., 2010). Further, learners with special and learning needs are referred to the Central Resource Center (CRC) for assessment but the Center experiences a backlog of cases due to huge number of referrals presently.

There have been remarkably few psychological assessment use studies in Botswana. Of those identified, they fall into three types: use of projective tests, regional comparative or benchmark studies, and policy support studies.

2.3.1   Projective Tests Study

Onyewadume (2005) carried out a study among adult Batswana, using Thematic Apperception Test (TAT) hero identification procedure. Findings of the study indicated that standard TAT cards from Western countries were not culturally appropriate tools for personality analysis for people in Botswana.

2.3.2   Regional Comparative or Benchmark Studies

Of studies that have examined the use of psychometric tests within a programmatic education services context, the study by Mpofu et al. (2005) is seminal. In a comparative study of psychometric test services in five sub-Saharan Africa countries, Mpofu et al. (2005) reported that psychometric test services were generally absent in the Botswana public school sector. The awareness of such services by the general population was low and human capital shortages high. Mpofu et al. (2005) noted that psychology assessment related services in school requiring test use, where they existed, were delivered in collaboration with the school guidance teacher, special education teacher, and social worker. However, the study focused primarily on views of teachers. It is likely that a different picture could have emerged if other stakeholders like psychologists, parents, and learners in education were surveyed for the areas in which they perceived psychometric tests to be helpful.

2.3.3   Policy Formulation and Support Studies

Mpofu et al. (2009) completed a study to advise education policy on the use of psychometric tests in school in the context of the Botswana guidance and counseling program. They concluded that psychometric tests would be best delivered by a multidisciplinary team to include educational psychologists, school counselors, remedial teachers, and speech therapists among others. They also recommended that tests for learner support were best provided as part of the school guidance and counseling program. The school guidance and counseling program is intended to prepare learners for life, citizenship, and the world of work and in the context of universal access to basic education, equity, and quality. It has been institutionalized in all schools in Botswana (Ministry of Education, 1996). The extent to which psychometric tests were used in the context of the school guidance and counseling program was unknown. Mpofu et al., (2015) conducted a study to develop and adapt culturally appropriate tests for use in schools to support student learning commissioned by the Botswana Department of Basic Education. They developed a Botswana Learner Appraisal System (BLAS) to support student learning and career advisement through the school guidance and counseling program.

The development of the BLAS (Mpofu et al., 2015) is a major advancement for assessment in Botswana. Psychological assessment and specifically psychometric tests used to guide learner support interventions in developing countries have typically been imported from Western countries, often with little regard for input from psychologists, educators, counselors, learners, and parents as co-partners in education. There is currently no generally acknowledged procedure for developing an inclusive, consumer-oriented framework for use of psychometric tests and test adaptation development in developing country education systems. The BLAS is used to assist learner support interventions informed by data on five major attributes important for school learning: cognitive ability, scholastic attainment, learning style preferences, social status, and career interest (for standard 1–12-year-old learners). The BLAS was reported to be useful among school personnel and students found the tests to be compatible or least disruptive of the school routine, suggesting that the tests could be similarly infused for use at other schools. The BLAS process is especially relevant to efforts that spur test development and use in developing countries.

At present educators and psychologists are actively contributing to the debate about the possibility of indigenizing psychology in African contexts through development and adaptation of culturally appropriate psychological tests to suit the Botswana context. The nation's education system is evolving to embrace the use of tests to support student learning (Ministry of Education's Revised National Policy on Education [RNPE], 1994; Ministry of Education, 1996; UNICEF/WorldBank, 2019). The education budget allowed for funding for projects on developing and adapting psychometric tests in Botswana school systems.

2.4   Psychological Assessment in Zimbabwe

Zimbabwe is a landlocked country in Southern Africa that borders Botswana, Mozambique, Namibia, South Africa, and Zambia. It has a population of about 14.8 million with 16 official languages, namely Shona, Ndebele, Chewa, Chibarwe, English, Ndau, Kalanga, Tonga, Sotho, Koisan, Shangani, Nambiya, Sign language, Tswana, Xhosa, and Venda. Currently the country is facing economic challenges with high rate of inflation of over 700%. Zimbabwe is a former British colony with a colonial legacy spanning 90 years, from 1890 to 1980.

The use of psychological assessments in Zimbabwe dates back to the colonial era. Psychological testing in Zimbabwe can be traced back to 1971 where the Rhodesian parliament legislated regulations for psychological practice through the Rhodesian Psychological Practices Act. The Act was administered by the Medical and Allied Health Professions Council and specified qualifications and procedures for registration and practice as a psychologist (Mpofu & Nyanungo, 1998). The Act was amended after 1980. In terms of the Psychological Practices Act, the practice of psychology can only be done by a licensed psychologist with training in clinical, educational, or occupational psychology. The practice of psychology includes measurement, assessment or testing of intellectual abilities, occupational or educational aptitudes, or interest by the administration of any psychological test. Psychologists in Zimbabwe like psychologists in other developing countries carry out psychological assessments to observe, describe, predict, and explain behaviors and mental process. The psychological assessments in all the fields are mainly for diagnoses, education selection, placement, and training decisions (Mpofu & Nyanungo, 1998).

Much like South Africa, during the colonial era, black people[3] had no access to professional psychology. Black children had no access to psychological assessments to identify their learning difficulties (Mpofu & Nyanungo, 1998). That meant that they could not receive relevant instruction based on performance on psychological tests. The services were thus segregatory. Psychological assessments were only extended to black children after Zimbabwe's independence from Britain in 1980 (Mpofu & Nyanungo, 1998). However, the psychologists who were offering the psychological assessments to the black students were white,[4] posing a challenge to the culturally and linguistically diverse population of Zimbabwe. One may question the ability of the psychologist to demonstrate cultural competence toward clients with diverse values, beliefs and feelings in this context. Also the country only had about 16 licensed and trainee white psychologists at independence in 1980 further limiting access to assessment services for majority of the country (Mpofu & Nyanungo, 1998). Further, in educational testing, it was observed that the psychological tests used discriminated against rural students and girls in favor of urban students and boys possibly because of the different exposure and socialization experienced by the two groups. The different exposure and socialization leads to different levels of test wiseness among urban students and boys and rural students and girls (Mpofu & Nyanungo, 1998). To overcome this situation, Zindi (1989) advocated for pupil assessment to be more relevant to the country's new dispensation that focuses on developing a more equitable Zimbabwe.

A further challenge in the Zimbabwean context at the time was the use of imported tests typically from Britain or America. Examples of such imported tests are: Wechsler Intelligence Scale for Children-Revised, British Ability Scales, Wechsler Preschool and Primary Scale of Intelligence, Kaufman Assessment Battery for children-Revised, Wide Range Achievement Test-Revised, Daniels and Diacks's Spelling Test, Good-enough Draw A Person Test, the Rothwell-Miller Interest Blank Test and Differential Aptitude Test. There were

---

[3] Similar to South Africa, a skin colour based racial classification for people with a mid to dark brown complexion of African descent in Zimbabwe.

[4] Similar to South Africa, a racial classification and skin colour specifier used mostly and exclusively for people of Western descent in Zimbabwe.

also personality, interest and aptitude tests imported from South Africa (Mpofu & Nyanungo, 1998).

Most of the psychological tests used in Zimbabwe had not been subjected to any systematic restandardization on the local population nor were there studies that have evaluated their validity to the Zimbabwean context (Mpofu & Nyanungo, 1998). Mpofu and Nyanungo (1998) give examples of items or activities on the Vineland Social Maturity Scale and the SOMPA-Adaptive Behaviour Inventory for Children which some Zimbabwean children have no experience with or no opportunity to perform in their day to day social interactions. The items do not suit the explorations or experiences of the Zimbabwean children. As such most Zimbabwean psychologists do not do any personality or cognitive testing with children due to the probable invalidity of imported Western tests in Zimbabwe. The psychologists see these tests as not relevant to the Zimbabwean context. There is a need for locally developed tests.

Mpofu and Nyanungo (1998) argued that, the low level of adoption of African epistemology by psychology departments in Africa impedes the development of indigenous psychological tests in Africa in general and Zimbabwe in particular. Only the Wechsler Intelligence Scale for Children- Revised and Good-enough Draw-A-Man Test has some Zimbabwean norms. However, the Zimbabwe norms are from urban children (Mpofu et al., 2007).

Zimbabwe experiences difficulties with people not licensed as psychologist administering psychological tests in employment settings (Chireshe et al., in press). Further, universities had employed people who are not licensed psychologists to train graduate students. The Allied Health Practitioners' Council of Zimbabwe have now ensured that only licensed psychologists teach on graduate programs. Seven universities in Zimbabwe now offer a psychology degree that gives students the basis for registration as practicing psychologists by the Allied Health Practitioners' Council, increasing the pool of black psychologists in the country. However, the curriculum at Zimbabwean universities does not equip graduates with skills to produce local relevant psychological tests. This may be attributed to the fact that the Zimbabwe psychology degree program structure and content has largely remained unchanged since the colonial era. The psychologists are trained in the use of Western tests without adequate interrogation on the cultural relevance of the tests to the Zimbabwean context. Also, several African psychologists who teach on graduate programs were trained in Western universities and in the use of Western psychological tests, which they took to their countries without any mod-ifications (Mpofu & Nyanungo, 1998; Zindi, 1989).

There was some movement to address the issue of test development in Zimbabwe. In 1986 a few Zimbabwean educational psychologists received advanced training in test development from the US Educational Testing Service (Mpofu et al., 2007). Some educational psychologists received training in test development in the 1990s from Canadian professors with a grant from the Canadian International Development Agency. Besides training in test development, the Canadians also trained Zimbabwean educational psychologists in the assessment of children with autism and other atypical disorders. The International Test Commission (ITC) spon-sored conference participation of at least six Zimbabwean educational psychologists. However, there was no further continuation of these initia-tives (Mpofu et al., 2007).

Of note in Zimbabwe is the development of diagnostic tests for local and indigenous languages and mathematics by the Ministry of Primary and Secondary Education (Mpofu & Nyanungo, 1998). The locally developed tests include: Graded Word Reading List, Informational Reading Inventory, Maths Attainment Test, Maths Diagnostic Test, Shona Attainment Test, and Shona Diagnostic Test. These tests are still being used and have been viewed as culturally relevant. However, their usefulness has not been extensively examined empirically.

Currently the Zimbabwean assessment landscape uses tests imported from the West or South Africa. There is a need for training of assessment specialists as well as for local test development and validity studies looking at the utility of tests imported from other countries.

2.5   Psychological Assessment in Zambia

Zambia, like Botswana and Zimbabwe, is a landlocked country with a history of Christian missionary education and British colonial administra-tion. The nation attained political sovereignty in 1964 with a population of 3.4 million, that grew to 17.4 million by 2019. Ten different Bantu languages were claimed as their first language by 1% or more of the population at the last national census (each of which has several dialects), and seven of those are mandated as medium of initial literacy instruction in the public basic school system. Most Zambians are fluent in two or more languages, including English, which is dominant in all state institutions and in secondary and tertiary education.

The historical origins of psychological assessment in Zambia include two distinct lines of intellectual descent. The first was focused on educational and occupational selection, driven (top-down) by the efforts of the colonial administration in Northern Rhodesia to systematize the selection of candidates for secondary schooling (Heron, 1975; Irvine 1969; MacArthur et al., 1964) and for employment in the mining industry (Mwanalushi & Ng'andu, 1981). The second emerged (bottom-up) in the 1980s from basic studies of cognitive functioning in children of school-going age (Serpell, 1974, 1982). A further strand emerged in the period from 2010 onwards from a biological/clinical tradition of neuropsychology (Kabuba et al., 2017; Kalungwana-Mambwe, 2017).

Noteworthy, by comparison with the development of the field in Zimbabwe, was the virtual isolation of psychological research and professional development in Zambia from South Africa between 1964 when Zambia attained political independence from British colonial rule and 1994 following the end of apartheid. Heron (1967) cited the work of Biesheuvel (1943, 1949) as a source of inspiration, and Deregowski (1968) interacted with and challenged empirically the work of Hudson (1967) on pictorial perception. Serpell (1982, 1984) regarded those studies as theoretically biased by an ideological premise that indigenous African cultures are deficient (which informed the racist policies of South Africa's government) and preferred to distance Zambian research from its legacy.

Heron's commitment to the inclusion of psychology among the social sciences to be recognized in the basic curriculum of Zambia's first university (UNZA), established in 1965, informed the establishment of the Human Development Research Unit (HDRU), devoted to basic research on perception and learning among young children (Deregowski, 1972; Heron, 1975; Serpell, 1974). Out of HDRU grew a continuing interest in issues of human development (Kingsley, 1977) in the Psychology Department of the School of Humanities and Social Sciences, which offered a four-year batchelor degree program with a major in psychology. Several outstanding, indigenous Zambian scholars graduated from the program in the 1970s, received post-graduate training abroad under UNZA's Staff Development program, and returned to staff the department with a broadening range of applications of psychology. In the late 1980s a separate department was established at UNZA in the School of Education, combining the fields of educational psychology, sociology, and special education.

Two of Zambia's first three indigenous scholars to qualify for the award of a doctoral degree in psychology, Mwanalushi and Ng'andu (1981), surveyed in detail the research literature on application of the discipline in Zambia in the first two decades after independence. They advanced a critical analysis of the limited impact achieved to date by psychology on national development, attributing the widely acknowledged socioeconomic problems of modern industry in Zambia to a "mismatch" between the nation's "cultural heritage" and "the requirements of modern work" (73). More fundamentally they challenged a "tacit assumption that theories derived from the experience of white (sic) people aimed at explaining those experiences can be transplanted in total to the explanation of the African experience" (74).

The Zambian history of assessment is marked by a discontinuity from 1985 to 2005, which was a fallow period of research in Zambia across disciplines due to a profound national economic recession beginning in the1980s that severely impacted the higher education sector (Machungwa et al., 1984; Peltzer & Bless, 1989). The early twenty-first century saw a renewal of academic research and advanced studies at the national university with technical and financial support from various universities abroad, including Yale (United States), Leiden (Netherlands), and Jyvaskyla (Finland).

Since 2010, the two UNZA departments have collaborated on a number of research projects, including cumulative development and field testing of psychological assessment methods, with particular attention to early childhood and primary school education (Matafwali & Serpell, 2014; Mwanza-Kabaghe et al., 2015; Stemler et al., 2009), and more recently to neuropsychological assessment of adults (Hestad et al., 2015; Kalungwana-Mambwe, 2017). In the fields of inclusion and educational provision for children with special educational needs, applied research in Zambia has built eclectically on that research literature to evaluate optimal methods of screening, placement, instructional support, and teacher training (Ndhlovu et al., 2016; Serpell & Folotiya, 2011).

A number of new assessment instruments have been developed and field-tested in Zambia over the years. Those designed for educational or occupational selection are for the most part unpublished for reasons of security, for example, Special Papers I and II of the national Secondary School Selection Examination (SSSE) standardized on large samples of Grade 7 students in the 1960s and the Zambia Advanced General Ability Test (ZAGAT) standardized on large samples of Grade 12 students in the 1970s. But systematic psychometric refinement has been cited in support of their application for selection purposes by the government Ministries of Education and Labour and by parastatal industrial corporations. Notable among Zambian tests for which standardization data have been published are the Panga Munthu Test (PMT), a nonverbal cognitive test for the assessment of child development (1970s), the Zambia Achievement Test (ZAT) (2000s), the Zambia Child Assessment Tool (ZamCAT) (2010s), and the Zambia Neurobehavioural Test Battery (ZNTB) (2010s). As with the locally developed tests in Zimbabwe, these tests would benefit from further research to establish their validity.

Complementary attention is needed on the one hand to the sociocultural context that determines the practical utility of psychological assessment, and on the other to technical issues of measurement. A detailed technical account of the development of the ZAT using Rasch scores concluded:

> Both technical and cultural factors play an important role in the quest to develop culturally sensitive measures; however, the development of psychometrically strong measures brings with it tremendous advances in our capacity to help both individuals and organizations better understand how best to improve upon their strengths and remediate areas of weakness. (Stemler et al., 2009, 182)

The Zambian Ministry of Education has in recent years strengthened the technical capacity of its Examinations Council (ECZ), and is planning to apply techniques of Item Response Theory to the refinement of its assessment tests administered annually nationwide for selection of candidates to progress in public schools from Grade 7 to 8 and from Grade 9 to 10. A number of test development initiatives are also under way within the Ministry designed to update and evaluate unpublished tests for the assessment of literacy and other competencies in the primary school population.

Applied research on initial literacy instruction, emergent literacy, and school readiness has generated several semi-standardized tests, including the Basic School Assessment Tool (BASAT) (Ketonen & Mulenga, 2002), the Decoding Competence (Spelling/Dictation) Test (Jere-Folotiya et al., 2014). And the Zambia National Campaign to Reach Disabled Children (1982–1985) gave rise to several instruments for screening individual children's special needs (Serpell & Jere-Folotiya, 2011). Follow-up to the campaign included feasibility studies of community-based rehabilitation (CBR) (Nabuzoka, 1986, 1993) and systematic development of a culture-sensitive approach to the assessment of family resources for home-based education of children with special needs, the Home Environment Potential Assessment inventory (HEPA) (Serpell & Nabuzoka, 2017).

In the field of medicine, following the gradual evolution of HIV infection into a chronic, usually non-fatal condition, increased attention has been given to hazards facing people living with HIV, including the possibility of neurocognitive impairment. A program of psychological test development was initiated at the University of Zambia in 2010 "to determine to what degree a Western neuropsychological test battery, with African American norms adjusted for age, gender, and education could be used in healthy Zambians." It concluded that "tests developed in the United States may be used in Zambia. Nevertheless, development and use of local cultural norms remains very important and is a must" (Hestad et al., 2015, 18).

A follow-up study recruited participants living with HIV and explored the diagnostic utility of the ZNTB, in the light of demographically corrected norms. "The algorithm for application of ZNTB applies a specific adjustment to the raw scores obtained by an individual based on that individual's rating relative to national norms on several demographic indices, such as years of schooling and residential location (rural vs urban)" (Kabuba et al., 2017). Eligibility for assessment with the battery in its present form is restricted to testees with a working knowledge of English and at least five years of basic education. While those prerequisites are met by a majority of Zambia's adult population, the restriction excludes a sizable proportion of elderly residents in rural areas. A sub-study examined the influence of the testing language in a sample of such adults and found that translating some of the verbal sub-tests into the local indigenous language not only improved overall performance but also differentiated more clearly between those living with HIV and a control group (Ndhlovu et al., 2013).

The rationale for intensifying the provision of care and education for children of preschool age includes early detection of children with special needs arising from organic impairment of visual, hearing, or motor functions, as well as intellectual functions attributable to central nervous system abnormalities such as cerebral palsy and Down's syndrome. Early detection affords opportunities for ameliorative interventions that are more difficult to implement in later phases of the child's development (Serpell & Nabuzoka, 1991). But a different theme that has received increasing attention from international agencies is that adverse conditions in early childhood place all children at risk for failure to attain their "full developmental potential" (Grantham-McGregor et al., 2007; Richter et al., 2017). This abstract theoretical idea has been deployed in conjunction with a universalistic interpretation of early childhood education to focus both intervention and assessment on "school readiness" (Britto et al., 2017). Adopting success in the formal school curriculum as a criterion of validity for assessment instruments in preschool childhood tends to reinforce a cultural deficiency view of indigenous child-rearing practices and to disregard the possibility that the current school curriculum deserves revision to meet the socialization goals of children's families (Ejuu, 2012; Oppong, 2015; Serpell & Nsamenang, 2015).

The political change in Zambia from colonial administration to democratically elected government shifted the focus of validation in the design of assessment instruments away from a universalistic conception of human psychological functioning toward addressing the competencies, needs, and aspirations of the indigenous population.

2.6   Conclusion

This chapter has presented the history of psychological assessment across four countries in Southern Africa, namely South Africa, Botswana, Zimbabwe, and Zambia. It is clear from all the histories that the legacy of colonialism impacted the development of assessment in these countries with them evidencing a strong reliance on tests imported from the West. The only exception to this is Zambia where Serpell makes it clear that an explicit decision was taken in the 1980s to focus on indigenous knowledge and assessment. Across the histories there is a strong call for assessment that is relevant and responsive to context and culture. Hence, the incorporation of indigenous knowledge into assessments appears to be core for assessment in Southern Africa. The work in Zambia on tests like the ZamCAT and ZNTB and the SAPI in South Africa provide excellent examples for how this may work. The HEPA in Zambia, the MSCI (Watson & McMahon, 2013), and Maree (2011) career instruments in South Africa also provide a way forward with regard to taking into account context when assessing.

Formal education, introduced in the early nineteenth century by Christian missionaries, was adopted in the newly independent nations of Zambia (1964), Botswana (1966), and Zimbabwe (1980) as a selection mechanism for matching the skills of the indigenous population to the task demands of industrial work, an applied psychology principle adopted in South Africa after the end of apartheid (1994). Cross-cultural variations in cognitive functioning arising from Western linguistic and cultural hegemony remain a pervasive challenge for educational and occupational assessment across the subregion, with instruments imported from

Western industrialized societies facing charges of ethnic, cultural, and class bias. The issues of urban and gender bias across tests as well as the lack of local norms feature strongly as factors impacting assessment when imported tests are used. The notion of test bias has been widely invoked in the interpretation of group differences in average levels of test performance. Various remedial strategies have been proposed, including local restandardization or adaptation of tests imported from abroad, demographically corrected norms, and construction of new local tests. Predictive validity, a popular indicator in occupational and educational psychology has been problematized in the contexts of training programs in industry and of curriculum development and inclusion in educational reform. At a more fundamental, theoretical level, cultural psychology has focused on construct validity, which was addressed systematically in the development of the SAPI and the HEPA (Fetvadjiev et al., 2018; Serpell & Nabuzoka, 2017)

Over and above psychometric considerations, an issue of great importance in all four countries is the political consideration of equity, between sociocultural groups (notably racial categories in South Africa), between socioeconomic strata (class and the rural/urban divide), and between genders (Mpofu & Nyanungo, 1998; Serpell & Jere-Folotiya, 2008). This challenge intersects in different ways with various indicators of validity used in the psychometric development and standardization of tests. Laher, Cheung, and Zeinoun (2020) discuss the need for a more intersectional approach to assessment that would involve greater consideration of issues linked to power and positionality.

In the fields of health care and rehabilitation, psychological assessment has also been dominated by imported methods, reflecting the cultural hegemony embedded in modern science and technology. Challenges to the validity of those methods in African societies arise from the difficulty of communication between professional practitioners and their clients or family advocates. Technical debates around emics and etics, universality and culture specificity have informed the growth of research and development in the field of psychological assessment attuned to the various demands of different contexts within the region, including rural subsistence economic activities, formal education, and technical work in modern industry. There is a need for such research to generate practical assessment instruments for use in the field.

The support from government structures across the countries demonstrates the need for political will beyond the psychology fraternity to (a) recognize the benefits offered by assessment for development in the country, (b) direct resources toward national assessment strategies for education and vocational planning among others, and (c) support policies for fair and unbiased testing. The role of national bodies like health councils and professional organizations are necessary to ensure fair and ethical assessment. Licensing seems to be another issue of concern in at least three of the nations. In Zambia the need for legislation in that regard is being advocated by the national Psychology Association (PAZ), drawing ideas from the South African situation.

Universities have a core role to play in terms of training professionals to be critical consumers of assessment. University curricula need to blend assessment knowledge from the West with indigenous knowledge to produce culturally competent practitioners. Across the countries, there is a need for psychologists to address psychological problems related to mental illness, stress, unemployment, suicide, student learning, and other social problems related to the fast evolving political and economic climates in each country.

Zambia and South Africa have a key role to play in terms of supporting the growth of test development in Botswana and Zimbabwe, as well as other countries in the region like Namibia or Malawi where psychology is still in its infancy. South Africa has a broad repertoire of experience across assessment fields from clinical and educational psychology through to occupational psychology across the developmental spectrum, but like other African countries it is still very much reliant on imported tests with few local norms. Zambia has progressed much in terms of locally developed assessments, but this has primarily been within the field of education and working with children. A collaborative approach across countries will ensure a richer and more relevant assessment amidst a context of low resources.

REFERENCES

Bemath, N. (2020). Relevance of the person-environment fit approach to career assessment in South Africa – A review. *African Journal of Psychological Assessment*, 2, 7 pages. https://doi.org/10.4102/ajopa.v2i0.22

Biesheuvel, S. (1943). *African intelligence*. Johannesburg: South African Institute of Personnel Relations.

(1949). Psychological tests and their application to non-European peoples. In G. B. Jeffery (ed.), *The yearbook of education* (pp. 90–104). London: Evans.

Britto, P. R., Lye, S. J., Proulx, K., Yousafzai, A. K., Matthews, S. G., Vaivada, T., ... & Bhutta, Z. A. (2017). Nurturing care: Promoting early childhood development. *The Lancet*, 389(10064), 91–102. https://doi.org/10.1016/S0140-6736(16)31390-3

Bohmke, W. & Tlali, T. (2008). Bodies and behavior: Science, psychology and politics in South Africa. In C. van Ommen & D. Painter (eds.), *Interiors: A history of psychology in South Africa* (pp. 125–151). Pretoria: UNISA Press.

Chireshe, R., Mudhovozi, P. & Nkoma, E. (in press). Introduction to professional practices in psychology. In *International handbook of psychological practices*.

Chowdhry, K. (1953). *An analysis of the attitudes of textile workers and the effect of those attitudes on work efficiency*. Ahmedabad: Atira Research Note.

Claasen, N. C. W. (1997). Cultural differences, politics and test bias in South Africa. *European Review of Applied Psychology, 47*(4), 297–307.

Deregowski, J. B. (1968). Difficulties in pictorial depth perception in Africa. *British Journal of Psychology, 59*(3), 195–204.

  (1972). Pictorial perception and culture. *Scientific American, 227*(5), 82–89.

Employment Equity Act (Act No. 55) (1998). Government Gazette Vol. 400, No. 19370, October 19, 1998.

Ejuu, G. (2012). Cultural and parental standards as the benchmark for early learning and development standards in Africa. *International Journal of Current Research, 4* (4), 282–288.

Feinstein, C. (2005). *An economic history of South Africa: Conquest, discrimination and development*. Cambridge: Cambridge University Press.

Fetvadjiev, V. H., Meiring, D., Vijver, F., Nel, J. A., & De Kock, F. (2018) Self–other agreement in personality traits and profiles across cultures: A multirater, multiscale study in Blacks and Whites in South Africa." *Journal of Personality, 86*(6), 935–951.

Foxcroft, C. & Davies, C. (2008). Historical perspectives on psychometric testing in South Africa. In C. van Ommen & D. Painter (eds.), *Interiors: A history of psychology in South Africa* (pp. 152–181). Pretoria: UNISA Press.

Foxcroft, C., & Roodt, G. (2013). *An introduction to psychological assessment in the South African context* (2nd ed.). Oxford: Oxford University Press.

Giliomee, H. & Mbenga, B. (2007). *New history of South Africa*. Cape Town: Tafelberg.

Grantham-McGregor, S., Cheung, Y. B., Cueto, S., Glewwe, P., Richter, L., & Strupp, B. (2007). International Child Development Steering Group. Developmental potential in the first 5 years for children in developing countries. *Lancet, 369*(9555), 60–70.

Harper, A. E., Jr. (1952). Adaptation of Iowa aptitude tests. *Teaching* Oxford Press, Bombay) 25, 45–46.

Heron, A. (1967). The years of transition; Psychology in Africa: The challenge of a new opportunity. *Bulletin* 2. University of Zambia, Institute for Social Research, 1–3, 54–6.

  (1975). Psychology and national development: The Zambian experience. In Berry, J.W. & Lonner, W.J. (eds.), *Applied cross-cultural psychology* (pp. 13–17). Amsterdam: Swets and Zeitlinger.

Hestad, K. A., Menon, J. A., Serpell, R., Kalungwana, L., Kabuba, N., Mwaba, S. O. C., Franklin, D. O. Jr., Umlauf, A., Letendre, R. K., & Heaton, R. K.

(2015). Do neuropsychological test norms from African-Americans in the United States generalize to a Zambian population? *Psychological Assessment, 28*(1), 18–38. https://doi.org/10.1037/pas0000147

Hudson, W. (1967). The study of the problem of pictorial perception among inacculturated groups. *International Journal of Psychology 2*(2): 89–107.

Irvine, S. H. (1969). Contributions of ability and attainment testing in Africa to a general theory of intellect. *Journal of Biosocial Science,* (Supplement 1), 91–102.

Jere-Folotiya, J., Chansa-Kabali, T., Munachaka, J. C., Sampa, F., Yalukanda, C., Westerholm, J. . . . & Lyytinen, H. (2014). The effect of using a mobile literacy game to improve literacy levels of grade one students in Zambian schools. *Educational Technology Research and Development, 62*(4), 417–432. https//:doi: 10.1007/s11423-014-9342-9

Jivan, A., Bischof, D. & Laher, S. (2020). Changing talent assessment landscape. Fact sheet published by South African Board for People Practices. Retrieved from https://cdn.ymaws.com/www.sabpp.co.za/resource/resmgr/ceanne/ceanne_2020/pdf_documents_2020/fact_sheet_august_2020v003.pdf.

Kabuba, N., Menon, J. A., Franklin, D. R., Heaton, R. K., & Hestad, K. A. (2017). Use of western neuropsychological test battery in detecting HIV-associated neurocognitive disorders (HAND) in Zambia. *AIDS and Behavior, 21*(6), 1717–1727.

Kaliski, S. (2006). *Psycho-legal assessment in South Africa.* Cape Town: Oxford University Press, Southern Africa.

Kalungwana-Mambwe, L. (2017). Influence of age and education on neuropsychological tests in Zambia. *Medical Journal of Zambia, 44*(2), 106–113.

Ketonen, R., & Mulenga, K. (2002). *The basic skills assessment tool for reading and writing (BASAT) and the users' guide.* Jyväskylä, Finland and Lusaka, Zambia: Niilo Mäki Institute and the Ministry of Education.

Kingsley, P. R. (1977). Psychology in Zambia: A bibliography. *HDRU Reports* 26. Lusaka, Zambia: University of Zambia Psychology Department (mimeo).

Laher, S., Cheung, F., & Zeinoun, P. (2020). Gender and personality research in Psychology: The need for intersectionality. In F. Cheung. & D. Halpern, (eds.), *The Cambridge international handbook on psychology of women* (pp. 167–179). Cambridge: Cambridge University Press.

Laher, S. & Cockcroft, K. (2013a). Current and future trends in psychological assessment in South Africa: Challenges and opportunities. In S. Laher & K. Cockcroft (eds.), *Psychological assessment in South Africa: Research and applications* (pp. 535–552). Johannesburg: Wits University Press.

(2013b). *Psychological assessment in South Africa: Research and applications.* Johannesburg: Wits University Press.

(2014). Psychological assessment in post-apartheid South Africa: the way forward. *South African Journal of Psychology, 44*(3), 303–314.

(2017). Moving from culturally biased to culturally responsive assessment practices in low resource, multicultural settings. *Professional Psychology: Research and Practice, 48*(2), 115–121.

MacArthur, R., Irvine, S. H., & Brimble, A. R. (1964). *The Northern Rhodesia mental ability survey*. Lusaka, Zambia: Rhodes-Livingstone Institute. (Communication no. 27).

Machungwa, P.D., Kathuria, R., & Westernholz-Bless, C. (1984). Occupational testing in Zambia. *Psychological Studies 4* (Reports of the Psychology Department, University of Zambia, mimeo).

Maree, K. (2011). *Career counselling: Techniques that work*. Cape Town: Juta & Company.

Matafwali, B., & Serpell, R. (2014). Design and validation of assessment tests for young children in Zambia. In R. Serpell & K. Marfo (eds.), *Child development in Africa: Views from inside. New directions for child and adolescent development* (pp. 146, 77–96). London: Palgrave Macmillan.

Ministry of Education. (1994). *The revised national policy on education*. Gaborone, Botswana: Government Printer.

 (1996). *Policy guide-lines on the implementation of guidance and counselling in Botswana education system*. Gaborone, Botswana: Guidance and Counselling Division.

Ministry of Finance and Development Planning. (2019). *Botswana budget speech*. Gaborone, Botswana: Government Printers.

Moerdyk, A. (2009). *The principles and practice of psychological assessment*. Pretoria: Van Schaik Publishers.

Mpofu, E., Maree, J. G., & Oakland, T. (2009). *Developing a framework for psychometric test use in Botswana Schools*. Gaborone, Botswana: Scholarship Development Enterprise Africa (ASDE).

Mpofu, E., Mutepha, M., Chireshe, R., & Kasayira, J. M. (2007). School psychology in Zimbabwe. In S. P. Jimerson, T. Oakland, & P. Farrel (eds.), *The handbook of international school psychology* (pp. 437–449). Thousand Oaks, CA: Sage Publications.

Mpofu, E. & Nyanungo, K. R. L. (1998). Educational and psychological testing in Zimbabwean schools: Past, present and future. *European Journal of Psychological Assessment*, 14(1), 71–90.

Mpofu, E., Oakland, T., Ntinda, K., Maree, J. G., & Seeco, E. G. (2015). Locality, observability and community action (LOCUM) in test development and use in emerging education settings. In Dixon, P., Humble, S., & Counihan, C. (eds.), *Handbook of international development and education* (pp. 326–342). Gloucester: Edward Elgar Publishing.

Mpofu, E., Oakland, T., Ntinda, K., Seeco, E., & Maree, J. G. (2014). Constructing a framework for the use of tests within a developing nation's school system. *International Perspectives in Psychology: Research, Practice, Consultation* 3(2): 106.

Mpofu, E., Peltzer, K., Shumba, A., Serpell, R., & Mogaji, A. (2005). "School psychology in sub-Saharan Africa: Results and implications of a six-country survey." In C. R. Reynolds & C. Frisby (eds.), *Comprehensive handbook of multicultural school psychology* (pp. 1128–1150). New York: John Wiley.

Mwanalushi, M. & Ng'andu, B. E. (1981). Psychology's contribution to national development in Zambia: past, present and future. *African Social Research, 32,* 55–82. (note: due to institution problems, this issue of the journal was only published in 1983).

Mwanza-Kabaghe, S., Mubanga, E., Matafwali, B., Kasonde-Ngandu, S., & Bus, A. G. (2015). Zambian preschools: A boost for early literacy? *English Linguistics Research, 4*(4), 1–10.

Nabuzoka, D. (ed.) (1986). *Reaching disabled children in Zambia: Reports and other articles on various aspects of the National Campaign to Reach Disabled Children (1980–1985).* Lusaka, Zambia: University of Zambia, Institute for African Studies (mimeo).

   (1993). How to define, involve and assess the care unit? Experiences and research from a CBR programme in Zambia. In H. Finkenflügel (ed.), *The handicapped community. The relation between primary health care and community based rehabilitation* (pp. 73–88). Amsterdam: VU University Press.

Ndhlovu, D., Mtonga, T., Serenje-Chipindi, J., & Muzata, K. (2016). Early childhood education in Zambia: inclusion of children with disabilities." *International Journal of Multidisciplinary Research and Development, 3*(8), 126, 132.

Ndhlovu, L., Serpell, R., & Mwanza, J. (2013). Effects of HIV status and linguistic medium on the test performance of rural low-literacy adults: implications for neuropsychological test development in Zambia. *Medical Journal of Zambia, 40*(2), 69–80.

Ntinda, K. (2012). Constructing a framework for use of psychometric tests in schools: A Consumer-oriented approach. Unpublished Doctoral dissertation, Gaborone, Botswana: University of Botswana.

   (2019). Parents and guardians: Their perceptions of psychometric test uses with learners in an emerging country's school system. *Journal of Psychology in Africa, 29*(6), 605–612.

Oakland, T. (2009). How universal are test development and use? In E. Grigorenko (ed.), *Assessment of abilities of competencies in an era of globalization* (pp. 1–40). New York: Springer.

Onyewadume, M. A. (2005). A study of the Thematic Apperception Test Hero Figure Identification with a sample of Botswana Adults: Concurrent and construct validation. *Mosenodi Journal of the Botswana Educational Research Association, 13*(1&2), 20–32.

Oppong, S. (2015). A critique of early childhood development research and practice in Africa. *Africanus: Journal of Development Studies, 45*(1), 23–24.

Peltzer, K., & Bless, C. (1989). History and present status of professional psychology in Zambia. *Psychology and Developing Societies, 1*(1), 53–64.

Pheko, M. M., Chilisa, R., Balogun, S. K., & Kgathi, C. (2013). Predicting intentions to seek psychological help among Botswana university students: The role of stigma and help-seeking attitudes. *Sage Open, 3*(3). https://doi.org/10.1177/2158244013494655.

Phelps, R. P. (2007). *Standardized testing primer*, vol. 21. New York: Peter Lang.

Pinto, X. & Myall, E. G. (2006). New ICSE History and Civics – Part I for Class IX, New Delhi: Frank Bros. & Co. (Publishers) Ltd.

Plake, B. S. (2005). Doesn't everybody know that 70% is passing? Teoksessa RP Phelps (toim.), Defending standardized testing.

Plattner, I. E., & Moagi-Gulubane, S. (2010). Bridging the gap in psychological service delivery for a developing country: Teaching the bachelor of psychology degree in Botswana. *Journal of Psychology in Africa*, *20*(1), 155–159.

Rajkhowa, S. C. (2005). Ancient European and Indian universities. In Sharma and Sharma (eds.), *Encyclopaedia of higher education: The Indian perspective* (vol. 1, pp. 1–6) New Delhi: Mittal Publications.

Richter, L. M., Daelmans, B., Lombardi, J., Heymann, J., Boo, F. L., Behrman, J. R., . . . & Bhutta, Z. A. (2017). Investing in the foundation of sustainable development: pathways to scale up for early childhood development. *The Lancet*, *389*(10064), 103–118.

Seedat, M. & Mackenzie, S. (2008). The triangulated development of South African psychology: Race, scientific racism and professionalization (pp. 63–91). In C. van Ommen & D. Painter (eds.), *Interiors: A history of psychology in South Africa*. Pretoria: UNISA Press.

Serpell, R. (1974) Aspects of intelligence in a developing country. *African Social Research*, *17*, 578–596.

(1982). Measures of perception, skills, and intelligence: the growth of a new perspective on children in a third world country. In W. W. Hartup (ed.), *Review of child development research, Vol. 6* (pp. 392–440). Chicago: University of Chicago Press.

(1984) Research on cognitive development in sub-Saharan Africa. *International Journal of Behavioural Development*, *7*(2), 111–127.

Serpell, R., & Jere-Folotiya, J. (2008). Developmental assessment, cultural context, gender, and schooling in Zambia. *International Journal of Psychology*, *43* (2), 88–96.

(2011). Basic education for children with special needs in Zambia: Progress and challenges in the translation of policy into practice. *Psychology and Developing Societies*, *23*(2) 211–245.

Serpell, R. & Nabuzoka, D. (1991). Early intervention in third world countries. In D. M. Mitchell & R. I. Brown (eds.), *Early intervention studies for young children with special needs* (pp. 93–126). London: Chapman & Hall.

(2017). Application of the Home Environment Potential Assessment scale (HEPA) for rural Zambian children with disabilities. Presentation in the Symposium on Psychological Assessment in an African Context: Experiences from Zambia at 1st *Pan-African Congress of Psychology*. Durban, South Africa: September 18–21, 2017.

Serpell, R. & Nsamenang, A. B. (2015). The challenge of local relevance: using the wealth of African cultures in ECCE programme development. In Marope, P. T. M. & Kaga, Y. (eds.), *Investing against evidence: The global state of early childhood care and education* (pp. 231–247). Paris: UNESCO.

Stemler, S., Chamvu, F., Chart, H., Jarvin, L., Jere, J., Hart, L., Kaani, B., Kalima, K., Kwiatkowski, J., Mambwe, A., Kasonde-Ng'andu, S., Newman, T., Serpell, R., Sparrow, S., Sternberg, R. J. & Grigorenko, E. L. (2009). Assessing competencies in reading and mathematics in Zambian children. In E. L. Grigorenko (ed.), *Multicultural psychoeducational assessment* (pp. 157–186). New York: Springer.

Statistics South Africa (2020). *Mid-year population estimates.* Retrieved on September 8, 2020 from www.statssa.gov.za/?p=13453

Stockton, R., Nitza, A., & Bhusumane, D. B. (2010). The development of professional counselling in Botswana. *Journal of Counselling & Development, 88*(1), 9–12.

Taylor, T. (2013). APIL and TRAM learning potential assessment instruments. In S. Laher & K. Cockcroft (eds.), *Psychological assessment in South Africa: Research and applications* (pp. 158–168). Johannesburg: Wits University Press.

Thompson, L. (2001). *A history of South Africa* (3rd ed.). New Haven: Yale University Press.

Tredoux, N. (2013). Using computerized and internet-based testing in South Africa. In S. Laher & K. Cockcroft (eds.), *Psychological assessment in South Africa: Research and applications* (pp. 424–442). Johannesburg: Wits University Press.

UNDP (2019). *Botswana human development report 2019.* Gaborone: United Nations Development Programme.

UNICEF/World Bank (2019). *Botswana public Expenditure review of basic education report.* Gaborone: UNICEF/ World Bank.

Watson, M. & McMahon, M. (2013). Qualitative career assessment in South Africa. In S. Laher & K. Cockcroft (eds.), *Psychological assessment in South Africa: Research and applications* (pp. 474–487). Johannesburg: Wits University Press.

World Bank (2019). Document3: Rural population. https://data.worldbank.org/indicator/SP.RUR.TOTL.ZS?locations=ZG).

Zindi, F. (1989). Pupil assessment techniques in Zimbabwe's secondary school (1984–1987). *Zimbabwe Journal of Educational Research, 1*(2), 161–179.

CHAPTER 3

Psychological Testing and Inclusive Schooling
Issues and Prospects in Central Africa

*Therese M. S. Tchombe, Asangha N. Muki, Melem L. Fangwi,
Lambert S. Wirdze, and Ndzetar E. Wirmum*

3.1 Introduction

One of the five defined subregions of Africa is Central Africa. This region is the heart or the core zone of the continent. In total, there are nine countries that fall within this region under the classification of the United Nations. These countries include Angola, Cameroon, Central African Republic, Chad, Democratic Republic of the Congo, Equatorial Guinea, Gabon, Republic of the Congo, São Tomé, and Príncipe. During the Scramble for Africa in 1884 and 1885, much of the region was shared between France, Britain, and Belgium. The Lake Chad basin was later forcefully added by the French to be a part of French West Africa with Britain getting parts of the basin as well. The Germans took the whole of Cameroon until the nations around the basin regained their independence.

Africa has been and remains a major recipient of external influences that have been imposed unsolicited (Nsamenang & Dawes, 1998). Scientific psychology as well as psychological testing arrived in Africa with colonization in the context of anthropological research (Peltzer & Bless, 1989) as well as in allied service sectors like health, education, and evangelism. Like every colonial import into Africa, it has retained an imperialistic and racist identity (Owusu-Bempah & Moffitt, 1995) in the sense that its theories and methods are still Eurocentric and its primary focus is on topics that reflect this externalized orientation, thereby largely losing "sight of the soil out of which the existing (African) society has grown and the human values it has produced" (Wastermann, 2001).

Compared with psychology's status in other world regions, the state of scientific psychology and psychological testing in Afrique noire or black Africa is inchoate (Nsamenang, 1993), except in South Africa where legislation and ethical codes in the discipline "are relatively well developed, compared with most European countries" and "second only perhaps to the USA and Canada." As the discipline stands today, Afrique noire occupies an outlier position in the psychology world and, given its limited capacity to generate and share its own psychology, it is a net importer rather than a generator of psychological knowledge. However, it is slowly evolving into a professional discipline, a fledgling science that still occupies only the fringes of academia and society in most African countries (Nsamenang, 1995).

The evolution and development of scientific psychology and psychological testing in sub-Saharan Africa has not been uniform. Variation exists across and within countries, regions, and language blocks in the orienting models, resources, conditions for training, research, and applications as well as in the number of psychologists and their integration into research, policy, and service programs. Whereas countries like Cameroon, Chad, and Gabon have been "struggling" to establish the discipline, formal psychology institutions and services already exist in Ethiopia, Ghana, Kenya, Liberia, Namibia, Nigeria, Uganda, Zambia, and Zimbabwe (Nsamenang, 2007). Psychology has long been established in South Africa, where it is said to be more similar than it is different from psychology elsewhere in the world. In general, psychology seems to be more "advanced" in English-colonized Africa than in those countries colonized by the French, Portuguese, and Spanish, a state of the field that reflects the mind sets of its Euro-American exporters and their Anglo-driven values.

Historically, the science of psychology and measurement of human behavior in sub-Saharan Africa has "advanced" from primary focus on the precocity of physical development of the African child through exploring various aspects of Africa's developmental ecocultures (e.g., Nsamenang, 1992; Weisner et al., 1997) to investigating specific domains of psychosocial development and attempting Africentric measures of cognitive abilities or intelligences (e.g., Kathuria & Serpell, 1999; Mpofu, 2002; Nsamenang, 2006b; Tchombe, 2011; Serpell, 1993).

Psychological testing is very important and advantageous with regards to the practice of inclusive schooling and education. UNESCO (1994) defines inclusive education/schooling "as a process of addressing and responding to the diversity of needs of all learners through increasing participation in learning, cultures and communities, and reducing exclusion in all ramifications within and from education." Thus, inclusive schooling/education involves changes and modifications in content, approaches, structures, and strategies, with the conviction that it is the responsibility of the state to educate all children. Education is intended to provide diverse students with the skills and competencies needed to enhance their lives. This includes assessment practices that enable teachers to identify students' current level of skills, their strength and weaknesses, target instruction at student's personal level, monitor student's learning, progress and plan to conduct adjustments in instruction and evaluate the extent to which students have met instructional goals.

Since 1994, when many countries ratified the renowned Salamanca Statement on social and educational inclusion, efforts have been made to include all children in general day care and school systems and thus reduce mechanisms of exclusion and the prominent role formerly ascribed to special needs education (UNESCO, 1994). In this light, the practice of psychological testing is very important in schools because it supports children in achieving success in school. If children have undiagnosed psychological, emotional, or behavioral difficulties, psychological testing can detect these challenges and help schools place students in the best learning environments to meet their needs. Psychological testing can also be used to benefit children with previously diagnosed conditions and to put them in classrooms where they can be challenged and motivated to grow both intellectually and personally (Mpofu & Nyanungo, 1998). The overall objectives for assessing students with special needs have changed with the movement toward inclusion. The earlier, traditional emphasis was on testing to establish a diagnosis and determine eligibility for services with norm-referenced assessment tools, whereas current emphasis is on developing a profile of student's strengths and weaknesses based on data obtained from a variety of sources and with a variety of approaches to assessment. This has resulted in increased use of assessment methods that go beyond traditional norm-referencing (Melem, 2016).

The purpose of this chapter therefore is to (a) identify the types of psychological tests in use in Central Africa, (b) determine whether or not validation studies have been conducted for the test, (c) point out some key problems associated with psychological testing in Central Africa, and (d) make recommendations for improving psychological testing in Central Africa.

3.2   Types of Psychological Tests and Inclusive Schooling in Central Africa

For most schools in Africa and in the Central African regions especially, the preferred approaches to assessment of special needs for inclusion in the regular classroom today are contextual, performance-oriented, holistic, interactive, multi-perspective, and real-world oriented (Kellaghan & Greaney, 2005). Relevant behaviors are observed and rated in natural contexts and performance-oriented assessments are used for evaluating selected behaviors from a holistic or focused-holistic perspective. Checklists and criterion-referenced probes have also been developed that focus on (a) basic skills and strategies for listening, speaking, reading, and writing, (b) responses to curriculum demands (e.g., social science), (c) classroom interactions between teachers, peers, and the student, and (d) effective classroom practices for management and instruction. The student is seen as a multifaceted entity with behaviors that change as a function of external demands. The assessment process is broad in scope and designed to provide opportunities to obtain authentic and sensitive indicators of performances in the real-world setting of the classroom and community (Sokopo, 2004). Machona and Kapambwe (2003) hold that the least restrictive environment for a student is the regular classroom, as such emphasis ought to be laid on using procedures that foster multi-perspective and collaborative processes. This allows the staff to profile a student's strengths and weaknesses, provide a baseline for intervention, and support dynamic, long-term educational planning as such achieving the goals of inclusion.

However, given differing levels of literacy and education, "taking a test" is not something that is necessarily within the everyday experience sphere of many people in Africa. According to Nell (1997), the extent to which a test-taker is "test wise" has a significant impact on test performance. Consequently, if an assessment practitioner wants to follow ethical testing practices, the extent to which it is possible to even consider administering a test is a decision that needs to be reached early on. In some instances, using other forms of assessment (e.g., behavioral observation) and obtaining information from key family members and community informants (e.g., parents, teachers, religious ministers/priests, a respected elder person in the community) may be preferable to administering a test to someone who has no test-taking experience. Not only will this eliminate the anxiety that taking a test could have for such a person, but it will also provide the assessment practitioner with more valid and authentic information about the person.

Norm-referenced tests allow educators to obtain quantitative measures for evaluating and comparing prerequisite language behaviors and other competencies for inclusion. The quantitative data from norm-referenced tests also play a role in establishing a student's need for special support services and the potential for learning in the inclusive classroom. In most countries in Central Africa according to Jatau, Uzo, and Lere (2002), educational specialists use norm-referenced tests to monitor academic achievement, intellectual ability, psycho-educational ability, or language and literacy as a first cut in the process of evaluating and diagnosing a child's learning difficulties. Olabisi (2005) holds that norm-referenced tests are designed to (a) obtain a preliminary diagnosis of a learning disorder, (b) determine the extent and nature of the deficit or disorder, (c) establish eligibility for specialized services or curriculum adaptations, and/or (d) determine eligibility for taking academic and college entry tests without time limits (Wiig & Secord, 1999).

According to Lerner (1993), within the educational sector of the Cameroonian, Chadian Central African Republic's educational sectors, norm-referenced tests mostly contain a range of items grouped into sub-tests, with each subtest designed to probe a specific aspect or dimension of the overall abilities tested. Subtests are often clustered to form composites designed to measure specific theoretical constructs, such as receptive and expressive language, or listening, speaking, reading, and writing. The standard scores on the total test and the composites provide performance constructs that are the best measures of the collective set of tasks. Ikpaya (2001) stipulates that individual norm-referenced tests vary in the content, tasks, and underlying models for subtests and constructs. They may also vary in the extent to which underlying neuropsychological functions and constructs are probed. They are, however, similar in the procedures used for standardization, analysis of data, scores reported, and interpretation of results. This makes it possible for a trained diagnostician to compare tests and test results, and evaluate a student's performances across a variety of tests.

Norm-referencing tests are used to identify inadequacies in basic skills and determine whether or not a student's inadequacies stem from factors related to differences in language or motivation or from inherent neuro-psychological deficits and disorders. When results from norm-referenced tests are available to teachers, performances and clinical interpretations are taken into account in complements to other information about the student (Ikujuni, 2005).

Kanjee (2003) postulates that criterion-referenced assessment uses a series of items to evaluate the acquisition of specific academic or language and communication skills and rules. Each probe is designed to contain items with a specific content, skill, or rule focus. Because the probes in a criterion-referenced inventory have such a specific focus and evaluate specific curriculum objectives or educational outcomes, they do not pro-vide a differential diagnosis of language or learning disabilities. The focus in criterion-referenced testing is on skill acquisition, and usually does not allow for evaluation of neuropsychological functions or deficits. Criterion-referenced test results validate norm-referenced test scores, teacher observations, or classroom evaluations of, for example, reading comprehension or mathematical skills. They are also used to determine focused targets for intervention, identify appropriate educational objectives, and establish educational outcomes (Crooks, 2002).

In countries of Africa and most especially countries of the Central Africa subregion, summative assessments and high-stake tests are designed to provide information on the learners' progression to the next class and teachers have tended to rely on these tests and examinations at the end of the school term and academic year in their assessment of learners. The results of these tests and examinations might tell teachers which learners in their classes have failed and which have not, but they do not tell us the kind of instruction the learners need to master and the outcomes or what errors in thinking led to the incorrect answers in the tests (Ahsan, 2016). In order to get that kind of information, teachers need the results provided by the consistent use of classroom-based formative assessment.

Formative assessment, also known as assessment for learning (Black & William, 1998), takes place anytime during a lesson. It identifies strengths and weaknesses of the learner and it is intended to enhance the learner's final performance. This means that it is not only used to support learning but also teaching. "Assessment for learning" is stressed as a way to improve teaching and the learning of learners, and also as an "integral part of the learning, teaching and assessment cycle." The teacher obtains and uses information about learners' progress toward the learning goals. A learner needs to know where he or she is and understand not only where they want to be but also know how to "fill the gap" between his or her current knowledge and understanding and desired level. Black and William (1998) further argue that formative assessment does not only serve as an effective classroom assessment tool but also as a "high-quality instructional feedback tool" that is timely, useful, and appropriate. Timely feedback, which is given as soon as possible after the assessment occurs, "can influence the next steps in the learning process." Black and William (1998) terms this as a "useful assessment" that is both diagnostic and prescriptive in reinforcing precisely what learners were expected to learn, identifies what was learned well, and describes what needs to be learned better. Black and William (1998) state that assessment becomes formative when the information is used to adapt teaching and learning to meet student needs. Table 3.1 shows the types of psychological tests and their level of usage in Central Africa.

Table 3.1. *Types of psychological tests and level of usage in Central Africa*

Sn	Type of tests	Level of usage
1.	Aptitude test	Rarely used.
2.	Achievement test	Highly used by schools to monitor learning progress among learners.
3.	Diagnostic tests	Rarely used in schools to understand category of learners but it is mostly used in hospitals to diagnose health related problems among individuals.
4.	Placement test	Rarely used by schools to place learners in specific programs.
5.	Intelligence test	Rarely used by schools and other organizations to place people according to their different intelligences.
6.	Personality test	Rarely used by schools and other organizations in society.
7.	Vocational test	Some industries/companies use it in terms of studying candidates portfolios, oral interviews and observation of performance on the job.
8.	Attitude test	Rarely used by schools and other organizations in society.
9.	Teacher made tests - Written, performance, and Oral) - Formative and summative	Highly used by schools to monitor learning progress among learners
10.	Examination board made tests	Highly used to monitor academic achievement among learners at the end of the study programme. For example, Cameroon General Certificate of Education Board (CGCEB).
11.	University admission tests	Some university departments use it to select students for specific programs.

Source: Tchombe, Wirdze, Asangha, Melem, & Ndzetar (2020), adapted from the study

From Table 3.1 it can be seen that schools in Central African regions mostly make use of achievement tests such as teacher-made tests and examination board tests in order to monitor students' progress and academic achievement. The other categories are rarely used by schools.

3.3   Issues/Problems Associated with the Current State of Psychological Testing in Central Africa

In Central Africa and most of sub-Saharan Africa, like in many developing regions of the world, the lack of psychological research has significant implications for intervention and research (Nsamenang, 2006a; Nsamenang, 2007;

Mpofu, 2002). The interest here is on the absence of culturally and inclusive appropriate, standardized, reliable, and valid psychometric measures to use in schools and societies to measure components of human behavior. More so, the lack/absence of trained personnel in psychological testing within school settings/societies also possess a big challenge (Holding et al., 2004; Kathuria & Serpell, 1998; Nsamenang, 2007).

Importing standardized tests from Western countries may seem to provide the easiest solution for this shortage. However, the transfer of tests to a non-Western context is frequently accompanied by test bias/measurement errors and limited validity (Greenfield, 1997; Van de Vijver, 2002). This bias may be due to a lack of familiarity with test demands (Mulenga, Ahonen, & Aro, 2001), poor translation of test items (Van de Vijver, 2002), stimulus unfamiliarity (Sigman et al., 1988; Sonke et al., 1999), and incomplete coverage or poor sampling of behaviors associated with a construct (Sternberg et al. 2002; Van de Vijver & Tanzer, 2004).

Education examination boards in most Central African countries do not provide their teachers with assessment resources that include access to item banks for different levels and subject areas, software to compile high-quality classroom tests linked to the curriculum, and software to analyze, interpret, and monitor learners' performance levels (Nsamenang, 2009), neither do they carry out placement, diagnostic, personality, or even intelligence tests for appropriate inclusive practices.

In practice, however, most teachers are required to develop their own assessment instruments and tools. Machona and Kapambwe (2003) note that it is unrealistic to expect teachers, especially those working in disadvantaged schools, to develop high-quality instruments to assess learners given their limited expertise and the significant amount of time required to do so. In their review of assessment practices in Africa, Kellaghan and Greaney (2005) also found that the poor quality of classroom assessment can be attributed to the shortage of learning and teaching materials as well as to poorly qualified teachers.

3.4   Prospects of Psychological Testing and School Reforms in Central Africa

According to Malda and Van de Vijver (2005), two approaches, namely adaptation and assembly, seem to provide the most satisfactory solutions to the shortage of assessment measures in Central African countries, sub-Saharan African countries, and less developed countries of the world. Adaptation involves retaining some and changing other features of a Western instrument to increase the suitability of the instrument for the new context; while assembly involves the construction of a new assessment measure. Participant consultation, through techniques such as focus group discussions, in-depth interviews, and participant observations may provide a useful means of gaining the necessary insight to carry out adequate adaptation or assembly (Vogt et al., 2004).

To begin with, validation or standardization of imported tests is needed to address the problems of reliability, validity, and interpretation of scores. To address the ecological and cultural influences, psychologists within Central African countries are encouraged to seriously consider constructing Africentric psychological tests rather than relying heavily on the imported Eurocentric ones. Imported tests should be translated into the different spoken ethnic languages of the different countries that constitute Central Africa. To ensure the reliability, validity, and the appropriate interpretation of scores, the translated versions should also be subjected to validation studies.

To address the low adoption and use of the existing test norms, awareness should be created through dissemination of the norms. This can be achieved by means of (a) incorporating discussions on validated tests in Central African countries into the teaching and learning of psychometrics at the universities and (b) provision of technical reports on the validated tests. Test developers and administrators should adopt an emic approach in which human behavior is examined using criteria related to a specific culture as opposed to using behavioral criteria that are presumed to be universal (etic approach).

In constructing and administering psychological tests within school settings and the society, test developers/administrators should take into consideration the concerns of equality, equity, and quality. In this light, psychological tests should be eco-culturally and inclusively friendly and thus reducing exclusion in all ramifications within and without school settings.

Apart from teacher-made tests that are mostly used among countries in Central Africa to determine the learning progress of learners, it is highly recommended that schools/societies should make use of other types of psychometric tests such as diagnostic tests, placement tests, vocational tests, aptitude tests, attitude tests, personality tests, and so on to gain information about the client's personality characteristics, symptoms, and problems in order to arrive at practical decisions about their behavior.

3.5   Conclusion

This chapter has highlighted the meaning of psychological testing vis à vis its importance to the practice of inclusive schooling within countries of

Central Africa. Different types of tests used in Central African countries have been examined and it was realized that most of the tests that were evident are mostly teacher-made tests and examination board tests. A good number of issues/problems associated with the current state of psychological testing in Central Africa were equally identified as well as some ethical issues to be considered before, during, and after administering psychological tests.

REFERENCES

Ahsan, S. & Smith, W. C. (2016). Facilitating student learning: A comparison of classroom and accountability assessment. In W. C. Smith (ed.), *The global testing culture: Shaping educational policy, perceptions, and practice* (pp. 131–152). Oxford: Symposium Books.

Black, P. & William, D. (1998). Assessment and classroom learning. *Assessment in education: Principles, policy and practice, 5*(1), 7–74.

Crooks, T. J. (2002). Educational assessment in New Zealand schools. *Assessment in education: Principles policy & practice, 9*(2), 237–253.

Greenfield, P. M. (1997). You cannot take it with you: Why ability assessments don't cross cultures. *American Psychologist, 52*(10), 1115–1124.

Holding, P. A., Taylor, H. G., Kazungu, S. D., Mkala, T., Gona, J., Mwamuye, B., Mbonani, L., & Stevenson, J. (2004). Assessing cognitive outcomes in a rural African population: Development of a neuropsychological battery in Kilifi District, Kenya. *Journal of the International Neuropsychological Society, 10*(2), 246–260.

Ikpaya B. O. (2001). *Exceptional children and youth introduction to special education.* Calabar: Clear Lines Publications.

Jatau, M. N., Uzo, C. C., & Lere, M. M. (2002). *Elements of special education for prospective teachers.* Jos: Deka Publications.

Kanjee, A. (2003). *Using assessment resource banks to improve the teaching and learning process, in improving the quality of primary education: Good practices and emerging models of district development* (pp. 59–71). Pretoria: District development support program/Research Triangle Institute.

Kathuria, R., & Serpell, R. (1998). Standardization of the Panga Munthu Test-A nonverbal cognitive test developed in Zambia. *Journal of Negro Education, 67* (3), 228–241.

Kellaghan, T. & Greaney, V. (2005). Monitoring performance: Assessments and examinations. In A. M. Verspoor (ed.), *The challenge of learning: Improving the quality of basic education in Sub-Saharan Africa* (pp. 271–292). Paris: Association for the Development of Education in Africa.

Lerner, G. (1993). *The creation of feminist consciousness: From the middle ages to eighteen-seventy.* New York: Oxford University Press.

Machona, P. E. & Kapambwe, W. (2003). *Enhancing teacher capacities and capabilities in learner assessment: The implementation of the Grade 4 basic*

Competence Testing Programme, Paper presented at the sub-regional conference on assessment: Learner assessment for improved educational quality. Livingstone, Zambia, June 30 to July 2.

Malda, M. & Van de Vijver, F. J. R. (2005). Assessing cognition in nutrition intervention trials across cultures. In H. H. Vorster, R. Blaauw, M. A. Dhansay, P. M. N. Kuzwayo, T. L. Moeng, & E. Wentzel-Viljoen (eds.), *Annals of Nutrition and Metabolism* (p. 5). Durban: Karger.

Melem L. F. (2016). Development and validation of a diagnostic test for the identification of children with functional cognitive learning disabilities. *African Journal of Social Sciences, 7*(4), 73–85.

Mpofu, E. (2002). Indigenization of the psychology of human intelligence in Sub-Saharan Africa. *Online Readings in Psychology and Culture (Unit 4)*. Retrieved from http://scholarworks.gvsu.edu/orpc/.

Mpofu, E. & Nyanungo, K. R. L. (1998). Educational and psychological testing in Zimbabwean schools: Past, present and future. *European Journal of Psychological Assessment, 14*(1), 71–90.

Mulenga, K., Ahonen, T., & Aro, M. (2001). Performance of Zambian children on the NEPSY: A pilot study. *Developmental Neuropsychology, 20*(1), 375–384.

Nell, V. (1997). Science and politics meet at last: The insurance industry and neuropsychological norms. *South African Journal of Psychology, 27*(1), 43–49.

Nsamenang, A. B. (2009). Conceptualizing developmental assessment within Africa's cultural settings. In E. L. Grigorenko (ed.), *Multicultural psychoeducational assessment* (pp. 95–131). London: Springer.

Nsamenang, A. B. & Dawes, A. (1998). Developmental psychology as political psychology in sub-Saharan Africa: The challenge of Africanisation. *Applied Psychology: An International Review, 47*(1), 73–87.

(1992). *Human development in cultural context: A Third World perspective*. Newbury Park, CA: Sage.

(1993). Psychology in sub-Saharan Africa. *Psychology and Developing Societies, 5* (2), 171–184.

(1995). Factors influencing the development of psychology in sub-Saharan Africa. *International Journal of Psychology, 30*(6), 729–739.

Nsamenang, A. B. (2006a). Origins and development of indigenous psychologies in Cameroon. In C. M. Allwood & J. W. Berry (eds.), *Origins and development of indigenous psychologies: An international analysis. International Journal of Psychology, 41*(4), 258–259.

(2006b). Human ontogenesis: An indigenous African view on development and intelligence. *International Journal of Psychology, 41*(4), 293–297.

(2007). Origins and development of scientific psychology in Afrique Noire. In M. J. Stevens & D. Wedding (eds.), under the supervision of John G. Adair. *Psychology: IUPsyS global resource (2007 edition)*. London: Psychology Press. www.psypress.com/iupsys/contents.asp.

Olabisi A. P. (2005). *Therapies for children with problems, a handbook for pre-primary and lower primary schools*, Vol. 1. Jos: Centre for Learning Disabilities and Audiology.

Owusu-Bempah, J. & Howitt, D. (1995). How Eurocentric psychology damages Africa. *The Psychologist: Bulletin of the British Psychological Society* (October): 462–465.

Peltzer, K., & Bless, C. (1989). History and present status of professional psychology in Zambia. *Psychology and Developing Societies, 1*(1), 51–64.

Serpell, R. (1993). *The significance of schooling: Life-journeys into an African society.* Cambridge: Cambridge University Press.

Sigman, M., Neumann, C., Carter, E., Cattle, D. J., D'Souza, S., & Bwibo, N. (1988). Home interactions and the development of Embu toddlers in Kenya. *Child Development, 59*, 1251–1261.

Sokopo, Z. N. (2004). *The interactional effects of different assessment policies on the assessment practices of Grade 9 teachers* (Unpublished PhD Thesis, Tshwane University of Technology, South Africa).

Sonke, C. J., Poortinga, Y. P., & De Kuijer, J. H. J. (1999). Cultural differences on cognitive task performance: The influence of task familiarity. In W. J. Lonner, D. L. Dinnel, D. K. Forgas, & S. A. Hayes (eds.), *Merging past, present, and future in cross-cultural psychology* (pp. 146–158). Lisse: Swets and Zeitlinger.

Sternberg, R. J., Grigorenko, E. L., Ngorosho, D., Tantufuye, E., Mbise, A., Nokes, C., Jukes, M., & Bundy, D. A. (2002). Assessing intellectual potential in rural Tanzanian school children. *Intelligence, 30*(2), 141–162.

Tchombe, T. M. (2011) Cultural strategies for cognitive enrichment in learning among the Bamiléké of West Region of Cameroon. In Nsamenang, A. B. & Tchombe, M. T. (eds.), *Handbook of African educational theories and practices: A generative teacher education curriculum* (pp. 205–216). Bamenda: HDRC.

UNESCO (1994). *The Salamanca statement and framework for action on special needs education.* Paris: UNESCO.

Van de Vijver, F. J. R. (2002). Cross-cultural assessment: Value for money. *Applied Psychology: An International Review, 51*(4), 545–566.

Van de Vijver, F. J. R., & Tanzer, N. K. (2004). Bias and equivalence in cross-cultural assessment: An overview. *European Journal of Applied Psychology, 54* (2), 119–135.

Vogt, D. S., King, D. W., & King, L. A. (2004). Focus groups in psychological assessment: Enhancing content validity by consulting members of the target population. *Psychological Assessment, 16*(1), 231–234.

Wasterman, D. (2001). The place and function of vernacular in African education. The International Review of Missions 1925. 14. Cited in Kishani, B. T. On the interface of philosophy and language in Africa: Some practical and theoretical considerations. *African Studies Review, 44*, 27–45.

Weisner, C. Bradley, & C. P. Kilbride (eds.). (1997). *African families and the crisis of social change.* Westport, CT: Bergin & Garvey.

Wiig, E. H. & Secord, W. A. (1999). *Diagnostic speech and language profiler. Experimental Edition.* Arlington, TX: Schema Press.

CHAPTER 4

Psychological Assessment in West Africa

Seth Oppong, Kwaku Oppong Asante, and Adote Anum

4.1 Introduction

The field of psychological assessment has seen consistent growth for almost a century with significant expansion of the literature centered largely around research in Western Europe and North America. Comparatively, there has not been as much progress in sub-Saharan Africa and this is typical of what pertains in many other non-Western countries. The measurement of constructs and development of psychological tests in sub-Saharan Africa therefore have largely been based on Eurocentric theories and philosophies (Durojaiye, 1984; Foxcroft, 2011; Oppong, 2016). This, according to Mpofu (2002), is partly because in sub-Saharan Africa scientific psychology is modeled on Western theories. There has not been enough research in sub-Saharan Africa to develop relevant indigenous African theories. Therefore, assessment is still closely tied to Western theories that inform development of tests and measurements. In this chapter we trace the history of psychological assessment in Anglophone West Africa. We discuss the trajectory of the psychological assessment, the need for the development of indigenous psychological assessment in order to wean itself from its Eurocentric roots, and finally the challenges and the prospects in West Africa.

West Africa, comprising 16 countries, lies between the Equator (latitude 0°) to the south and the Tropic of Cancer (latitude 23° 27′N of the Equator) to the north as well as longitude 15°E and longitude 15°W. These countries include Benin, Burkina Faso, Cape Verde, The Gambia, Ghana, Guinea, Guinea-Bissau, Ivory Coast, Liberia, Mali, Mauritania, Niger, Nigeria, Senegal, Sierra Leone, and Togo, as well as the United Kingdom Overseas Territory of Saint Helena, Ascension, and Tristan da Cunha (Masson & Pattillo, 2001; United Nations 2019). The region, with a population of about 391 million people, is home to the Economic Community of West African States (ECOWAS), which functions both as a political and economic union. This region also has two subregional blocs, namely (a) West African Economic and Monetary Union (UEMOA as the French acronym) comprising mainly the Francophone countries with CFA franc as their currency and (b) West African Monetary Zone (WAMZ), consisting mainly of the Anglophone countries, aimed at adopting ECO[1] as its currency. Later Ivory Coast joined WAMZ but the UEMOA backed by France has, without the consent of the majority of WAMZ members, launched ECO as their new currency. This region plays host to the headquarters of African Development Bank in Abidjan (Ivory Coast), Association of African Universities in African Research Universities Alliance in Accra (Ghana), and the African Continental Free Trade Area (AfCFTA) in Accra.

Several indigenous languages are spoken in West Africa, of which Hausa is the most widely spoken in the subregion (Heine & Nurse, 2007; Meshesha & Jawahar, 2007). The influence of colonization is a legacy of three co-official languages: French, English, and Portuguese. At the Berlin Conference of 1885 and 1886, West Africa was partitioned among the British, French, Portuguese, and Germans. However, the German territory (largely present-day Togo and part of Ghana) was shared between the British and the French after World War II. Liberia became the first free Black Nation in Africa in 1847 while Ghana the first colonized sub-Saharan African country to regain its independence in 1957 (Fynn, 1975). Prior to the encounter with Europe, West Africa had several great empires and kingdoms. The notable ones include empires of Old Ghana, Mali, and Songhai as well as the kingdoms of Asante, Oyo, Dahomy, and others. It is worth mentioning that the University of Sankore at Timbuktu was established in the Old Ghana Empire in 989 CE (Oppong, 2017a). Unfortunately, this region has also experienced many forms of political instability. This includes several coup d'etats and civil wars including the Nigerian (Biafra) Civil War, First Liberian Civil War, Second Liberian Civil War, Guinea-Bissau Civil War, Ivorian Civil War, and Sierra Leone Rebel War (Annan, 2014). The countries (Guinea, Liberia, and Sierra Leone) in this region were severely hit by the Ebola Virus outbreak from 2014 to 2016 (Secor et al., 2020).

West Africa is arguably one of the regions with a long and distinct history of psychology (see Oppong, 2014, 2016, 2017a; Oppong Asante & Oppong, 2012). Advanced studies of philosophy and physiology took place at the University of Sankore at Timbuktu, which was established

---

[1] The Authority of ECOWAS Heads of State and Government adopted in 2019 "ECO" as the name of the single currency to be issued in January 2020 but it did not materialise.

before European education. In this regard, the early precursors of scientific psychology were likely to have been studied at the University of Sankore (see Oppong, 2017a). In 1734, Anton Wilhelm Amo (from present-day Ghana) obtained his doctorate by defending a thesis, *De Humanae Mentis "Apatheia"* (on the apathy of the human mind or the absence of sense and of the faculty of sensing in the human mind and the presence of these in our organic and living body) (Archampong, 2012; Meyns, 2019; Oppong, 2017a). Amo's philosophy of mind focused on cognition and sensation, perception and the mind–body problem while critiquing René Descartes (Meyns, 2019). It has been argued that Amo's contributions belong to the modern precursors of psychology (Oppong, 2017a).

Despite this, scientific psychology as understood in the West/Global North arrived in the region as a colonial import (Nsamenang, 2007; Oppong Asante & Oppong, 2012; Oppong, et al., 2014; Oppong, 2014, 2017a). Within this region, the first formal Department of Psychology was established in Ghana at the University of Ghana (Nsamenang, 2007; Oppong Asante & Oppong, 2012). Psychology is more developed in the Anglophone countries than in the Francophone ones and it is more established in Ghana and Nigeria driven largely by the influence of the academic institutions and the professional associations. Thus, the region plays a key role in the development of psychology in Africa. This chapter therefore focuses on four English-speaking West African countries: Ghana, Nigeria, Liberia, and Sierra Leone. Liberia and Sierra Leone do not have well-developed programs in psychology but are included nevertheless. Liberia and Sierra Leone have experienced protracted civil war and were severely devastated by the 2014 Ebola outbreak – two events that had noticeable impacted on the mental health of both countries (Harris et al., 2020; Secor et al., 2020; WHO, 2017). The University of The Gambia has begun a psychology program. However, The Gambia will be excluded from this critical history because scientific psychology is in its infancy there. Similarly, through the efforts of the Association of Psychologists in Senegal (established in 2017), a department of psychology has been recently opened at the University of Dakar (American Psychological Association, 2021). However, Senegal (a Francophone country) is also excluded for the same reason as The Gambia. Histories of psychological assessment in Ghana, Nigeria, Liberia, and Sierra Leone are therefore presented. This is then followed by a reflection on current challenges for assessment and discussion of future developments in the region.

4.2   Psychological Assessment in Ghana

With a population of about 30 million, Ghana is located between Ivory Coast in the west, Burkina Faso in the north, Togo in the east, and the Gulf of Guinea and Atlantic Ocean in the south. The Equator and Greenwich Meridian pass through the territory of Ghana, making it the center of the world geographically. Ghana translates as "Warrior King" in the Soninke language (Jackson, 2001). The territory, then called the Gold Coast, was renamed Ghana when it regained its independence from the British in 1957. Ghana is a multiethnic country with several indigenous languages. English is the official language in which all formal business is conducted. The Akan language is the most widely spoken language, used mainly in the middle to southern parts of the country. The history of modern psychology in Ghana is similar to other parts of Africa (Nsamenang, 2007). Study of psychology likely commenced with the inception of teacher training and training of health professionals (Nsamenang, 2007; Oppong Asante & Oppong, 2012) prior to Ghana attaining independence in 1957. The study of psychology as a science commenced at the University of Ghana with different elements of the course taught in sociology, prison administration, and again in nursing. There are different dates one can reference as the origin of psychology in Ghana ranging from the establishment of the University of Sankore, Timbuktu established in 989 CE through to the establishment of Basel Seminary (now Presbyterian College of Education) in 1898, and the founding of the Department of Psychology at the University of Ghana in 1967 (see Oppong, 2017a).

In spite of this potential claim to different origins, it is well noted that the first academic department of psychology in West Africa was established in Ghana (Nsamenang, 2007; Oppong Asante & Oppong, 2012). The first clinical psychologist in West Africa was the late Prof. Samuel A. Danquah (from Ghana) who qualified in 1971 (see Mensah-Sarbah, 2005; Oppong, 2019b). While there is no documentation about the exact date of commencement of psychological assessment in Ghana, one can make references to the earliest application of psychological assessment in educational settings. Adopting a lose definition of psychological assessment as the use of interviews, observations, and testing to make decisions about people in education (Oppong, 2016, 2017b), it is reasonable to assume that psychological assessment began as achievement testing in Ghana.

The application of psychological assessment in other settings (clinical, counseling, industrial, and neuropsychology) came much later after 1967. The training of clinical psychologists in Ghana is reported to have begun in

1974 at the Department of Psychology of the University of Ghana (Mensah-Sarbah, 2005). The genesis of psychological assessment in Industrial and Organizational (I-O) psychology is not well documented but anecdotal evidence suggests that H. C. A. Bulley, a psychometrician, a consultant, and a lecturer with the Department of Psychology at University of Ghana was the first to employ psychological assessment for selecting personnel into the Ghana Armed Forces, Ghana Police Service, and several organizations, notably Unilever Ghana Limited. Graduate training of I-O psychologists began in the 1980s (Oppong, 2013). Historically, the I-O Psychology program at University of Ghana has not included a module on psychological assessment but it has often been taught as part of personnel psychology in the area of personnel selection. On the other hand, assessment is core to the training in clinical psychology. Currently, doctoral students in psychology take an examinable course in advanced psychological assessment. Clinical psychology training is now available at the University of Cape Coast and University of Ghana (Oppong, 2016). Plans are underway for the University of Cape Coast to introduce master's degree and doctoral programs in I-O Psychology.

Essuman (1999) provides a good summary of the history of guidance and counseling in Ghana. Suffice to say that 1955 marked the beginning of formalized guidance in Ghana when the Ministries of Labour, Social Welfare, and Education collaborated to set up a Youth Employment Department. By 1961, about 30 such youth employment centers had been established in Ghana (Essuman, 1999). By 1976, the Ghana Education Service (GES) had developed a guidance and counseling policy that required all second cycle institutions to have guidance and counseling coordinators (Essuman, 1999); this was extended to basic schools in 1982. The first batch of "about 200 guidance coordinators had been trained [by University of Cape Coast] and were working in second cycle institutions, regional and district offices of the GES" (Essuman, 1999, 31–32). In 1976, graduate studies in counseling commenced at University of Cape Coast. University of Ghana established its Counselling and Placement Centre in November 1970 (Agbodeka, 1998; Essuman, 1999). Advanced training in counseling psychology and educational psychology is available at University of Cape Coast and University of Education, Winneba, with the Methodist University College of Ghana and University of Ghana also providing advanced training in counseling psychology (Oppong Asante & Oppong, 2012; Oppong et al., 2014). University of Cape Coast offers master's and doctoral training in educational measurement and evaluation.

Other major developments in Ghana include the establishment of the Ghana Psychology Council (GPC) by the Health Professions Regulatory

Bodies Act, 2013 (ACT 857) and the Ghana Psychological Association in 1998 (Ghana Psychological Association [GPA], 2020), as well as the indigenization movement and/or the realization of the shortcomings of the currently used psychological instruments (see Foxcroft, 2011; Oppong, 2016, 2017b). Using Western imported tests without appropriate norming has the potential to result in epistemological violence in practice and research (see Oppong, 2015, 2019a, 2020; Osei-Tutu et al., 2020). The GPC accredits psychology programs as well as licenses psychologists in order to ensure public safety in the use of psychological services (including psychological assessment). The GPC has currently made recommendations for revising the curriculum of the counseling and guidance curricula and to rename the programs counseling psychology. The GPA plays important disaster management roles in Ghana, including its activities during the June 3 fire and flooding, the banking crises, and its role in the fight against the COVID-19 pandemic. It makes the GPA one of psychological associations (and therefore Ghanaian psychologists) globally to be heavily involved in national development issues. In its five-year strategic plan, the GPA (2020) commits itself to standardizing psychological tools not validated for use in Ghana. The need for culturally sensitive tests is an ethical requirement for professional practice in psychology (Asumeng & Opoku, 2014; Foxcroft, 2011; Opoku, 2012; Oppong, 2017b). It is also important for the development of psychology for teaching test development and validation procedures as well as clinical practice. It is an important step toward ensuring that attention is drawn to the need for collective efforts to develop tests.

There have been several efforts to validate psychological scales for both industry and clinical practice. In Table 4.1, we have summarized the commonly used tests in Ghana. These generally fall within three broad categories: school or achievement tests, personnel selection tests, and clinical/neuropsychological tests. The Wide Range Achievement Test (WRAT 4) is an achievement test but is used mainly in clinical settings for school placement and to diagnose school-related problems. The National Education Assessment (NEA) is used primarily to estimate the extent to which Ghanaian school children are reaching criterion for literacy and numeracy skills (see Oppong, 2017b).

In Ghana, tests are more commonly used for clinical purposes, mainly diagnosis and decision on intervention, and therefore a lot more tests fall within this category. The challenge, however, is that very few of these tests are standardized on the Ghanaian population and therefore the utility of the tests depends solely on the expertise of the practitioner.

Table 4.1. *Some of the commonly used psychological tests in Ghana*

Setting	Types of Tests	Source/Reference
School/educational	Teacher-made tests (e.g., class exercises, homework, oral examinations, essay tests, objective tests, and assignments)	GES, technical reports
	Examination board-made tests	Kniel & Kniel (2008)
	University admissions tests	Dept. of Psychiatry, UGMS; unpublished data
	English (essay, comprehension, grammar, and usage)	
	General paper (quantitative methods, critical thinking and current affairs)	
	NEA*	
	Draw a Person Test for Ghana*	
	Wide Range Achievement Test (WRAT 4)*	
	Self-search career interest test	
Clinical, neuropsychological, and counselling	Basic Personality Inventory*	Oteng-Yeboah (2005), unpublished data.
	Wechsler Intelligence Scale for Children (WISC-III UK)*	Edwin (2002), unpublished data
	Wechsler Adult Intelligence Scale (WAIS-III and IV)*	Miezah (2015), unpublished data
	Kaufman Assessment Battery for Children (KABC - II)*	Quartey (2014), unpublished data
	Comprehensive Test of Nonverbal Intelligence (CTONI)	Appiah et al. (2020); Lenz et al. (2018)
	Multidimensional Aptitude Battery	Anum et al. (in press); Appiah et al. (2020)
	Coping Inventory for Stressful Situations	Adjorlolo (2019)
	SWLS*	Anum (2014); Yawson (2008), unpublished data
	ADHD test	Debrah (2002); unpublished data
	Bender Visual Motor Gestalt Test (Bender-Gestalt Test)	Adjorlolo (2016)
	Patient Health Questionnaire*	Adjorlolo (2016); Frempong-Boakye (2017); unpublished data
	Generalised Anxiety Disorder-7 scale*	
	Beck Depression Inventory (BDI)	

Table 4.1. (*cont.*)

Setting	Types of Tests	Source/Reference
	Brief Symptom Inventory (BSI)	Adjorlolo et al. (2020)
	Beck Anxiety Inventory (BAI)	Anum et al. (2020)
	Raven's Progressive Matrices (Colored and Standard)*	
	General Health Questionnaire	
	Woodcock Johnson Test for Cognition and Achievement – WJ-III	
	Childhood Autism Rating Scale	
	Minnesota Paper Form Board Test	
	Montreal Cognitive Assessment	
	PTSD Test (Civilian and military)	
	Minnesota Multiphasic Personality Inventory	
	Hopelessness Scale	
	Basic Personality Inventory	
	Coping Inventory for Stressful Situations	
	Multidimensional Aptitude Battery*	
	Depression, Anxiety Stress Scale (DASS 42)	
	Basic Personality Inventory	
	Quality of Life Test	
	Facial Recognition Test	
	Mini-Mental Status Exams	
	Trail Making Test*	
	Revised Quick Cognitive Screening Test (QCST-R)*	
	Alzheimer's disease Assessment Scale-Cognitive Subscale	
	Suicide Behaviour Questionnaire*	
	WHOQoL_OLD*	

This situation is changing gradually and in the last 10 years, the research in standardization has increased significantly (see Table 4.1).

The first of such standardizations were done on the Raven's Coloured Progressive Matrices (Anum, 2014) and Raven's Standard Progressive Matrices (Yawson, 2008). Two other intelligence tests, the Wechsler Intelligence Scales for children and adults (Edwin, 2001; Miezah, 2015) and the Kaufman Assessment Battery for Children (Quartey, 2014) have also been standardized. The use of psychological tests for the measurement of psycho-pathology is widespread for research and clinical purposes. As reported for intelligence tests, several of these measures have been standardized on the local population. The most common instruments are the Revised Quick Cognitive Screening Test (Adjorlolo, 2016; Frempong-Boakye, 2017); the Generalised Anxiety Disorder-7 scale (Adjorlolo, 2019); the Satisfaction with Life Scale, Short Grit Scale, General Mattering Scale, Brief Resilience Scale (Lenz et al., 2018); Patient Health Questionnaire-9 (PHQ-9) (Anum et al., 2019); and the Akan versions of Affectometer-2 (AFM-2), Automatic Thought Questionnaire–Positive (ATQ-P), Generalized Self-Efficacy Scale (GSEs), PHQ-9, and Satisfaction with Life Scale (SWLS) (Appiah et al., 2020).

Appiah et al. (2020) validated Akan (Twi) versions of the AFM-2, ATQ-P, GSEs, PHQ-9, and SWLS for use in Ghana. The World Health Organization (WHO) quality of life measure for older adults was also translated into three indigenous Ghanaian languages and validated (Anum et al. 2020). These suggest there is a shift to creating cross-culturally sensitive measures for research and clinical work. Many of these validation studies are driven largely by research needs that require the measurement of mental health constructs rather than for clinical purposes. The focus therefore is on a healthy general population. Findings from these, however, provide benchmarks that help designate a range of scores considered to be normal. Developing clinical benchmarks is therefore not difficult. There are a few validation studies that have used clinical popula-tions; these include the Stroop Test, Controlled Oral Word Association Test, Trail Making Test (TMT) (Adjorlolo, 2016), and the general cog-nitive screening test, Revised Quick Cognitive Screening Test (RQCST) (Adjorlolo, 2016; Frempong-Boakye, 2017).

Two factors have hampered the dissemination of findings from these validations. First, the efforts at publishing these studies for cross-cultural comparisons have been slow. Second, very little effort is made to modify tests to suit nonurban and less literate populations therefore limiting the extent of generalizability of these findings. To date there has been only one study in which an entire battery of tests was modified to develop a culture-sensitive assessment (Holding et al., 2018).

Two facts emerge from this critical history: that there is an increasing drive to validate and normalize foreign instruments and that there is very little effort in developing indigenous psychological instruments. Developing new instruments is usually more difficult, requiring large sample size and substantial funding. Psychological assessment has not received much attention in research. With growing interest in this field, it is likely that needed funds will become available for instruments to be developed locally. Furthermore, the development of the Characterological Interpersonal Coping Styles Diagnostics (CICS-D) – a theory-informed assessment tool in Ghana – is worth mentioning. The CICS-D was designed to assist clinicians and other assessors to determine preferred styles of social interaction (Oppong, 2019c).

4.3 Psychological Assessment in Nigeria

Located between Niger in the north, Chad in the northeast, Cameroon in the east, and Benin in the west with its southern coast as the Gulf of Guinea in the Atlantic Ocean, the Federal Republic of Nigeria comprises 36 states and the Federal Capital Territory with Abuja as its administrative capital and Lagos as its commercial capital. With a total area of about 923,768 km^2, Nigeria is estimated to have a population of around 203.5 million (United Nations, 2019; World Factbook, 2019). It is a multiethnic nation comprising more than 250 ethnic groups with over 500 distinct languages: the Hausa–Fulani in the north, Yoruba in the west, and Igbo in the east constituting over 60% of the total population are the three largest ethnic groups in Nigeria (World Factbook, 2019). The major languages spoken in Nigeria are English (official), Hausa, Yoruba, and Igbo. This oil-producing country is the home to the headquarters of ECOWAS and a member of Organization of the Petroleum Exporting Countries (OPEC). As is the case with many African countries, scientific psychology was also a colonial import. Its origin is often traced to the establishment of the first psychology department in Nigeria that was founded about 1964 at the University of Nigeria, Nsukka, with around 16 students and two lecturers (Allwood, 2018; Mayer, 2002). Another key historical event is the international cross-cultural psychology conference (the Ibadan Conference) convened by Herbert Kelman and Henri Tajfel in January 1967 in Ibadan.

Nigeria is among the countries in Africa with the most psychology departments (Allwood, 2018; Mayer, 2002). Its history of psychological testing can be traced to educational testing as it may have been broadly practiced by the Islamic scholars in the northern part of Nigeria in the early fourteenth century (see Adeyemi, 2016). This is because the scholars tested the performance of their students before they were deemed fit to bring their education to an end at their madrasa. However, it is reasonable to suggest that psychological testing in the broader sense may have commenced either in 1955 when organized and formal guidance and counseling services became available at St. Theresa's College or with the founding of psychological academic departments, particularly the establishment of the Department of Behavioural Science and Clinical Behaviour Therapy at the College of Medicine of the University of Calabar. Mensah-Sarbah (2005) has noted, prior to Prof. S. A. Danquah being engaged by the Federal Government in 1982, that there were other departments of clinical psychology at Ibadan, Ife, and Lagos. He stated that "those departments at the Nigerian Universities were concerned with the traditional roles of psychological testing and measurements" (Mensah-Sarbah, 2005, 32). The implication is that psychological assessment practices may have begun earlier than the 1980s. This focus on psychological testing is collaborated by Njoku (2012, 5) who suggests that "it appears that all psychologists are tending towards similar areas of emphasis, namely, testing and in academic settings" in Nigeria. She has called on Nigerian psychologists "to distinguish them-selves in the specific focus areas of their specialty" (Njoku, 2012, 5).

The existence of Nigerian Psychological Association (NPA) as well as the Counselling Association of Nigeria has contributed to the professionalization of psychology in Nigeria. Despite these efforts, it is said that psychology is not legally regulated nor very organized as is the case in Ghana or South Africa (see Allwood, 2018; Njoku, 2012). Though the Nigerian Council for Psychologists Act (Est) Bill is said to have been passed by the National Assembly, NPA is advocating for immediate assent so that the Nigerian Council for Psychologists (NCfP) can be established ("Association urges President" May 2019). Nigerian psychology has also been characterized as problem oriented rather than theoretically oriented (Mayer, 2002) resulting in a poorly developed psychological research community in Nigeria (Allwood, 2018). It is important to note that *Ife PsychologIA* is a very prominent journal published in Nigeria by the Ife Centre for Psychological Studies and Services. Other developments in Nigeria that have shaped testing include the estab-lishment of the following: Nigeria Aptitude Testing Unit (now defunct) in 1964; Test Development and Research Office (now Test Development and Research Unit of WAEC) in 1966; and the Joint Admission and Matriculation Board (JAMB) in 1976 (Nweze, 2009).

A literature search failed to yield any significant result about commonly used psychological assessment tools in Nigeria. For instance, Njoku (2012) only mentions the fact that Nigerian psychologists are largely involved in psychological testing while Omoniyi (2016) intimates that there are limited availability of psychological tests for counseling in Nigerian schools. Obot (1996) also reported that Nigerian psychologists are employed in the health care system, both in the training of physicians and practice in the psychiatric establishments. These clinical psychologists provide psychological assessment services as well. In spite of the limited information about the commonly used tests in Nigeria, it is acknowledged that psychological testing is important. However, many commentators decry the use of Western imported tests without appropriate Nigerian norms (Adejumo, 2008; Olowookere, 2011; Omoniyi, 2016). Though Olowookere (2011) acknowledged the need for locally made psychological tests, she identified the following as some of the challenges associated with developing psychological tests in Nigeria: (a) limited availability of psychometricians, (b) limited funding and time constraints, (c) heavy work overload on the academics who are also expected to develop the tests, (d) limited training and mentoring of new test developers, and (e) unattractiveness of psychometrics as a domain for practice among psychology trainees. These challenges may similarly account for lack of activities in the development of psychological tests in West Africa as a whole and in other regions of Africa as well.

In spite of the limited literature on psychological assessment in Nigeria, there are several studies that report use of assessment in the measurement of psychological constructs as observed in emotional intelligence (Adeyemo & Adeleye, 2008), work-related outcomes (Karatepe, 2011), and well-being (Emasealu & Popoola, 2016; Mazzucato et al., 2015). The GHQ-12, Hospital Anxiety and Depression Scale, Kessler-6 (Mughal et al., 2020) and Draw a Person Test (Bakare, 1972; Ebigbo & Izuora, 1981) have been standardized. These are by no means exhaustive but serve to illustrate the fact that psychological assessment exists in Nigeria.

4.4 Psychological Assessment in Liberia and Sierra Leone

Liberia and Sierra Leone are neighboring countries. They are located west of Ivory Coast and both share a border with Guinea. Both countries have been devastated by protracted civil wars in the 1990s and severely by the Ebola outbreak. They share a similar history. Liberia was founded by the free slaves from the United States (and declared its independence in 1847 from the American Colonization Society) while Sierra Leone was founded by free slaves from the United States and West Indies (and attained its independence in 1961 from the British). In Sierra Leone, the Temne and Mende are the two largest and most influential ethnic groups. There are 16 officially recognized ethnic groups in Liberia including the Americo-Liberians (descendants of the free slaves); of the 16 ethnic groups, the Kpelle is the largest with more than 20% of the population. Both countries have different versions of the creole language. Liberia has a population of about 4.1 million (WHO 2017) while Sierra Leone has a population of about 7.09 million (Harris et al., 2020).

Psychology is not well established in both countries (Harris et al, 2020; Davis-Russell, 2013; Oppong, 2019d; WHO, 2017). Both countries have few practicing psychologists and no regulatory bodies for the practice of psychology (Harris et al., 2020; WHO, 2017). The limited availability of trained psychologists in these countries does not suggest that there are no trained psychologists; they have citizens who are qualified as psychologists in the diaspora but are largely uninterested in relocating to the home countries. Within the Faculty of Social Sciences, the University of Makeni, Sierra Leone has a Department of Counselling Psychology while the only psychology program in Liberia is located at the William V. S. Tubman University; in October 2016, the University of Liberia also commenced a degree program in social work. Neither country has graduate training programs in psychology. They have mostly received the services of foreign psychologists attached to the many international nongovernmental organizations that provided psychosocial support in the wake of both the civil wars and the Ebola outbreak. The WHO (2017) has pointed out that cultural competence is required for offering psychosocial services to the victims of war and Ebola survivors in Liberia.

The current state of psychology in both countries suggests that there are no norming of psychological tests and possibly only Western imported tests are being used by the few psychologists who may be practicing there without regulations. The concerns raised about the use of nonvalidated tests equally apply here (see Foxcroft, 2011; Olowookere, 2011; Omoniyi, 2016; Opoku, 2012; Oppong, 2017b). The Child War Trauma Questionnaire, Oxford Refugee Studies Program's psychosocial adjustment measure (Betancourt et al., 2010), UCLA Post-Traumatic Stress Disorder Reaction Index, Family Relations Scale of the Childhood Trauma Questionnaire, Everyday Discrimination Scale (Betancourt et al., 2013), and Life Events Checklist, PTSD Checklist, Center for Epidemiologic Studies Depression Scale, and GHQ (Akinsulure-Smith & Keatley, 2014) have been used in Sierra Leone with PHQ-9 and

GAD-7 being applied in Guinea, Liberia, and Sierra Leone (Secor et al., 2020). The factor structure for the Post-Traumatic Stress Diagnostic Index has been examined in Sierra Leone (Vinson & Chang, 2012). Perhaps, the most remarkable thing to say here is that it was in Liberia that Glick (August 1968, cited in Triandis, 2009, 4) discovered that "what Western psychologists use as a clue for intelligence is used by the Kpelle is a clue for stupidity," giving us preliminary evidence of cross-cultural variations in the conceptions of cognitive abilities.

4.5 Current Challenges

Psychological assessment has not developed significantly in West Africa when we consider history and trends in the discipline. The growth is hindered by a number of inter-connected challenges. These challenges include (a) use of Western imported tests without suitable norms in the region, (b) limited opportunities for advanced training in psychometrics in the region, (c) limited research funding for test development and standard-ization, (d) issue of multiplicity of cultures and languages in each country, and (e) absence of test development companies. Development of an original and culturally appropriate test involves a lengthy and laborious process; a task that requires expertise and significant funding. A less expensive alterna-tive is to standardize or create comparative norms on local populations. When local norms are developed, scores of the local population are com-pared to similar individuals and therefore they are not unfairly characterized by their responses on the instruments. Another approach is to replace images or items with more culturally sensitive ones so that they are familiar to the local population, an approach called adaptation. Holding et al. (2018), for example, used this approach when studying long-term neuropsychological effects of severe malaria in a rural population of children and adolescents in Ghana. This approach has been used successfully in Kenya in measuring neurocognitive ability of children in rural communities or among children with little education (e.g., Kitsao-Wekulo et al., 2013).

A lack of indigenous test development is an outcome of a narrow focus in training of psychologists. Graduate training in psychology in Ghana and Nigeria focuses on three key programs: clinical/counseling, health, and industrial and organizational psychology. The unintended effect is that it creates a deficit in the expertise and a knowledge gap in other psychology disciplines. Universities teaching psychology will need to expand graduate programs to train and provide expertise in psychometrics, a necessary condition for test construction and standardization.

The ideal solution to the challenges of testing in West Africa is for the indigenous development of measurement instruments that directly measure psychological constructs defined within the local cultural contexts. This is not only hindered by funding and expertise constraints but also influenced by the diversity in indigenous languages. West African countries are multi-lingual and multicultural. In Ghana, for example, there are at least 11 cod-ified languages referred to as "government sponsored" languages. The use of multiple languages means psychological constructs are not likely to have equivalences across languages thereby making it difficult to have a single measure for a construct. Developing multiple measures for two or more languages or culture groups for a construct increases the potential for bias. For example, it is not uncommon that crucial words cannot be translated or for those words not to exist in another language (Abubakar et al., 2009). This is no different from the problem of Western bias that has dogged assessment in African and non-Western contexts (Van de Vijver, 2002).

Ghana and Nigeria will have to provide leadership in the discipline in the subregion to improve psychological assessment. With a significant number of psychologists and researchers, the responsibility rests on aca-demics in these two countries to continue to validate and test ecological validity of measures for the subregion. Collaborative research with aca-demics in countries with limited capacity across the subregion will accel-erate the instrument validation and improve cross-cultural research. This can be done by conducting research in multiple countries or collaborating with academics in cognate fields to gather data in the other West African countries. Equally needed is an effort on the part of the centers of excellence in psychology (the University of Ghana and the University of Ibadan) in the region to reach out to the entire region by way of offering scholarships for graduate studies in psychology. This also calls for more collaboration between Ghana and Nigeria. The growth of psychology and psychological assessment in Ghana and Nigeria should stimulate its growth in the entire region. Inability to do the aforementioned may undermine the growth of psychology as a profession in the entire subregion.

4.6 Future Prospects

There are opportunities for growth in the practice of psychological assess-ment in the region. The transfer of tests to a non-Western context causes bias and frequently leads to reliability and validity problems in psycholog-ical assessment (Van de Vijver 2002). This does not allow for cross-cultural comparisons and thereby creates the realization that many of the commonly used tests have deficiencies. This has sparked interest in standardization studies in the region.

Mental health is gradually gaining recognition as a national public health issue in the region. There are also early signs that the training in and practice of psychology will expand given that new psychology departments have been established in Liberia, Sierra Leone, and The Gambia. Researchers in Ghana are leading the way in the translation of tests into indigenous languages for the purposes of validation (e.g., Appiah et al., 2020; Hamzat et al., 2009). In Mali, Thalmayer et al. (2019) have developed and examined the personality structure among the Supyire-Senufo people using a lexical survey of their indigenous language. The accumulating scientific literature on psychological assessment including this book chapter also provides opportunities for individuals intending to use tests, develop new tests, or standardize tests in the region. It is expected that psychological assessment will grow in the region when these opportunities are exploited. Teachers of psychology, particularly those teaching psychological assessment and psychometrics, should improve their pedagogical approaches to make this subfield attractive to the new generation of psychologists being trained. It will be useful for the centers of excellence in psychology in the region to develop postgraduate programs focusing on psychometrics. There are graduate programs in educational measurement and evaluation in the region; however, the nature of the training prepares the students better for assessment in educational settings without adequate orientation for the other setting of applications of psychological assessment. Research supervisors should encourage their doctoral students to consider conducting validation studies on existing tests or daring to improve the existing tests or even constructing new ones.

4.7 Conclusion

This chapter has reviewed the history of psychological assessment in West Africa with special focus on Ghana, Nigeria, Liberia, and Sierra Leone. Generally, psychology and psychological assessment are well established in Ghana relative to Nigeria. However, both Ghana and Nigeria have more advanced practice and training in psychology than the rest of the countries in the region. There are fewer or no locally developed tests in the region leading to overreliance on imported tests. These imported tests are often without suitable norms for use in the region because the rate of standardization studies does not match the rate of proliferation of tests. Noting the challenges and prospects for psychological assessment in the region, it is reasonable to conclude that Ghana and Nigeria have enormous responsibility to create and sustain interest in the research and practice. It is equally reasonable to conclude that the demand for psychological services (including psychological assessment) will rise. Owing to this, advanced training in psychometrics including computer applications in testing will be in great demand for locally developed tests. Developments in Ghana and Nigeria will shape the future of psychological testing in the region. As a result, the growth of psychology and psychological assessment in Ghana and Nigeria should stimulate its growth in the entire region else we fail as a profession. This will require regional thinking instead of national orientation. Psychological assessment in the region should be approached as an ECOWAS project. Thus, we implore psychologists in Ghana and Nigeria to call for a regional meeting to strategize for the growth of psychological assessment in West Africa.

REFERENCES

"Association urges President." (May 2019). *Association urges President Buhari to sign bill to establish psychological council.* Retrieved from www.vanguardngr.com/2019/05/association-urges-president-buhari-to-sign-bill-to-establish-psychological-council/

Abubakar, A., Van de Vijver, F. J. R., Van Baar, A. L., Wekulo-Kitsao, P., & Holding, P. (2009). Enhancing psychological assessment in sub-Saharan Africa through participant consultation. In A. Gari, & K. Mylonas (eds.), *Quod erat demonstrandum: From Herodotus' ethnographic journeys to cross-cultural research* (pp. 169–181). Athens: Pedio Books Publishing.

Adejumo, G. O. (2008). Scope, nature and uses of psychological test. In E. M. Hassan, S. E. Oladipo, & Owoyele, J. W (eds.), *Reading in counselling psychology.* Department of Counselling Psychology, College of Applied Education and Vocational Technology, Tai Solarin University of Education, Ijebu-Ode, Silver print Communication.

Adeyemi, K. A. (2016). The trend of Arabic and Islamic education in Nigeria: Progress and prospects. *Open Journal of Modern Linguistics, 6*(3), 197–201. http://dx.doi.org/10.4236/ojml.2016.63020

Adeyemo, D. A., & Adeleye, A. T. (2008). Emotional intelligence, religiosity and self-efficacy as predictors of psychological well-being among secondary school adolescents in Ogbomoso, Nigeria. *Europe's Journal of Psychology, 4* (1), 22–31.

Adjorlolo, S. (2016). Ecological validity of executive function tests in moderate traumatic brain injury in Ghana. *The Clinical Neuropsychologist 30*(sup1): 1517–1537. https://doi.org/10.1080/13854046.2016.1172667

(2019). Generalised anxiety disorder in adolescents in Ghana: Examination of the psychometric properties of the Generalised Anxiety Disorder-7 scale.

African Journal of Psychological Assessment, *1*(0), a10. https://doi.org/10 .4102/ajopa.v1i0.10

Adjorlolo, S., Anum, A., & Amin, J. M. (2020). Validation of the Suicidal Behaviours Questionnaire-Revised in adolescents in Ghana. *Journal of Mental Health*, 1–7. Advance online publication. https://doi.org/10.1080/ 09638237.2020.1739239

Agbodeka, F. (1998). *A history of university of Ghana: Half a century of higher education (1948–1998)*. Accra: Woeli.

Akinsulure-Smith, A. M., & Keatley, E. (2014). Secondary trauma and local mental health professionals in post conflict Sierra Leone. *International Journal for the Advancement of Counselling*, *36*(2), 125–135. https://doi.org/ 10.1007/s10447–013-9197-5

Allwood, C. M. (2018). *The nature and challenges of indigenous psychologies*. Cambridge: Cambridge University Press.

American Psychological Association. (2021, May). Psychological practice in Senegal: Challenges and opportunities. Global Insights Newsletter. https:// www.apa.org/international/global-insights/psychological-practice-senegal

Annan, N. (2014). Violent conflicts and civil strife in West Africa: Causes, challenges and prospects. *Stability: International Journal of Security & Development*, *3*(1), 1–16. http://dx.doi.org/10.5334/sta.da

Anum, A. (2014). A standardisation study of the Raven's Coloured Progressive Matrices in Ghana. *Ife PsychologIA: An International Journal*, *22*(2), 27–35.

Anum, A., Adjorlolo, S., & Kugbey, N. (2019). Depressive symptomatology in adolescents in Ghana: Examination of psychometric properties of the Patient Health Questionnaire-9. *Journal of Affective Disorders*, *256*, 213–218.

Anum, A., Adjorlolo, S., Akotia, C. S., & de-Graft Aikins, A. (2021). Validation of the multidimensional WHOQOL-OLD in Ghana: A study among population-based healthy adults in three ethnically different districts. *Brain and Behavior*, *11*(8), e02193. https://doi.org/10.1002/brb3.2193

Appiah, R., Schutte, L., Fadiji, A. W., Wissing, M. P., & Cromhout, A. (2020). Factorial validity of the Twi versions of five measures of mental health and well-being in Ghana. *PLoS One*, *15*(8), e0236707. https://doi.org/10.1371/ journal.pone.0236707

Archampong, C. B. K. (2012). Amo's philosophy of mind and Cartesian episte- mology. *Journal on African Philosophy*, *1*(5), 59–76.

Asumeng, M. A. & Opoku, Y. J. (2014). Psychological testing. In C. S. Akotia & C.C. Mate-Kole (eds.), *Contemporary psychology: Readings from Ghana* (pp. 39–49). Accra: Digibooks Ghana Ltd.

Bakare, C. (1972). Social class differences in the performance of Nigerian children on the draw-a-Man Test. In L. J. Cronbach & P. J. D. Drenth (eds.), *Mental tests and cultural adaptation* (pp. 355–363). Netherlands: Mouton.

Betancourt, T. S., Borisova, I. I., Williams, T. P., Brennan, R. T., Whitfield, T. H., de la Soudiere, M., Williamson, J., & Gilman, S. E. (2010). Sierra Leone's former child soldiers: A follow-up study of psychosocial adjustment and community reintegration. *Child Development, 81*(4), 1077–1095. https://doi.org/10.1111/j.1467-8624.2010.01455.x

Betancourt, T. S., Newnham, E. A., McBain, R., & Brennan, R. T. (2013). Post-traumatic stress symptoms among former child soldiers in Sierra Leone: Follow-up study. *The British Journal of Psychiatry, 203*(3), 196–202. https://doi.org/10.1192/bjp.bp.112.113514

Davis-Russell, E. (2013). Pan-African psychology: A view from Liberia. *Journal of Black Psychology, 39*(3), 333–335.

Debrah, L. A. (2002). Standardization of the Multidimensional Aptitude Battery (MAB). Unpublished master's dissertation, University of Ghana, Accra, Ghana.

Durojaiye, M. O. A. (1984). The impact of psychological testing on educational and personnel selection in Africa. *International Journal of Psychology, 19*(1–4), 135–144.

Ebigbo, P. O. & Izuora, G. I. (1981). *Draw a person test: Standardization, validation and guidelines for use in Nigeria.* Enugu, Nigeria: Chuka Printing Company Ltd.

Edwin, A. K. (2001). *Is the Wechsler Intelligence Scale for Children (WISC-IVUK) applicable?* (Unpublished master's dissertation, University of Ghana, Accra, Ghana).

Emasealu, H. U. & Popoola, S. O. (2016). Information needs, accessibility and utilization of library information resources as determinants of psychological well-being of prison inmates in Nigeria. *Brazilian Journal of Information Science: Research Trends, 10*(2), 29–46. https://doi:10.36311/1981-1640.2016.v10n2.05.p29.

Essuman, J. K. (1999). The History of Guidance and Counselling in Ghana. *Ife PsychologIA: An International Journal, 7*(2), 22–43. https://doi: 10.4314/ifep.v7i2.23555

Foxcroft, C. D. (2011). Ethical issues related to psychological testing in Africa: What I have learned (so far). *Online Readings in Psychology and Culture 2*(2). https://doi.org/10.9707/2307-0919.1022

Frempong-Boakye, T. (2017). *Validation of the revised quick cognitive screening test in a Ghanaian sample.* Unpublished master's dissertation, University of Ghana, Accra, Ghana.

Fynn, J. K. (1975). *A junior history of Ghana.* Accra, Ghana: Sedco.

Ghana Psychological Association. (2020). *5 year strategic plan (2021–2026).* Accra, Ghana: Author.

Hamzat, T. K., Samir, M., & Peters, G. O. (2009). Development and some psychometric properties of Twi (Ghanaian) version of the visual analogue scale. *American Journal of Biomedical Research, 12* (2), 145–148.

Harris, D., Endale, T., Lind, U. H., Sevalie, S., Bah, A. J., Jalloh, A., & Baingana, F. (2020). Mental health in Sierra Leone. *BJPsych International, 17* (1), 14–16. https://doi.org/10.1192/bji.2019.17

Heine, B. & Nurse, D. (2007). African languages: An introduction, In B. Heine & D. Nurse (eds.), *A linguistic geography of Africa* (pp. 1–10). Cambridge, UK: Cambridge University Press.

Holding, P., Anum, A., van de Vijver, F. J., Vokhiwa, M., Bugase, N., Hossen, T., . . . & Hasan, R. (2018). Can we measure cognitive constructs consistently within and across cultures? Evidence from a test battery in Bangladesh, Ghana, and Tanzania. *Applied Neuropsychology: Child, 7*(1), 1–13.

Jackson, J. G. (2001). *Introduction to African civilizations.* New York: Citadel Press.

Karatepe, O. M. (2011). Procedural justice, work engagement, and job outcomes: Evidence from Nigeria. *Journal of Hospitality Marketing & Management, 20* (8), 855–878.

Kitsao-Wekulo, P. K., Holding, P. A., Taylor, H. G., Abubakar, A., & Connolly, K. (2013). Neuropsychological testing in a rural African school-age population: Evaluating contributions to variability in test performance. *Assessment,* 20(6), 776–784.

Kniel, A. & Kniel, C. (2008). *The draw a person test for Ghana.* Winneba, Ghana: University of Education.

Lenz, A. S., Watson, J.C., Luo, Y., Norris, C., & Nkyi, A. (2018). Cross-cultural validation of four positive psychology assessments for use with a Ghanaian population. *International Journal for the Advancement of Counselling, 40,* 148–161. https://doi.org/10.1007/s10447–017-9317-8

Masson, P., and Pattillo, C. (2001). Monetary union in West Africa (ECOWAS): Is it desirable and how could it be achieved? Retrieved from www.imf.org/ external/pubs/nft/op/204/

Mayer, S. (2002). Psychology in Nigeria: A view from the outside. *Ife PsychologIA: An International Journal, 10*(1), 1–8. https://doi:10.4314/ifep.v10i1.23481

Mazzucato, V., Cebotari, V., Veale, A., White, A., Grassi, M., & Vivet, J. (2015). International parental migration and the psychological well-being of children in Ghana, Nigeria, and Angola. *Social Science & Medicine, 132,* 215–224.

Mensah-Sarbah, C. (2005). *An evaluation of various contributions of the nation's clinical psychologists to health care in Ghana from 1972–2005.* Unpublished master's dissertation, University of Ghana, Accra, Ghana.

Meshesha, M., and Jawahar, C. V. (2007). Indigenous scripts of African languages. *Indilinga: African Journal of Indigenous Knowledge Systems, 6* (2), 132–142.

Meyns, C. (2019). Anton Wilhelm Amo's philosophy of mind. *Philosophy Compass 14*: e12571. https://doi.org/10.1111/phc3.12571

Miezah, D. (2015). *Validation of Wechsler adult intelligence acale-fourth edition (WAIS-IV) in the Ghanaian population.* Unpublished master's dissertation, University of Ghana, Accra, Ghana.

Mpofu, E. (2002). Psychology in sub-Saharan Africa: Challenges, prospects and promises. *International Journal of Psychology 37*(3): 179–186.

Mughal, A.Y., Devadas, J., Ardman, E., Levis, B., Go, V. F., & Gaynes, B. N. (2020). A systematic review of validated screening tools for anxiety disorders and PTSD in low to middle income countries. *BMC Psychiatry, 20,* 338. https://doi.org/10.1186/s12888–020-02753-3

Njoku, M. G. C. (2012). *Nigerian Psychological Association: The way forward.* A Paper Presented at the First Nigerian Psychological Association Southeast Regional Meeting/Professional Development Seminar, Nigeria.

Nsamenang, A.B. (2007). Origins and development of scientific psychology in Afrique Noire. In M. J. Stevens and D. Wedding (eds.), under the supervision of John G. Adair. *Psychology: IUPsyS Global Resource* (2007 ed.). London: Psychology Press. www.psypress.com/iupsys/contents.asp.

Nweze, T. (2009). Management of examinations: Ethical issues. *Edo Journal of Counselling*, 2(1), 90–102.

Obot, I. S. (1996). Psychologists in the Nigerian health care system: A brief report. *Psychology & Health*, *12*(1), 39–42. https://doi.org/10.1080/08870449608406919

Olowookere, E. I. (2011). Challenges associated with the development of locally made psychological tests in Nigeria. *Journal of Functional Management*, 4(1), 48–57.

Omoniyi, M. B. I. (2016). History and development of guidance and counselling: The missing dimension of Nigeria school counselling services. *International Journal of Education and Research*, 4(11), 413–424.

Opoku, J. Y. (2012). Some theoretical and practical problems associated with using western instruments to measure cognitive abilities on the African continent. In H. Lauer & K. Anyidoho (eds.), *Reclaiming the Human Sciences and Humanities through African Perspectives* (vol. 1, pp. 537–559). Accra, Ghana: Sub-Saharan Publishers.

Oppong Asante, K. & Oppong, S. (2012). Psychology in Ghana. *Journal of Psychology in Africa*, 22(3), 473–478. https://doi:10.1080/14330237.2012.1082055.

Oppong, S. (2013). Industrial and organizational psychology in Ghana. *The Industrial-Organizational Psychologist*, 50(3), 79–83.

(2015). A critique of early childhood development research and practice in Africa. *Africanus: Journal of Development Studies*, 45(1), 23–41. https://doi.org/10.25159/0304-615X/252.

(2016). The Journey towards Africanizing psychology in Ghana. *Psychological Thought*, 9(1), 1–14. https://doi:10.5964/psyct.v9i1.128.

(2017a). History of psychology in Ghana since 989AD. *Psychological Thought*, 10(1), 7–48. https://doi:10.5964/psyct.v10i1.195.

(2017b). Contextualizing psychological testing in Ghana. *Psychologie a její kontexty/Psychology & its Contexts*, 8(1), 3–17.

(2019a). Overcoming obstacles to a truly global psychological theory, research and praxis in Africa. *Journal of Psychology in Africa*, 29(4), 292–300. https://doi.org/10.1080/14330237.2019.1647497

(2019b). Doing 'history of psychology' in Ghana: A long, frustrating, lonely journey without directional signs but rewarding. *HAP: Newsletter of History of Applied Psychology*, 10, 4–8.

(2019c). *Characterological interpersonal coping styles diagnostics (CICS-D)*. Department of Social Sciences, William V. S. Tubman University, Liberia. Retrieved from www.academia.edu/38857571/Characterological_Interpersonal_Coping_Styles_Diagnostics_CICS_D_

(2019d). On becoming a psychologist in Liberia: Career prospects with a degree in psychology. *Tubman University Times*, III(2), 5–6.

(2020). When something dehumanizes, it is violent but when it elevates, it is not violent. *Theory & Psychology, 30*(3), 468–472. https://doi.org/10.1177/0959354320920942

Oppong, S., Oppong Asante, K., & Kumaku, S. K. (2014). History, development and current status of psychology in Ghana. In C. S. Akotia & C. C. Mate-Kole (eds.), *Contemporary psychology: Readings from Ghana* (pp. 1–17). Accra, Ghana: Digibooks Ghana Ltd.

Osei-Tutu, A., Dzokoto, V. A., Affram, A. A., Adams, G., Norberg, J., & Doosje, B. (2020). Cultural models of well-being implicit in four Ghanaian languages. *Frontiers in Psychology, 11*, 1798. https://doi: 10.3389/fpsyg.2020.01798

Oteng-Yeboah, N. Y. A. (2005). *Standardization of the basic personality inventory in Ghana.* Unpublished master's dissertation, University of Ghana, Legon.

Quartey, D. S. (2014). *Performance of Ghanaian school children on The Kaufman Assessment Battery for Children – Second Edition (KABC-II) – An exploratory validation study.* Unpublished master's dissertation, University of Ghana, Accra, Ghana.

Secor, A., Macauley, R., Stan, L., Kagone, M., Sidikiba, S., Sow, S., Aronovich, D., ... & Sanderson, J. (2020). Mental health among Ebola survivors in Liberia, Sierra Leone and Guinea: Results from a cross-sectional study. *BMJ Open, 10*: e035217. https://doi:10.1136/bmjopen-2019-035217

Thalmayer, A. G., Saucier, G., Ole-Kotikash, L., & Payne, D. (2019). Personality structure in East and West Africa: Lexical studies of personality in Maa and Supyire-Senufo. *Journal of Personality and Social Psychology.* Advance online publication. https://doi.org/10.1037/pspp0000264

Triandis, H. C. (2009). The Ibadan conference and beyond. *Online Readings in Psychology and Culture, 1*(1). https://doi.org/10.9707/2307-0919.1002

United Nations, Department of Economic and Social Affairs, Population Division (2019). World population prospects 2019: Volume I: Comprehensive tables. Retrieved from https://population.un.org/wpp/Publications/Files/WPP2019_Volume-I_Comprehensive-Tables.pdf

Van de Vijver, F. J. R. (2002). Cross-cultural assessment: Value for money. *Applied Psychology: An International Review, 51*(4), 545–566.

Vinson, G. A. & Chang, Z. (2012). PTSD symptom structure among West African War trauma survivors living in African refugee camps: A factor-analytic investigation. *Journal of Traumatic Stress, 25*(2), 226–231. https://doi.org/10.1002/jts.21681

World Factbook. (2019). *Nigeria.* CIA. Retrieved from www.cia.gov/library/publications/the-world-factbook/attachments/summaries/NI-summary.pdf

World Health Organization. (2017). *Culture and mental health in Liberia: A primer.* Geneva: WHO.

Yawson, S. (2008). *Standardization of the Standard Progressive Matrices: A case study of Accra.* Unpublished master's dissertation, University of Ghana, Legon.

CHAPTER 5

Psychological Assessment in the Levant

Karma El Hassan and Pia A. Zeinoun

5.1 Introduction

Arab Levant refers to the Arab-speaking countries of Lebanon, Syria, Jordan, and the West Bank and Gaza (Palestinian Occupied Territories). These countries are geographically close, and considered ethnically and culturally similar with diversity in religious sects. The territory is historically rich, being the birthplace of two of the world's monotheistic religions (Judaism and Christianity), and the location of some of the oldest continuously inhabited cities in the world (Harb 2015). The Arab population is young with the majority under 25 years of age, and they are described to be on the collectivist end of the individualistic–collectivist continuum (Ayyash-Abdo 2001). Despite some differences, there are broad commonalities in religion, language, and psychosocial trends that are part of the shared cultural heritage (Ibrahim 2013).

5.1.1 Historical Development

The following sections will provide a brief overview of the development of psychological practice and science in the region in the last century, and how it was impacted by various cultural, social, and geopolitical changes that occurred in this period. The developments are grouped into three periods: late nineteenth and first half of the twentieth centuries, the second half of the twentieth century, and recent developments in the twenty-first century.

In the last quarter of the nineteenth century, the first publication was "Elementary Lessons in Mental Philosophy" by Daniel Bliss (1894), the founder of the American University of Beirut. The textbook contained the primary principles in philosophy and psychology and dealt with a range of psychological topics such as feelings, will, memory, and forgetfulness (Al-Soud 2000). Another notable psychology publication was the

Al-Mukhtataf magazine, founded in Beirut in 1876. This magazine had great credit for bringing Western sciences closer to Arab readers, and enriching the Arabic library with their translations, writings and studies in science and philosophy especially in publishing a set of articles related to important psychological topics and psychology in general for the Lebanese scientist Yaqoub Sarrouf, and these contributed to presenting psychology topics in a scientific framework (Al-Soud 2000).

The inception of modern psychology as a scientific discipline began in most Arab countries in the early decades of the twentieth century. It emanated mainly in the four Arab countries in which the first Arab universities appeared, and they were forerunners in psychological studies and literature, namely Syria, Iraq, Lebanon, and Egypt. Egypt was the first Arab country to model scientific psychological approaches in research, teaching, and practice, with the establishment of independent departments of psychology in two major universities: Cairo University and Ain Shams University (Ibrahim 2013). Thus, as early as 1911, modern scientific psychology became available to students in Egypt in schools of arts and education, although it was initially taught under the umbrella of philosophy. It was very strongly influenced by British universities and there was close alliance between psychology and education (Prothro & Melikian, 1955).

The Egyptian experience was transplanted across the Arab region. In Syria, Lebanon, and Palestine, many private schools were established by Western missionaries. These schools with foreign support, continue to exercise great influence on the education of the area. According to Prothro and Melikian (1955), "psychology in Arab Near East spring from and is nourished by Western psychology. British, French, and American influences can be seen – and distinguished- in the work of psychologists throughout the area" (304). In Syria and Lebanon, psychology has been influenced by the French tradition, while in Palestine by the British. Where the French academic tradition prevails, psychology is closely allied with philosophy and emphasizes psychoanalysis and phenomenological psychological theories, with less focus on psychometric and statistical analyses, and a near absence of experimental studies (Ibrahim 2013). When British academic tradition prevails, psychology is allied with education, and there is a strong emphasis on testing and measurement (Prothro & Melikian, 1955). This strong link to Western psychology led to dependence on Western universities for advanced training, reduced contact among Arab researchers, and to restriction of publishing activity to translation of important Western books and adaptation to local use of Western tests (Prothro & Melikian, 1955).

So, although the Egyptian experience was replicated in the Levant, there were differences due to various national traditions, such as the language used in scientific practice (Arabic, English, and French), the prominence and influence of different psychological traditions (British, French, and American), differences in psychology's role in national development, psychology's relation with the lay community, and the varying relations that psychology had with psychiatry, sociology, education, anthropology, philosophy, or the natural sciences (Kazarian & Khoury, 2003; Zebian et al. 2007).

The growth of psychology accelerated after 1960. There was an increase in the number of universities offering psychology and accordingly an increase in number of students. Growth of psychological research was facilitated and encouraged by a variety of professional, organizational, and cultural factors. Similarly, there was an increased need for psychological specialists, and different forms of psychological writing (Ibrahim, 2013). The earliest psychological association in Arab countries was the Egyptian Psychological Association established in 1929. Since that time, psychologists have established national societies in Levant countries, including Lebanon (2004) and Syria (2013), and several psychological periodicals were issued. Studies covering a wide variety of topics especially in developmental, educational, social, cross-cultural, and abnormal clinical psychology were published (Gielen, 2006).

According to a review of published psychological research in 114 developing countries by Sánchez-Sosa and Riveros (2007), psychologists in Jordan, Lebanon, Egypt, Kuwait, and Iraq have been particularly active. While prior to 1998, 70% of investigations were conducted by Egyptian psychologists, Jordan and Iraq were leading in the number of psychology publications in 2007. Around the same period, studies in assessment gained prominence. For example, Ibrahim and colleagues (Ibrahim et al. 1993; Ibrahim & Ibrahim, 2003) began a series of studies focused on development and standardization of behavior assessment tools and behavior therapy techniques with emphasis on Arab children.

Although the Levant countries have always been exposed to conflict, occupation, and political instability, the situation aggravated with the start in 2010 of the Arab Spring. This period had great impact on local psychology, specifically the notable interest in mental health services and displaced populations, and hence the measurement of related constructs.

5.2   Psychological Assessment Research in Levant

A good number of reviews have highlighted issues on psychological assessment in the past two decades. Fasfous, Al-Joudi, Puente, and Pérez-García

(2017) presented a review of studies (384) done on neuropsychological measures in Arab countries before 2016, while more recently Zeinoun, Iliescu, and El Hakim (2021) conducted a systematic review of the methodologies used in the development of 138 Arabic tests from 1998 to 2019. Other reviews have focused on topics related to assessments, such as a content analysis of psychological studies (random sample of 99 from database) published in English from 1950 to 2004 to evaluate their cultural sensitivity (Zebian et al., 2007), the mental health impact of trauma in the region for the period 1995–2012 (Amawi et al., 2014), and research on creativity, intelligence, and giftedness in the region, subsuming 50 studies from 1984 to 1997, to study the extent they are sensitive to the local or indigenous culture (Khaleefa, 1999). Additionally, several reviews in Arabic are published on an electronic forum, Arab Psychnet (http://arabpsynet.com/).

The number of studies has increased over the years, with a slow but steady move away from simple translation to adaptation, validation, and norming. Zeinoun et al. (2021) note that among the reviewed 138 Arabic tests that screen/diagnose or plan treatment for psychological disorders, there was an upward trend of publications, ranging from 25 in the first decade (average 2.5 publications per year), to 113 in the second decade (average 10.3 per year). Similarly, Fasfous et al. (2017) reports that included studies that have used cognitive measures with Arabic speakers had the rate of approximately 7.7 publications per year (22 studies from 1961 to 1989, and 204 from 2011 to 2015). Very few tests have been assembled, and a good number of research studies focused on neuropsychological and mental health measures as there was a high need for them due to political instability, especially in Palestine and Lebanon.

In the field of Arab-related cognition, Egypt took the lead followed by Saudi Arabia and GCC countries (Fasfous et al., 2017) and this could be because of the number of universities and advanced medical training institutions in these countries. There were studies involving norming and validation of the Wechsler, Stanford Binet, and other cognitive ability tests. Adaptation across tests varied in quality and most of the studies utilized nonverbal tests and executive functioning tasks and mostly on children (Abdul Razzak, 2013). This was at the expense of thorough examination of verbal skills, as nonverbal abilities were erroneously assumed to be culture free. As the focus in this review is on the Levant, the following subsections will outline examples of psychological assessment research done in Jordan, Lebanon, Palestine, and Syria.

5.2.1   Jordan

Jordan has witnessed intense psychological assessment research activity in the last decades, especially by psychologists associated with institutions. Sánchez-Sosa & Riveros (2007) rank Jordan as 13 among 114 developing countries in psychological research, and Fasfous et al. (2017) state that validating or norming (or both) was reported for 63% of cognitive tests used in Jordanian publications. Some notable studies from Jordan include the Jordanian Bayley Scale of Infant Development-II (Al-Razouq, 2006), Beery Visual- Motor Integration Test (Al-Razouq, 2014; Al-Waqfi, 1998), Arabic Receptive-Expressive Vocabulary Test (Wiig and Al-Halees, 2000), and the Token Test (Alkhamra and Al-Jazi, 2015), and several other cognitive (Al-Zoubi & Green, 2015) achievement (Abu-Hamour and Al-Hmouz, 2016), and behavioral/mental health tools (Hamid et al., 2004). In 2011, Abu Asaad compiled a three-volume guide of educational and psychological tests and measures in Arabic language for use by practitioners. The guide provides detailed information on around 100 Arabized tests with description of their purpose, use, psychometric properties, research, and so on.

5.2.2   Lebanon

Testing has become popular in Lebanon in the past decade, with more interest on the level of universities and national organizations. In 2014, the Lebanese Psychological Association became a member of the International Test Commission (ITC) to help disseminate the international standards on test usage in Lebanon (Zeinoun & Maroun, 2015).

Many practitioners in Lebanon use some form of "testing" within their practice. Methodologies and practices range from a psychodynamic test usage (e.g., projective tools) to educational testing (e.g., vocational inventories), to special education and psychoeducational assessments (Zeinoun & Maroun, 2015). Graduate programs in clinical and educational psychology, and programs of speech/language pathology, psychomotor therapy, and occupational therapy offer courses in tests and measurement, psychoeducational evaluation, projective testing and personality assessment. Availability of these programs and the rising need for services, has led to a sharp rise in psychology related services in Lebanon. In 2010, there were 45 practitioner psychologists in Lebanon (Khoury and Tabbarah, 2010), while today there are more than 300 mental health professionals registered as psychotherapists or practicing psychologists (Zeinoun & Maroun, 2015).

Lebanese research on assessment has traditionally dealt with achievement, mental ability, and psychosocial stress-related measures, and has primarily involved test development and cross validation studies. As per the Fasfous et al. (2007) review, validation or norming or both was reported for 53% of cognitive tests used in Lebanon. Early examples include the Lebanese Intelligence Scale for Adults (LISA) (Saigh, 1986) and the Goodenough Draw A Man Test (Atiyeh, 1993), while more recent tools encompass behavioral rating scales for children (e.g., Conners-3 Teachers and Parents Rating Scales; El Hassan & Haidar, 2020), and adults (e.g., PHQ-9 and GAD-7; Sawaya et al., 2016), quality of life scales (e.g., Quality of College Life; El Hassan, 2011), education-related tests (e.g., Watson Glaser Critical Thinking Appraisal; El Hassan & Madhun, 2007), achievement tests (e.g., Test of Auditory Comprehension of Language-Revised; El Hassan & Jammal, 2005), cognitive tests (WISC-IV; Touma & Moussallem, 2016), and structured interviews (DAWBA; Zeinoun et al. 2013). In addition, due to the political instability in Lebanon, the country (along with Palestine and Iraq) has produced several tools for war-related psychopathology (Amawi et al., 2014), such as the Children's Posttraumatic Stress Disorder Inventory (CPTSDI) (Saigh, 1989).

While most of these tests were adapted from English versions, recently more tests have been assembled indigenously including those for Arabic vocabulary and picture naming (Kanj & El Hassan, 2021), verbal memory (Zeinoun, 2020), and personality variables indigenous to the Levant (Zeinoun et al., 2017).

5.2.3   Palestine

Collective trauma has been passed down from one generation of Palestinians to another. However, it is only recently, namely since the first Intifada in 1987, but with new momentum during the second Intifada in 2000, that research on mental health and war-related psychological distress among the Palestinian people has proliferated (Makkawi, 2015). The focus of this research has been on consequences of individual exposure to military violence and trauma and its relationship with mental health, coping strategies, and psychopathology (e.g., Thabet et al., 2013). However, according to Haj-Yahia (2007), empirical research in Palestine has suffered from several methodological flaws such as the use of traditional quantitative research methods, the use scales that were initially developed in English and merely translated into Arabic with no cultural relevance. A possible reason for this is that Palestinian universities, despite

their anti-colonial inception, continue to teach mainstream Western individualistic knowledge (Makkawi, 2015). For instance, the problems in the
use of the Western diagnosis of PTSD have been widely debated
(Summerfield, 1999), and several researchers have tried to improve the
measurement of PTSD by using more culturally sensitive items and
adaptation procedures for instruments such as the Harvard Trauma
Questionaire (Mollica et al., 1992).

Moving forward, research conducted with colonized communities such
as the Palestinian people ought to be decolonizing praxis, be indigenously
informed, and transformative, and utilize methodological flexibility
including qualitative methods (Smith, 1999).

Another area of research lies along in the assessment and monitoring of
subjective well-being (SWB) and its related factors in Palestinian territories
(Harsha et al., 2016; Veronese et al., 2017). The developed Arabic SWBAS
may be used both as a reliable diagnostic screening tool for identifying and
profiling at-risk individuals and longitudinally to monitor the effectiveness
of psychological and social intervention programs. The findings of the
study provide support for the idea that understanding well-being requires
the contribution of social, environmental, and individual factors and calls
for a focus on both protective and risk factors. It supports the view of
enhancing the resources available to individuals for dealing with adverse
life circumstances and it demands that risk factors (e.g., human insecurity
and negative functioning) be counteracted by the promotion of protective
factors (Veronese et al., 2017). Harsha et al. (2016) aimed to study the
levels of well-being and its associated factors using data from the National
Time Use Survey and building a well-being scale from the WHO Well-
being Index.

As little has been reported about the emotional well-being of children
growing up in war-like conditions, or the factors affecting it, a series of
studies investigated positive and negative affect (PA, NA) of children living
in refugee camps in Gaza using a culturally adapted Arabic Palestinian
version of the PANAS-C (Veronese & Pepe, 2017). The leading research
aim was to present a culturally adapted Palestinian version of the measure
and report its psychometric proprieties, as found in a sample of 6- to 11-
year-old children living in refugee camps. Having such a tool will help
identify the sets of emotions, affective mapping, that are most salient to the
individuals under occupation. The results of the factor structure revealed
interesting findings that reflect the Palestinian context. For example, and
as part of the NA dimension, items of *afraid-scared-frightened* had high
factor loadings, reflecting the significant role played by fear in their lives.

Similarly, group of items *mad-blue-sad* made significant contribution to NA in Palestinian children, though this was not found in other studies. The item *alert* also had high factor loading on PA reflecting the military occupation (Veronese & Pepe, 2017). Developing and adapting the PANAS-C has enabled the reliable mapping of affect in a unique and sensitive context, that of Palestinian refugees under occupation.

5.2.4   Syria

There are major milestones in the march of psychological sciences in Syria that are related to the history of Syria and its political, social, and cultural development. The opening of the Institute of Arab Medicine (1903) and the School of Law (1913) formed the first nucleus of the Syrian University (now Damascus University), which became a hub for research and teaching. After the proclamation of Syria's independence, the Minister of Education gave special care to educational and psychological studies. Syrian psychology was a mixture of American, English, and French approaches, and several textbooks have been authored, or translated to teach psychology in local universities (Al-Soud, 2000). While psychological textbooks in Syria have been enormously helpful in building capacity, most of the books were designed for purely academic purposes, with a strong focus on theory. For this reason, in addition to social stigma, psychological sciences were restricted to theory and academic setting, with very few psychological services offered in Syrian schools or communities (Al-Soud, 2000).

With the advent of the Arab Spring and resulting political instability, displacement, and violence, research started focusing on the effect of trauma and PTSD especially among displaced and refugees' population (Alpaket et al., 2015; Ibrahim & Hassan, 2017), mental health of Syrian children (Perkins et al., 2018), and psychosocial sequels of Syrian conflict (Marwa, 2016), Syrian coping strategies with conflict (Hedar, 2017), and so on.

The Syrian Association for Mental Health (SAMH) was established in 2013 as an independent professional association for psychologists, psychiatrists, and clinical social workers to enhance mental health and provide psychological and social services according to the best, evidence-based practice. On its webpage (www.syriasamh.com/enIndex.htm), SAMH provides a list of studies, tests and measures used, and conferences held in the last few years. They focus mostly on assessment, treatment, and interventions dealing with stress, trauma, and depression using some tools developed in collaboration with humanitarian associations.

5.3 The Current Impact of Sociocultural Factors on Assessment

The review in section 5.2 has provided evidence of the development of the field of psychology and assessment in the Levant. What started as sporadic Westernized research has now become more focused on national issues. With these changes, there were several challenges that psychologists had to deal with in their endeavor to build an evidence-based science of psychology and assessment.

5.3.1 Arabic Language

While the Arabic language, referred to as Modern Standard Arabic (MSA), is the official language of the Levant countries, and the lingua franca of written text and formal spoken language, each country has its own vernaculars. Local vernaculars are a variation of MSA and are used in everyday speech. This plurality of Arabic dialects and the fact that spoken Arabic is distinct from the written language has been termed "diglossia"(Kaye, 2001) and poses unique challenges in psychology (Daouk-Öyry et al., 2016). One major challenge is the dilemma of whether to use MSA or local vernaculars in test stimuli and instructions. Some researchers have circumvented this issue by focusing on developing and using nonverbal tests instead of verbal tests (Al-Joudi, 2015; Mahmoud, 2015), leading to a scarcity in properly developed language-based tests that are crucial for neuropsychological and educational decision-making. Others have proposed solutions such as more rigorous methodologies to identify the most appropriate language needed for population while using MSA as a blueprint (see Daouk-Öyry et al., 2016 for such solutions).

5.3.2 Bilingualism

Another related issue is the high percentage of bilingual or trilingual people, especially in Lebanon. As an example, a bilingual Arab may feel more comfortable performing verbal memory tasks and responding to questionnaires in Arabic but prefer English or French when performing tasks involving mathematical computations (Mahmoud, 2015). This highlights the need for a bilingual assessment for this population, and consequently the inclusion of bilingual people in norms selection (Ardila, 2003).

5.3.3 Intellectual Dependency

Several reviewers of Levant psychological research and assessment have noted an uncritical acceptance of theories and findings from Western psychology (Abou Hatab, 1997; Ahmed & Gielen, 1998;Al-Soud, 2000; Gielen, 2006; Khaleefa, 1999). Abu Hatab (1997) called it a "one-way relationship" where theories, concepts, and methods are imported in a random, uncritical, and unplanned way that subsequently reinforces unhealthy forms of intellectual dependency. In psychological assessment, the trend of adopting an etic approach is reflected by several authors. Khaleefa (1999) noted that the measures of intelligence and creativity reviewed were not sensitive to the local or indigenous culture, while Zebian (2007) also noted that regional researchers do not engage in high levels of culturally sensitive research. Similarly, Zeinoun et al. (in press) found that more than 80% of Arabic tests published between 1998 and 2019, were translated and adapted from existing tests, often without ensuring cultural or linguistic equivalence. Authors recommended that this disproportionate preference for adapting existing English or French tests into Arabic, instead of creating (assembling) indigenous tests, limits the breadth and depth of psychological assessment research and practice.

The etic approach to test-related research has critical implications on clinical assessment. Adapted tests are often used for high-stake decisions (e.g., diagnoses, policies) and when the tools used in such decisions have not been appropriately developed and tested, they may lead to a detrimental effect on individuals, organizations, societies, and science in general.

Several authors have called for more locally grounded research. Zeinoun et al. (2013, 2017) called for covering the indigenous conceptualizations and measures of personality and mental illness by using mixed methods such as open-ended questions to provide richer information about indigenous expressions. Similarly, Ismail (2012) argued that the process of importing mental health knowledge needs to be tempered by careful consideration and contemplation of indigenous resources; as without awareness of existing practices, interventions will fall short of offering a meaningful addition.

While these issues seem to permeate the research and clinical aspects of psychological assessment, there is promising progress in the field of psychology and mental health in the Arab region. A bibliometric study of 760 mental health articles published by Arab-based researchers shows that research output has increased by 160% from 2008 to 2019 in comparison with an increase of 57% in the rest of the world (Zeinoun et al., 2020).

5.3.4   Economic and Sociopolitical Context

There are several issues that can be related to the Levant in terms of economic, social, and geopolitical contexts as these have impacted the development and progress of psychological assessment. Lebanon, Syria, Jordan, and Palestine are classified by the World Bank as low to middle income countries (LMICs), which is reflected in limited financial resources, infrastructure, and capacity to conduct research on psychological assessment.

While research on test development has increased in the past decade (Zeinoun et al., in press), this is often with limited financial support. In higher education, most psychology departments lack adequate infrastructure (labs, library, recent books, journals, etc.) to facilitate education and research (Ibrahim, 2013). The economic and sociopolitical strain is also noted in clinical practice. Service users may avoid undergoing formal psychological and psychoeducational assessments as these are often costlier and more time-consuming than other mental health services and are rarely covered by insurance. In some regions like the Palestinian territories, importing psychological tests and using foreign currency are problematic. Finally, the geopolitical instability witnessed intermittently by the Levant countries has led to a so-called brain-drain whereby many qualified academics and clinicians are forced to immigrate instead of investing in the growth of local capacity.

5.3.5   Education, Training, and Professional Regulation

While several graduate programs in clinical and educational psychology offer courses on testing, there are no doctorate or master programs in clinical neuropsychology or applied psychometrics. Professionals who want to refine their skills in assessments must rely on "workshops" that train participants on test administration. However, such training emphasizes technical test usage, leaving professionals without the advanced theoretical understanding and the use of assessment results for diagnosis and treatment planning.

Finally, a major challenge to the practice of psychological assessment has been the relative absence of professional regulation, which was only recently established in some countries (Saigh, 1984; Zeinoun &

Maroun, 2015; Zebian et al., 2007). For example, while Lebanon passed a law in 2017 to regulate the professional practice of clinical and educational psychologists, the law does not mandate any specific training in assessment.

5.3.6 Collaboration

Another note made by reviewers of the discipline is the limited level of communication among Arab psychologists themselves and with colleagues in other cultures (Ibrahim, 2013). This was also noted in the early development of the discipline by Prothro and Melikian (1955) and was attributed then to the dependence of the psychologists on Western universities for advanced training, which reduced the amount of contact among Arabs. In recent years, there has been some improvement in collaboration. Zeinoun et al. (in press) found that the proportion of papers with international collaboration published by Arab countries was at 29% in 2009, but this number steadily increased to 50% by 2018. The improved collaborations have been bolstered by many factors, including the establishment of professional associations in Levant countries and Arab region, the holding of many local and international conferences and symposia, and the publication of Arab periodicals and establishment of online networks.

5.4   Conclusion and Recommendations

The chapter has presented an overview of research and practice in psychological assessment in the Levant. Based on this discussion and for assessment-related research and practice to meet the diversified psychosocial needs of Arab society, the following transformations are recommended.

The field needs to appreciate the indigenous perspective of psychology and integrate that with etic and global perspectives. That is, the Levant culture needs to be understood on its own terms, in relation to its culture, history, and path to development, and carefully weaved with Western applications. To be relevant and meaningful, research needs to build on national heritage and balance it with contemporary needs. It must move away from the current "decontextualizing" movement – and be culturally sensitive – and take contextual variables and psychosocial processes into consideration to better understand the construct investigated and to choose the appropriate indigenous tools to study it. The concern should not be only with the cross-cultural equivalence of the various measures and tools used but with their relevance and sensitivity to culture. Melikian's (1984) call 25 years ago for a "grass roots psychology linked to the intellectual history and thought of the Arab and even to the present folk psychology and developed within the framework of scientific psychology" (12) is more valid today than ever. Such a move would help Arab researchers to define their own vision and establish their own priorities that better reflect their communities' needs. However, such transformation and development take time, and we are then faced with the dilemma that if there is an immediate need for providing care and relief, can these wait until these tools have been developed?

Levant psychological research should embark on development of locally reliable, valid, and culturally appropriate assessment tools and procedures covering educational, psychological, and mental health. Such a meticulous task requires expertise from several domains like subject matter (e.g., mental health), psychometrics, linguists, and cross-cultural psychologists. Accordingly, there is a need to develop a cadre of professionals who are technically and scientifically qualified to undertake this task and at same time enhance the role of professional associations to ensure stronger collaboration among researchers and across disciplines. Strengthening research infrastructure and resource availability would also help in the development of the culturally appropriate tools.

The transformation should also cover content of research to be more relevant to current needs of the Levant. Topics such as mental and emotional health, trauma, depression, aggression, and child/adolescent psychology all need to be investigated in terms of their indigenous conceptualization in the region. Tools used should include quantitative and qualitative approaches and should shift between emic and etic approaches to appropriately capture cultural characteristics. In this regard focusing on "what works" and on strengths rather than problems only would yield more useful information for interventions.

To further address linguistic challenges, it is important to keep working on developing and updating currently used and available psychology dictionaries and lexica. Also, working on word frequency databases for different dialects would help in the development of verbal tests in Arabic that are greatly needed in the Levant.

Other domains that need to be worked on include professionalizing the discipline in terms of setting appropriate governmental regulations for licensing and practicing the profession. In addition, the societal "stigma" associated with psychology and mental health needs to be addressed. Possibly, once research becomes more relevant and meaningful to the community resulting in better diagnosis and intervention, the negative perceptions will gradually fade away and the discipline will attain societal recognition.

In sum, for psychological research and assessment to better fulfill their societal role and function, they need to better meet psychosocial needs of the Arab society, develop their professional cadre of experts who collaboratively work on their research, and address various issues related to infrastructure, language, and governmental regulations.

REFERENCES

Abdul Razzak, R. (2013). A preliminary study on the Trail-making Test in Arabic-English bilingual young adults. *Applied Neuropsychology*, *20*(1), 53–60. https://doi:10.1080/09084282.2012.670163.

Abou-Hatab, F. (1997). Psychology from Egyptian, Arab, and Islamic perspectives: Unfulfilled hopes and hopeful fulfillment. *European Psychologist*, *2*(4), 356–365.

Abu Asaad, A. (2011). *Guide of psychological and educational tests and measures* (3 volumes). (dalil alikhtibarat wa almakaiis alnafsia wa altarbawiya). Depone Center for Teaching Thinking: Amman, Jordan.

Abu-Hamour, B. & Al-Hmouz, H. (2016). Prevalence and pattern of learning difficulties in primary school students in Jordan, *Australian Journal of Learning Difficulties*, *21*(2), 99–113. doi:10.1080/19404158.2017.1287104

Ahmed, R. & Gielen, U. (1998). *Psychology in the Arab countries*. Cairo, Egypt: Menoufia Press.

Al-Joudi, H. (2015). Availability of Arabic language tests in the Middle East and North Africa. *INSNET*, *35*, 6–8.

Al-Soud, N. (2000). The progress of the science of psychology in the Arab world and its prospective development [in Arabic]. *Intellectual Studies Magazine*, *1*, 155–183

Alkhamra, R. A. & Al-Jazi, A. B. (2015). Validity and reliability of the Arabic Token Test for children. *International Journal of Language & Communication Disorders*, Advance online publication. doi:10.1111/1460-6984.12198.

Alpak, G., Unal, A., Bulbul, F., Sagaltici, E., Bez, Y., Altindag, A., Dalkilic, A., & Savas, H. A. (2015). Post-Traumatic stress disorder among Syrian refugees in Turkey: a cross- sectional study. *International Journal of Psychiatry and Clinical Practice*, *19*(1), 45–50.

Al-Razouq, T. H. (2006). Al-khasais al-saikumitriya lemiqyas Bayley lilnumow al-'aqli walharaki 'omr 1-42 shahr [Psychometric properties of the Jordanian version of Bayley Mental and Motor Scales for Child Development (Age: 1 Month-42 Months)]. *Educational Sciences*, *36*(1), 96–112.

(2014). Ma'ayir al-idrak al-basari-al-haraki lilatfal 'omr 2-7 sanawat [Visual-Motor/Integration Scale for Children from two to seven years]. *Educational Sciences*, *41*(S1), 464–477.

Al-Waqfi, R. (1998). *Sensory Motor Integration Test*. Amman: Princess Tharwat College.

Amawi, N., Mollica, R., Lavelle, J., Osman, O., & Nasir, N. (2014). Overview of research on the Al-k mental health impact of violence in the Middle East in light of the Arab Spring. *Journal of Nervous and Mental Disease*, *202*(9), 625–629.

Ardila, A. (2003). Language representation and working memory with bilinguals. *Journal of Communication Disorders*, *36*(3), 233–240

Atiyeh, N. (1993). *Thka' al atfal min khilal al rusum (measuring children's intelligence through drawing Goodenough Draw A Man Test)*. Beirut, Lebanon: Dar El Talia.

Ayyash-Abdo, H. (2001). Individualism and collectivism: The case of Lebanon. *Social Behavior and Personality*, *29*(5), 503–518(16). http://dx.doi.org/10.2224/sbp.2001.29.5.503.

Al-Zoubi, M., & Green, M. (2015). Developing a mental ability test to be used in vocational guidance for fresh university graduates in Jordan (In Arabic). *Jordan Journal of Social Sciences*, *8*(1), 1–27.

Bliss, D. (1894). Elementary lessons in mental philosophy. Beirut (In arabic).

Daouk-Öyry, L., Zeinoun, P., Choueiri, L., & Van de Vijver, F. (2016). Integrating global and local perspectives in psycholexical studies: A GloCal approach. *Journal of Research in Personality*, *62*, 19–28. doi:dx.doi.org/10.1016/j.jrp.2016.02.008.

El Hassan, K. & Jammal, R. (2005). Validation and development of norms for the Test of Auditory Comprehension of Language-Revised (TACL-R). *Assessment in Education: Principles, Policy & Practice*, *12*(2), 183–202.

El Hassan, K. & Madhun, G. (2007). Validating the Watson Glaser Critical Thinking Appraisal. *Higher Education Journal*, *54*, 361–383. https://doi.org/10.1007/s10734-006-9002-z.

El Hassan, K. (2011). Quality of college life (QCL): Validation of a measure of student well-being in the Middle East. *International Journal of Educational and Psychological Measurement*, *8*(1), 12–22.

El Hassan, K. & Haidar, Z. (2020). *Adaptation and validation of Conners-3 teacher and parent rating scales on Lebanese children*. Manuscript in press.

Fasfous, A., Al-Joudi, H., Puente, A., & Pérez-García, A. (2017). Neuropsychological measures in the Arab world: A systematic review. *Neuropsychological Review*, *27*, 158–173. https://doi.org/10.1007/s11065-017-9347-3.

Gielen, U. P. (2006, December). Arab psychology and the emerging global psychology movement: A modest Proposal. Paper presented at Third International Conference: Social Sciences and Interdisciplinary Studies: An Integrated Perspective, Kuwait University.

Haj-Yahia, M. (2007). Challenges in studying the psychological effects of Palestinian children's exposure to political violence and their coping with this traumatic experience. *Child Abuse and Neglect, 31*(7), 691–697.

Hamid, H., Abu-Hijleh, N., Sharif, S., Raqab, M., Mas'ad, D., & Abbas, A. (2004) A primary care study of the correlates of depressive symptoms among Jordanian women. *Transcultural Psychiatry, 41*(4), 487–496.

Harb, C. (2015). *The Arab Region from: Handbook of Arab American Psychology.* Routledge. Retrieved from www.routledgehandbooks.com/doi/10.4324/9780203763582.ch1

Harsha, N., Ziq, L., Ghandour, R., & Giacaman, R. (2016). Well-being and associated factors among adults in the occupied Palestinian territory. *Health and Quality of Life Outcomes, 14*(122), 1–7. doi:10.1186/s12955-016-0519-2.

Hedar, M. (2017). Mental health during the Syrian crisis: How Syrians are dealing with the psychological effects. *International Review of the Red Cross, 99* (3), 927–935. doi:10.1017/S1816383119000080.

Ibrahim, H. & Hassan, C. Q. (2017). Post-traumatic stress disorder symptoms resultingfrom torture and other traumatic events among Syrian Kurdish refugees in Kurdistan region, Iraq. *Frontiers in Psychology, 8*(281), 1–8. doi:10.3389/fpsyg.2017.00241.

Ibrahim, A. S., Dukhayyil, A., & Ibrahim, R., (1993). Two waves of growth in psychological behavioral therapy (Mowjatan mena attawattur fi alilaj also-loooki). *Journal of Psychology, 26,* 16–26.

Ibrahim, A. S., (2013). Arab World Psychology. In K. D. Keith (ed.), *The Encyclopedia of Cross-Cultural Psychology* (1st ed.). John Wiley and Sons, Inc.

Ibrahim, A. S. & Ibrahim, R. (2003). Anxiety, depression, hostility, and general psychopathology: An Arabian study. In A. J. Giuliano, K. N. Anchor, & J. B. Barth (eds.), *Advances in medical psychotherapy and psychodiagnosis* (pp. 173–184). Dubuque, IA: Kendall-Hunt Publishing Company.

Ismail, G. (2012). Cognizing omitted contexts and implicit paradigms: Toward a valid mental health discourse. In S. Jabour (ed.) *Public Health in the Arab World* (pp. 191–199). Cambridge University Press.

Khoury, B., Tabbarah, S (2012). Lebanon. In Baker, B. D. (ed.), *The Oxford handbook of the history of psychology: Global perspectives.* Oxford: Oxford University Press. doi:10.1093/oxfordhb/9780195366556.013.0017

Kaye, A. S. (2001). Diglossia: The state of the art. *International Journal of the Sociology of Language,* 117–130.

Kazarian, S. & Khoury, B. (2003, December). *Psychology in Lebanon: Challenges and prospects.* Paper presented at the Middle East and North Africa Regional Conference in Psychology, Dubai, United Arab Emirates.

Khaleefa, O. (1999). Research on creativity, intelligence and giftedness: The case of the Arab World. *Gifted and Talented International, 14*(1), 21–29. doi: 10.108015332276.1999.11672902.

Maalouf, F., & Akl, E. (2019). Mental health research in the Arab region: Challenges and call for Action. Elsevier Editorial System(tm) for The Lancet, THELANCETPSYCH- D-18-01069R1.

Mahmoud, O. (2015). Neuropsychological assessment in the Arab World: Observations & challenges. *International Neuropsychological Society (INS) NET, 35*(1), 4–6.

Makkawi, I. (2015). Critical psychology in the Arab world. In I. Parker (ed.) *Handbook of critical psychology* (pp. 415–424). London: Routledge.

Marwa, J. (2016). Psychosocial sequels of Syrian conflict. *Psychiatry, 19*(2). doi:10.4172/2378-5756.1000355.

Melikian, L. (1984). The transfer of psychological knowledge to the third world countries and its impact on producing states development, the case of five Arab Gulf oil- producing countries. *International Journal of Psychology, 19*, 65–77. https://doi.org/10.1080/00207598408247516.

Mollica, R. F., Caspi-Yavin, Y., Bollini, P., Truong T., & Lavelle, J. (1992). The Harvard Trauma Questionnaire: Validating a cross-cultural instrument for measuring torture, trauma, and posttraumatic stress disorder in Indochinese refugees. *Journal of Nervous Mental Disorders, 180*(2), 111–116.

Perkins, J. D., Ajeeb, M., Fadel, L. & Saleh, G. (2018). Mental health in Syrian children with a focus on post-traumatic stress: a cross-sectional study from Syrian schools. *Social Psychiatry and Psychiatric Epidemiology, 53*(11), 1231–1239.

Prothro E. T. & Melikian, L. (1955). Psychology in the Arab Near East. *Psychological Bulletin, 52*(4), 303–310.

Rama Kanj & Karma El-Hassan (2021). Measurement of expressive vocabulary in multilingual children using the dual-Focus approach method for test development, International Journal of Multilingualism, DOI: 10.1080/14790718.2021.1895171.

Sánchez-Sosa, J. J., & Riveros, A. (2007). Theory, research, and practice in psychology in the developing (majority) world. In M. J. Stevens & U. P. Gielen (eds.), *Toward a global psychology: Theory, research, intervention, and pedagogy* (pp. 101–146). Mahwah, NJ: Erlbaum

Sawaya, H., Atoui, M., Hamadeh, A., Zeinoun, P., & Nahas, Z. (2016). Adaptation and initial validation of the Patient Health Questionnaire–9 (PHQ-9) and the Generalized Anxiety Disorder–7 Questionnaire (GAD-7) in an Arabic speaking Lebanese psychiatric outpatient sample. *Psychiatry Research, 239*, 245–252. https://doi.org/10.1016/j.psychres.2016.03.030.

Sayed, M. A. (2003). Psychotherapy of Arab patients in the West: Uniqueness, empathy, and "otherness." *American Journal of Psychotherapy 57*(4), 445–459.

Saigh, P. A. (1984). School psychology in Lebanon. *Journal of School Psychology, 22*(3), 233–238.

(1986). *The Lebanese General Intelligence Scale (Forms A, B, and C).* Beirut: American University of Beirut, Office of Research and Development

(1989). School psychology research in Lebanon: A retrospective analysis and a look ahead. *Professional School Psychology*, *4*(3), 201–208.

Smith, L. T. (1999). *Decolonizing Methodologies: Research and Indigenous People*. London: Zed Books Ltd.

Soueif, M. I. (1998). Conclusions. In R. A. Ahmed & U. P. Gielen (eds.), *Psychology in the Arab countries* (pp. 569–582). Menoufia, Egypt: Menoufia University Press.

Summerfield, D. (1999). A critique of 7 assumptions behind psychological trauma programs in war-affected areas. *Social Science Medical*, *48*(10), 1449–1462.

Thabet, A. A., Abu Tawahina, A., El Sarraj, E., Henely, D., Pelleick, H., & Vostanis, P. (2013). Comorbidity of post-traumatic stress disorder, attention deficit with hyperactivity, conduct, and oppositional defiant disorder in Palestinian children affected by war on Gaza. *Health*, *5*(6), 994–1002. www.scirp.org/journal/health/.

Touma, V. M. & Moussallem, Y. (2016). La nécessité de l'adaptation d'un test cognitif à la culture arabe–le cas du WISC-IV. *Pratiques Psychologiques*, *22* (1), 75–85.

Veronese, G. & Pepe, A. (2017). Positive and negative affect in children living in refugee camps: Assessing the psychometric proprieties and factorial invariance of the PANAS-C in the Gaza Strip. *Evaluation and the Health Professions*, *40*(1), 3–32.

Veronese, G., Pepe, A., Dagdouke, J., Addimando, L., & Yaghi, S. (2017). Measuring well-being in Israel and Palestine: The Subjective Well-Being Assessment Scale. *Psychological Reports*, *120*(6), 1160–1177.

Wiig, E. H. & Al-Halees, Y. (2000). Developing a language screening test for Arabic- speaking children. *Folia Phoniatrica et Logopaedica*, *52*(6), 260–274.

Zayour, A. (1996). Towards an Arab psychology (nahu psychologia arabia). (Psychnet forum interview). file:///E:/ITC%20Chapter/Zayour% 20Arabpsynet.pdf.

Zebian, S. Alamuddin, R., Maalouf, M., & Chatila, Y. (2007). Developing an appropriate psychology through culturally sensitive research practices in the Arabic speaking world. *Journal of Cross-Cultural Psychology*, *38*(2), 91–122. doi:10.1177/0022022106295442.

Zeinoun, P., Akl, E. A., Maalouf, F. T., & Meho, L. I. (2020). The Arab Region's contribution to global mental health research (2009–2018): A bibliometric analysis. *Frontiers in Psychiatry*, *11*, 182. https://doi.org/10.3389/fpsyt.2020 .00182.

Zeinoun, P., Daouk-Öyry, L., Choueiri, L., & Van de Vijver, F. J. R. (2017). A mixed method study of personality conceptions in the Levant: Jordan, Lebanon, Syria, and the West Bank. *Journal of Personality and Social Psychology*, *113*(3), 453–465.

Zeinoun P. & Maroun, M. (2015). Neuropsychology in Lebanon: History and future directions. *INSNET*, *35*(2), 1–3.

Zeinoun, P., Bawab, S., Atwi, M., Hariz, N., Tavitian, L., Khani, M., ... & Maalouf, F. (2013). Validation of an Arabic multi-informant psychiatric diagnostic interview for children and adolescents: Development and Well Being Assessment-Arabic (DAWBA-Arabic). *Comprehensive Psychiatry 54*(7), 1034–1041.

Zeinoun, P., Iliescu, D., & El-Hakim, R. (2021). Psychological tests in Arabic: A review of methodological practices and recommendations for future use. *Neuropsychology Review.* https://doi.org/10.1007/s11065-021-09476-6.

Zeinoun, P., Farran, N., Khoury, S., & Darwish, H. (2020). Development, Psychometric Properties, and Pilot Norms of the first Arabic Indigenous Memory Test: The Verbal Memory Arabic Test (VMAT). *Journal of Clinical and Experimental Neuropsychology.* doi:10.1080/13803395.2020.1773408.

The History of Assessment in the Nordic Countries

Sverre L. Nielsen and Dave Bartram

6.1 Introduction

This chapter covers the history of assessment and its development in the Nordic countries with emphasis on Norway, Sweden, and Denmark, with some reference to Finland. When it comes to the socioeconomic structure and functioning, the first three are quite similar in many ways, with analogous political and governmental structures (kingdoms). The languages are also quite similar. Denmark and Norway were one kingdom from 1380 to 1814. Although Norway became an independent country in 1814, it went into a union with Sweden from 1814 to 1905, after which Norway became completely independent. Finland is a republic with a history partly linked to Sweden and Russia (Kirby, 2006). Table 6.1 shows the populations and languages in these countries.

The history of psychology in general and of assessment in particular in the Nordic countries is not very well covered in the relevant international literature. The few articles and books one can find are mostly written in the respective native languages of these countries. The information in this chapter is taken mainly from K. H. Teigen (2015), as well as a number of articles and additional sources as cited.

6.2 Scandinavian Psychology Prior to the World Wars

The start of psychology as an autonomous discipline in the Scandinavian countries came later than in the United Kingdom and the rest of Continental Europe. In Germany, and eventually many other places, the development of experimental psychology led to the rise of applied psychology and to a field of study that came to be known as "psychotechnics." These evolutions were delayed in the Scandinavian countries, and the introduction of various forms of assessment therefore also came later.

Table 6.1. *Populations and languages in the four countries*

Country	Population (millions)	Official languages
Denmark	5.6	Danish
Finland	5.5	Finnish and Swedish
Norway	5.0	Norwegian
Sweden	9.5	Swedish

Prior to World War II, the influence on Scandinavian psychology came mainly from German psychology. However, after World War II the trend shifted, and the main influences came from the United States. The different schools of psychology were not formally created or represented in Scandinavia; therefore Scandinavian psychologists could choose to wait for the developments that were taking place elsewhere, and then take an eclectic attitude and make use of these developments in their practice. Teigen (2015) maintains that this situation has led to specific developments of the various disciplines and aspects of psychology in Scandinavia, and this of course includes tests and testing.

The first Danish textbook with "psychology" on the title page was published in 1752 and was written by Jens Kraft (1720–1765), a professor of mathematics and philosophy. His textbook was inspired by German philosopher Christian Wolff. Although lectures on psychology had been given in Scandinavian universities as early as 1750 in Sweden, 1788 in Denmark, and 1813 in Norway, psychology was taught within the context of philosophy. The development of psychology as a separate university discipline was connected to the rise of the experimental psychology laboratories in Germany, especially Wundt's laboratory. Scandinavian academics visited Wundt's laboratory in Leipzig to study the new science and later went back to their homelands and established their own institutes of psychology: Denmark (Copenhagen) in 1886, Sweden (Uppsala) in 1902, and Norway (Oslo) in 1909 (Christiansen, 1984). This can be seen as the period of birth for modern psychology, with an accent on experimentation and measurement, in these three countries.

In Denmark, Alfred Lehman (1858–1921) was one of the many young Scandinavians who visited Germany and studied the new psychology in Leipzig. After his return to Denmark, he was the driving force in starting an independent psychophysical laboratory in 1886. He also became increasingly interested in problems of applied psychology, eventually becoming completely absorbed by issues of measurement of individual differences, especially in industrial and work psychology, with applications in personnel selection and the utility of the workforce in economic life. In many ways Lehman can be described as the father of applied psychology and assessment in Scandinavia.

The founder of the first Swedish psychological research laboratory in 1902 was Sydney Alrutz (1868–1925). Unfortunately, he never got a professorship or a university position because psychology at that time was regarded as a branch of either philosophy or pedagogy. But he became instrumental in the development of Nordic collaboration in psychology when he founded the first Nordic journal of psychological research in 1906. However, Alrutz was regarded in his time and in our time as leaning too much toward a metaphysical orientation. It is therefore Gustav Axel Jeaderholm (1882–1936) who is described, at least by Teigen (2015), as the first significant Swedish representative of applied psychology and psychotechnics. He studied with Karl Pearson in London to learn basic statistical concepts. He was appointed professor in 1919 and became quite internationally oriented, successfully absorbing influences from German psychotechnics, American functionalism, Adler's individual psychology, and Piaget's developmental psychology.

Teigen (2015) appoints Anathon Aall (1867–1943) as the most important influencer on the start of the "new psychology" in Norway. Aall had spent many years at various universities in Europe, and in 1908 he became a professor of philosophy at the University of Kristiania (Oslo). Even though nominally a professor of philosophy, his position was first of all responsible for the teaching of psychology. His comprehensive activity led in 1909 to the establishment of a psychological institute at the University of Kristiania. Through this movement, psychology became accepted as a discipline in the academic world in Norway.

Helga Eng (1875–1966) must also be mentioned, especially in relation to the development of assessment theory and practice. She started her scientific career with visits to Germany and maintained this connection over many years. Eng became Norway's first exponent of applied test psychology, i.e., "psychotechnics." She was the first director of the newly established psychotechnical institute in Oslo in 1925, where she developed ability tests for various trades and offered occupational and vocational guidance to young people.

Teigen (1996) points to the years around 1910 as an important epoch in the development of psychology and assessment in Norway. It is fair to assume that this is also true for the other Scandinavian countries. He also writes that "some historians of psychology have maintained that the development of an applied psychology, that took place at the same time, was even more important. It was not only about finding applications for results in experimental psychology, but also about submitting practical problems to independent psychological analyses." He especially highlights in this context the influence in the Nordic countries of two scientists – Hugo Münster (1863–1916) in the United States and William Stern (1861–1938) in Germany – as the two most influential spokesmen of applied psychology. This also demonstrates the increasing impact of US psychology in Scandinavia. Stern developed assessment methods (tests) in areas including pedagogical and educational psychology, psychotherapy, forensic psychology, military psychology, and industrial psychology. Together with the establishment of psychological institutes and, later on, "psychotechnical institutes," history shows the presence of assessment methods in the Nordic countries. It shows that assessment methods were copied, translated, and adapted, and were also developed *de novo* for use in the Scandinavian countries.

The psychology historian Kurt Danziger (1985) has described three different basic models used in psychological research and assessment: the Leipziger model, the Paris model, and the Anglo-American model. The Leipziger model (associated with Wundt) is geared toward psychological research in the normal, or usual, range of phenomena and manifestations. It uses a small number of test takers who are measured in-depth and often obtains results in the form of qualitative data. The Paris model (associated with Charcot, Janet, and Freud) adopts a clinical approach to the study of "unusual" mental life events, and also relies heavily on qualitative data or case studies. The Anglo-American model (associated with Galton, Hall, and others) uses bigger groups of test takers, resulting in large amounts of quantitative data that need statistical analysis. While psychoanalysis and qualitative studies had a good standing in the Scandinavian countries, it is obvious that the development of assessment methods within the afore-mentioned specific areas has leaned on the Anglo-American school of assessment, tests, and testing.

Already before World War I, psychological assessment had been used in the occupational field (in early forms of industrial and work psychology) and especially, following the trends in the United States, in schools (educational assessment) and the health service (clinical assessment). These trends were present in the Scandinavian countries, which were connected to such evolutions. For example, the new ideas and techniques generated by Alfred Binet came to the Nordic countries from the psycho-logical laboratory in France (at the Sorbonne). The intelligence tests that were being published by Binet from 1905 onward spread quickly to other countries. In Norway, the Binet scale published in 1908 was used in Bergen already in the same year as it was published in France.

With this backdrop, how did the field of assessment develop in Scandinavia? It is interesting to note that while there are similarities between these three countries, which is natural with all the common international inspirations and trends that were present especially in the earlier years, the development of assessment has also taken slightly different paths in each of them.

6.3   Psychology and Assessment in Scandinavia during the World Wars (1923–1945)

A common trend was the adoption of measures developed in other cultures and later their standardization and adaptation. The Binet scales, which later were developed into the Stanford–Binet tests, were being used in all three Nordic countries, but it was some time before they were standardized. The first standardizations took place in Denmark in 1930 and in Norway between 1923 and 1931 (Christiansen, 1984). Another common trend was the establishment of "psychotechnical institutes," a result of an increasing interest in occupational psychology and the measurement of abilities, which was necessary within particular trades and certainly in recruitment sessions for the drafting of military personnel. Psychotechnical institutes were established in Norway in 1925, in Denmark in 1929, and in Sweden 1944. The first group tests of ability (i.e., tests used for mass testing of personnel, developed mainly in the armed services in the United States and known as the "Army Alpha tests") were used in Norway in the 1920s. Several other group tests were developed (e.g., "maturity tests") in 1925.

In the earlier days of psychological measurement, testing, and assessment, various professionals (both trained scientists and lay people) used the scales, often changing them as they saw fit. This led to a rising demand for restricting use of such tests to professionals only. The demand for test use to be restricted to psychologists only rose in parallel to the development of the psychology professions in the Scandinavian countries – it came naturally, as a result of a developing professional identity based on competence, to argue that only psychologists had the relevant competence to use such tests. This is also where the three countries differ. Norway became more and more attached to US psychology, especially during and after World War II, while Sweden and Denmark became more attached to

European psychology. Norwegian military personnel who were trained in the United Kingdom and the United States, including officers, psychologists, and physicians, made contacts within the UK and US military psychology establishments. These contacts continued and were reinforced in the years after 1945 and have continued onward ever since. A typical example is that of the psychology program established in Bergen in 1969 – at that time, many of the new positions were filled by American psychologists. The program was the first in Scandinavia that was built on the Boulder model (Frank, 1984), and it was not a coincidence that this program was the first to include "psychometrics" as a separate subject from 1972. It should also be noted though that the main textbook for this subject was Swedish (Magnusson, 1961).

6.4   Scandinavian Psychology Post the World Wars

Another factor that has influenced the partial divergence of the development of psychological assessment in the three Nordic countries discussed here was how the countries came out of World War II. Sweden had been neutral, and Denmark had relatively little destruction of its infrastructure. Norway, on the other hand, had tremendous challenges in rebuilding infrastructure. The great help Norway received from the United States in this respect (the Marshall Aid Program) resulted in many ties, also between universities. It was clear to the Norwegian leaders that Norway urgently needed competent craftspeople and engineers. When the first Nordic conference of psychology was opened in Oslo in June 1947, the prime minister in his opening address pointed to the need for psychologists especially to help assess and find the best candidates for education and training, when building up the country. Already from the founding of the psychotechnical institute in Oslo, occupational tests had been developed for certain trades. After five years in business, 2,200 candidates within 11 fields had been tested by the psychotechnical institute. In 1947, the director of occupational affairs established an advisory committee to assist the directorate of work life to develop the public work of occupational counseling. This process resulted in the establishment of "occupational psychology offices" in the main cities in Norway. Here young people could come and receive counseling on choosing a career, based on both testing and qualitative interviews (Knoff, 1994). The tests were mainly intelligence and ability tests, but they were not very strong from a scientific point of view. For example, the Norwegian intelligence tests that were used in the 1950s were poorly normed, based on norms only applicable for boys – who were the preferred and expected target for Norway's high need for engineers. Later on, the use of intelligence testing switched to the Wechsler Adult Intelligence Scale (WAIS), and the main usage of this test was for a long time connected to the military – especially the testing of young men who were conscripted to military service. The norms used in Norway for the WAIS were for many years those developed in and for the United Kingdom.

Work and organizational psychology has gradually grown in Scandinavia as a separate and distinct field. This branch of psychology was present and developed from the very start of the psychotechnical institutes in the 1920s, with their emphasis on assessing and recruiting people for various trades and jobs in the public sector. Psychological testing in schools and in clinical settings also developed and used. The increasingly diverse situation in the postwar 1945–1950s, while encouraging especially the development of occupational testing, kept testing as a relatively undifferentiated repertoire across all specializations in psychology. It is therefore fair to say that it took a long time before the field of occupational testing developed into a more established form.

6.5   Scandinavian Psychological Assessment: 1960s–1970s

Kile (1987) has named the period between the 1960s and 1970s as "the long incubation time." During this time, testing in general and occupational testing especially gradually developed, but without notable breakthroughs. Then two things happened at the same time. One was the increasing awareness in business that there was much to gain from cooperation with professionals in matters of leadership, organization, and recruitment. The other was that university programs began to include work and organizational psychology as separate subjects. The first university institute teaching these subjects separately was established in Bergen in 1977. This development is more or less similar in all the Scandinavian countries.

We also note that the Scandinavian psychological associations involved themselves in the "assessment business": each of the three psychological associations established test publishing businesses around 1970. They obtained the rights to publish tests such as the Wechsler test batteries, the Minnesota Multiphasic Personality Inventory (MMPI), and the Sixteen Personality Factor Questionnaire (16PF). In the beginning these tests were just translated and sometimes slightly adapted to the local culture. National norming was expensive and, with the limited populations (and limited sales) that were typical in Scandinavia, could only be completed much later.

6.6   Psychological Assessment: 2000–Present

Based on the common developments described here, and also driven by the increasing internationalization of all aspects of psychology, we note that the "assessment policy" in these Scandinavian countries has become more similar during the past years. Also, cooperation between the three test companies has arisen to a certain degree, especially on the development and sale of tests.

In the beginning of the twenty-first century, a rising concern around issues of quality assurance of both tests and test use, especially in the occupational field, has arisen in Scandinavia. This was influenced by discussions both in the International Test Commission (ITC) and in the European Federation of Psychologists' Associations (EFPA). In Norway, a certification scheme, organized by DNV GL, was introduced for tests and test users within the occupational field. This certification scheme also came into effect in Sweden. Initiatives to do the same in Denmark have not succeeded so far.

Recent data on this evolution suggests that the certification of tests has worked and has had an effect in improving the quality of tests. The DNV GL's certification scheme on tests within the occupational field is based on the "EFPA review model for the description and evaluation of psychological and educational tests." This certification scheme started in 2007, and today 41 tests are certified (24 in Norway, 15 in Sweden, and 2 in Denmark). However, the certification of test users has had more limited success in Scandinavian countries. The certification scheme, accredited by EFPA, has now been used to validate the test user qualifications in the United Kingdom and Poland. Sweden has also been accredited by EFPA to award the EuroTest EFPA Level 2 qualification in testing.

With the knowledge the authors have of the present situation in Scandinavian psychological associations, it must be stated, as a sad fact, that the issue of development and quality control of psychometric tests and test use is not high on their priority lists. This applies both for the clinical and occupational fields and gives little or no support for the few certification schemes carried out by a neutral third party. Within the clinical field the public healthcare system is reluctant to use much money on proper adaptations of tests, which leave the quality assurance to the publishers themselves, with more or less positive results. Strong competition between various consultant companies within the occupational field, especially in selection and leadership training, is a hindrance for joining forces to promote and support neutral schemes for quality control of tests and test users.

In 2011 an important ISO standard was published (ISO, 2011: ISO 10667), and Norway has been an significant contributor to this effort. High expectations were connected to it, but no evidence of the impact of this standard has been published as far as we know. All efforts of establishing guidelines and or standards that can lead to better regulations and quality control of psychological assessment should be welcomed and supported. This development is slow, but internationally heading the right way.

6.7   Conclusion

At present, psychological assessment in the Scandinavian countries is a valued activity intrinsically bound to psychological services in work, clinical, forensic, and educational contexts. Significant efforts are made in universities for the development of good assessment skills in future psychologists; ethical considerations are especially observed and discussed. The Scandinavian countries are active participants in the EFPA Board of Assessment. Most of the important psychological measures that are used internationally as "gold standards" are adapted and normed in the Scandinavian countries, and a number of indigenous measures have been developed in each of these countries – so that psychologists have access to a good portfolio of valid tests.

REFERENCES

Christiansen, B. (1984). Om psykologprofesjonens røtter [About the roots of the psychology profession]. In Holter, P. A., Magnussen, S., & Sandsberg, S. (eds.), *Norsk Psykologi i 50 år [50 years of Norwegian psychology]* (pp. 13–49). Oslo: Scandinavian University Press.

Danziger, K. (1985). The origins of the psychological experiment as a social institution. *American Psychologist, 40*(2), 133–140. Referred to in Teigen, K. H. (2004). *En psykologihistorie [A history of psychology]*. Bergen: Fagbokforlaget.

Frank, G. (1984). The Boulder Model: History, rationale, and critique. *Professional Psychology: Research and Practice, 15*(3), 417–435.

ISO (2011). *ISO 10667-1:2011 Assessment service delivery – Procedures and methods to assess people in work and organizational settings – Part 1: Requirements for* the client and *"ISO 10667-2:2011 Assessment service delivery – Procedures and methods to assess people in work and organizational settings – Part 2: Requirements for service providers*. Retrieved from www.iso.org/standard/56441.html

Kile, S. M. (1987). Psykologar i arbeidslivet [Psychologists in working life]. In Myklebust, J. P. & Omundsen, R. (eds.), *Psykologprofesjonen mot år 2000 [Psychology profession towards the year 2000]* (pp. 325–339). Oslo: Scandinavian University Press.

Kirby, D. (2006). *A concise history of Finland*. Cambridge: Cambridge University Press.

Knoff, R. H. (1994). Psykologi i arbeids – og organisasjonspsykologi før og nå [Psychology in work and organizational psychology before and now]. In Reichelt, S. (ed.), *Psykologi i forandring [Psychology in change]* (pp. 189–205). Oslo: Norsk Psykologforening.

Magnusson, D. (1961). *Testteori*. Stockholm: Almquist & Wiksell.

Teigen, K. H. (1996). *Psykologi. Universitetet I Bergens historie [Psychology. The history of the University of Bergen]* (vol. 2, pp. 710–742). Bergen: University of Bergen.

(2015). *En psykologihistorie [A history of psychology]*. Bergen: Fagbokforlaget.

CHAPTER 7

Key Episodes in The History of Testing in Central Western Europe

Jonas W. B. Lang and Jan Corstjens

7.1 Introduction

This chapter focuses on the development of modern testing in the Dutch, German, and French-speaking parts of Europe (France, The Netherlands, Belgium, Luxembourg, Germany, most parts of Switzerland, Austria, and the South Tirol region of Italy). Some early forms of selection testing in this region of the world can be traced back as far as the Roman Empire where officers and soldiers were selected through systematic assessment procedures during a period of probation before they were fully accepted into the Roman army (Stout, 2018). However, the start of modern psychometric testing happened much more recently toward the end of the nineteenth century and early twentieth century, and the region has played a pivotal role in this development. The purpose of this chapter is to highlight some key moments in this history.

7.2 Wilhelm Wundt, Experimental Psychological Laboratories, and Early Testing

An important antecedent of the development of psychometric testing was the development of experimental psychology. In 1879, Wilhelm Wundt had opened the first psychological laboratory at the University of Leipzig, then a part of the newly formed German Empire. Wundt had worked with the famous psychophysiologist Hermann von Helmholtz at the University of Heidelberg and was interested in applying rigorous scientific measurement methods developed for psychophysiological measurement to the systematic measurement of psychological experiences. Soon after Wundt opened his laboratory in Leipzig, other psychological laboratories followed like the ones of Gustav Elias Müller in Göttingen and Hermann Ebbinghaus at the University of Berlin (Sprung & Sprung, 2001). Psychological laboratories typically had a set of devices to record reaction times, movements, or perceptions. One characteristic of early experimental psychology that resulted from its development from psychophysiology and psychology was a keen interest in the scientific measurement of psychological states. Early experimental psychologists defined psychological experiments by rigorous and repeatable measurement of psychological states and not necessarily by experimental manipulations (Stern, 1911; Wundt, 1883).

The development of experimental psychology was not restricted to its origin in Germany and soon spread to other countries like the United States and France. Frequently, foreign students traveled to Leipzig to study with Wundt and learn the new science of psychology. These students then took their knowledge and expertise home and psychological laboratories opened at universities such as Clark (Nicolas & Young, 2014), Cornell, and later Harvard in the United States. Several famous early American and UK psychologists wrote their doctoral thesis with Wundt in German. Notable figures include Charles Spearman from the United Kingdom and Titchener from the United States. The founding father of psychology in the United States – William James – also studied briefly with Wundt but never worked in his laboratory (Gundlach, 2018). He later hired another former doctoral student of Wundt, Hugo Münsterberg, to build the psychological laboratory at Harvard University (Blatter, 2014). The new discipline was also well received in France, Belgium, and the Netherlands where psychological laboratories were opened at the Sorbonne University and the Salpêtrière University Hospital in Paris (Nicolas, 2006; Nicolas & Young, 2014), at the Catholic University Leuven in 1891 (Richelle et al., 1992), and at the University of Groningen in 1892 (Busato et al., 2013), respectively.

From an early point in time, experimental psychologists that were trained and inspired by Wundt were interested in studying individual differences in mental capacity and talent. This work extended an article on the measurement of psychological states by Wundt himself (Wundt, 1883). The most well-known of these students was James McKeen Cattell. Cattell wrote a dissertation with the title *Psychometrische Studien* (Cattell, 1886a) that was also published in Wundt's journal *Philosophische Studien* (Cattell, 1886b). This early work studied relatively basic tasks such as, for instance, the time it takes to recognize German words. In addition to the work of his doctoral advisor Wundt, Cattell was also inspired by the work of the English statistician and eugenicist Francis Galton who advocated the use of statistical methods and argued that human characteristics follow a bell-shaped normal distribution. Cattell later developed a series of basic cognitive measures at Columbia University in a first attempt to measure intelligence. However, one of his own students, Clark Wisseler, found evidence that these basic measures did not correlate highly with each other or with relevant outcome variables (Wissler, 1901), which was discouraging to Cattell and many of his contemporaries especially in the eugenics movement (Fancher, 1985; Wickett, 1998; Wissler, 1901).

Another Wundt-trained psychologist who contributed to the early development of psychological measurement was Charles Spearman. Spearman's seminal work on general intelligence (Spearman, 1904) was related to Cattell's earlier work and was also inspired by Galton. Both Cattell and Spearman relied on combining Galton's work with ideas around psychometric and psychological measurement that they had picked up in Wundt's lab in order to apply these insights in practice. Their focus on application differed from the perspective of their mentor who had high methodological and philosophical standards and believed that this type of application could only happen after the young discipline had developed – these views typically led to some distance between Wundt and the scholars he had trained (Fahrenberg, 2012). Spearman also focused on developing new statistical and psychometric methods like correlation coefficients and factor analysis methodology. He presented some of this work at the first congress of the newly founded German association for experimental psychology (later the German Psychology Association) in 1904 (Schumann, 2004).

7.3   Alfred Binet and the Measurement of Intelligence

In 1891, the experimental psychological laboratory of the Sorbonne University in Paris was joined by an ambitious young researcher, Alfred Binet. The Sorbonne laboratory had been founded and was led by the physiologist Henry Beaunis on the initiative of the founding father of French psychology Théodule Ribot. Binet had previously worked with Jean Martin Charcot at the Salpêtrière Hospital. Charcot was famous for his work on hypnosis, but he also had an interest in experimental psychology and had started his own psychological laboratory at the Salpêtrière University Hospital. Binet quickly became an important member of the Sorbonne laboratory and finally its director in 1893. He was ambitious in trying to ensure that French experimental psychology would catch up with German and American experimental psychology (Binet, 1894; Nicolas & Young, 2014). In addition to his work on hypnosis with Charcot, he had developed an interest in developmental psychology and had monitored the development of his two daughters (Siegler, 1992). However, the young Binet was not really satisfied with these earlier approaches and was thus interested in the new discipline of experimental psychology and the work in laboratories. In his laboratory work, Binet showed an interest in measurement early on and developed or refined several devices to measure basic individual differences (Nicolas, 2006). Binet was a member of the Society for the Psychological Study of the Child and in this capacity he and other members were approached by the governmental Commission for the Retarded with the request to advise on a test for identifying children with learning disabilities. In response to this request, Binet collaborated with the then young medical student Théodore Simon and combined his earlier experiences from developmental psychology with his expertise with measuring psychological states. The result was the first modern approach to intelligence testing (Binet & Simon, 1907; Schneider, 1992). Binet and Simon's contribution was especially noteworthy because they went beyond earlier approaches that mainly focused on measuring perceptual speed and basic cognitive function. In contrast, Binet and Simon included more complex cognitive tasks into their scale. Their work was mostly concerned with individual diagnosis but in allowing for individual diagnosis they also gathered normative information for populations in the way Galton and his followers had recommended. Binet and Simon's work is remarkable because modern intelligence testing is still heavily based on the core task that they suggested more than a century ago. The Binet–Simon test became popular internationally because it solved the issues that Cattell was confronted with and thus was enthusiastically received and popularized especially in the United States by Goddard and Terman (Benjamin, 2009; Terman, 1916). Although popular abroad, Binet's work gained less traction in France (Schneider, 1992). One potential reason was that French researchers and the French public in large parts were interested and fascinated by graphology (the idea that the style of handwriting – not its content – allows for insights into the writer's personality or psychological state). Binet initially rejected graphology but subsequently worked on graphology in collaboration with a graphologist in the years in which he also conducted work on intelligence in children (Nicolas et al., 2015). Binet suggested the use of the Binet–Simon intelligence scale or similar measures in the military after reading about the use of tests with mentally ill German soldiers, but those ideas did not gain the same traction as in the United States where a modified form of the test was used to systematically screen soldiers for World War I. One reason why intelligence testing was less popular in France in Binet's time and was largely used for children and psychiatric patients was the fact that France traditionally had a central-ized system with a governmentally organized education system. This system included state exams. Because these exam scores were available for all recruits/school graduates and widely accepted there was less need to introduce a standardized measure in comparison to the United States with its more decentralized and heterogenous educational system (Schneider, 1992).

7.4   William Stern and the Foundation of Differential Psychology

A German psychologist who was inspired by Cattell's work on the appli-cation of statistical methods to testing was William Stern. Stern had studied under Herman Ebbinghaus at one of the early experimental psychology laboratories at the University of Berlin and also had a keen interest in developmental psychology. Today, Stern is mostly known for suggesting the term "IQ" or "*Intelligenzquotient*" to track children's cog-nitive development (Stern, 1914). Arguably, his most important influence on the field of individual difference research and testing is his work on differential psychology (Stern, 1900, 1911) and especially his book *Die differentielle Psychologie in ihren methodischen Grundlagen* (Stern 1911). The book introduced key conceptual ideas on individual differences. While earlier work had typically discussed "measurement," Stern devel-oped the conceptual foundation of modern individual difference and personality research. He first discussed traits ("*Merkmale*") and described differential psychology and testing as a separate applied discipline. The book is less well-known outside the German-speaking world because it was not translated but early individual difference researchers in other parts of the world read and cited it heavily. For instance, Gordon Allport was a student of William Stern in the 1920s in Hamburg and the first chapter of Allport's classic personality introduction book not only discusses Wundt's work but also many of Stern's ideas and cites both (Allport, 1937; Asendorpf, 1999).

7.5   Hugo Münsterberg and the First Selection Tests

Another former doctoral student of Wundt, already briefly mentioned because of his association to Harvard and William James, is Hugo Münsterberg (Benjamin, 2006; Blatter, 2014; Stern, 1917). Münsterberg wrote several influential books on the application of psychological methods. His 1912 book *Psychologie und Wirtschaftsleben: Ein Beitrag zur angewandten Experimental-Psychologie* (Münsterberg, 1912) is commonly seen as the starting point for modern industrial and organizational psychology and Münsterberg is therefore also typically seen as the or one of the two founding fathers of industrial and organizational psychology in the United States (Spillmann & Spillmann, 1993; Vinchur & Koppes, 2007). The book was initially published in German and then translated by the author and published in English a year later as *Psychology and Industrial Efficiency* (Münsterberg, 1913). Relevant to the history of testing, the 1912 book includes arguably one of the first successful applications of psychometric testing in an applied setting beyond educational and developmental contexts. A common problem at the time was the high number of traffic accidents. Modern cities increasingly adopted electric trams and these trams were responsible for a large number of traffic victims. Münsterberg successfully developed psychometric tests designed to select tram drivers and normed them on the basis of comparing tram drivers with many accidents with those with less accidents. Münsterberg also reported selection procedures for sailors and ideas about vocational tests. A new element in the 1912 book that went beyond earlier testing was the idea to match tests to the specific requirements of the job.

7.6 Otto Lipmann, William Stern, Institutes of Applied Psychology and the First Journal of Applied Psychology

While testing and particularly intelligence testing were less commonly used in the military, especially German psychologists initially enthusiastically applied testing in the military for more specific selection tasks, in organizations, and in vocational counseling (Gundlach, 1996, 2002; Vinchur & Koppes, 2010). William Stern is today widely known as an individual difference researcher and developmental psychologist. However, Stern was also an early industrial and organizational psychologist. Stern had come up with the German term *"Psychotechnik"* (psychotechnology) that Münsterberg popularized in Germany (Gundlach, 1996, 2002) and captured the idea that psychology could be utilized as a form of technology. Stern extensively collaborated with Otto Lipmann – also a former student of Ebbinghaus. Lipmann and Stern led a trend toward the formation of a series of institutes of applied psychology in Germany. Most of these institutes sought collaboration with business organizations but also more broadly with educational institutions and the government. Some of these institutes were linked to universities and directly sought to apply psychological methods and particularly testing methods in organizations just like Münsterberg had suggested (Vinchur & Koppes, 2010; Viteles, 1923). Psychotechnology as a movement also caught on in the Netherlands, where the lab at University of Groningen conducted early testing for selection of telephonists and high-currency workers and the city of Amsterdam opened one of the first psychotechnics laboratories (Haas, 1995; Van Strien & Dane, 2001), and Switzerland, where Edouard Claparède founded the Association Internationale de Psychotechnique (later the International Association of Applied Psychology) in 1920 (Roland-Lévy, 2020).

The most well-known of the early psychotechnology/applied psychology institutes was Stern and Lipmann's *Institut für Angewandte Psychologie und psychologische Sammelforschung* in Berlin. Stern and Lipman implemented one of the first systematic approaches for vocational consulting at the Weimar Republic department of labor in the late 1920s and early 1930s. Stern and Lipmann also founded the *Zeitschrift für Angewandte Psychologie und Psychologische Sammelforschung* in 1908 (known as the *Zeitschrift für Angewandte Psychologie* from 1916 onward). The journal existed until 1933 when it was banned by the newly appointed Nazi regime. It published many early papers on the application and development of tests and preceded the American *Journal of Applied Psychology* by almost a decade even though the contents of the journal did not only include topics related to testing. Stern and Lipmann also initiated an influential book series with the title *Schriften zur Psychologie der Berufseignung und des Wirtschaftslebens* (*Papers on the Psychology of Vocational Aptitude and Industrial Efficiency*). This paper series had almost the character of a journal and included many early papers on the use of testing in applied settings and the young field of vocational testing (e.g., Lipmann, 1921). Contributors to the series were also two of the first widely known female applied psychologists, Hildegard Grünbaum-Sachs and Franziska Baumgarten. Baumgarten later also wrote several books on applied psychology and especially on testing that were widely circulated in the 1930s (Daub, 2011; Richebächer, 2010) including the seminal book *Die Berufseignungsprüfungen: Theorie und Praxis* (*Vocational Testing: Theory and Practice*; Baumgarten, 1928). Another well-known early applied psychologist was Walter Moede. Moede was a former assistant of Wundt (Moede, 1919, 1920) and studied selection. He was also an early pioneer of the assessment of teams and contributed to the emergence of social psychology.

7.7   The Exodus from Germany

Many leading figures in German and Austrian psychology of the late 1920s and early 1930s including Stern and Lipman were Jewish or were critical of the right-wing parties and the general political climate that started to emerge in the Germany of the 1920s. One key element of the climate of the time was the so-called *Dolchstosslegende*. According to this widely circulated story, the German army was never defeated in the field and was actually close to winning World War I. The Nazis finally took power in Germany in 1933 with the election of Hitler to the chancellor position (equivalent of a prime minister). This change ended the career of many leading figure in psychological testing with a Jewish background but also created many new opportunities for others like Moede who was a member of the Nazi party.

The victims of the Nazi regime among psychologists include not only psychologists interested in testing and measurement like William Stern and Otto Lipman, but also important figures of the broader discipline of psychology like Wolfgang Köhler, Max Wertheimer, Kurt Lewin, or Otto Selz (Lück, 2011; Sprung & Sprung, 2001). A large number of these important figures left Germany and Austria in the 1930s and mostly found a new home in the United States. However, some scholars like Otto Selz were directly killed by the Nazi regime. Otto Selz fled to the Netherlands but was caught in Amsterdam and deported back to Germany; he died in the Auschwitz concentration camp. The Lipmann-Stern era in Berlin and Hamburg found an infamous end when students who were members of the Nazi organization SA (Sturmabteilung) destroyed Lipmann's Berlin institute. Lipmann decided to end his life (von Rosenstiel, 1985). Shortly thereafter, Stern emigrated to the United States via the Netherlands and taught at Duke university until his death. Past his prime, he started his first lecture in the United States with the words "First: I realize that my English is imperfect ... This is the first English lecture I have ever given, and so you will have not only instruction, but also occasion for amusement" (Probst, 2014).

7.8   *Wehrmachtpsychologie* Testing

The new regime fostered psychological research that seemed closer to the new Nazi ideology and also to related disciplines such as, most notably, heredity research that were later heavily associated with war crimes like the work of Otmar Freiherr von Verschuer at the Kaiser Wilhelm Institute of

Anthropology focusing on eugenics and human heredity. Within psychology, the change was mostly gradual. Psychologists still endorsed the experimental-scientific ideas of psychotechnology but tried to combine them with theoretical framework known as *Ausdruckspsychologie* (expression psychology). Ausdruckspsychologie was developed from the start of the twentieth century from graphology and largely was based on the idea that careful observation of nonverbal behavior would allow inferences about an individuals' personality characteristics (Haas, 1995; Manteufel, 2006). Ausdruckspsychologie ideas had links to Gestalt psychologists like Karl Bühler (1933) and the notion that a person should be judged "as a whole" (Fitts, 1946; Highhouse, 2002). However, during the time of the Nazi regime, Ausdruckspsychologie was also linked with physiogonomy-related ideas (the practice of assessing a person's character or personality from their outer appearance) and associated with psychologists like Ludwig Klages, who was openly antisemitic, and Philipp Lersch, who enthusiastically supported Hitler and the Nazi euthanasia programs (Ellgring, 1981; Geuter, 1985).

The exodus of leading figures in German vocational testing because of their Jewish heritage or opposition to the Nazi regime opened up space for another group of psychologists. During the years of the Weimar Republic, the newly founded army of the new republic faced selection problems. The Treaty of Versailles had limited the number of soldiers in the army considerably so that systematic selection of officers was necessary. The world economic crisis emphasized this trend even more so that even the selection of soldiers required selection procedures. To address this need, the army of the Weimar Republic started a special military psychology unit that was led by Max Simoneit from the 1930s and exclusively included male psychologists (Geuter, 2008). The unit saw massive growth during the 1930s and conducted careful selection examinations of all officers and later also with specialists of lower ranks. Simoneit was initially not a member of the Nazi party when he was appointed (Bönner, 1986; Lück, 2015). He wrote several books on the psychology of soldiers and today is possibly most well-known for extending and further developing the heterogenous batteries of psychometric tests and practical tasks under observation both individually and in groups used by the Wehrmachtspsychologie. This battery later provided the inspiration for test batteries developed and used by the British War Officer Selection Board and the US Office of Strategic Services (OSS Assessment staff, 1948, 3) and subsequently the basis for the use of similar methods in business organizations after the war where they developed into what is today known as the *assessment center* (Wiggins, 1973).

As the war progressed, the Wehrmachtpsychologie lost a lot of its influence during 1942 because of the need to recruit rather than select in the changed circumstances of the war and the number of tests markedly decreased during 1942 (Geuter, 2008). In this time period, Simoneit joined the Nazi party – possibly in an effort to improve the standing of the organization he lead (Lück, 2015). Nevertheless, the Wehrmachtspsychologie was ultimately dissolved at the end of 1942 and Simoneit became a soldier and fought on the east front (Geuter, 1985; Lück, 2015). After the war, former members of the Wehrmachtpsychologie took over many of the vacant faculty positions in postwar Germany so the ideas of the former Wehrmachtspsychologie had a latent influence on German psychology into the 1960s and 1970s (Bönner, 1986; De Lorent, 2017). Simoneit himself did not get a position and instead worked as an independent scholar/psychologist after the war (Bönner, 1986; Lück, 2015).

7.9   Dutch Psychometrics and the Centraal Instituut voor Toetsontwikkeling

Before and during World War II, Dutch interest in assessment and testing was largely restricted to efforts by individual researchers in the Groningen lab and in industry to apply psychotechnology to practice (Haas, 1995; van Strien & Dane, 2001). The majority of Dutch university psychology had largely been influenced by sociological thinking and testing rarely went beyond a Dutch translation of Binet-styled intelligence testing and its pragmatic application (Mulder & Heyting, 1998). This situation broadly changed in the 1950s when Dutch psychologists became interested in the methods that American testing researchers had developed during the 1930s (Heijden & Sijtsma, 1996). One important figure in the early development of testing in the Netherlands was Adriaan de Groot – a professor at the University of Amsterdam. de Groot had worked with Otto Selz during his time in Amsterdam but was also a former head of the psychology section of the Philipps company (Frijda & de Groot, 1981). He was thus familiar with both fundamental cognitive psychology and applied work. de Groot founded the Research Instituut voor de Toegepaste Psychologie in 1957 where he developed tests for education and selection. de Groot visited the Educational Testing Service in 1958 and tried to implement ideas and technologies developed there in the Netherlands. His school tests were widely used from the 1950s and his efforts culminated in the founding of the *Centraal Instituut voor Toetsontwikkeling* (CITO; National

Institute for Educational Measurement) at Arnhem in 1968 as a central body for the development of tests in the Netherlands.

Dutch testing psychology from early on was interested in the development and application of item-response theory (IRT) and Rasch methods. These methods (see Lang & Tay, 2021, for a recent overview) had developed in the 1960s after pioneering work by Frederic Lord and others in the US and the initial publication of the Rasch model by the Danish mathematician Georg Rasch. An important figure in this movement was Robert Mokken – a political scientist by training who worked on the application of item-response theory methods at the University of Amsterdam. Another important figure in the development of testing in the Netherlands was John van de Geer – a professor at the University of Leiden who organized several meetings on the new methods of Rasch and IRT measurement in the 1960s and 1970s and created a climate that was fruitful for young psychometricians and led to the success of many well-known Dutch testing and psychometric scholars like Jan de Leeuw, Wim van der Linden, Jos ten Berge, Ivo Molenaar, Klaas Sijtsma, or Rob Meijer (Heijden & Sijtsma, 1996).

7.10 Internationalization and Critical Psychology

The years after World War II were characterized by the adoption of US assessment instruments for clinical, organizational, and educational practice in especially the Dutch-speaking part of Central Western Europe and increasing internationalization (Haas, 1995; Van Strien & Dane, 2001). In German-speaking areas, a similar adoption occurred to a lesser degree and with some delay (Pawlik, 1994; Sprung & Sprung, 2001). Two developments hampered internationalization. First, many of the former Wehrmachtpsychologen were accepted into influential university positions, continued to focus on Ausdruckspsychologie after the war and into the early 1970s, and affected the policies of the German society of psychology (that also includes members from Austria and Switzerland). A second development that led to clashes within the German-speaking world was the emergence of the critical psychology movement. The early West German state still had many former Nazis in important positions and especially young students rebelled against this situation, which ultimately fueled the West German student protests of the late 1960s and early 1970s. Critical psychology partly fulfilled a desire for questioning the status quo. The core idea behind the critical psychology movement led by Klaus Holzkamp was a critique of the third-person perspective of "traditional" psychology, its focus on method over content, and the neglect of the role of society and the context in especially the development of clinical "disorders" (Motzkau & Schraube, 2015; Teo, 1998). The goal of proponents of critical psychology was to substitute critical psychology with a psychology from the perspective of the subject. One element of critical psychology was a critique of tests as a method in daily clinical practice because of the artificial nature of test situations and the tendency of tests to be removed from the specific situation of the individual (Rexelius, 1988).

In the French-speaking part of Central Europe, internationalization occurred even slower than in the German-speaking part. As noted previously, the tests that Binet had developed were widely used but surprisingly not very frequently in France in his time. However, this trend continued after World War II and until today to some degree. In addition to cultural differences with other countries like the United States (Carson, 2007), one reason for the low popularity of Binet's work was likely his early death and the comparably greater attention to more fundamental researchers like Piaget (Lautrey & Ribaupierre, 2004; Schneider, 1992). Some authors have also suggested that Binet had few followers because of how he interacted with his coworkers (Schneider, 1992). Instead of a focus on testing and assessment, French psychology and especially clinical psychology has long been influenced by psychoanalytic work and especially the psychoanalytic theories of the Frenchmen Jacques Lacan (Botbol & Gourbil, 2018; Hook, 2017). Lacan had critical views on +behavioral methods and also psychoanalytic work in the ego-psychology tradition that is popular in the United States. During the student protests of the late 1960s that also occurred in France, tests were also frequently criticized by left-leaning intellectuals in a somewhat similar way that German critical psychology did (Lautrey & Ribaupierre, 2004).

7.11   University Entry Selection in Belgium, Germany, and the Netherlands

The aforementioned Dutch CITO example did not necessarily broadly translate to the surrounding countries. However, one notable exception is traditionally the selection of medical students. At the start of this chapter, the situation of testing in France was already discussed and the fact that a largely standardized education system typically makes the broad use of tests for entry to university and the military less of a necessity when school exam grades can be used for selection (Carson, 2007). France and Germany have traditionally used this system. Validity studies also typically find that selection tests do not predict much additional variance beyond these central exams (Schuler & Hell, 2008). Other central European countries such as Belgium and Austria refrain from explicit selection and instead use the first year of university education to select students. Although costly, the approach typically leads to broader acceptance in society and the common hope is that it increases fairness especially when paired with non-existing or low student fees. One notable exception to the broad absence of tests in university selection, however, has traditionally been medical education because of the high costs of educating medical professionals. The need for selection medical education has led to the development of specific selection tests. The largest of these programs is likely the *German Test für medizinische Studiengänge* (TMS), which is also used in Austria and Switzerland in somewhat adapted form. The TMS was developed in the 1970s. Because of declining interest in medical education the test fell out of favor for a time but since 2007 it has experienced a resurgence and is now very widely used again in combination with school grades and may be the largest European selection program with more than 15,000 yearly participants (Chenot, 2009; Trost et al., 1998; Zimmerhofer & Trost, 2008). Belgium also successfully uses a centralized test for the selection of medical students (Lievens et al., 2009).

The specific characteristics of Central European education systems notwithstanding the globalization of education and the fact that a larger percentage of the population seeks to attend university have recently led to an increased interest in the use of selection tests to select international and graduate students. Traditionally, most Central European university education systems did not distinguish between bachelor and master level so that a selection from undergraduate to master-level graduate education was not necessary. This situation has recently changed with the Bologna reforms also broadly separating European university education into undergraduate and graduate and there is new interest in the use of tests for graduate student selection (Schwager et al., 2015).

7.12 Modern Use of Tests in Organizations

In more recent years, the use of tests in governmental and business organizations in Central Europe shows some variation across countries and industries (Lievens, 2007) and with the more commonly studied US context. However, overall, these variations are typically smaller than many applied psychologists may expect. One important difference between

Central Europe and other parts of the world has long been that the legal situation made the use of inappropriate selection devices and procedures much less of a risk than, for instance, in the United States. This situation has traditionally opened up the markets for nonscientific procedures (Kanning, 2010). One reason for this situation is that Central European laws typically penalize the loss of immaterial goods in civil law not very highly. Accordingly, the risk in using an inappropriate selection procedure for an organization is typically lower than in countries with UK/US-style legal systems. Additionally, countries in Central Europe – with the exception of the Netherlands and France to some degree – mostly do not have easily identifiable racial minorities and instead have cultural, linguistic, and religious minorities making it more complex to identify and systematically study minority differences. An exception was a debate in Germany after the reunification when researchers discovered that East German test participants in personnel selection typically had lower scores on certain measures (Kersting, 1995).

Overall, the legal and political situation in Western Europe leaves the decision to implement evidence-based selection programs more strongly to the initiative of specific organizations and decision-makers. One example for such an initiative is the use of Thurstonian-inspired selection tests in the selection of German governmental employees. This research program was initiated by a newly founded institute after World War II – the German Society for Personnel Selection (DGP; Deutsche Gesellschaft für Personalwesen) and its head Adolf Otto Jäger and resulted in the development of the Wilde Intelligence Test (Althoff & Jäger, 1981). This measure was used more than 500,000 times in the 1950s and 1960s and is longer and more comprehensive than most other measures of intelligence (Lang et al., 2010). Jäger later became a professor at the University of Berlin and focused on more fundamental intelligence research. However, a revised version of his more modern test – the BIS-r-DGP – is still widely used in selection in Germany (Beauducel & Kersting, 2002).

Another initiative with the goal to improve the use of tests in Western Europe is the development of testing quality criteria systems in the Netherlands and Germany (Evers et al., 2010; Hagemeister et al., 2012; Hornke & Kersting, 2004; Kersting, 2008). These evaluation systems go somewhat beyond the US standards for testing by providing not only a set of guidelines but also an institutional structure that supports the implementation of these guidelines. The German DIN33430 system builds on the infrastructure of the widely known institute for normation that focuses on norms for technical products or services across a large range. The DIN33430 includes the requirement for special training and focuses on the certification of people. People who want to get certified simply need to pass an exam. Psychology departments increasingly make an effort to teach the key skills for passing this exam already in their curriculum. An initiative related to the DIN33430 is the TBS-TK system (Diagnostik- und Testkuratorium der Föderation Deutscher Psychologenvereinigungen, 2018). TBS-TK focuses on tests (and not people). Tests are reviewed by two independent reviewers who write a report together. The test reviews are then published by a leading German psychology journal. Like TBS-TK, the Dutch COTAN system also focuses on evaluation tests (Evers et al., 2010). While TBS-TK is based on evaluations by reviewers, COTAN focuses more on threshold-based guidelines. Like the DIN33430 system, COTAN also publishes test evaluations of Dutch-speaking tests.

7.13   Outlook and Trends

Our review of key episodes in the development of testing in Central Western Europe has shown that many key innovations came from this region of the world until the middle of the last century. We conclude this chapter with some speculation about future developments in selection and testing specific to this part of the world.

One recent trend is the increasing use of testing and assessment for quality control in education especially in the Netherlands and Germany so that psychometric methods have a more indirect role in improving education and higher education outcomes. Universities in Central Europe are increasingly interested in recruiting international students and this creates a new need to assess foreign applicants for Western European universities and organizations and there is also an increasing trend for students within Europe to study in other countries. A similar trend toward globalization also exists in business organizations and this trend creates an increasing need to use testing to compare applicants and employees across countries and language barriers. We expect that these trends will continue.

A second trend affects the education and training of psychologists as one major source of psychometric knowledge and expertise in testing. Traditionally, the education of psychologists in Central Western Europe was relatively institutionalized with the majority of training organized by state universities on the basis of a relatively standardized curriculum and a four to five years of education to become a psychologist. The Bologna reforms with the introduction of a master and bachelor system have changed this general makeup. There is a trend for shorter and more specialized courses with a focus on specific subdisciplines of psychology like clinical or work and organizational psychology. At the same time, the number of students in most countries have increased. An important question for the future is how this changed landscape with a larger number of psychologists but with a shorter and more specialized education will change the future of psychological testing in applied settings. The European Federation of Psychologists Associations has tried to address this trend by establishing a European quality standard for psychologists, the EuroPsy (European Federation of Psychologists Associations, 2013). However, this initiative has so far not yet had a profound impact because the labor markets and quality standards are still largely focused on the national level.

REFERENCES

Allport, G. W. (1937). *Personality: A psychological interpretation*. New York: Henry Holt.

Althoff, K. & Jäger, A. O. (1981). Zur Struktur des Wilde-Intelligenz-Tests (WIT) und zu seiner Stellung im Strukturmodell von Jäger 1967 [The structure of the Wild Intelligence Test (WIT) and its position in the structural model of Jäger1967]. *Diagnostica, 27*(3), 215–226.

Asendorpf, J. (1999). *Psychologie der Persönlichkeit [Psychology of personality]* (2nd ed.). Heidelberg: Springer.

Baumgarten, F. (1928). *Die Berufseignungsrüfungen: Theorie und Praxis [The career aptitude: theory and practice]*. Bern: A. Francke.

Beauducel, A., & Kersting, M. (2002). Fluid and crystallized intelligence and the Berlin Model of Intelligence Structure (BIS). *European Journal of Psychological Assessment, 18*(2), 97–112. https://doi.org/10.1027//1015-5759.18.2.97

Benjamin, L. T. Jr. (2006). Hugo Münsterberg's attack on the application of scientific psychology. *Journal of Applied Psychology, 91*(2), 414–425. https://doi.org/10.1037/0021-9010.91.2.414

(2009). The birth of American intelligence testing. *Monitor on Psychology, 40*(1), 20.

Binet, A. (1894). *Introduction à la psychologie expérimentale [Introduction to experimental psychology]*. Paris: Alcan.

Binet, A. & Simon, T. (1907). *Les enfants anormaux [Abnormal children]*. Paris: Armand Colin.

Blatter, J. T. (2014). The psychotechnics of everyday life: Hugo Münsterberg and the politics of applied psychology, 1887–1917. *ProQuest Dissertations and Theses*, 191. Retrieved from https://search.proquest.com/docview/1557761517

Bönner, K. H. (1986). *Das Leben des Dr. Max Simoneit [The life of Dr. Max Simoneit]*. https://doi.org/10.23668/psycharchives.265

Botbol, M. & Gourbil, A. (2018). The place of psychoanalysis in French psychiatry. *British Journal of Psychology International, 15*(1), 3–5. https://doi.org/10.1192/bji.2017.3

Bühler, K. (1933). *Ausdruckstheorie: Das System an der Geschichte aufgezeigt [Theory of expression: The system of history shown]*. Jena: Gustav Fischer.

Busato, V., van Essen, M., & Koops, W. (2013). *Vier grondleggers van de psychologie [The founders of psychology]*. Amsterdam: Bert Bakker.

Carson, J. (2007). *The measure of merit: Talents, intelligence, and inequality in the French and American republics, 1750–1940*. Princeton, NJ: Princeton University Press.

Cattell, J. M. (1886a). *Psychometrische Untersuchungen [Psychometric examinations]*. Leipzig: Wilhelm Engelmann.

(1886b). Psychometrische Untersuchungen [Psychometric examinaions]. *Philosophische Studien: Erste Abtheilung/Philosophical Studies: Erste Abtheilung, 3*, 305–335.

Chenot, J.-F. (2009). Undergraduate medical education in Germany. *German Medical Science: GMS e-Journal, 7*, Doc02. https://doi.org/10.3205/000061

Daub, E. (2011). Franziska Baumgarten-Tramer: Für die Wissenschaftlichkeit praktischer Psychologie [Franziska Baumgarten-Tramer: For the scientificity of practical psychology]. In S. Volkmann-Raue & H. E. Lück (eds.), *Bedeutende Psychologinnen des 20. Jahrhunderts* (2nd ed.). Wiesbaden: VS Verlag.

de Lorent, H.-P. (2017). Peter R. Hofstätter. In *Täterprofile: Die Verantwortlichen im Hamburger Bildungswesen unterm Hakenkreuz und in der Zeit nach 1945, Band 2 [Perpetrator profiles: Those responsible in the Hamburg education system under the swastika and in the period after 1945, vol. 2]* (pp. 742–797). Hamburg: Landeszentrale für politische Bildung Hamburg.

Diagnostik- und Testkuratorium der Föderation Deutscher Psychologenvereinigungen [Diagnostic and Test Curatorium of the Federation of German Psychologist Associations]. (2018). Föderation Deutscher Psychologenvereinigungen [Federation of German psychologists' associations]. *Psychologische Rundschau/Psychological Review, 69*(2), 109–116. https://doi.org/10.1026/0033-3042/a000401

Ellgring, H. (1981). Nonverbal communication: A review of research in Germany. *German Journal of Psychology, 5*(1), 59–84.

European Federation of Psychologists Associations. (2013). *EuroPsy: European certificate in psychology*. Brussels: Author.

Evers, A., Sijtsma, K., Lucassen, W., & Meijer, R. R. (2010). The Dutch review process for evaluating the quality of psychological tests: History, procedure, and results. *International Journal of Testing, 10*(4), 295–317. https://doi.org/10.1080/15305058.2010.518325

Fahrenberg, J. (2012). *Wilhelm Wundt – Pioneer in psychology and outsider?* Retrieved from http://psydok.psycharchives.de/jspui/handle/20.500.11780/669

Fancher, R. E. (1985). *The intelligence men: Makers of the IQ controversy*. New York: W.W. Norton & Company.

Fitts, P. M. (1946). German applied psychology during World War II. *American Psychologist, 1*(5), 151–161. https://doi.org/10.1037/h0059674

Frijda, N. H. & de Groot, A. D. (1981). (eds.). *Otto Selz: His contribution to psychology*. The Hague: Mouton.

Geuter, U. (1985). Polemos panton pater – Militär und Psychologie im Deutschen Reich 1914–1945 [Polemos panton pater – military and psychology in the German Reich]. In M. G. Ash & U. Geuter (eds.), *Geschichte der deutschen Psychologie im 20. Jahrhundert [History of German psychology in the 20th century]* (pp. 146–171). Opladen: Westdeutscher Verlag.

(2008). *The professionalization of psychology in Nazi Germany*. Cambridge: Cambridge University Press.

Gundlach, H. (1996). Faktor Mensch im Krieg Der Eintritt der Psychologie und Psychotechnik in den Krieg [The man factor in war: The entry of psychology and psychotechnology into war]. *Berichte Zur Wissenschaftsgeschichte/Reports on the History fo Science, 19*(2–3), 131–143. https://doi.org/10.1002/bewi.19960190211

(2002). *Psychologie und Psychotechnik bei der Eisenbahn [Psychology and psychotechnology at the Railways]*. Retrieved from https://psydok.psycharchives.de/jspui/bitstream/20.500.11780/3466/1/gundlach_01.pdf

(2018). William James and the Heidelberg fiasco. *History of Psychology, 21*(1), 47–72. https://doi.org/10.1037/hop0000083

Haas, E. (1995). *De opkomst van de bedrijfs- en schoolpsychologische beroepspraktijk in Nederland [The rise of business and school psychology in the Netherlands]*. Hilversum: Uitgeverij Verloren.

Hagemeister, C., Kersting, M., & Stemmler, G. (2012). Test reviewing in Germany. *International Journal of Testing, 12*(2), 185–194. https://doi.org/10.1080/15305058.2012.657922

Heijden, P. G. M. & Sijtsma, K. (1996). Fifty years of measurement and scaling in the Dutch social sciences. *Statistica Neerlandica, 50*(1), 111–135. https://doi.org/10.1111/j.1467-9574.1996.tb01483.x

Highhouse, S. (2002). Assessing the candidate as a whole: A historical and critical analysis of individual psychological assessment for personnel decision making. *Personnel Psychology, 55*(2), 363–396. https://doi.org/10.1111/j.1744-6570.2002.tb00114.x

Hook, D. (2017). The subject of psychology: A Lacanian critique. *Social and Personality Psychology Compass, 11*(5), e12316. https://doi.org/10.1111/spc3.12316

Hornke, L. F., & Kersting, M. (2004). "Checkliste" zur DIN33430 ["Checklist" for DIN33430]. In L. F. Hornke & U. Winterfeld (eds.), *Eignungsbeurteilungen auf dem Prüfstand: DIN33430 zur Qualitätssicherung [Self-assessments on the test bench: DIN33430 for quality assurance]* (pp. 273–324). Retrieved from http://eprints.uanl.mx/5481/1/1020149995.PDF

Kanning, U. P. (2010). *Von Schädeldeutern und anderen Scharlatanen: Unseriöse Methoden der Psychodiagnostik [From skull deuters and other charlatans: Unserious methods of psychodiagnosis]*. Lengerich: Pabst.

Kersting, M. (1995). Der Einsatz "westdeutscher" Tests zur Personalauswahl in den neuen Bundesländern und die Fairnessfrage: Auswirkungen der Testleistungsdisparität zwischen Ost und West auf die Auswahlentscheidung [The use of "West German" tests for personnel selection in the new Länder and the question of fairness: impact of test performance disparity between East and West on the selection decision]. *Report Psychologie/Psychology Report, 20*(7), 32–41.

   (2008). *Qualität in der Diagnostik und Personalauswahl – der DIN-Ansatz* [*Quality in diagnostics and personnel selection – the DIN approach*]. Retrieved from www.gbv.de/dms/zbw/568932684.pdf%5Cnhttp://d-nb .info/988964112/04

Lang, J. W. B., Kersting, M., Hülsheger, U. R., & Lang, J. (2010). General mental ability, narrower cognitive abilities, and job performance: The perspective of the nested-factors model of cognitive abilities. *Personnel Psychology, 63*(3), 595–640. https://doi.org/10.1111/j.1744-6570.2010.01182.x

Lang, J. W. B., & Tay, L. (2021). The science and practice of item response theory in organizations. *Annual Review of Organizational Psychology and Organizational Behavior, 8*, 311–338. https://doi.org/10.1146/annurev-orgp sych-012420-061705

Lautrey, J., & Ribaupierre, A. de. (2004). Psychology of human intelligence in France and French-speaking Switzerland. In R. J. Sternberg (ed.), *International handbook of intelligence* (pp. 104–134). Cambridge: Cambridge University Press.

Lievens, F. (2007). Research on selection in an international context: Current status and future directions. In M. M. Harris (ed.), *Handbook of research in international human resource management* (pp. 107–123). Mahwah, NJ: Erlbaum.

Lievens, F., Ones, D. S., & Dilchert, S. (2009). Personality scale validities increase throughout medical school. *Journal of Applied Psychology, 94*(6), 1514–1535. https://doi.org/10.1037/a0016137

Lipmann, O. (1921). Wirtschaftspsychologie und psychologische Berufsberatung [Economic psychology and psychological career guidance]. *Schriften Zur Psychologie Der Berufseignung Und Des Wirtschaftslebens/*Writings on the Psychology of Professional Aptitude and Economic Life, *1*(1), 1–24.

Lück, H. E. (2011). Anfänge der Wirtschaftspsychologie bei Kurt Lewin [Beginnings of business psychology with Kurt Lewin]. *Gestalt Theory, 33* (2), 91–114.

   (2015). Simoneit, Max. In U. Wolfradt, E. Billmann-Mahecha, & A. Stock (eds.), *Deutschsprachige Psychologinnen und Psychologen 1933–1945. Ein Personenlexikon, ergänzt um einen Text von Erich Stern* [*German-speaking psychologists 1933-1945. A personal lexicon, supplemented by a text by Erich Stern*] (pp. 418–419). Wiesbaden: Springer.

von Rosenstiel, L. (1985). Lipmann, Otto. In Historische Kommission bei der Bayerischen Akademie der Wissenschaften [Historical Commission at the Bavarian Academy of Sciences] (eds.), *Neue Deutsche Biographie [New*

german biography] *14* (p. 645). Munich: Author. Retrieved from https://
www.deutsche-biographie.de/downloadPDF?url=sfz51743.pdf

Manteufel, A. (2006). "Von den Möglichkeiten einer psychologischen
Menschenauslese" – Psychodiagnostik im Kriegsdienst der deutschen
Wehrmacht [From the possibilities of psychological selection of people" –
psychodiagnosis in the military service of the German Wehrmacht]. In G.
Lamberti (ed.), *Intelligenz auf dem Prüfstand: 100 Jahre Psychometrie*
[Intelligence put to the test: 100 years of psychometry] (pp. 59–79).
Göttingen: Vandenhoeck & Ruprecht.

Moede, W. (1919). *Die Experimentalpsychologie im Dienste des Wirtschaftslebens*
[Experimental psychology at the service of economic life]. Berlin: Julius Springer.

(1920). *Experimentelle Massenpsychologie [Experimental mass psychology].*
Leipzig: S. Hirzel.

Motzkau, J. & Schraube, E. (2015). Kritische Psychologie: Psychology from the
standpoint of the subject. In I. Parker (ed.). *Handbook of Critical Psychology*
(pp. 280–289). London: Routledge.

Mulder, E. & Heyting, F. (1998). The Dutch curve: The introduction and
reception of intelligence testing in the Netherlands, 1908–1940. *Journal of*
the History of the Behavioral Sciences, 34(4), 349–366. https://doi.org/10
.1002/(sici)1520-6696(199823)34:4<349::aid-jhbs1>3.0.co;2-m

Münsterberg, H. (1912). *Psychologie und Wirtschaftsleben: Ein Beitrag zur ange-*
wandten Experimental-Psychologie [Psychology and economic life: A contribution
to applied experimental psychology]. Leipzig: Barth.

(1913). *Psychology and industrial efficiency.* Cambridge, MA: The Riverside Press.

Nicolas, S. (2006). The importance of instrument makers for the development of
experimental psychology: The case of Alfred Binet at the Sorbonne
Laboratory. *Journal of the History of the Behavioral Sciences, 42*(July), 3–18.
https://doi.org/10.1002/jhbs.21790

Nicolas, S., Andrieu, B., Sanitioso, R. B., Vincent, R., & Murray, D. J. (2015).
Alfred Binet and Crépieux-Jamin: Can intelligence be measured scientifically
by graphology? *Annee Psychologique/Anne Psychological, 115*(1), 3–52. https://
doi.org/10.4074/S0003503315001013

Nicolas, S., & Young, J. L. (2014). A French description of the psychology
laboratory of G. S. Hall at Clark university in 1893. *American Journal of*
Psychology, 127(4), 527–535. https://doi.org/10.5406/amerjpsyc.127.4.0527

Pawlik, K. (1994). Psychology in Europe: Origins and development of psychology
in German-speaking countries. *International Journal of Psychology, 29*(6),
677–694. https://doi.org/10.1080/00207599408246558

Probst, P. (2014). "Um den Bedürfnissen des praktischen Lebens entgegenzukom-
men" – ein Einblick in Biografie und Werk William Sterns ["To meet the
needs of practical life" – an insight into the biography and work of William
Stern]. In M. Spieß (ed.), *100 Jahre akademische Psychologie in Hamburg. Eine*
Festschrift [100 years of academic psychology in Hamburg. A commemorative
publication] (pp. 87–115). Hamburg: Hamburg University Press.

Rexelius, G. (ed.). (1988). *Psychologie als Gesellschaftswissenschaft: Geschichte, Theorie und Praxis kritischer Psychologie [Psychology as social science: history, theory and practice of critical psychology]*. Opladen: Westdeutscher Verlag.

Richebächer, S. (September 2010). Franziska Baumgarten (1883–1970): Psychotechnikerin, Pionierin, Professorin, Pazifistin [Psychotechnician, pioneer, professor, pacifist]. *Punktum*, 5–7. Retrieved from http://psydok.psycharchives.de/jspui/handle/20.500.11780/21?offset=0.

Richelle, M., Janssen, P., & Bredart, S. (1992). Psychology in Belgium. *Annual Review of Psychology, 43*(1), 505–529. https://doi.org/10.1146/annurev.ps.43.020192.002445

Roland-Lévy, C. (2020). The first hundred years of IAAP towards the future. *IAAP Bulletin, 2*(1), 9–10. Retrieved from https://iaapsy.org/site/assets/files/1082/apaw_2020_jan_vol2_1_-_final.pdf

Schneider, W. H. (1992). After Binet: French intelligence testing, 1900–1950. *Journal of the History of the Behavioral Sciences, 28*(2), 111–132. https://doi.org/10.1002/1520-6696(199204)28:2<111::AID-JHBS2300280202>3.0.CO;2-W

Schuler, H. & Hell, B. (2008). *Studierendenauswahl und Studienentscheidung [Student selection and study decision]*. Göttingen: Hogrefe.

Schumann, F. (2004). *Bericht über den 1. Kongress für experimentelle Psychologie in Gießen vom 18. bis 21. April 1904: Wiederabdruck der Erstausgabe Leipzig 1904 im Auftrag der Deutschen Gesellschaft für Psychologie [Report on the 1st Congress for Experimental Psychology in Gießen from 18 to 21 April 1904: Reprint of the first edition Leipzig 1904 on behalf of the German Society for Psychology]*. Göttingen: Hogrefe.

Schwager, I. T. L., Hülsheger, U. R., Bridgeman, B., & Lang, J. W. B. (2015). Graduate student selection: Graduate record examination, socioeconomic status, and undergraduate grade point average as predictors of study success in a western European university. *International Journal of Selection and Assessment, 23*(1), 71–79. https://doi.org/10.1111/ijsa.12096

Siegler, R. S. (1992). The other Alfred Binet. *Developmental Psychology, 28*(2), 179–190. https://doi.org/10.1037/0012-1649.28.2.179

Spearman. (1904). "General intelligence," objectively determined and measured. *American Journal of Psychology, 15*(2), 201–292.

Spillmann, J., & Spillmann, L. (1993). The rise and fall of Hugo Münsterberg. *Journal of the History of the Behavioral Sciences, 29*(4), 322–338. https://doi.org/10.1002/1520-6696(199310)29:4<322::AID-JHBS2300290403>3.0.CO;2-I

Sprung, L., & Sprung, H. (2001). History of modern psychology in Germany in 19th- and 20th-century thought and society. *International Journal of Psychology, 36*(6), 364–376. https://doi.org/10.1080/00207590143000199

Stern, W. (1900). *Über Psychologie der individuellen Differenzen: Ideen zu einer "differentiellen Psychologie" [On Psychology of Individual Differences: Ideas for a "Differential Psychology"]*. Leipzig: Barth.

(1911). *Die differentielle Psychologie in ihren methodischen Grundlagen [Differential psychology in its methodological foundations]*. Leipzig: Barth.

(1914). *Die psychologischen Methoden der Intelligenzprüfung: und deren Anwendung an Schulkindern [The psychological methods of intelligence testing: and how to apply them to school children]*. Leipzig: Barth.

(1917). Hugo Munsterberg: In memoriam. *Journal of Applied Psychology*, *1*(2), 186–188. https://doi.org/10.1037/h0074508

Stout, S. E. (2018). Training soldiers for the Roman Legion. *The Classical Journal*, *16*(7), 423–431.

Teo, T. (1998). Klaus Holzkamp and the rise and decline of German critical psychology. *History of Psychology*, *1*(3), 235–253. https://doi.org/10.1037/1093-4510.1.3.235

Terman, L. M. (1916). *The measurement of intelligence: An explanation of and a complete guide for the use of the Stanford revision and extension of the Binet-Simon intelligence scale*. Cambridge, MA: Houghton Mifflin.

The OSS Assessment staff. (1948). *Assessment of men: Selection of personnel for the Office of Strategic Services*. New York: Rinehart & Company.

Trost, G., Blum, F., Fay, E., Klieme, E., Maichle, U., Meyer, M., & Nauels, H.-U. (1998). *Evaluation des Tests für medizinische Studiengänge (TMS): Synopse der Ergebnisse [Evaluation of the medical degree test (TMS): synopsis of results]*. Bonn: Institut für Test- und Begabungsforschung [Institute for Test and Talent Research].

van Strien, P. J. & Dane, J. (2001). *Driekwart eeuw psychotechniek in Nederland: de magie van het testen* [Three quarters of a century of psychotechnics in the Netherlands: the magic of testing]. Arnhem: Nederlandse Stichting voor Psychotechniek [Dutch Foundation for Psychotechnics].

Vinchur, A. J. & Koppes, L. L. (2007). Early contributions to the science and practice of industrial psychology. In L. L. Koppes, P. W. Thayer, A. J. Vinchur, & E. Salas (eds.), *Historical perspectives in industrial and organizational psychology* (pp. 37–58). New York: Psychology Press.

(2010). A historical survey of research and practice in industrial and organizational psychology. In S. Zedeck (ed.), *APA handbook of industrial and organizational psychology, Vol 1: Building and developing the organization* (pp. 3–36). https://doi.org/10.1037/12169-001

Viteles, M. S. (1923). Psychology in business-in England, France, and Germany. *The Annals of the American Academy of Political and Social Science*, *110*, 207–220. Retrieved from www.jstor.org/stable/1015087.

Wickett, J. C. (1998). Hans J. Eysenck' s influence on intelligence research. *Psihologija*, *31*(3), 249–256.

Wiggins, J. S. (1973). *Personality and prediction: Principles of personality assessment*. Reading, MA: Addison-Wesley.

Wissler, C. (1901). The correlation of mental and physical tests. *The Psychological Review: Monograph Supplements*, *3*(6), i–62. https://doi.org/10.1037/h0092995.

Wundt, W. (1883). Über die Messung psychischer Vorgänge. *Philosophische Studien*, 1, 251–260. Retrieved from http://vlp.mpiwg-berlin.mpg.de/.

Zimmerhofer, A. & Trost, G. (2008). Auswahl- und Feststellungsverfahren in Deutschland – Vergangenheit, Gegenwart und Zukunft [Selection and identification procedures in Germany - past, present and future]. In H. Schuler & B. Hell (eds.), *Studierendenaushal und Studienentscheidung* [*Student education and study decision*] (pp. 32–42). Göttingen: Hogrefe.

CHAPTER 8

The Beginnings of Psychological Assessment in Spain and Portugal

Jaime Pereña Brand

8.1 Introduction

In this chapter we deal with the evolution of psychological assessment in Spain and Portugal, paying special attention to the early days, which largely explain and condition what has happened in more recent times.

Spain and Portugal share the territory of the Iberian Peninsula at the southwestern end of the European continent. They are two countries with remarkable similarities but also with marked peculiarities of their own. They form two of the oldest states in Europe and both experienced a period of splendor and glory during the fifteenth to seventeenth centuries, as a result of the great maritime expeditions undertaken, and the vast territories first explored by European countries. Both Spain and Portugal suffered an extended period of decline from the eighteenth century onwards, from which they have only been able to recover in the second half of the twentieth century.

This historical evolution has strongly conditioned, as it could not be otherwise, the development of economic and scientific activities in both countries, which logically also applies to the use of psychological assessment instruments.

Portugal is a small country, with an area of 92,090 km^2 and just over 10 million inhabitants. It has more than 1,700 km of coastline on the Atlantic Ocean, a geographical fact that explains the country's traditional maritime and commercial vocation and the fact that many Portuguese have taken the sea route to emigrate. Although it is a country essentially oriented toward the Atlantic Ocean, the climate of the central and southern regions is largely the same as that of the Mediterranean regions.

Spain is the second largest country in the European Union, after France, with an area of 506,000 km^2, and the fifth most populous, with just over 46 million inhabitants. It is a country with various regions that have very varied geographical characteristics that have conditioned the demographic, social, and economic evolution of the country. The northern zone is humid and participates in the characteristics of the Atlantic climate. The Mediterranean coastal regions are the most fertile and populated, also those that concentrate most of the important tourist activity. Most of the territory is made up of a large central plateau with high average altitudes and a continental climate that presents very marked changes, cold in winter and warm in summer. It also has two island regions, the Balearic Islands in the Mediterranean and the Canary Islands in the Atlantic, two archipelagos of great importance for tourism.

This chapter briefly describes the evolution of psychological assessment techniques in Spain and Portugal, following a chronological order, paying greater attention to the early days, which are generally less well-known, and identifying the most outstanding milestones or those that have had the greatest impact in the scientific field and in professional practice.

8.2   Huarte de San Juan, a Precursor

When considering the beginnings of the practice of psychological assessment in the Iberian Peninsula it is most appropriate to refer to the distant but very significant precursors. In the sixteenth century, when Spain and Portugal were still two great powers, Juan Huarte de San Juan read medicine at the then prestigious University of Alcalá de Henares. Although he was a polymath, he was particularly interested in the psychological aspects of medicine, which led him to publish his highly successful *Examen de Ingenios Para Las Ciencias* that was published in several European countries. The word "*ingenios*," which could be translated today as "abilities," is the basis of differential psychology and of psychological assessment because Huarte, anticipating by several centuries modern psychological concepts, affirmed that there is "diversity of abilities" and that, both for the common good and for personal satisfaction, it is necessary that individuals dedicate themselves to those tasks for which they are best qualified, and avoid those others for which they do not have natural abilities (Huarte de San Juan, 1989).

8.3   Psychological Assessment in the Nineteenth Century

Psychological assessment was established as a scientific discipline in most European countries during the nineteenth century, a period of decline for Spain and Portugal, and a time strongly marked by very turbulent sociopolitical circumstances starting with the traumatic invasion of the

Peninsula by the Napoleonic troops, which seriously endangered the very survival of the two nations and forced enormous war efforts that left them both badly weakened and strongly divided. As a result, once Napoleon was expelled from the Peninsula, political instability was the dominant note throughout the century.

The nineteenth century also saw the move to independence of the vast colonies that Spain and Portugal had in America, which aggravated the serious economic, social, and political problems of the motherland.

In the second half of the nineteenth century, the Industrial Revolution arrived in Spain, and to a lesser extent in Portugal, with a notable delay in comparison with what had happened in the more advanced European countries. A significant mining industry was developed, important textile and steel industries were installed, the road network was improved, and railway communications were developed. Therefore, the two countries began to modernize, which meant a significant change, but a change that did not affect the whole territory and was restricted to a few places, mainly Bilbao, Barcelona, and Porto areas.

Some scientists were concerned about the underdevelopment of the Iberian Peninsula and interested in importing the ideas and techniques that were in force in countries such as France, Germany, or the United Kingdom.

Giner de los Ríos (1839–1915) had a great influence from his chair at the Central University of Madrid and stood out for his efforts to improve teaching and education. His influence in the field of psychological assessment derives from the fact that he knew the laboratory that Wundt had created in Leipzig in 1879 (Calonge & Calles, 2016). In Barcelona, Dr. Turró was very well-known, an outstanding example of some doctors who were at that time trying to explain human behavior from the English Empiricism viewpoint.

The most important author for the scientific field that interests us is undoubtedly Luis Simarro (1851–1921), a physician who studied psychiatry with Charcot in Paris and who, upon his return to Spain, founded the Laboratory of Anthropology, the first scientific laboratory in the country dedicated to studying psychological aspects related to human behavior. In addition, Simarro held the first chair of experimental psychology instituted in a Spanish university, specifically at the University of Madrid. For all these reasons, Dr. Simarro had a decisive influence on the training of the professionals who promoted psychological assessment in the following century.

8.4 Psychological Assessment in the Twentieth Century (1900–1949)

In the first part of the twentieth century, the political turbulence in the Peninsula continued. A terrible three-year civil war broke out in Spain in 1936, which was followed by the almost 40 years of General Franco's regime, while, between 1926 to 1974, Portugal was under the rule of General Salazar.

These traumatic sociopolitical circumstances resulted in a high degree of international isolation for both countries and a notable delay in development in the technical and scientific fields, which significantly impacted on the progress of psychology and psychological evaluation.

Psychological studies had traditionally come from two very different areas of knowledge, medicine and philosophy. In the nineteenth century, psychology made rapid progress in many countries becoming an independent discipline with its own research base. In Portugal and Spain this was significantly delayed, with university studies in psychology not acquiring an independent status until the last decades of the century.

Despite this, there had been authors who made significant contributions to the field of psychological assessment in the Peninsula, following in the footsteps of Luis Simarro at the end of the previous century. The first of these outstanding authors of the twentieth century are Achúcarro and Rodríguez Lafora, who, in 1914, founded the first laboratory of applied psychology in Spain. Rodríguez Lafora published in 1917 a work entitled *Los niños mentalmente anormales* (*Mentally Abnormal Children*) in which he dealt extensively with the Binet–Simon test, published a few years earlier in France. The Binet–Simon test was widely used in Spain for several decades (Calonge & Calles, 2016).

The revision of this psychometric scale undertaken in Stanford and known as the Stanford–Binet or Terman–Merrill scale was adapted and published in Spain in 1930 by Professor Germain, who can be considered the father of Spanish psychometry. However, this was not a true standardization of the test.

Another of the most recognized pioneers of that time was Emilio Mira y López (1896–1964), a physician and psychiatrist who achieved great international prestige. He introduced modern professional orientation in Spain through a Psychotechnical Institute that he founded. He was the first Professor of Psychiatry in Spain and his activity is especially relevant for us because he had an intense dedication to the field of psychological assessment. Unfortunately for Spain he had to emigrate abroad after the civil war, but this was an advantage for countries such as Argentina, Uruguay, and Brazil where he carried out fruitful professional work. One of his great contributions was the development of the PMK, an evaluation instrument called Myokinetic Psychodiagnosis or Mira Test, which was widely used in Latin America. In an article published in 1968 he was considered one of the most influential authors in the history of psychology (Annin et al., 1968).

Although these first attempts to create or adapt psychological assessment instruments in Spain and Portugal were highly meritorious from a scientific point of view, they were isolated events with little practical impact. In Spain, the civil war and the harsh social conditions of the post-war period resulted in a radical interruption of scientific research. In Portugal, the Salazar dictatorship also produced conditions of isolation from the progress being made in other countries.

After the Civil War, José Germain (1897–1986) was appointed director of the Department of Experimental Psychology, established in 1948 within the Consejo Superior de Investigaciones Científicas (CSIC), the powerful government agency responsible for promoting research in Spain. Germain coordinated the formation of a large group of young and enthusiastic researchers, who gave a decisive impulse to psychological assessment, both from the scientific perspective and in terms of practical application. José Luis Pinillos, María Eugenia Romano, Miguel Siguán, Francisco Secadas, Mariano Yela, Jesús Amón, Alfonso Álvarez del Villar, among others, laid the foundations of modern psychometry in Spain and carried out extraordinary research and translation work. Many of them had studied abroad and had excellent training in the most advanced techniques and methodologies.

As it was the case in other countries (and still is), the educational background of these scholars was diverse. Some came from the field of philosophy, others were educators, some were physicians or psychiatrists, etc. They had been inspired by a range of very different psychological schools, from those with a psychoanalytic approach to those more focused on psychometry and statistics. This gave Spanish psychological assessment a variety and richness that would not be found in other countries that had a more homogeneous approach.

8.5   Further Developments in Psychological Assessment (1950–1969)

In the 1950s, several organizations that would contribute decisively to the development of psychology in Spain were created. In 1952, Germain established the Spanish Society of Psychology and a year later the School of Psychology and Psychotechnology of Madrid, which played a very relevant role in the education of future psychologists. In 1956, the National Institute of Applied Psychology and Psychotechnology of Madrid, a pre-existing body that would also play a significant role, was reorganized, and strengthened.

In the field of psychoanalysis, María Eugenia Romano (1917–1987) stood out. She had studied philosophy and medicine but always with the determination of dedicating herself to clinical psychology (Calonge, 1988). Romano applied various projective techniques, both in her clinical work and in her teaching activity, and she was especially known for her mastery of the Rorschach test, contributing decisively to the training of hundreds of specialists in this technique.

In the educational field, Francisco Secadas (1917–2012) played a key role as director of the psychotechnical laboratory of the Virgen de la Paloma vocational training college in Madrid. In this college, Secadas promoted psychological assessment using numerous tests including *Otis Sencillo, Palancas, Laberintos*, and *Memoria de Formas*. Later on, he became a professor at University of Valencia where he developed several original instruments in the educational field related to child development and to reading or writing skills.

One of the most brilliant psychologists of that generation was José Luis Pinillos (1919–2013), a philosopher who, as well as in Madrid, had studied in London, Bonn, and Michigan. During his long academic life, he was a professor at the universities of Valencia and Madrid, wrote numerous works, and received many important awards. His role in the field of psychological assessment was very prominent in the 1960s particularly in relation to personality questionnaires. In 1960 he published the *Cuestionario de personalidad* (CEP), a personality questionnaire he had developed, although inspired by those previously designed by Guilford and Eysenck. Sixty years later, the CEP is still one of the most widely used personality tests in Spain, Portugal, and Latin America.

Nevertheless, Mariano Yela (1921–1994) deserves a special mention because his contributions had a decisive practical impact on psychological assessment in Spain. After reading philosophy in Madrid, he worked at the Thurstone laboratory in Chicago and at the University of Louvain with Michotte. Upon his return to Spain he promoted a new style of working in the field of psychology, with the scientific rigor he had learned from his mentors and with a robust and systematic use of mathematical and statistical techniques (Rozo, 1995).

Yela returned from the United States with the deep conviction that psychologists needed to improve their scientific background and to use effective and well-developed tools to be able to carry out their work in a professional and objective manner. As a result of his experience in the United States, he brought to Spain some simple paper and pencil tests. He also began to develop innovative instruments of his own, several of which became popular and were widely used by psychologists. All this meant a radical change and a decisive impulse to Spanish psychological assessment.

In the 1950s and 1960s a major economic change begun to take place. Spain left behind the era of self-sufficiency and began a rapid process of development. Numerous industrial companies appeared, some with strong government support, and hundreds of thousands of people migrated from the countryside to the cities to work in the new factories. After 150 years of delay came an Industrial Revolution that would radically change the economic and social landscape of Spain and Portugal.

In one of those industrial companies, Standard Eléctrica, Yela met Miguel Siguán (1918–2010) and Roberto Cuñat, (1909–1989) two professionals who were going to be very important in the field of psychological assessment. Siguán had studied philosophy in Barcelona, his hometown, and after the Civil War he had trained with Piaget in France and in industrial psychology at the London School of Economics in London. He was also a prolific writer and renowned linguist, and from his chair at the University of Barcelona he was one of the main promoters of the development of scientific psychology and psychological assessment in Catalonia.

Cuñat was an economist but he had a great interest in the management of human resources in organizations. In fact, in 1958 he published a book on this matter, which was very advanced for his time, *Productividad y mando de hombres en la empresa Española* (*Productivity and Manpower Management in the Spanish Company*; Pereña Brand, 2006). In this work, Cuñat defended the need for professional personnel selection in organizations and was a strong supporter of the use of aptitude and personality tests, insisting that assessment instruments should be properly developed, their validity should be scientifically proven, they should be well administered, and they should only be used by trained experts (Cuñat, 1958).

Yela, Cuñat, and Siguán therefore agreed that the new companies that were being formed required more and more rigorous psychological assessment tools in order to manage their human resources properly. Unlike what had happened with other previous academic scientists, their practical relevance was extraordinary because they were able to develop and make available to professional people new assessment instruments developed with the appropriate technical characteristics. In particular, the Yela–Cuñat tandem was decisive, the first acting from the university, the second from the industrial field.

Cuñat had been one of the founders of the consulting firm Técnicos Especialistas Asociados (TEA) in 1952. Five years later its subsidiary Ediciones TEA was born with the aim of publishing business management books. In 1958 TEA's Department of Psychology was created under the direction of Cuñat and with the technical advice of Yela.

At that time, TEA's objective was to have assessment tests for its own use in consulting and personnel selection work. Under the coordination of Yela, existing tests across different Spanish institutions were compiled, some of which were elaborated by Yela, and others created or adapted by other already mentioned authors such as Siguán, Pinillos, or Secadas. Given the needs of the Spanish market, tests began to be adapted and published almost exclusively for the organizational field and mainly for the industrial sector. They were aimed at assessing constructs such as spatial aptitude, mechanical comprehension, manual skills, or visual–motor coordination. Some of the tests developed or adapted by Yela are classic works of that time: Otis–Yela, Figure Rotation, Motor Speed, Visual–Motor Coordination, Faces, Levers, and so on. Hundreds of thousands of peasants leaving the countryside to join newly established industrial companies were assessed using these tests.

Soon the idea emerged at TEA that the psychological tests could not only be used to support the company's own activities but also be marketed and made available to other customers who needed them. In this way, TEA Ediciones was born, and has led these activities since then. The shift into commercial activities meant a radical change that would have extremely beneficial effects for psychological assessment. Up until that moment, the creation or adaptation of tests had been very informal and carried out in an ad hoc manner usually for research purposes or for self-use in narrow areas.

Commercialization required more representative standardizations, to develop better presented materials, to assess systematically the validity and reliability, to produce technical manuals, and to respect intellectual property rules. All this had not existed until then.

Cuñat and Yela were aware that Spain needed to adapt certain tests published in other countries that at that time had a much higher level of development. Even though the principle of autarchy prevailed in official policy, Cuñat, with the support of Yela, made a great effort to keep windows open to the outside world (Pereña Brand, 2006). Thus, in

1960 the first publishing contract was signed with a foreign publisher, the leading publisher in this field, The Psychological Corporation. Following a common practice at the time, this was an omnibus contract that covered the publication of various works, and thus opened the door to a stable collaboration between the two companies.

A year later, a contract was signed with the French publishing house Centre de Psychologie Appliquée in order to publish one of its most widely used tests, the D-48 dominoes test. In this manner, psychological evaluation in Spain was brought in line with the scientific currents that were being developed in the rest of Europe and America, a trend that would no longer be abandoned (Calonge & Calles, 2016).

Yela was a psychologist specialized in psychometry and statistics who put great emphasis on methodological rigor, but he was also an enterprising man with a strong personality, capable of exerting a remarkable influence on others. For this reason, although he was never an employee of TEA Ediciones, he maintained a consulting role for a long time, and he had a decisive influence on the development of the company. That is why, unlike what has happened in other test publishers, TEA hired, from the very beginning, high-level psychometricians who were able to make robust adaptations as well as create new tests of their own. Yela collaborated in the selection of the people who would carry out these research and development tasks and imposed methodological rigor when elaborating or adapting new tests. Three people played a key role in this area.

Agustín Cordero (1928–2020) directed the TEA's test department from its beginnings and effectively balanced his managerial role with his lectures at the university and his work adapting tests and creating his own assessment tools. Until his retirement in 1992 he led the transformation of the small department of the 1960s into the company TEA Ediciones, and together with Nicolás Seisdedos (1937–2016) and María Victoria de la Cruz was responsible for the publication of hundreds of tests.

In the early days, in addition to those tools already mentioned, TEA published emblematic tests as the Mac Quarrie and Thurstone's Primary Mental Abilities Test (PMA), still one of the most used in Spain today. A bit later, the Differential Aptitude Test (DAT) was adapted through a thorough scientific study that became the model for the adaptation methodology to be followed (Pereña Brand, 2006).

In 1964, another company dedicated to the publication of tests that played an important role at that time, MEPSA, was set up in Madrid. It began by distributing the editorial collection of the French company Établissements d'applications psychotechniques (EAP) and especially the

Bonnardel tests, which became widely used in Spain. From 1967 onwards, MEPSA distributed and standardized the Raven's Progressive Matrices, a test of particular relevance that was also widely used in Spain mostly in the educational and military settings (Calonge & Calles, 2016).

8.6 Psychological Assessment in Spain and Portugal (1970–1990)

In the early 1970s, TEA Ediciones made a definitive shift in its publishing activity and began to adapt and publish works specifically aimed at the educational and clinical fields, especially the great scales of individual administration and the main personality questionnaires. A major milestone was the publication of the adaptation of the famous Minnesota Multiphase Personality Inventory (MMPI), carried out by Seisdedos. A particularly risky and challenging project was the publication of the adaptation of the most prestigious scales existing for the individual assessment of intelligence in adults and children. Thus, in 1971 the Wechsler Adult Intelligence Scale (WAIS), whose adaptation was still coordinated by Yela, was published, followed in 1974 by the Wechsler Children Intelligence Scale (WISC), adapted by Seisdedos and De La Cruz (Pereña Brand, 2006).

Thus, from that moment on, Spanish psychologists were able to have access to the main psychological assessment instruments adapted in accordance with generally accepted technical standards and marketed in a stable and controlled manner. Some tests had been elaborated, adapted, and used in previous years, but in most cases, they were unfinished studies and works that were spread in an informal way and without the pertinent norms and manuals.

Also published at that time, after signing an agreement with IPAT (Institute for Personality and Ability Testing), was Raymond B. Cattell's famous 16PF. It was adapted by Seisdedos and De La Cruz with the collaboration of Professor José María Prieto of the Complutense University of Madrid and was published in 1975. The commercial success of the 16PF in Spain was extraordinary and it became the most widely used personality test for decades, both in organizations and in clinical and educational fields.

Cordero, Seisdedos, and De la Cruz continued to integrate for many years the technical department of TEA Ediciones and followed the path that Yela had initially laid out. They not only carried out the adaptations and the standardizations of the main tests coming from abroad but also developed numerous tests of their own, a policy which had two main purposes: (a) as a means of giving a quick and efficient answer to the needs of the national market and (b) to promote the technical and financial independence of the publishing activity, avoiding an excessive dependence on the big foreign publishers. Some of the first tests developed were the dominoes tests TIG-1 and TIG-2, the General Intelligence Tests, the MAI (Immediate Auditory Memory), the TICV (Verbal Comprehension Test) and the TN, Numerical Tests (Pereña Brand, 2006).

The work carried out between 1960 and 1990 by Cordero, Seisdedos, and De la Cruz in favor of psychological evaluation was enormous. The scientific work of Seisdedos, should be highlighted. He inherited the methodological rigor of his teacher Yela and, with his enormous creativity, produced highly original tests that have been widely used in Spain and other countries, such as the Coins (the "most ingenious test" according to Hans Eysenck), the Keys (High Ability Test), or the Tables and Graphs (Prieto, 2016).

The National Institute of Applied Psychology and Professional Orientation published in 1976 the book entitled *Tests used in Spain. Technical-bibliographical Information*, a work of great relevance because it explained all the psychological assessment tests used in the country describing their technical characteristics. It was carried out in collaboration by the two publishers then in existence (TEA Ediciones and MEPSA) and Juan García Yagüe, an author who had created several tests for the educational field.

In 1966, the EOS Institute for Psychological Guidance was founded in Madrid, a company dedicated mainly to educational psychology and vocational guidance. EOS has developed a prominent role in the field of psychological assessment in schools and has created several assessment tools, some of which have played a prominent role in the educational field and have been a notable help not only to psychologists but also to educators and parents of students. Among the tests published by EOS that have had the most impact in Spain and Latin America, three very useful batteries in the school field can be mentioned: *The Cognitive Assessment of Reading and Writing Battery* (BECOLE), the *EOS Psychopedagogical Battery*, and the *EVALÚA Psychopedagogical Battery*.

In the 1970s, the first psychology faculties were created and the pioneers (Yela, Pinillos, Secadas, Siguán, and Romano) trained and educated new generations of psychologists who would give a strong boost to psychology studies in Spain and Portugal and would soon begin to develop new assessment tests. In 1972, the *Inventory of Study Habits* by Fernández Pozar was published, an important step that reflected the beginning of the period of maturity of Spanish psychology. From that moment on, the development of psychology, and consequently of psychological assessment, has been very fast and solid, both in Spain and in Portugal. It can be said, without fear of exaggeration, that not only has the secular backwardness that existed around 1930 been recovered but that some countries with a much older tradition have been overcome.

Dozens of Spanish authors have followed this trail and have elaborated new works of great scientific and practical value: Alonso Fernández, Fernández Ballesteros, Cuetos, Yuste, Corbalán, Pedro Hernández, Miguel Tobal, Cano Vindel, and many others (Pereña Brand, 2006).

The peculiar political situation conditioned the evolution of the psychological assessment in Portugal. The Carnation Revolution of 1974 began the process of democratization of the country and led to the emergence of the first faculties of psychology. However, this happened at a time when the golden age of psychometry had passed and there was a certain distrust throughout the world toward the scientific usefulness of the tests, which led to significant delay (Almeida et al., 2013).

Two Portuguese authors are particularly relevant. Leandro Almeida, professor at the University of Minho, published in 1986 the *Bateria de Provas de Raciocínio Diferencial* and in 1988 the *Escala de Competências Cognitivas* (ECCO-4/7). Mario Simões, Professor at the University of Coimbra and Director of the Laboratório de Avaliação Psicológica e Psicometria, carried out the Portuguese adaptation of the WISC-III and prepared, together with other authors, the *Bateria de Avaliação Neuropsicológica de Coimbra* (BANC) (Simões et al., 2002–2008).

From the commercial point of view, the company CEGOC followed the steps of TEA in Spain and started to publish tests in the 1980s with the D-48 and D-70 being published in 1983, the PMA the following year, and the *Quadrado de Letras* one year later.

8.7   Psychological Assessment in Spain and Portugal Post 1990

University studies in psychology had traditionally been linked to the faculties of Philosophy and Medicine. The recognition of psychology as a science with its own entity was slow and full of obstacles, and in Spain and Portugal it was quite late. In Spain, a School of Psychology and Psychotechnique was created in 1968, dependent on the Complutense University of Madrid, which was a very important step toward institutionalizing the studies of psychology, but it was not until 1980 that the first Faculty of Psychology was created, whose first dean was Jesús Amón, a professor specialized in statistics and assessment. As a consequence of this institutional change, the number of students grew vertiginously at the end of the 1980s and psychology experienced a scientific flowering of great proportions, becoming a rapidly expanding profession.

Something similar happened in Portugal. Psychology and pedagogy studies were present in Portuguese universities since 1930, mainly in Coimbra and Lisbon, but inserted in the Faculties of Arts. The situation did not change significantly after the educational reforms of 1957 and 1968. Finally, in 1980, the first Faculties of Psychology and Educational Sciences were created as autonomous higher education centers, although the studies of psychology and educational sciences were kept in the same faculty (Magalhães).

Although in Spain and Portugal the studies of psychology reached that university level with a certain delay, it is necessary to emphasize that throughout the twentieth century psychology experienced a deep progress in most of the world, trying to evolve toward more and more scientific and objective methods. This is particularly true in the field of psychological assessment, where from the beginning statistics have played an essential role and reliability, validity, and standardization studies have been considered indispensable.

However, there has been a phenomenon that I consider to be paradoxical, and which has undoubtedly occurred in Spain and Portugal, but also in most parts of the world. Despite the great scientific development experienced in the field of psychological assessment, some of the most widely used tests in the world today are direct heirs to those that were designed and developed in the first decades of the twentieth century. Great had been the progress made in that century, but the main classical tests have experienced small changes. Projective tests such as the Rorschach Test or the TAT, conceived by Murray in 1935, are still widely used. The Wechsler scales have been updated several times, but their basis is still the Wechsler–Bellevue scale that the author developed when he was chief psychologist at Bellevue Hospital in the 1930s. Hathaway and McKinley developed the famous MMPI in the late 1930s. The Raven's Progressive Matrix test was first published in 1938. Cattell developed his 16PF by applying factorial analysis techniques in the 1940s.

Taking this into account, the evolution of psychological assessment instruments in Spain since 1990 is characterized by four main features. The first is the modernization of products. Many of the classic tests had become somewhat obsolete, and a great effort was made to adapt, to standardize, and to publish the most recent and best carried out versions of the most modern existing tests: MMPI-2, 16PF-5, WISC-III, WAIS-III, and DAT-5. At the same time, the presentation of the materials was modernized and improved to make them more attractive and in line with the demands of a more modern and advanced society.

The second feature of this evolution derives from the strong impulse that psychology was experiencing in Spain and Portugal with the arrival of thousands of psychologists trained in the new university faculties. This was both a challenge and an opportunity. A challenge because there was a growing demand for more modern, better developed, and more varied assessment tools, capable of responding to more specific assessment needs. An opportunity because hundreds of highly trained psychologists capable of developing new assessment instruments began to emerge. Many of the teachers in the new psychology faculties had not only a solid scientific base but also a high level of creativity and a strong motivation. All this made feasible the publication of many new tests that have been very useful and well accepted by the markets.

Some of the most representative works are the *Commercial Action Battery* by Seisdedos; the *Personal and Professional Interests* by De la Cruz; the *Reading Process Assessment Battery* by Cuetos, Rodríguez, Ruano, and Arribas; the *Assessment of Attention Deficit with Hyperactivity* by Farré and Narbona; the *Child Neuropsychological Maturity Test* by Portellano, Mateos, Martínez Arias, Granados, and Tapia; the *Work Climate Questionnaire* by Corral and Pereña; the *Creative Intelligence Test* by Corbalán et al.; the *Factorial Assessment of Intellectual Aptitudes* by Santamaría, Arribas, Pereña, and Seisdedos; the *Multifactorial Self-Assessment Test of Childhood Adaptation* by Hernández-Guanir; and the *TEA's Competences Test* by Arribas y Pereña.

A third characteristic feature of the 1990s is the intense and accelerated process of internationalization that was taking place worldwide, and in which Spain and Portugal actively participated. In July 1994, the XXIII World Congress of the International Association of Applied Psychology was held in Madrid, coordinated by José María Prieto, a milestone of special relevance for the international consolidation of Spanish psychology. Several publications echoed this event, highlighting the strength that applied psychology had acquired in the Iberian Peninsula (Fernández Ballesteros, 1994).

Many of the most famous test authors became aware of the importance of adapting and publishing their works in Spanish and Portuguese languages, while local publishers, mainly TEA Ediciones, made a great effort to adapt relevant works that had not been published in those countries until now. Several times the authors themselves were involved in facilitating the needed agreements between original and local publishers. The adaptations of works by such outstanding authors as L. V. Gordon, Theodore Millon, Alan and Nadeen Kaufman, Randy Kamphaus, Cecil Reynolds, Leslie Morey, Robert Hare, Rolf Brickenkamp, Paul Costa, Robert McCrae, Charles Spielberger, and so on reached our markets this way.

But the unstoppable phenomenon of globalization produced much deeper changes that in this case do not have to do with the scientific facet of psychological assessment but with its business and commercial side. Test publishers have traditionally been very stable companies, well positioned in national markets, and committed to ensuring the quality and good use of assessment tools. In the 1990s this stability was radically broken and the market worldwide witnessed drastic changes in the form of the appearance of new publishers, the disappearance of classic companies, company mergers, international acquisitions, agreements between business groups, and so on. Spain and Portugal were fully involved in this earthquake, which results in a completely new configuration of the market worldwide in terms of publishing and distribution of psychological assessment tests.

The fourth feature of the evolution experienced since 1990 is the use of new technologies related to computers and communications. A particularly laborious and delicate part of the process of psychological assessment is the scoring and the interpretation of the results obtained. This task, which is essential for an accurate assessment, is very costly when the number of subjects to be assessed is high, as is the case in the educational, military, or government fields.

The prominent test publishers in Spain, mainly TEA Ediciones and EOS, have been very active in offering advanced technological solutions to facilitate the work of scoring and interpreting the tests. In the early 1970s, TEA Ediciones started to offer automatic scoring services based on optical mark reading performed on answer sheets designed to be captured by optical reading machines. This system was widely used in the United States and had been highly developed by companies such as National Computer Systems. In Spain it was also widely used for more than three decades in which TEA Ediciones and EOS, among other companies, read and scored millions of answer sheets, many referring to psychological assessment tests, and many others on tests of various types of knowledge.

Personal computers appeared in 1980, and the BASIC programming language became popular, allowing the use of computers to become widespread and reach millions of new users. At TEA Ediciones,

Seisdedos began to develop programs to score some popular tests such as the 16PF, the SMAT, the Kuder, the CPI, and the MBTI. They were still simple and handmade solutions, but they would decisively mark the way forward.

In 1994, a product was launched in the market that today seems an obvious solution but at that time was very advanced not only for Spain but for many other countries, the TEA-SYSTEM. It was a platform designed to score and interpret a wide range of tests, not just one. It allowed the administration, the scoring, and the elaboration of a narrative report of the test. The TEA-SYSTEM was of great importance not only as a very relevant product in itself but also because it was a model that was followed and perfected from that moment on.

From 1995 onwards, many of the tests published by TEA Ediciones included what was called a scoring disk, that is, a diskette that performed as a traditional scoring template and was rather effective in making the process of obtaining the test scores easier.

At the end of the 1990s, the use of communication networks, mainly the Internet, began to become popular worldwide, something that would eventually affect the lives of billions of people and, of course, the business of psychological assessment. Many doubts and debates arose about how to adapt such traditional instruments – as most tests are – to the new technologies, and how to do so while respecting ethical standards on the use of the tests and copyright. A pioneering international experience was the launch of the 16PFWorld.com platform in which TEA Ediciones participated together with several other publishers from different countries.

In 2002 the *e-teaediciones* platform was launched, a very advanced technological solution that enabled performing the whole assessment process over the Internet: administration, scoring, and interpretative report. It incorporated both aptitude tests and numerous personality questionnaires. The system was initially sold on a personal basis to ensure that only trained professionals could access the tests. Dozens of tests were gradually incorporated into *e-teaediciones*, a solution that has been extraordinarily successful, has been used to assess hundreds of thousands of test-takers, has been imitated in many countries, and has been the basis for many technical developments in more recent times.

8.8   Conclusion

The chapter has provided a summary of the rapid and profound transformations that have taken place in the instruments, the methods, and the market of psychological assessment in Spain and Portugal during the twentieth century, proving that both countries started from positions of weakness and backwardness but have been able to incorporate themselves into the most modern scientific trends and have been able to reach pre-eminent positions in some aspects.

REFERENCES

Almeida, L. S., Araújo, A. M., & Diniz, A. M. (2013). Avaliaçao psicológica e o uso dos testes em Portugal. *PSIENCIA Revista Latinoamericana de Ciencia Psicológica, 5*(2), 144–149.

Annin, E. L., Boring, E. G., & Watson, R. I. (1968). Important psycologists, 1600–1967. *Journal of the history of behavorial sciences, 4*, 303–315. Retrieved from www.miraylopez.com/espanol.htm.

Calonge, I. (1988). María Eugenia Romano. Apuntes biográficos. *Paples del Psicólogo, VI*(35). Retrieved from www.papelesdelpsicologo.es/resumen?pii= 365.

Calonge, I., & Calles, A. M. (2016). *Tests psicológicos en España 1920–1970*. Madrid: Complutense University of Madrid.

Cuñat, R. (1958). *Productividad y mando de hombres en la empresa española*. Madrid: Euramérica.

Fernández Ballesteros, R. (1994). Psychological Assessment. *Applied Psychology: An International Review, 43*(2), 157–174.

Huarte de San Juan, J. (1989). *Examen de ingenios para las ciencias* (ed. G. Serrés) Madrid: Cátedra.

Magalhães, J. (s.f.). Apontamento sobre a história de Faculdade de Psicologia e de Ciências da Educação de Universidade de Lisboa. In S. C. Matos (ed.), *A Universidade de Lisboa, Séculos XIX–XX*. Lisboa: University of Lisbon. Retrieved from https://repositorio.ul.pt/bitstream/10451/10461/1/hist% C3%B3riaFPCE-UL.pdf.

Pereña Brand, J. (2006). *Una tea en la psicometría española*. Madrid: TEA Ediciones.

Prieto, J. M. (December 22, 2016). *El Colegiado D. Nicolás Seisdedos un referente de la Psicología española*. Madrid: Obtenido de Colegio Oficial de la Psicología de Madrid. www.copmadrid.org/web/comunicacion/noticias/ 499/el-colegiado-d-nicolas-seisdedos-referente-la-psicologia-espanola

Rozo, J. (1995). Mariano Yela (1921–1994). *Revista Latinoamericana de Psicología, 27*(3), 527–531.

Simões, M. R., Machado, C., Gonçalves, M. M., & Almeida, L. (2002–2008). *Avaliação psicológica: instrumentos validados para a população portuguesa* (vols. I–III). Coimbra: Quarteto Ed.

CHAPTER 9

Histories of Psychological Assessments in the United Kingdom

Dave Bartram

9.1 Introduction

The United Kingdom is more properly called the United Kingdom of Great Britain and Northern Ireland, where Great Britain includes the nations of Scotland, England, and Wales. The United Kingdom covers some 93,638 square miles and has a population of around 66.5 million people (56 million in England, 1.9 million in Northern Ireland, 3.1 million in Scotland, and 5.4 million in Wales). English is the main language, being spoken by 98% of the population over the age of three years. Some 62% of the population only speak English. There is a total of 14 indigenous languages used across the British Isles: 5 Celtic, 3 Germanic, 3 Romance (e.g. Angloromani), and 3 sign languages, with various regional dialects. There are also many languages spoken by people who arrived more recently in the British Isles, within inner-city areas; these languages are mainly from South Asia and Eastern and Western Europe. The population is culturally diverse with many people descended from families that emigrated to United Kingdom from countries of the British Empire in the late nineteenth century and early twentieth century. The United Kingdom is a union of nations and a monarchy, with Christianity (the Anglican Church) as its "official" State religion. According to the 2011 Census, this is followed by Islam, Hinduism, Sikhism, Judaism, and Buddhism in terms of number of adherents. This variety together with the relatively large number of individuals with nominal or no religious affiliations, has characterized the United Kingdom as a post-Christian, multi-faith, secularized society.

In this chapter we will see that the development of psychological assessment as a science in the United Kingdom, and more widely, proceeded in parallel and interaction with the development of psychometrics as a set of measurement tools, which in turn was used to support a worldview at that time that saw psychological differences as relatively fixed attributes that were only primarily changeable through genetic changes.

We also track the development of assessment methods that were influenced strongly by the two world wars. The greatest changes and developments in testing and assessment in the United Kingdom took place in occupational job selection and training settings before they had an impact on practice in clinical and educational assessment. As a consequence, this chapter focuses on the history of occupational assessment rather than on developments in the clinical and educational fields.

9.2   The Early Development of Psychological Assessment (1859–1890)

The year 1859 marked the publication of Charles Darwin's *The Origin of Species*. It sparked off developments in the arts and sciences, but of particular interest for the current theme of assessment is that it proposed a model for understanding how "intelligent" behavior develops and changes over time and encouraged the development of scientific rigor in the measurement of individual differences.

Not long after, in 1879, Wundt established his experimental psychology lab in Leipzig, Germany. This is generally regarded as the date that psychology as a formal discipline began. However, the foundations of psychological assessment in the United Kingdom were built by Sir Francis Galton (1822–1911), and strongly influenced by his half-cousin, Charles Robert Darwin (1809–1882). Darwin had introduced the theory that the branching pattern of evolution resulted from a process of natural selection, whereby the ability to adapt to one's environment is key in increasing the chances of survival of a species (Darwin, 1859). What is more, these differences in ability to adapt to the environment were seen as being driven by genetic mechanisms (i.e., natural selection) and not subject to modification through environmental changes or learning.

Galton was particularly interested in the inheritance of intelligence and the degree to which intelligent behavior was a function of nature or nurture. In 1884 at the International Health Exhibition in London, Galton established the first anthropometric laboratory, to measure people's characteristics and determine their heritage. Galton was interested in how science could be used to improve society and considered Britain's growing underclass a cause for concern. The proposal that one could improve the human population through a statistical understanding of heredity and use this to encourage "good" breeding strategies was linked to Darwin and to the theory of natural selection – and was often referred to as Social Darwinism. Based on his research, Galton in accordance with Darwin believed that desirable human qualities were hereditary traits. Galton (1883) first coined the term "eugenics" and he and his followers are now criticized for their philosophical stance on eugenics and race, but it should be remembered that within the cultural milieu at the time Galton's work was not only acceptable but was seen as "leading edge." This approach became associated with genetic determinism: the belief that variability in human character is entirely or in the main caused by genes, and relatively unaffected by education or living conditions. While it is difficult from the perspective of today to feel comfortable about the wholehearted embracing of eugenics in the latter part of the nineteenth century and early part of the twentieth century, it is important to understand that the zeitgeist of the time had a major influence over the choice of what to study and the perceived need to become more "scientific" in the processes used to make the measurements.

When Galton began his work around the middle of the nineteenth century, measurement methodology was in its infancy. Methods for measuring intangible attributes like intelligence and making causal inferences about its antecedents were yet to be developed. Galton developed the tools of correlation and regression to the mean, applied statistical techniques to the study of human individual differences and developed the use of questionnaires and surveys for collecting large volumes of data from large groups of people in the United Kingdom.

Galton's most significant contribution was recognizing that a different body of tools was needed to work with individual differences than those developed for use in experimental psychology. Galton's work on the measurement of correlations was placed on a rigorous mathematical base by Hamilton-Dickson (1886) and developed into the more general framework of linear regression by Karl Pearson (1920), who originally called a correlation (what we now call "r") the Galton coefficient of reversion. Galton invented the term "regression" to describe the fact that predicted measures, using correlation as the basis of prediction, tend to regress toward the mean. The lower the correlation, the greater the degree of regression (Galton, 1889; Stigler, 1997).

Galton is well-known as the founder of psychometrics and differential psychology in modern psychology. Less well-known is that he developed the lexical hypothesis of personality (Caprara & Cervone, 2000; Galton, 1884) over half a century before the idea was picked up again by Allport and Odbert (1936). The lexical hypothesis derives from the concept of linguistic relativity, and postulates that those personality characteristics that are important to a group of people will eventually become a part of that group's language. From this it follows that important personality characteristics are more likely to be encoded into language as a single word. The lexical hypothesis has been a major influence on the development of the "Big Five" (e.g., Goldberg, 1993, and see Goldberg et al., 2006 for information about the open source online IPIP) and the foundation of current hierarchical models of personality as we shall see later. The approach has been criticized and challenged for a range of reasons but its importance in the development of trait-based psychological models of personality cannot be underestimated (Ashton & Lee, 2005).

9.3   From the 1890s to the Great War of 1914–1918

The three countries most central to the developments in assessment that started in the 1890s were the United Kingdom, Germany, and the United States. In the late 1800s psychology was still regarded as a branch of philosophy in most of Europe including the United Kingdom. The exception to this was of course Germany – where Wilhelm Wundt established the new "experimental science" of psychology in Leipzig in 1879 and was followed by others such as Ebbinghaus and Stern. In Germany, Wundt's laboratory acted like a magnet attracting psychologists from all over Europe and North America and helped to establish links that developed into the international bodies of psychology that we see today (e.g., see Boring, 1960).

This became the epicenter for all those who were interested in developing psychology as a *science* rather than a branch of philosophy, both in the assessment of individual differences and in the "experimental" approaches. "German psychology" led to the rise of applied psychology, and to a field that came to be known in much of continental Europe as "psychotechnics." This is the practical or technological application of psychology, especially as applied to commercial, social, or economic problems. In the United Kingdom it was called occupational psychology (Shimmin & Wallis, 1994).

This period is also pertinent to the history of psychometrics and psychological assessment due to the continued acceptance of eugenics. Worldviews were quite different around the turn of the nineteenth century than they are now. At that time, University College London (UCL) welcomed Galton's request for a legitimate establishment in which he could research eugenics. In 1904 he established the Eugenics Record Office at 88 Gower Street, and he went on to fund the UCL Galton Eugenics Laboratory in 1907, as well as endowing a Fellowship in National

Eugenics. While eugenics was new as a construct, what it referred to was not and Waller (2001) has argued that there was little innovation occasioned by the eugenics movement.

Be that as it may, by the end of World War II it had become evident that eugenics promoted discrimination and oppressive socio-political ideologies (e.g., see Friedman, 2011).

9.4 The Development of Psychometrics

The period post 1890 was also a time when a number of significant developments were taking place in the development of psychometrics that underlie robust assessment methods. To support this, new mathematical statistical methods were being developed by people like Pearson, Spearman, and Fisher.

Karl Pearson (1857–1936) was a statistician who is credited with establishing the discipline of mathematical statistics. He founded the world's first university statistics department at UCL in 1911 and along with Galton was a proponent of Social Darwinism and eugenics. He was appointed professor of mathematics at UCL in 1884. As a supporter of Galton and his work, Pearson continued his legacy by becoming UCL's chair of eugenics, a position funded directly by Galton.

Charles Spearman (1863–1945) produced a theory of intelligence (Spearman, 1904) which he regarded as the most important of his many contributions. However, he is now best known for the Spearman rank order correlation, a non-parametric version of the "product–moment" coefficient calculated by Pearson. He was one of those who had studied with Wundt and was keen to develop an objective experimental world of measurement. Spearman pioneered the use of factor analysis in developing his theory of intelligence using factor analysis to determine the common variance across scores on tests of various different abilities. He was the first to introduce the concept of what he called "g," the general factor of intelligence.

The development of the tools of Analysis of Variance by Ronald Fisher (1890–1962) was of fundamental importance to those following the experimental psychology approach pioneered by Wundt, rather than Galton's focus on individual differences. Fisher was another close follower of Galton who held similar views on eugenics. In 1933, Fisher became head of the Department of Eugenics at UCL. While his prominent support of eugenics led to the positive outcomes of his work on statistics and genetics, on the negative side he was a dissenting voice in UNESCO's statements on "The Race Question" (see UNESCO, 1950, 1952, 1969,

1978), insisting instead on the inherent nature of racial differences. His reputation as a eugenicist is now more controversial than it was in his lifetime and he was recently the subject of protests at Gonville and Caius College Cambridge where a commemorative memorial window to him is to be removed (Turner, 2020).

9.5   The Great 1914–1918 War

At this time, the influences of Galton and his colleagues in the United Kingdom and Wundt and his colleagues in Germany focused on the statistical analyses of large numbers of measures from large groups of people, resulting in large bodies of quantitative data that needed new methods of statistical analysis. This crossed the Atlantic to seed the US growth of assessment, which soon outgrew its European roots and now is the major commercial driver of European assessment. However, this parallelism of approaches occurred again and again between the war years of the twentieth century, with a focus on methods for improving large-scale assessment, prediction, and classification, rather than individual more clinical approaches to assessment.

Although the systematic study of individual differences began with the work of Francis Galton in the United Kingdom in the late 1800s, his focus was on measurement for description rather than for prediction. As such his work had a strong impact on all areas of assessment: clinical, educational, and occupational. By 1910, though, the concept of validation as measured by correlation coefficients (the "test-criterion method") and concepts of reliability had become established. By the 1920s, validity and reliability were defined and accepted as key requirements for tests and the model of basing occupational assessment on job analysis was well established in occupational assessment. It was in the occupational field that assessment developed most through the needs for effective officer selection training, and the optimal assignment of men to roles in the armed forces.

The North Atlantic alliance of psychologists was developing just as Germany and the United Kingdom, and later the United States, were going to war with each other. The Great War provided the opportunity for the first large-scale use of testing for military selection, placement, and classification. However, little was done in the United Kingdom as the powers-that-be were seemingly unaware of the potential expertise they had in their country (Shepard, 2015). Spearman, for example, spent most of the war guarding a depot in the north of England. Because of the military's lack of knowledge of what they could have done with psychologists working on important issues like assessment and human factors, those

British academic psychologists who were medically trained were confined to working as psychiatrists with victims of shellshock in hospitals. These included William Halse Rivers and two of his graduate medical students, Charles S. Myers and William McDougall.

Treatment for "shellshock" was developed by Rivers and his team of students. The first paper that used the term shellshock was published in *The Lancet* (Myers, 1915). As well as being the founder of the *British Journal of Psychology*, Rivers and later Myers had considerable impacts on the developments of academic psychology and psychological assessment in the United Kingdom. Rivers's contributions to the development of science in general and psychology in particular in the United Kingdom are much underestimated.

In Germany, the military were better prepared and had engaged with psychologists. The impact of the United Kingdom on the evolution of psychological assessment during this period was indirect. People like Spearman, Pearson, and Fisher were primarily methodologists and thought leaders of the time. Influences were strongest on the models that underpinned test design and development (notably Spearman's model of intelligence). The developments of psychometrics, which owed so much to people like Spearman, Pearson, and Fisher, ultimately led to the development of more efficient multi-aptitude test batteries like those developed for military use in the United States.

9.6   The Inter-war Years (1918–1939)

Charles Myers (1873–1946) was one of the stand-out figures in British psychology during the first half of the century. He was one of the ten founding members of The Psychological Society in 1901, which would later become the British Psychological Society in 1906. Myers was its president from 1920 to 1923. He is best known for his founding and development of the National Institute for Industrial Psychology (NIIP) and for its pioneering work between the world wars. The Institute conducted research into problems of general interest to the industrial and commercial sector and published the results. It also undertook research consulting into the problems of particular organizations and suggested solutions. He remained director of the NIIP until 1938 when Elton Mayo from the United States was invited to take over. However, World War II interrupted his plans for that (Shimmin & Wallis, 1994).

At this time Taylorism was still dominant in manufacturing. Taylor (1911) believed that the task of management was to determine the best way for the worker to do a job, with any unnecessary motion eliminated, the worker should follow a machinelike routine, to became far more productive. In contrast, the emphasis of the NIIP under Myers was more enlightened and on well-being rather than methods of squeezing more out of the workers. In the 1920s, the NIIP was seen as leading the world in industrial psychology and vocational guidance (see Zibarras & Lewis, 2013).

Key developments in Germany during this period saw the military psychologists develop what we would now call assessment centers, including performance tests and situational tests as well as or instead of paper and pencil tests of ability, personality, motivation, and so on. Major features of the German assessment center programs were seen in the efforts to select German officers in the 1930s. The United Kingdom was now following these trends and work had been done on applying some of the German concepts of assessment centers to the UK military, especially in relation to leadership selection and development. Cooperation between psychologists in Germany, the United Kingdom, and the United States became increasingly difficult with the rise of Hitler in 1933.

9.7 World War II and the Post-war Years (1940s–1970s)

One of the most influential British psychologists working at this time was British-born Philip E. Vernon (1905–1987). He was psychological research advisor to the Admiralty and War Office during World War II, creating training methods and selection tests. He was best known for his work on models of intelligence and the development of Spearman's model. He developed a hierarchical model with Spearman's g at the top beneath which sat two major group factors: verbal–educational ability (v:ed) and practical–spatial–mechanical abilities (k:m). These could be deconstructed into smaller factors. He wrote important books on measurement of personality including, *Personality Tests and Assessments* in 1953 and *Personality Assessment (Psychology Revivals): A Critical Survey* in 1964.

Looking back to the War years, Vernon and Parry (1949) provided a very full account of the problems and procedures of psychological assessment and selection for all three of the armed services. Shimmin and Wallis (1994) note that "this book is the earliest technical and narrative account of the applications of differential psychology on a significantly wide scale in Britain, with appropriate 'follow-up' data to demonstrate its effectiveness" (14). By the end of the war, three million recruits had taken part in a psychological assessment procedure.

9.8   The Development of Assessment Centers

The War Office Selection Board (WOSB) picked up on the Wehrmacht's methods from 1942 through to 1946. WOSBs were developed by psychiatrists and psychologists, such as J. R. Rees and W. R. Bion (see Vinden, 1977). They improved on the German model with more empirical and less holistic approaches to leadership and through numerous reliability and validity studies. Australia and Canada went down similar lines and followed the UK model. After World War II, the UK WOSB procedures were picked up by the British Civil Service Selection Board (CSSB) and were used to create the first non-military application of what we now call assessment centers (see Garforth, 1945; Morris 1949).

The CSSB and the "Fast Stream" selection procedures for identifying future leading civil servants (referred to as Extended Interviews) continue to the present day, though much refined in terms of measurement procedures and content. In the United Kingdom, widespread use of assessment centers in the private sector did not really start until the late 1960s/early 1970s. Before that it was mainly military and public sector organizations that used and developed the methodology (Shimmin & Wallis, 1994).

9.9   The 1970s and 1980s: Assessment Centers in the Private Sector

This period was important in the history of psychological assessment in the United Kingdom for several reasons. Firstly, the period saw assessment centers become strongly entrenched in assessment. Legislation was passed that eventually led to the Equality Act (2010), which outlawed discrimination in assessment. The eugenics debate arose again with the debate over the work of Cyril Burt, and personality assessment became increasingly part of the occupational assessment process.

The use of psychological assessment in assessment centers and individual "clinical interviews" in the public sector continued and grew after World War II and the decades that followed. Its use in the private sector, especially for senior managers and leaders, however, lagged behind developments in the United States. The stimulus that encouraged firms to adopt Assessment center methodology in the United Kingdom is often attributed to the influence of Sir Michael Edwardes in the late 1970s (Adeney, 2019). At the time there were troubles at British Leyland (BL), the agglomeration of British motor marques from Austin to Jaguar that had been set up after the war. Edwardes's focus was on saving BL.

He arrived at BL with a small team that included his communications director from Chloride, John Mackay, and a psychologist who was to put BL top management through his tests. Communication and the empowerment of management were Edwardes's priorities. His success and his emphasis on the importance of objective assessment resulted in other leading private-sector companies getting their own psychologists on board to deal with senior management assessments (Adeney, 2019).

9.10   Concerns over Bias and Fairness in Testing

The increasing use of testing in selection, from shop floor to boardroom, together with the growing struggles of ethnic minorities and women to gain fair and equal representation in the workplace, led to a host of legislation that required test developers to ensure that their tests were unbiased and used fairly. This had a big impact on occupational assessment in the United Kingdom in the 1960s and 1970s. The movement against racial and gender discrimination had started in the United States with the US Civil Rights Act (1964). The anti-discrimination acts in UK legislation came a decade later: the Equal Pay Act (1970), the Sex Discrimination Act (1975), and the Race Relations Act (1976). These made it illegal to discriminate on the basis of marital status or gender, race, ethnicity, color, nationality, or national origin in recruitment, promotion, and training. The acts cover direct and indirect discrimination, and victimization. This legislation opened the way for people to take organizations to industrial tribunals on grounds of inappropriate or inadequate consideration having been given to disabilities and for bias in selection testing resulting in unfair discrimination on the grounds of age, race, religion, and gender. The Equal Pay Act was improved in 1983 and toward the end of the century two new acts came into being: the Disability Discrimination Act in 1995 and the Human Rights Act in 1998. These acts were finally all brought together in the Equality Act (2010), which brought disability, race, gender, and all other grounds of discrimination under one piece of legislation.

9.11   The Cyril Burt Saga and the Continuing Eugenics Issue

One cannot discuss the development of assessment in the United Kingdom without mentioning Cyril Burt (1883–1971). His "official" biography was written by Leslie Hearnshaw (1979) who notes that Burt was the leading educational psychologist in his time. His research on factor analysis and the genetics of intelligence was groundbreaking and formed a major part of the body of work on the heritability of intelligence that had been done by Galton, Spearman, Pearson, and Thurstone. His research was heavily predicated on the similarities and differences between the intelligence scores of identical twins (monozygotic) reared apart (same genes, different environment). By looking at the correlations between these twins it was possible to provide estimates of the heritability of the intelligence test scores they had obtained.

Shortly after Burt's death in 1971, however, he was accused of fraud by Kamin (1974) and Oliver Gillie (1976) who argued that the two research assistants who were supposed to have tested twins for him did not exist. It was argued that they were fictitious names and that Burt had invented the data. Since these claims, there has been a series of investigations made by people in support of Burt's position and against it (e.g., Blinkhorn, 1989; Eysenck, 1977; Gould, 1996; Hernshaw, 1992; Joynson, 1989; Mackintosh, 1995; Tucker, 1997). While there has been no resolution, it is fair to say that this has discredited him as an authority and discredited the "science" that was claimed to be behind the social changes taking place in the postwar years.

9.12   The Growth in Use of Personality Assessment

The 16PF Questionnaire (Cattell, 1949) had been developed by Raymond B. Cattell and his colleagues in the 1940s and 1950s. It was first published in 1949 and is now in its fifth edition (1994). Throughout the 1960s and 1970s it was the "standard instrument" to use in a wide range of personality assessment settings, both for clinical use and for occupational assessment. It was notable when it was first produced in being directed toward the measurement of normal personality rather than being just for clinical use. As the five-factor instruments started to gain traction, research on the 16 factors continued and analyses identified five group factors underlying the 16 scales. The 16PF was the forerunner of a number of new instruments developed in the United Kingdom during the 1980s and early 1990s (see Bartram et al., 1995 for a review of the main instruments in use at this time).

In 1965, Guion and Gottier had summarized 12 years (1952–1963) of research on the use of personality tests in selection by saying "It is difficult in the face of this summary to advocate, with a clear conscience, the use of personality measures in most situations as a basis for making employment decisions about people" (Guion & Gottier, 1965, 160).

This resulted in a dearth of new academic research on the validity of personality in work settings.

9.13   The Growth of Occupational Assessment in the United Kingdom (1970s–1990s)

The rejection of personality assessment by Guion and Gottier in 1965 was largely ignored by UK practitioners who continued to use personality inventories in the 1970s and onwards because they found that, in practice, the information they provided was important and relevant to their clients. These practitioners felt vindicated when the publication of two meta-analyses on the validity of personality tests for personnel selection (Barrick & Mount, 1991; Tett et al., 1991) showed evidence of validity for personality assessment. The current status of personality assessment for occupational assessment has been comprehensively summarized by Rothstein and Goffin (2006).

The NIIP expanded rapidly in the mid-1960s, however, it faced acute problems by the middle of the 1970s. The NIIP suspended activity in 1973, and finally closed in 1976. It was an influence on the career paths of many important figures in UK psychology at this time, not least of whom was Peter Saville (Forsythe, 2019). Together with Roger Holdsworth, who had worked for NIIP, he formed the first of what became a growing number of small entrepreneurial companies dedicated to the use of tests designed specifically for use in the workplace and developed in the United Kingdom. Saville and Holdsworth Ltd. started to produce original tests developed in the United Kingdom in 1977. As a business designed to develop and promote psychometric testing, theirs was the first UK company to be set up that developed its own range of psychometrically sound tests that were also visually appealing to the modern business user. Most competitors were still focused on adapting instruments imported from the United States (like the 16PF, CPI, MBTI, Gordon's GPPI, Jackson's PRF, and the NEO) many of which had been developed originally for clinical use (like the MMPI-2) (see Muniz et al., 2001).

While other instruments developed in the United States were also used in the United Kingdom, it was not until Saville's work on the Occupational Personality Questionnaire (OPQ) that there was a serious "home-grown" alternative. He had done his Ph.D. on the 16PF and was familiar with its strengths and weaknesses. The OPQ suite of tests were the first designed specifically for use in the world of work. Built using "business language" and with the engagement of industrial sponsors it was published in 1984. This suite of instruments included the first commercially available Big Five instrument (called Pentagon) and two forms of a 30-scale "Concept Model." One used a traditional normative format with five-point Likert rating scales. The other used a forced-choice format and produced ipsative scales.

During the end of the 1980s and early 1990s a host of smaller companies began providing consultancy in occupational assessment and training in test use. In 1995, the British Psychological Society (BPS) published its first set of test reviews covering personality scales available in the United Kingdom (Bartram et al., 1995) including tests developed over this period by a number of UK-based companies. There were reviews of 30 instruments. Of these 16 were US instruments adapted for use in the United Kingdom, mainly instruments from the early post-World War II years. The OPQ tests were the first to be developed in the United Kingdom and were followed by a small number of new UK tests published by various developers between 1987 and 1993 (see Bartram et al., 1995 for details of publishers of these 30 tests). Also see Bartram et al. (1997) for reviews of 44 UK ability and aptitude tests and Bartram et al. (1990) for 70 reviews of a variety of assessment instruments using in occupational guidance.

9.14   The Technological Revolution in the 1980s to the Late 1990s

As we proceed through the 1980s to the present day, we see assessment being dominated by the developments in computing and the growing accessibility and power of computers. This began slowly in the 1980s with expensive stand-alone machines – so called micro-computers. Moore's Law (that the number of transistors in an integrated circuit doubles every two years) correctly predicted the tremendous increase in power and decrease in cost of computing equipment (Schaller, 1996); which made the Internet and associated developments possible. This rapidly resulted in the ubiquitous availability of the Internet and inexpensive access to it by the early 2000s (Bartram & Tippins, 2017).

The 1980s saw the growing use of computers for report generation and printing of standardized interpretations and score-reports for well-known tests like the WISC, WAIS, MMPI, OPQ, 16PF, and so on (Bartram & Baylis, 1984). Also, computers were used in clinical and educational testing settings for supporting users in the interpretation of complex assessment systems. Actual computer-based tests were relatively rare and not widely used. They focused on niche areas such as use of tests by people with disabilities, clinical performance assessments, educational diagnostic tests, and the use of testing in the military (Scott et al., 2018).

9.15   Item Response Theory

While Lord and Novick's (1968) classic work on Item Response Theory (IRT) had been published back in the 1960s, widespread adoption of IRT in test design and development was slow to pick up in the United Kingdom. It was being used by organizations like NFER (National Foundation for Educational Research) in the development of attainment tests, especially for use in large-scale educational testing. Tests were still delivered on paper, but many were developed and scored by computer. It was not until the 1980s and 1990s that IRT applications started to emerge as the basis for general test design and construction. The lack of connectivity between computers restricted the use of these technologies in test design to organizations that had access to worldwide distribution networks (see Scott et al., 2018 for recent reviews).

9.16   The British Ability Scales

Most of the clinical and educational tests available for use in the United Kingdom were US imports, with intelligence testing being dominated by the Stanford–Binet and Wechsler range of scales. One major development in the United Kingdom that stands out, however, was the production of the British Ability Scales (BAS). This was led by Colin Elliot in 1979 at NFER. He used Rasch scaling and the battery has become recognized as a leading standardized battery for assessing a child's cognitive ability and educational achievement across a wide age range. The BAS is now in its third edition.[1] In addition, Elliot developed the Differential Ability Scales (DAS) –the first edition of which was published in 1990, with a second edition in 1997. The DAS has three levels: the first is the Lower Pre-school, the second level is the Upper Pre-school, and the School-Age level is for students from ages 6 to 17 years, 11 months old. The DAS is the US Version of the BAS.[2]

9.17   Item Generation and Test Generation

The main innovations that emerged in the United Kingdom in the 1980s were from the work of Sidney Irvine and his team in Plymouth University

---

[1] For further details see: www.gl-assessment.co.uk/products/british-ability-scales-bas3/.
[2] For information on the DAS see: www.pearsonassessments.com/professional-assessments/products/authors/elliott-colin.html.

on automated item generation for use in army selection testing (Irvine et al., 1990) and that of the present author and his colleagues at Hull University on the development of computer-based information management and adaptive tests for pilot selection in the British Army Air Corps and the Royal Navy (Bartram, 1987). Both programs were funded by the UK Ministry of Defence.

Whenever the critical properties of test items can be well specified, it becomes possible to provide rules for the generation of items. Item-writing is replaced by rule-writing. As a result, there is no fixed set of test items as in a traditional test. This approach was used in all the Micropat tests (Bartram, 1995, 2002; Bartram & Dale, 1991) where the forcing functions for tracking tasks, the items in a test of speed of mental arithmetic, and the stimulus sequences and screen positions in a signal detection task were all generated by rules. As a result, psychometric properties are a function of the rules that create items and not a function of any specific items themselves.

Irvine (Irvine, 2002; Irvine et al., 1990) developed a system for creating parallel tests using item generation and a well-defined cognitive model. Each item could be defined in terms of elements that were either "radicals" or "incidentals." The radicals determined the psychometric characteristics of the item such as what it measured, and how difficult it was. The incidentals defined the content in terms of the features that could vary from item to item without affecting its psychometric properties. The theory was that if one can define these sufficiently well, then items can be generated from a set of variable definitions with values of each variable either being generated or picked at random from a limited set of options. This approach was used for the British Army Recruit Battery (BARB), a set of ability tests designed for use in quick assessments of intelligence for army recruiting. The volume of tests needed was large and it was necessary to develop secure multiple forms of tests to ensure security.

Bartram and Dale started development of the Micropat test battery for the Army Air Corps and the Royal Navy pilot selection programs in 1981 (Bartram, 1987). The main innovation in Micropat is that many of the new tests were derived from cognitive psychology models. The aim was to develop useful and reliable measures of individual differences using material that came from the experimental psychology literature. Bartram's approach was to start with models of what cognitive factors affected a person's behavior, then to consider how measures could be derived from tasks designed to capture that behavior and to explore the psychometric properties of those attributes.

This came at the end of a decade of intensive work in which most researchers in the field were exploring the potential role of computers in testing. In particular it addressed the need to look at item and test generation methods that could be based on clear cognitive models of what the test taker is doing; that were psychometrically robust in that they had properties akin to reliability, validity, and scaling that are needed from any measurement process; that provided the needed degree of control over administration and that were cost-efficient.

The book describing work on item and test- or task-generation (Irvine & Kyllonen, 2002) was based on a conference held by ETS in 1998. It contained contributions from all the main researchers at the time. They came from Germany, the United States, and the United Kingdom. The North Atlantic Alliance begun in the late 1880s remains strong.

9.18   The Internet (Late 1990s to Now)

Most of the early use of the Internet was for logistic convenience, and the delivery of paper and pencil tests online. In general, research showed that self-report measures were stable across modes of delivery while some ability tests, especially speeded ones, were not (Bartram & Brown, 2004). In the United Kingdom, there was growing use of the Internet for managing the process of assessing applicants for jobs and indeed the whole recruitment and selection process (Bartram, 2000).

The other potential opened up by the Internet, together with the developing levels of bandwidth with 4G and now 5G networks, was the viability of high-fidelity simulations that can load and unload data very rapidly to give real-time interactions of great complexity (Adler et al., 2018). In particular technologies like virtual reality seem to offer great potential for future immersive realistic assessments. Coming under the general heading of gamification (see Hawkes et al., 2018), this is where a lot of the innovation is now taking place. Where this will lead, we cannot tell.

9.19   Conclusion

Francis Galton was among the first individuals to propose modern mental testing and psychometrics with his development of procedures for measuring reaction time and sensation and his "invention" of the correlation. It is unfortunate that he also aligned himself with and drove forward the eugenics movement. However, the value of what he and his "school" achieved in psychometrics and measurement science should be looked at in terms of what it provides now, without the discredited views on eugenics.

There have been many innovations in test design and use in the United Kingdom since then. One of the most significant recently has been the development of a multi-dimensional IRT scoring tool that produces "pure" normative scales from forced-choice item data (Brown & Maydeau-Olivares, 2011). While the outer appearance of personality instruments may have changed little over the past few decades, this new scoring procedure is as far away from traditional classical test scoring models as a Tesla is from a car with a petrol engine. The development in sophistication of psychometric tools since Galton's pioneer work is staggering.

Moving from the early 1900s to the early 2000s, there were growing concerns around quality assurance of tests, test use practices, and the competence of test users. This was especially true in the occupational field where there was a growing body of law that meant one had to avoid bias and unfairness in job selection. From 1987 onwards, the BPS had led the development of test user competence standards and competence models (Bartram, 1996). The BPS, which encompasses all four nations in the United Kingdom, worked with the European Federation of Psychologists' Associations (EFPA)'s Standing Committee on Tests and Testing (later renamed the Board of Assessment) to develop a three-level qualification model. EFPA accredited the BPS to award the EuroTest certificate of competence from September 2011 (Bartram, 2011). Over 30,000 people have now been certified. During this period of technical innovation, the International Test Commission also engaged in a lot of work on the development of guidelines on good practice including guidelines that defined minimum competences for proper and fair test use (Bartram, 1998).

Today psychological testing is a part of the Internet world, an accessible and routine process for people of all ages. We get tested as children, as adults, as elderly people, and as job applicants, for health reasons and for educational reasons. Great care is now taken to ensure that tests are valid and fair. We also focus on issues of validity to know what it is that we are measuring and the consequences for people of their results in terms of educational, work, health, and life outcomes.

REFERENCES

Adeney, M. (2019). *Sir Michael Edwardes obituary*. Guardian Newspapers. Published 18 September 2019.

Adler, S., Boyce, A. S., & Caputo, P. M. (2018) Employment testing. In J. C. Scott, D. Bartram, & D. H. Reynolds (eds.), *Next generation technology-enhanced assessment* (pp. 3–35). Cambridge: Cambridge University Press.

Allport, G. W.; Odbert, H. S. (1936). *Trait-names: A psycho-lexical study*. Albany, NY: Psychological Review Company.

Ashton, M. C., & Lee, K. (2005). A defence of the lexical approach to the study of personality structure. *European Journal of Personality, 19*(1), 5–24.

Barrick, M. R. & Mount, M. K. (1991). The Big Five personality dimensions and job performance: A meta-analysis. *Personnel Psychology, 44*(1), 1–26.

Bartram, D. (1987). The development of an automated pilot testing system for pilot selection: the MICROPAT project. *Applied Psychology: An International Review, 36*(3/4), 279–298.

(1995). Validation of the Micropat Battery. *International Journal of Selection and Assessment, 3*(2), 84–95.

(1996). Test qualifications and test use in the UK: The competence approach. *European Journal of Psychological Assessment, 12*(1), 62–71.

(1998). The need for international guidelines on standards for test use: A review of European and international initiatives. *European Psychologist, 3* (2), 155–163.

(2000). Internet recruitment and selection: Kissing frogs to find princes. *International Journal of Selection and Assessment, 8*(4), 261–274.

(2002). The MICROPAT Pilot Selection Battery: Applications of generative techniques for item-based and task-based tests. In S. Irvine & P. Kyllonen (eds.), *Item generation for test development*. Mahwah, NJ: Lawrence Erlbaum.

(2011). Contributions of the EFPA Standing Committee on Tests and Testing to Standards and Good Practice. *European Psychologist, 16*(2), 149–159.

Bartram, D. & Baylis, R. (1984). Automated testing: Past, present and future. *Journal of Occupational Psychology, 57*, 221–237.

Bartram, D. & Brown, A. (2004). Online testing: Mode of administration and the stability of the OPQ32i scores. *International Journal of Selection and Assessment, 12*(3), 278–284

Bartram, D. (senior ed.) with Lindley, P. A., & Foster, J. (eds.). (1990). *Review of psychometric tests for assessment invocational trainings*. Sheffield: Training Agency, Employment Department Group.

Bartram, D. (senior ed.) with Anderson, N., Kellett, D., Lindley, P.A., & Robertson, I. (consulting eds.). (1995). *Review of personality assessment instruments (level B) for use in occupational settings*. Leicester: BPS Books.

Bartram, D., (senior ed.) with Burke, E. B., Kandola, R., Lindley, P. A. Marshall, L., & Rasch, P. (eds.). (1997). *Review of Ability and Aptitude tests (Level A) for use in occupational settings*. Leicester: BPS Books.

Bartram, D. & Dale, H. C. A. (1991). Validation of the MICROPAT battery of pilot aptitude tests. In P. L. Dann, S. H. Irvine, & J. M. Collis (eds.), *Advances in computer-based human assessment* (pp. 149–170). Dordrecht: Kluwer Academic Publishers.

Bartram, D. & Tippins, N. (2017). *The potential of online selection*. In H. W. Goldstein, E. D. Pulakos, J. Passmore, & C. Semedo (eds.), *Wiley Blackwell handbooks in organizational psychology. The Wiley Blackwell handbook of the psychology of recruitment, selection and employee retention* (p. 271–292). Oxford: Wiley-Blackwell.

Blinkhorn, S. F. (1989). Was Burt stitched up? *Nature, 340*(6233), 439–440.

Boring, E. G. (1960). *A history of experimental psychology* (2nd ed.). Englewood-Cliffs: Prentice-Hall.

Boroditsky, L. & Liberman, M. (December 13–23, 2010). For and Against Linguistic Relativity. *The Economist*. The Economist Newspaper Limited. Archived from the original on 15 February 2012. Retrieved 19 September 2019. (A debate between university professors.)

Brown, A. & Maydeu-Olivares, A. (2011). Item response modelling of forced-choice questionnaires. *Educational and Psychological Measurement, 71*(3), 460–502.

Caprara, G. V. &Cervone, D. (2000). *Personality: Determinants, dynamics, and potentials*. New York: Cambridge University Press.

Cattell, R. B. (1949): *The sixteen-personality factor questionnaire*. Champaign, IL: Institute for Personality and Ability Testing

Darwin, C. (1859). *The origin of species*. London: John Murray, Albemarle Street.

Eysenck, H. J. (1977). The case of Sir Cyril Burt. *Encounter, 48*(1), 19–23.

Forsythe, A. (2019). *Key thinkers in individual differences: Ideas on personality and intelligence*. New York: Routledge.

Friedman, J. C. (2011). *The Routledge history of the holocaust*. London: Taylor & Francis.

de la P. Garforth, F. I. (1945). War office selection boards (O.C.T.U.). *Journal of Occupational Psychology*, 19, 97–108.

Galton, F. (1883). *Inquiries into human faculty and its development*. London: Macmillan Publishers.

(1884). Measurement of character. *Fortnightly Review. 36*, 179–185.

(1889). *Natural inheritance*. London: Macmillan.

Gillie, O. (1976). Crucial data was faked by eminent psychologist. *London:* Sunday Times, October [24], 1976.

Goldberg, L. R. (1993). The structure of personality traits: Vertical and horizontal aspects. In D. C. Funder, R. D., Parke, C. Tomlinson-Keasey, & K. Widaman (eds.), *Studying lives through time: Personality and development* (pp. 169–188). Washington, DC: American Psychological Association.

Goldberg, L. R., Johnson, J. A., Eber, H. W., Hogan, R., Ashton, M. C., Cloninger, C. R., & Gough, H. C. (2006). The International Personality Item Pool and the future of public-domain personality measures. *Journal of Research in Personality*, 40, 84–96.

Gould, S. J. (1996). The real error of Cyril Burt factor analysis and the reification of intelligence. In Gould, S. J., *The Mismeasure of Man* (ch. 6). London: W. W. Norton & Company.

Guion R. M. & Gottier R. F. (1965). Validity of personality measures in personnel selection. *Personnel Psychology, 18*(2), 135–164.

Hamilton-Dickson J. D. (1886). Appendix to Galton, *Proceedings of the Royal Society. London, 40*, 63–66.

Hawkes, B., Cek, I., & Handler, C. (2018). The gamification of employee selection tools: An exploration of viability, utility and future directions. In J. C. Scott, D. Bartram, & D. H. Reynolds (eds.), *Next generation technology-enhanced assessment* (pp. 288–316). Cambridge: Cambridge University Press.

Hearnshaw, L. (1979). *Cyril Burt: Psychologist.* Ithaca, NY: Cornell University Press.

(1992). Burt Redivivus. *The Psychologist, 5*(4), 169–170.

History.com (eds.). (2020). *Eugenics.* Downloaded from www.history.com/topics/germany/eugenics, October q0, 2020. Last updated May 26, 2020.

Irvine, S. H., Dann, P. L., & Anderson, J. D. (1990). Towards a theory of algorithm-determined cognitive test construction. *British Journal of Psychology, 81*(2), 173–195.

Irvine, S. H. (2002). The foundations of item generation for mass testing. In Irvine, S. H. & Kyllonen, P. (eds.), *Item generation for test development.* Mahwah, NJ: Lawrence Erlbaum.

Irvine, S. H. & Kyllonen, P. (eds.) (2002). *Item generation for test development.* Mahwah, NJ: Lawrence Erlbaum

Joynson, R. B. (1989). *The Burt affair.* New York: Routledge.

Kamin, L. J. (1974). *The science and politics of IQ.* Potomac, MD: Lawrence Erlbaum Associates.

Lord, F. M. & Novick, M. R. (1968). *Statistical theories of mental test scores.* Menlo Park: Addison-Wesley.

Mackintosh, N. (ed.). (1995). *Cyril Burt: Fraud or framed?* New York: Oxford University Press.

Morris, B. S. (1949). Officer selection in the British army 1942–1945. *Occupational Psychology 23*(4), 219–234.

Muñiz, J., Bartram, D., Evers, A., Boben, D., Matesic, K., Glabeke, K., Fernandez-Hermida, J. R., & Zaal, J. N. (2001). Testing practices in European countries. *European Journal of Psychological Assessment 17*(3), 201–211.

Myers, C. S. (1915). The study of shell shock. *The Lancet* (February 13), 316–320.

Pearson, K. (1920). Notes on the history of correlation. *Biometrika, 13*(1), 25–45.

Rothstein, M. G. & Goffin, R. D. (2006). The use of personality measures in personnel selection: What does current research support? *Human Resource Management Review. 16*(2), 155–180.

Schaller, B. (1996). The origin, nature, and implications of "MOORE'S LAW." Microsoft. (September 26, 1996), Retrieved September 10, 2014. http://research.microsoft.com/en-us/um/people/gray/moore_law.html

Scott, M., Milbourn, B., Falkmer, M., Black, M., Bölte, S., Halladay, A., Lerner, M. Taylor, J., & Girdler, S. (2018). Factors impacting employment for people with autism spectrum disorder: A scoping review. *Autism 23*(4), 1–33.

Shephard, B. (2015). Psychology and the great war, 1914–1918. *The Psychologist, 28*(11), 944–946.

Shimmin, S. & Wallis, D. (1994). *Fifty years of occupational psychology in Britain.* Leicester: The BPS.

Spearman, C. (1904). "General intelligence," objectively determined and measured. *The American Journal of Psychology, 15*(2), 201–293.

Stigler, S. M. (1997). Regression toward the mean, historically considered. *Statistical Methods in Medical Research, 6*(2), 103–114.

Taylor, F. W. (1911). *Principles of scientific management.* New York: Harper & Brothers Publishers.

Tett, R. P., Jackson, D. N., & Rothstein, M. (1991). Personality measures as predictors of job performance: A meta-analytic review. *Personnel Psychology, 44*(4), 703–742.

Tucker, W. H. (1997). "Re-reconsidering Burt: Beyond a Reasonable Doubt." *Journal of the History of the Behavioral Sciences.* 33 (2): 145-162.

Turner, C. (2020). College to take down eugenicist memorial. *Daily Telegraph,* June 27, 2020.

Vernon, P. E. & Parry, J. B. (1949). *Personnel selection in the British forces.* London: London University Press.

Vinden, F. H. (1977). The introduction of war office selection boards in the British Army: A personal recollection. In B. Bond & I. Roy (eds.). *A yearbook of military history* (vol 2). London: Croom Helm.

UNESCO. (1950). *The race question.* Paris: UNESCO.

   (1952). *The race concept: Results of an inquiry.* Paris: UNESCO.

   (1969). *Four statements on the race question.* Document code: COM.69/II.27/A.

   (1978). *Draft Declaration on Race and Racial Prejudice.* Presented at the 20th UNESCO General Conference in Paris.

Waller, J. C., (2001). Ideas of heredity, reproduction and eugenics in Britain, 1800–1875. *Studies in History and Philosophy of Biological and Biomedical Sciences, 32*(3), 457–489.

Zibarras, L. & Lewis, R. (2013). *Work and occupational psychology: Integrating theory and practice.* London: Sage Publishing.

CHAPTER 10

The Early History of Psychological Testing in Eastern Europe and Russia

Dragoş Iliescu, Andrei Ion, and Krunoslav Matešić

10.1 The General Context of Eastern Europe

Sitting at the confluence of Middle Eastern, Eastern, and Western influences, Central and Eastern Europe has gone during the twentieth century through more social, economic, and political convulsions than any other region of the globe. The late nineteenth century was a period characterized by great social and political turmoil. A series of political upheavals known as the Spring of Nations swept across Europe, leading to the creation of national states. In Eastern Europe this movement started in 1848 with the creation of new states such as Romania, continuing until the end of World War I, when the dismantling of the Austro-Hungarian Empire led to the creation of the sovereign states of Yugoslavia, Czechoslovakia, Hungary, Greater Poland, and modern-day Ukraine (Galicia). The newly emerged nations were in a constant struggle to shake off the dominion and influences of the more powerful states, such as the Ottoman Empire, Russia, or the Austro-Hungarian Empire.

The social situation and associated societal challenges and struggles inherited by these new states from their former political status as provinces and peripheries of empires massively influenced their evolution. Education and health especially would become a major challenge for all of these states. For example, while we know that in the early years of the twentieth century approximately 79% of the world population was illiterate (Roser & Ortiz-Ospina, 2019), we also know that this figure is an average based on literacy rates reported beginning with the late 1870s of above 75% in the United Kingdom and France (Roser & Ortiz-Ospina, 2019) and extremely low literacy rates even 50 years later in Eastern Europe (e.g., in 1930, when the first official census was conducted in Romania, approximately 38% of the population were *de facto* illiterate). During most of the late nineteenth century and early twentieth century, these countries struggled with ensuring basic access to health and education, while trying to assert themselves as independent and self-determining national states. This would set the stage and provide the context for the development of psychology in general and of psychological testing in particular.

The political situation of the whole area is a second important force that shaped the evolution of these countries during the entire twentieth century, and that is important for our focal theme. In 1914, the Bosnian-Serb Gavrilo Princip assassinated the heir to the Austro-Hungarian throne, Franz Ferdinand, starting World War I and putting in motion a series of events that shaped the world irreversibly. In 1917, in the middle of World War I, the Bolshevik Revolution led to the installment of a new social and political system that would influence most of the Central and Eastern European countries throughout the entire century. In the aftermath of World War II, at the Yalta convention, on the premise of ensuring a buffer zone that would prevent future Western aggression on Russia, communism was imposed in Albania, Bulgaria, the Czechoslovak Republic, Eastern Germany, the Federal Republic of Yugoslavia, Hungary, Poland, and Romania. Several countries were annexed by the USSR, namely Byelorussia, Estonia, Latvia, Lithuania, Moldavia, and Ukraine. This shift brought about radical changes in the entire academic environment, reshaping the agenda and research focus within Russia and subsequently in the entire Central and Eastern European area.

In spite of these convulsions, science in general has fared reasonably well in this geographical space. In a ranking based on Nobel prize winners, Russia and Eastern Europe was second only after Western Europe and the United States, with Russia alone accounting for 31 different laureates throughout the past century. Names such as Dmitri Mendeleev, Nicola Tesla, V. V. Dokuchaev, Nikolay Semyonov, Emil Palade, or the French-naturalized Polish researcher Maria Salomea Skłodowska (Marie Curie) made outstanding scientific contributions. Ivan Pavlov and Lev Vygotsky are some of the most cited psychologists, being ubiquitous in every introductory psychology textbook. However, one wonders why so few contributions to the development of psychological testing and/or the psychology of individual differences can be traced back to this part of the world. In the chapter to follow, we summarize the anfractuous evolution of psychological science in general and psychological testing specifically within the social and political context of the past century for Central and Eastern Europe. This region includes several national states most easily identified as "former communist block" states: Bulgaria, Hungary, Moldavia, Poland, Russia, Romania, Serbia, and the ex-Yugoslav Republic countries, The Czech Republic, Slovakia, and Ukraine. All these countries have emerged as national states in the mid-nineteenth century, each having a relatively unique language and national identity. The region has over 290 million inhabitants, with Russia alone accounting for over 145 million. The dominant religion across these countries tends to be Orthodox Christianity, with some notable exceptions such as the Czech Republic, Slovakia, Poland, Croatia, and Slovenia. Approximately 70% of the population lives in urban areas. All the countries included in this region have undergone important political, social, and economic changes throughout the past century.

10.2 Psychology in Eastern Europe: The Early Days

The first psychological association founded in this geographical space was the Moscow Psychological Society, founded in Russia in 1885 (http:// psyrus.ru/en/about). In the next few years, psychology departments were established in most of the large Russian universities. Despite the less favorable social and political context, psychology departments or psychological laboratories emerged in most of the other Eastern European countries. Although the development of psychological assessment took a sudden turn in Russia in 1918, in the aftermath of the Soviet Revolution, the advancement of psychology continued in the still democratic countries from Eastern Europe.

As in other areas of the globe, research and practice in psychological assessment was focused on two areas: psychotechnics and vocational testing. In most of the Eastern European countries psychological testing consisted mainly in the measurement of various psychophysiological functions such as spatial processing, resistance to dizziness, static balance, or various forms of attention (Pitariu, 1992) with the aim of avoiding workplace accidents or improving worker productivity. Vocational testing occurred mostly in educational settings, consisting in the administration of measures capturing intellectual functioning, cognitive development, and functioning in children, adolescents, and young adults. The evolution of psychological assessment across all the countries in Eastern Europe followed a similar pattern to the ones encountered in other regions of the world where psychological science flourished.

In terms of sources of inspiration, research and practice of psychological assessment had in the early days two distinctive branches: first, a combination of strong Germany-derived experimental and psychotechnical assessment that was used in a Munsterberg-inspired fashion in applied, work-related settings; second, the translation and/or construction of measures tapping into intellectual and cognitive functioning with a child-developmental twist.

10.2.1 Russia

Russia in the 1920s had a complicated social and historical situation, and the evolution of psychology and pedagogy, and more specifically of testing associated with these disciplines, should be considered in this context. Specifically, Russia had just passed through seven years (1914–1920) of unabated conflict: international wars and a civil war/revolution, coupled with the famine and terrible individual abuse that goes with such historical contexts. Leopoldoff (2014) reports that one of the priorities of the government was reintegration of the (supposedly two) millions of orphaned and abused children and teenagers. She also suggests that this was reflected in strong support given by the Bolshevik government to "pedology" (i.e., the science of child rearing), that was supposed to contribute its share to the creation of the envisioned "new man," having an explicit science-embracing stance. Tests and the quantitative and statistical methods that were indissolubly related to tests were perceived as objective science and thus encouraged, in this context. This came as a continuation of the strong interest in early education that was shown in Russia even before the communist revolution and that was reflected in the existence of over 50 laboratories of experimental psychopedagogy (mainly in Moscow and Sankt Petersburg; Fradkin, 1990) and the organization of five congresses by Russian experts up until 1916 (Leopoldoff, 2014).

Russian scholars in this field seem to have had mostly a medical background (Leopoldoff, 2014) and were trained in international, predominantly European laboratories such as Wilhelm Wundt's laboratory in Leipzig. Important names were Vladimir Behterev (1857–1927), Alexandre Necaev (1970–1948), Alexandre Lazurskij (1874–1917), Gregori Rossolimo (1860–1928), and Alexandre Bernstein (1870–1922). They were active internationally and correspondence has been uncovered between these early founders and prominent scholars such as Wilhelm Wundt (Leipzig), Alfred Binet (Paris), Edouard Claparede (Geneva), and Stanley Hall (Cambridge and Worcester, MA).

This incipient tradition of maybe two decades was embraced by the new Soviet regime, with a strong agenda to push education from both ideological and economic reasons. Ideologically, education was perceived as a form of enlightenment – probably the motive for the supervision of schools beginning in 1919 by the People's Commissariat for Enlightenment.

Economically, the rapidly industrializing country had a strong need of qualified workforce and a predominantly rural and illiterate population was no help in this respect. The need to measure and classify cognitive ability and personal style seems thus to have been central to both the vision and the need of the new leadership. Pedology, the science of child rearing, was central to this effort to reform society – it was the leading force behind education and coordinated other disciplines that also contributed, such as psychoneurology, sociology, pedagogy, health, and life sciences. Several scholars (Leopoldoff, 2014; Petrovskij, 1991) actually underline that it may be impossible to understand Russian psychology and testing without understanding this preeminent position of pedology in its early stages of development.

The tests that were used at that time were the Binet–Simon cognitive ability tests, Rossolimo's psychological profiles, Necaev's tests, and Lazurskij's "Seven Stars profile" (Leopoldoff, 2014). The Binet–Simon test was adapted into Russian in several forms, but the 1911 version of the test seems to have been dominant – this was translated by Anna Subert (Leopoldoff, 2014) and was officially published in Moscow in 1923 (Necaev, 1925). Although apparently efficient, this test was considered boring for young children due to its lack of illustrations. The most frequently used psychological measures in the 1920s and 1930s in the USSR were the Russian translations of Binet–Simon and the indigenous Rossolimo test batteries. Terman's measures appear also to have been translated and used, although not on a broad scale (Leopoldoff, 2014). Apparently, despite the incompatibilities with the Soviet doctrine, an association of psychological testers was founded in Moscow as late as 1927. A number of papers appeared in the Russian outlet *L'Annee Psychologique* summarizing the work of Russian psychometricians and psychological assessment researchers, including mentions of large-scale assessments of cognitive functioning (over 13,000 school children).

10.2.2   Romania

By the late 1920s, a number of psychologists trained in Wundt's laboratory managed to officially introduce psychophysiological departments as standalone academic programs in several universities. The Romanian Psycho-technic Society was established in 1930. At this time, psychological assessment was confined mainly to a number of industrial laboratories, such as the laboratory of the Bucharest Tram Society, the Aeronautical Medical Center, or the Romanian General Industrial Association, from where psychotechnical measures slowly found their way into army recruiting centers, transportation, or industrial companies (Ion et al., 7). A number of well-established measures of cognitive functioning, such as the Army Alpha, were translated into Romanian in the mid-1930s. During the same period, the first handbook of psychological assessment, *Selecting Capacities and Professional Orientation*, was published in Romania by Florian Ştefănescu-Goangă (1939).Another important figure was Nicolae Margineanu, a student of Ştefănescu-Goangă, who published important books related to assessment, such as *Psychotechnics in Germany* (1929), *Elements of Psychotechnics* (1938), *Psychotechnics in Industrial Settings* (1942), and *Psychotechnics* (1943).

10.2.3   Poland

In 1903 the first Polish laboratory of experimental psychology was established at the Jagellionian University of Krakow, and laboratories were established quickly after that in Warsaw and Lvov. As documented by Salgado, Anderson, and Hülsheger (2010), psychotechnical testing centers were active at this time, specialized in testing employees from specific lines of work, mainly for jobs related to industry or transportation (e.g., a testing center for engine drivers). National institutions began to appear at that time, generating more advancement. For example, the Polish Psychotechnical Institute was founded in 1925 (Dryjanska, 2016) and two psychotechnical laboratories were established in Krakow and in Warsaw. The Polish Psycho-technical Society was founded around the same time, and it started publishing the quarterly journal *Psycho-Technica* (Dryjanska, 2016). In the next few years, 18 different laboratories were founded across the country. Psychological testing in Poland included a range of psycho-physiological measures (ranging from reaction time to attention span) mainly aimed at assessing various individual characteristics deemed to be essential for performing work-related tasks in industrial fields of work.

10.2.4   The Former Kingdom/Republic of Yugoslavia

The birth of psychological science followed slightly different pathways in Yugoslavia. First of all, we need to mention the federative nature of Yugoslavia, composed of six former states; two of them, Croatia and Serbia, were especially active in the domain of testing in these early days.

In Croatia, an early moment is the two-volume *Introduction to Experimental Pedagogy*, (Radosavljevic, 1912) published in Zagreb in

1910/1912 by Paja Radosavljevic (1879–1958), a post-graduate student of Ernst Meumann; Radosavljevic later emigrated to the United States, where he was a professor at the University of New York. The second volume, entitled *Introduction to Experimental Didactics*, is especially important for testing, as it includes a translation and adaptation of the 1908 version of the Binet–Simon scale (Radosavljevic, 1912, 257–267), enriched with some items from Goddard's American translation from 1910.

Having been trained at the Karl Franzen University of Graz, Ramiro Bujas (1879–1959) rapidly became influential in this geographical space, establishing the first laboratory for experimental psychology in 1920, the Institute of Psychology in 1923, and the School of Psychology at the Faculty of Philosophy in Zagreb in 1929 (Pavlina, 1986, 1989). In 1932, he founded the journal *Acta Instituti psychologici Universitatis zagrabiensis*, which published articles in German, French, and later English. Also in 1932, he co-founded the counseling center for career choice within the Bureau for Trade Advancement of the Chamber of Commerce, Trade and Industry; many consider this as the beginning of systematic applied psychology in Croatia and the then Yugoslavia. Though going through several changes in structure and activities and changing its name a number of times, this center remained active until the end of 1948 when the Bureau for Psychology and Occupational Physiology was disbanded (Matešić, 2017; Zebec-Silj & Zebec, 2018). In this whole time, the Center and Bureau tested about 19,000 candidates for the purpose of career guidance; their main thrust was the selection of underprivileged boys who were selected to receive a trade education.

With a Ph.D. in philosophy, systematized to the workplace of a "psychotechnician," Zlatko Pregrad (1903–1983) developed different tests to measure intellectual abilities, mostly adaptations of accepted psychodiagnostic instruments of the time – among these was an adaptation of the Binet–Simon scale that was completed by Pregrad in 1933 (Pregrad, 1933) starting from an earlier German language adaptation of that test by Otto Bobertag (1879–1934), a psychologist from Stern's circle in Wroclaw (Matešić, 2011). Two years later, Pregrad (1935) adapted the Binet–Terman test from a Czech adaptation done by Cyril Stejskal (1890–1969). However, the most important was academician Zoran Bujas (1910–1994), who began work at the center in 1935 where he, along with his colleagues, developed around 40 psychological tests, primarily intended for the assessment of intellectual abilities (Matešić, 2011).

In Serbia, the development of psychodiagnostic instruments was closely tied to the establishment of the Seminar for Psychology in Belgrade, which transitioned into the Group for Psychology in the late 1920s. Credit is due to academician Borislav Stevanovic (1891–1971), Spearman's doctoral student who prepared the Belgrade revision of the Binet–Simon test in 1934 (Stevanovic, 1934).

The primary focus in Serbia was also on experimental and educational psychology; for example, the first Serbian psychological association was the Serbian Society for School Psychology. However, while Croatian psychological assessment practices had an applied focus, in Serbia the use of psychological measures was mostly developmental oriented. When the Psychological Department was established as part of the University of Belgrade, Stevanovic introduced a course on "The Assessment of Aptitudes of Children and Adults." His research work focused mostly on the development and structure of intelligence, drawing from Spearman's factorial model. Most of the psychological testing going on was coordinated by the Psychotechnic Institute in Belgrade. Well-established measures of general mental ability such as the Simon–Binet scales were translated during the 1920s, and in the early 1930s the "Belgrade Revision of Binet–Simon Scale for Children" was published (Marinkovic, 1992). Some of the research work of Serbian psychologists was presented during the International Congress of Psychology in 1932 and 1937, and most of their work was loaded on topics directly related to assessment: norming of intelligence tests, test-bias by socioeconomic status, and so on.

10.2.5   Czechoslovakia

The history of Czechoslovakian applied psychology began with the establishment of the Psychotechnic Institute as part of the Masaryk Academy of Labor in 1920. Not fewer than 11 psychotechnical laboratories were established in Czechoslovakia up until World War II. William Forster, the most reputed Czechoslovakian psychologist of that time (the 1930s), led the cutting-edge work of the Prague Psychotechnics Institute, developing a renowned apparatus for assessing reaction time and distributed attention. The International Congress of Psychotechnics of 1934 was hosted in Prague, and the practice of psychological and psychotechnical assessment flourished throughout a large number of vocational guidance centers (Klikperova-Baker et al., 2019).

10.2.6   Hungary

Drawing from the Austrian and German school of psychological thought, early Hungarian psychology was a mélange between philosophical and experimental orientations. The National Institute of Psychology was established in 1928 and psychology was taught at that time as a subdiscipline of philosophy. The psychotechnical tradition was present in Hungary; five different psychotechnics centers were active during the 1930s (Salgado et al., 2010). The most popular test batteries were the Russian-imported Rossolimo tests and the German-imported Dresden Method. A significant part of the work of psychotechnicians was focused on the selection of transportation and industry workers.

10.3   The Dark Days

One of the tenets of communist doctrine emphasized homogeneity as opposed to heterogeneity in respect to between-individual psychological functions and capabilities. The entire "New Man" dogma was based on a negation of such fundamental and enduring differences in the psychological fabric of citizens. It is therefore no wonder that psychology was among the first sciences heavily impacted by censorship with the advent of communist regimes. Psychological assessment was especially deemed as a threat to the Soviet view on human beings and was consequently eliminated from university curricula and applied settings. This ideological position was imposed by Soviet Russia and we should therefore take a closer look at why and how this position was shaped.

As noted earlier, faith in tests and testing in the Soviet Union was based on, and connected to, pedology (i.e., the new science of child rearing). Testing was therefore linked to developmental and educational settings and was sanctioned and encouraged by the state. This initial positive situation changed in the late 1920s and early 1930s, in the context of debates about the consequences of psychological measurement applied to children that were fueled by discontent teachers and parents, as well as by the realization of the fundamental incompatibility between testing and the "New Man" framework. Gradually increasing state-driven censorship was initially imposed on work-related testing – although some reports state that during the early 1920s the Dresden approach to selecting engine drivers was still in use in the USSR (Salgado et al., 2010) – but research and application of cognitive developmental measures for children remained high and psychological assessment still survived as an essential branch of pedology. We also feel compelled to mention that in that period one of the important figures of Soviet testing – credited by many as one of the founding fathers of Soviet psychotechnics – was Isaak N. Spielrein who, among others, organized between September 8 and 13, 1931 the Seventh International Conference of Psychotechnics in Moscow (Koltsova et al., 1990).

During the 1930s, as ideologically based state censorship crept its way into all aspects of society, all the psychotechnical laboratories and institutes were shut down in the USSR, their staff being forced to specialize in other areas of face the purge of the Stalinist regime (Salgado et al., 2010). During the same period, the practice of psychological measurement was officially banned across the USSR, being largely regarded as incompatible with Soviet doctrine (Leopoldoff, 2014) – in line with the principle "if it cannot be measured, it does not exist," the state-driven censorship found a very effective way of making sure that individual differences did not exist, by outlawing the practice of psychological measurement. This evolution culminated with an official prohibition of testing practices in the mid-1930s: the entire science of pedology was officially forbidden by the Decree issued by the Central Committee of the Communist Party of the Soviet Union (Bolsheviks) (on July 4, 1936), announcing the start of the Dark Days of Psychological Science.

By this measure alone, the USSR finally found a solution to problems such as mental retardation, learning disabilities, and other problematic behaviors interfering with the formative effect of Soviet education.

This is likely one of the major specific events in the history of Russian and Eastern European psychology. This single measure was the official signal announcing the demolition of psychology across the entire Eastern Block – that is, the states that would become communist states less than 10 years later. This political act alone set in motion a series of events that gradually dismantled the solid foundations of psychological science across the entire region.

During the late 1950s, in the Czechoslovakian Republic Psychology ceased to exist as a standalone academic discipline: it was declared unscientific and was replaced with the study of cerebral physiology and neural activity. The countless vocational centers and psychotechnical laboratories were dissolved, the practice of psychological assessment surviving only in very specific areas of industry or work-related contexts, as it did in most of the communist countries.

In the Republic of Yugoslavia, the specific Stalinist approach to the dismantling of psychology is well documented. As an effect of the Radio Bucharest broadcast of a Resolution of the Informbiro on June 28, 1948 in which Yugoslavia was accused of "straining from the party line" the Fifth Congress of the Communist Party of Yugoslavia was held only three weeks later and concluded on the need to "ideologically deal with the class enemy" (Matković, 2003). Following the congressional demand to deal with the intelligentsia who opposed the establishment of the "people's democracy," communist students of the Faculty of Philosophy in Zagreb conducted an ideological confrontation with professors, assistants, and students whom the Party determined to be "enemies of the people." The confrontation with professors at the Department of Psychology, mainly such eminent figures as Ramiro Bujas, Zoran Bujas, and assistant Adela Ostojcic (1908–2008), occurred on December 18, 1948. In these proceedings, it was determined that tests, as a Western ideological procedure aiding class reproduction, should be labeled as a "nonscientific method" and banned, as in the Soviet Union. Psychological knowledge was reduced to Russian psychological textbooks, psychological testing being regarded as a particularly dangerous and consequently unscientific practice.

As Yugoslavia was undergoing an intense industrialization, practices of psychophysiological assessment were heavily regulated but still permitted within institutions such as the Industrial Hygiene Institute (Marinkovic, 1992); the only real testing existed within the framework of professional guidance (Matešić, 2006).

We also note that Yugoslavia likely resisted more than any other ex-communist country and used the first occasion to reconstruct testing: the official ban on tests and testing lasted only until 1951, when Yugoslavia joined the International Labour Office. Due to international demands, the Counselling Centre for Professional Guidance was re-established in 1952, headed by one of the psychologists fired in 1948, and since the archives had been preserved, the tests also survived and vocational guidance was immediately revitalized.

The Association of Psychologists of the Federal Peoples Republic of Yugoslavia was established in February 1953 and Ramiro Bujas (Zagreb) was elected president. The Psychological Society of the Peoples Republic of Serbia was established in June of the same year, counting about 15 members, with Borislav Stevanovic (Belgrade) being elected as president. The group grew into what is now the Serbian Psychological Society, active today in running the Centre for Applied Psychology (CAP), a company that publishes a number of psychodiagnostic instruments, aside from a journal (*Psychology*), a newsletter ("Psychological News"), and books written by its members, primarily university professors (Stojanovic, 2003). Interestingly, while nominally part of the same country (Yugoslavia), psychologists from the various states did not cooperate very much. Tests developed in Serbia were not administered in Croatia and Slovenia; the same applied to tests created in Croatia. The only notable exception may well be the publication of tests in the so-called "Serbo-Croatian" language in Slovenia, which were then distributed to the rest of the country (Bele-Potocnik, 1974, 1984).

In this context, it is also worthwhile to mention the contributions of Slovenian, Macedonian, and Bosniac psychologists to the development of tests and testing. Mihajlo Rostohar (1878–1966) is credited for the development of psychology in Slovenia. He studied psychology under Alexius Meinong in Graz, obtaining his doctorate in 1906 in Vienna. In 1911 he began his academic career at the Charles University in Prague, and following the fall of the Austro-Hungarian Empire, Rostohar participated in the establishment of the University of Ljubljana in 1919 but later left Slovenia, returned to Czechoslovakia, and became a professor at Masaryk University in Brno, where he remained until 1939. In 1950 he established the Department of Psychology in Ljubljana (Slovenia), working in the field of child psychology. The center of psychodiagnostic instruments established in Ljubljana, Slovenia was very active in publishing psychological measures. In Bosnia and Herzegovina, the development of testing began in the early 1960s when psychologists primarily educated in Serbia and partially in Slovenia and Croatia returned to their state of origin. The Department of Psychology of the University of Sarajevo was only established in 1989; however, the School of Pedagogy and Psychology was established at the same university in 1969, educating pedagogist-psychologists as experts for work in schools. These specialists were using a limited repertoire of tests developed mainly in Croatia, Serbia, and Slovenia. In the Republic of North Macedonia, the study of psychology was established in the early 1970s at the Faculty of Philosophy of the St. Cyril and Methodius University. Tests from the Belgrade Centre for Applied Psychology were primarily used; some of these tests were translated into the Macedonian language.

In Poland only two Silesian institutes of psychology survived the Soviet purge against the profession (Dryjanska, 2016). Similar developments followed in most Eastern European countries. In Romania a particularly brutal oppression against psychology occurred during the late 1970s (Iliescu et al., 2007). All the psychology departments were disbanded and professional practice was outlawed with many academics and practitioners being forced to find other areas of work, mostly in positions for which they were overqualified (Ionet al., 2017). In most of the Eastern European countries the practice of psychological assessment was completely expelled from educational and clinical fields, surviving only in those areas where it was deemed as a necessity – industry and transportation. The accelerated development of a centralized but otherwise inefficient industrialization depended on a large number of workers, and this necessity was responsible for the survival of psychological assessment practices in factory-based psychological laboratories. Psychologists working in such laboratories were allowed to use psychometric assessment only with the purpose of establishing the basic fitness for work (Ion et al., 2017).

Very little information about the practice of psychological assessment in the communist block is available after the Iron Curtain fell over Europe. In the 1957 issue of the French journal *Bulletin of the National Institute for the Study of Work and Vocational Guidance*, an article authored by members of the Moscow Academy of Pedagogy mentioned "the method of *tests* pretends to allow an exact and objective diagnosis and even prediction. One knows that as a group, Soviet psychologists do not favor the method. They are not opposed to short tasks furnishing quantitative results, but on the condition that one has an understanding of their psychological foundations" (Fraisse & Piaget, 1968). As outlined by Cervin (1964), the university curriculum for psychology included general psychology (developmental psychology, consciousness, cognition and thinking, internal regulation of behavior, psychophysics, and sensory-motor processes), natural sciences (human biology and physiology, highly loaded with Pavlovian thought), mathematical sciences (probability theory and finite mathematics), philosophy, and advanced psychology courses (child psychology, psychology of work, physiological psychology, and abnormal psychology); psychological assessment and testing-related courses were nowhere to be found. A similar curriculum was adopted in the Czech Republic, with courses pertaining to individual differences and assessment being inexistent (Cervin, 1964).

With Czechoslovakia having such a strong psychotechnical tradition and a history of liberalism, a publisher specializing in editing psychological measures opened a business in Slovakia in 1968 (Psychodiagnostika; Klikperova-Baker et al. 2019), but the apparent resurrection of psychological testing did not last. In the aftermath of the Soviet military intervention from 1968, all the re-emerging psychological organizations were dismantled (Klikperova-Baker et al., 2019). The list of representative psychologists in Europe working in personnel selection before 1980, published by the International Association of Applied Psychology (IAAP, the former International Association of Psychotechnics) featured a total number of 12 psychologists from the Communistic Block, half of them representing the USSR, as compared to over 60 psychologists from France, Germany, Italy, Switzerland and the United Kingdom (Salgado et al., 2010).

A rare glimpse into the (communist) state of affairs on psychological assessment from behind the Iron Curtain was offered by Landy (1986). In the attempt to appear as a flexible and liberal leader, Ceausescu (Romania's dictator) allowed Frank Landy to visit Romania and to get in touch with a number of psychologists. The set of psychological measures available in the few industrial laboratories was, in reality, far wider than the authorities assumed to be the case or were aware of. Apart from a number of legacy measures from the "psychotechnical era," psychologists kept on using translated versions of renowned measures of cognitive ability and personality, such as Raven's Progressive Matrices or the California Psychological Inventory. When not having access to the international "gold standards," psychologists working in these laboratories used to devise their own replicas. A similar pattern unfolded in the other countries as well. In Poland, for instance, psychological assessment survived as part of the practice of workplace safety and engineering psychology, various measures being in use within the Central Institute of Labor Protection, in Warsaw. In the former Yugoslavia, a country that departed through its 1965 political and economic reforms from Moscow's hard-liner stance not only in their foreign policy but also in other domains – psychology being among them – the practice and use of psychological assessments was not completely outlawed, but was rather shifted toward research, mainly conducted at the Vocational Guidance Center and the Psychological Institute (Matešić, 2006).

Drawing from the strong psychotechnical tradition and fading glory of the early days when psychological science was beginning to flourish in most of the Eastern European countries, the practice of psychological assessment endured the hardship of censorship and state-exerted ideological control. Poor quality copies or replicas of celebrated American or Western European measures could be found in most psychological institutes and laboratories. Although officially banned, psychologists still learned how to use the respective measures. Since the 1950s until the fall of the communist regime, several generations overcame the brutal restrictions, managing somehow to pass knowledge pertaining to the administration and interpretation of psychometric measures, ranging from basic cognitive functions to the more intricate and elaborate measurements of individual differences. What basically was an uninterrupted practice of psychological assessment can be regarded nowadays as an expression of freedom of thought, an assertion of the strong professional identity of psychologists, that surpassed state-driven censorship.

10.4   The Revival

After the fall of communism and the return of the Eastern European states to democracy and independence from the Soviet Union, psychology quickly became re-established in all these countries – and psychological testing assessment re-emerged with a vengeance. Both indigenous test production and adaptations of established international "gold standards" emerged. Tests began to be taught in universities, and to be intensively used in practice in all domains, re-occupying the territory that had been denied to them previously. Test publishers were established in all these countries. The whole ecosystem of testing was reconstructed in an evolution that took about 15–20 years. At this moment, testing in all Eastern European countries is a mature activity, with ties to international and European practice.

Publishers from all these countries have joined the European Test Publisher's Group (ETPG), a trade association that promotes ethical testing and strong standards of quality in test publishing. Many of them are also members of the European chapter of the Association of Test Publishers (E-ATP). Researchers and practitioners from these countries are habitual participants in conferences of the International Test Commission (ITC), the European Association for Psychological Assessment (EAPA) and the Psychometric Society (PS).

Re-emergence of testing out of the dark ages imposed by communism was from many points of view difficult. First, in all these countries, testing survived "through the grapevine," with testing materials of low quality, often without authors, and almost always infringing on intellectual property. The natural and habitual practice of those psychologists who were using tests, a practice that was transmitted further in universities, was based on test usage without observance of intellectual property rights. This rampant copyright infringement gradually subsided, while psychologists began to see the advantages of professionally published, updated, and well-tended measures. Second, many of the tests in usage were outdated: old forms of international measures that had in the meantime undergone several revisions in the West were only slowly relinquished by psychologists and university professors and replaced in practice with the new and updated forms. Third, cultural test adaptation was not necessarily the intensively scientific process that is recommended by current consensus (ITC, 2017; Iliescu, 2017). Contemporary psychometric practices in test adaptation and norming were only slowly adopted and accepted.

At this moment, however, we consider this transition to be finished. The repertoire of professionally published tests available in each of these countries ranges from a few dozen to over 100. All domains of testing are represented in almost all these countries, from the work-related and vocational counseling related measures that had been timidly used historically, to newly adapted and adopted measures for usage in clinical, forensic, and other applied settings. We note in this context that test adaptation and construction in many of these countries is significantly impacted by the high costs and low return that is typical for countries with smaller populations. It costs just as much to develop a measure in the United States as in Montenegro – only that servicing a population of 327 million is different in return than servicing a population little above 0.6 million people.

10.5   Conclusion

The more than tumultuous past of the geographical region of Eastern Europe and Russia has had strong repercussions on the development of psychological testing practices. The development of assessment instruments and testing models still largely depends on the population volume and economic situation of the various individual states. In many Eastern European countries, testing was the object of state-driven censorship and professional ban, surviving only in laboratories where the use of psychological tests and measures was considered a necessity. After the fall of the communist regime, when the profession was reinstated, the influence of laboratory-like psychophysiological assessment ran high until the early 2000s. Gradually, as psychological research and practice developed, reconnecting with the psychological science in Western Europe and the United States, test publishers gradually emerged in each country, enabling the use of "gold standard" measures in all the areas of applied psychology. Nowadays, apart from the sporadic encounter with obsolete and poorly photo-copied outdated tests, the practice of psychological testing is virtually indistinguishable from that encountered in Western Europe or North America.

In the years to come, psychological testing is expected to follow a similar trend as the one encountered in the United States and most countries in Western Europe. Psychological assessments powered by intelligent technologies (e.g., artificial intelligence) are gradually becoming available in this region, especially in personnel selection. Features like computer-generated reporting and synchronous/a-synchronous virtual assessments are also expected to be more and more popular in several areas of applied psychology. In clinical psychology the pace of adopting such technologies is very likely to be slower compared to I-O psychology because most of the healthcare systems are still public, having a slower rate of adopting intelligent technologies compared to the private companies.

REFERENCES

Bele-Potocnik, Z. (1974). Dejavnost Zavoda SR Slovenije za produktivnost dela pri razvoju psihodiagnosticnih sredstev v Sloveniji. U *Posvetovanje psihologov Slovenije o psihodiagnosticnih sredstvih* [Activity of the Institute for work productivity of SR Slovenia in the development of psychodiagnostic instruments in Slovenia]. November 1973 (pp. 8–14). Ljubljana: Drustvo psihologov Slovenije/Society of Psychologists of Slovenia.

(1984). Prikaz i ocjena opremljenosti psiholoske djelatnosti raznih podrucja sa psihodijagnostickim instrumentima [Presentation and assessment of psychological practice in various fields as equipped with psychodiagnostic instruments]. In K. Matešić (ed.). *Prvo jugoslavensko savjetovanje o psihologijskim mjernim instrumentima [First Yugoslav Consultation on Psychology Measuring Instruments]* (pp. 23–32). Zagreb: Drustvo psihologa SR Hrvatske i Ljubljana: Zavod SR Slovenije za produktivnost dela, Center za psihodiagnosticna sredstva/Society of Psychologists SR Croatia and Ljubljana: Institute of Sr Slovenia for Work Productivity, Center for Psychodiagnostic Funds.

Bujas, R., Pregrad, Z., & Agapov, M. (1935). *Preradba americke tzv. Alfa-serije, sistema za ispitivanje inteligencije odraslih.* Za internu upotrebu [*The adaptation of the American Alpha series system for intelligence testing in adults.* For internal use]. Zagreb: Consulting station on the choice of vocation of the Chamber of Commerce and Industry in Zagreb/Stanica za savjetovanje o izboru zvanja Trgovinsko-indusrijske komore u Zagrebu.

Cervin, V. B. (1964). Comparison of psychological curricula at French, Russian, Czech and Canadian universities. *Canadian Psychologist/Psychologie Canadienne, 5*(2), 75.

Dryjanska, L. (2016). Industrial-organizational psychology in Poland: Past and current trends. *Организационная психология/ Organizational 6*(4), 8–13.

Fradkin, F. A. (1990). *A search in pedagogics.* Moscow: Progress.

Fraisse, P. (1955). Positions de la psychologie soviétique [Positions of Soviet psychology]. *Les Études Philosophiques/Philosophical Studies, 10*(3), 492–495.

Fraisse, P. & Piaget, J. (1968). *Experimental psychology: Its scope and Method.* New York: Basic Books.

Iliescu, D. (2017). *Adapting tests in linguistic and cultural situations.* Cambridge: Cambridge University Press.

Iliescu, D., Ispas, A., & Ilie, A., (2007). Psychology in Romania. *The Psychologist, 20* (1), 34–35.

ITC. (2017). *The ITC guidelines for translating and adapting tests* (2nd ed.). Retrieved from www.InTestCom.org.

Klicperová-Baker, M., Hoskovcová, S., & Heller, D. (2019). Psychology in the Czech lands: Bohemia, Czechoslovakia, and the Czech Republic. *International Journal of Psychology 55*(2), 133–143.

Koltsova, V. A., Noskova, O. G., & Oleinik, Y. N. (1990). Isaak N. Spielrein and Soviet psychotechnics. *Soviet Journal of Psychology, 11*(2), 95–122.

Landy, F. J. (1986). Psychology in Romania. *The Industrial-Organizational Psychologist, 24,* 21–25.

Leopoldoff, I. (2014). A psychology for pedagogy: Intelligence testing in USSR in the 1920s. *History of Psychology, 17*(3), 187–205. doi: 10.1037/a0035954.

Margineanu, N. (1929). Psihotehnica in Germania [Psychotechnics in Germany]. Cluj-Napoca: Publishing House of the Institute of Psychology of Cluj University.

(1938). Elemente de psihometrie [Elements of psychometry]. Cluj-Napoca: Publishing House of the Institute of Psychology of Cluj University.

(1942). Psihotehnica in marea industrie [Psychometrics in the great industry]. Cluj-Napoca: Publishing House of the Institute of Psychology of Cluj University.

(1943). Psihotehnica [Psychometrics]. Cluj-Napoca: Publishing House of the Institute of Psychology of Cluj University.

Marinkovic, K. (1992). The history of psychology in Former Yugoslavia: An overview. *Journal of the History of Behavioral Sciences, 28*(4), 340–351.

Matešić, K. (2006). Treće razdoblje razvoja testova i postupaka testiranja u Republici Hrvatskoj od 1952. do 1991. godine [The third period of test development and testing practices in the republic of Croatia from 1952 to 1991]. *Suvremena psihologija/Contemporary Psychology, 9*(2), 213–227

(2011). *80 years of lifelong career guidance in the Republic of Croatia: New challenges and approaches.* Zagreb: Croatian Employment Service (pp. 13–15). Retrieved from http:/Avww.hzz.hr/UserDocsImagcs/Zbomik_radova_konferencije_80_god_CPU_u_RH.pdf.

(2017). HR-DAZG -239. Zavod za psihologiju I fiziologiju rada. [HR-DTG-239 – Bureau for Professional psychology and physiology]. *Suvremena psihologija/Contemporary Psychology, 20*(2), 197–206. doi:10.21465/2017-SP-202-06.

Matković, H. (2003). *Povijest Jugoslavije – 1918–1991–2003. [The History of Yugoslavia – 1918–1991–2003]*. Zagreb: Naklada Pavičić.

Necaev, A. P. (1925). *Rukovodstvo k eksperimental'no-psihologiceskomu issledovaniju detej doskol'nogo i skol'nogo vostrasta* [Instructions for experimental and psychological study of preschool and school children]. Moscow: Moszdravotdel.

Pavlina, Z. (1986). Ramiro Bujas kao nas suvremenik [Ramiro Bujas as our Contemporary]. *Primijenjena psihologija/Applied Psychology, 7*(1–4), 144–152.

(1989). Bujas, Ramiro. In V. Faust & I. Kurelac, *Hrvatski biografski leksikon, sv. 2 – Bj – C [Croatian Biographical Lexicon, St. Peter's 2–Bj–C]* (pp. 451–453).

Zagreb: Yugoslav Lexicographic Institute "Miroslav Krleza"/Jugoslavenski Leksikografski Zavod "Miroslav Krleza."

Petrovskij, A. V. (1991). Zapret na komplejsnoe issledovanie deststva [Ban on complex research about childhood]. In M. G. Jarosevskij (ed.), *Repressirovannaja nauka [Repressed science]* (pp. 126–135). Moscow: Nauka.

Pitariu, H. D. (1992). I-O Psychology in Romania: Past, Present, and Intentions. *The Industrial-Organizational Psychologist, 29(4),* 29–33.

Pregrad, Z. (1933). *Preradba Binet-Bobertagova sistema ispitivanje inteligencije. Za internu upotrebu* [The adaptation of the Binet-Bobertag system of intelligence testing. For internal use]. Zagreb: Station for consultation on the selection of titles at the Chamber of Commerce in Zagreb/Stanica za savjetovanje o izboru zvanja pri Trgovinskoj komori u Zagrebu.

   (1935). *Preradba Binet-Termanova sistema za ispitivanje inteligencije* [The adaptation of the Binet-Terman system of intelligence testing; based on the Czech adaptation by C. Stejskal]. Zagreb Station for consultation on the selection of titles at the Chamber of Commerce in Zagreb/Stanica za savjetovanje o izboru zvanja pri Trgovinskoj komori u Zagrebu.

Pregrad, Z. & Agapov. M. (1937). *Preradba americke tzv. Beta-serije za ispitivanje opce intelektualne darovitosti nepismenih* [The adaptation of the American Beta series for testing general intellectual abilities of the illiterate]. Zagreb: Station for consultation on the selection of titles at the Chamber of Commerce in Zagreb/Stanica za savjetovanje o izboru zvanja Trgovinske komore u Zagrebu.

Radosavljevic, P. R. (1912). *Uvod u eksperimentalnu pedagogiju, drugi dio, Opca eksperimentalna didaktika* [Introduction to experimental pedagogy, part two, General experimental didactics]. Zagreb: Hrv. pedagosko-knjizevni zbor/ Croatian Pedagogical-Book Choir.

Roser, M. & Ortiz-Ospina, E. (2019). *Global rise of education.* Published online at OurWorldInData.org. Retrieved from: https://ourworldindata.org/global-rise-of-education.

Salgado, J. F., Anderson, N. R., & Hülsheger, U. R. (2010). Employee selection in Europe: Psychotechnics and the forgotten history of modern scientific employee selection. In J. L. Farr & N. T. Tippins (eds.), *Handbook of employee selection* (pp. 921–941). London: Routledge/Taylor & Francis Group.

Stefănescu-Goangă, F. (1935). *Selecţiunea capacităţilor şi orientarea profesională [Capacity selecting and professional orientation].* Cluj-Napoca: Cartea Românescă/Romanian Books.

Stevanovic, B. P. (1934): *Razvice decje inleligencije i Beogradska revizija Bine-Simonove skale* [The development of child intelligcnce and the Belgrade revision of the Binet–Simon Scale]. Belgrade: Posebna izdanja/Special Editions of SKA CII.

Stojanovic, M. (2003). *Pedeset godina Drustva psihologa Srbije* [Fifty years of the Serbian Psychological Society]. Belgrade: Drustvo psihologa Srbije/Society of the Psychologists of Serbia.

Zebec-Silj, I. & Zebec, M. (2018). Osnivanje i djelatnost Stanice za savjetovanje pri izboru zvanja od 1931 do 1948. godine – Pocetak primijenjene psihologije u Hrvatskoj [The establishment and activitics of The Vocational counseling center 1931–1948 – The beginning of applied psychology in Croatia]. *Suvremena psihologija/Contemporary Psychology*, *21*(1), 5–28. doi:10.214652018-SP211-01.

Ion, A., Sulea, C., Ilie, A, Ispas, D., & Iliescu, D. (2017). Industrial and organizational psychology in Romania. *The Industrial Organizational Psychologist*, *51*(1), 3–5.

CHAPTER II

Hearing the Untold
A Review of Central Asia's Contribution to the Expansion of Psychological Assessment

Mostafa Zarean and Fatemeh S. Tarighat[1]

11.1 Introduction

In regional studies with a Central Asian focus, the countries of Pakistan, Afghanistan, Tajikistan, Uzbekistan, Kazakhstan, Turkmenistan, and Kyrgyzstan are usually grouped together. Moreover, depending on the nature and objectives of the study, Iran might also be considered in this group. Throughout the vast historical and political developments in the region in the past century, Iran has been affiliated with both Middle Eastern and Central Asian countries. It is true that Iran has had a significant role in the political transformations in the Middle East due to sharing closer ties in religious motivations and oil reserves with its Middle Eastern counterparts. However, when it comes to cultural and anthropological analyses, Iran also fits the profile of a Central Asian country. In this study, Iran is included in the Central Asian chapter because of its stronger association with the other countries in this region in culture, language, social approaches to education, and recent psychological advancements.

The regional information gathering is important for a better understanding of the population in each region. Central Asia is constantly undergoing significant social and political changes. In some cases, the chance to study the local populations has come up for the first time. The countries in this region have experienced multiple wars, famine, regime changes, territorial modifications, and economic advancements and setbacks throughout the past decades, which have all contributed to their current state. These struggles have imposed, and are imposing, tremendous mental strain on the individuals in the region. While some countries have begun the healing process, and have been working toward the improvement of the collective mental health, some are still far behind

---

[1] The authors would like to take this opportunity to thank Dr. Sayed Jafar Ahmadi at Kabul Education University of Rabbani for his insightful comments on the section 11.4 on Afghanistan.

socially and scientifically. Therefore, it seems that a glance at the psychological state of the countries through the lens of assessment would be beneficial in identifying the strengths and weaknesses of each country as a small step in serving the goal of maintaining mental health in the region.

Through data collection for this chapter, it became clear that of the countries included in this chapter, Iran and Pakistan possess the largest number of official records for research and country-specific contributions to the field of psychological assessment. Taking into account the historical background of the countries in the past six decades, the lack of evidence in certain areas of psychology is justified. In Afghanistan, for instance, the decades-long social and political turmoil has prevented the scholars of almost all fields from doing research in their respective areas of expertise. In many cases, the local researchers have been forced into exile out of the fear of execution, especially under the Taliban rule, or have had to halt their studies as a result of lack of funding, the instability of the educational system, or the fact that the dire social state in the country has called for realization of the basic human needs rather than fulfilling the secondary ones (Barfield, 2010; Lee, 2018; Wahab & Youngerman, 2010). Moreover, in the cases of Tajikistan, Uzbekistan, Kazakhstan, Turkmenistan, and Kyrgyzstan, it is important to consider the aftermath of the dissolution of the Soviet Union in 1991. Once socialist republics in the Soviet Union, all five countries have undergone tremendous social, political, and economic changes, and have had to face many challenges after declaration of independence (Dadabaev, 2017; Hiro, 2009).

For this study, because of the scarcity of online books and records, and a need for translation from the local languages, a questionnaire in English was designed to address the main issues specific to each country (Appendix 1). The questionnaire was divided into two sections. Section 1 included six questions addressing the basic information about psychological assessment in each country such as its origin in the county, its status as a university program, and its main local figures. Section 2 had two descriptive questions inquiring about the respondents' evaluation of psychological assessment in their country, and any further comments. The questionnaire was e-mailed to a number of current psychology professors and researchers in each country. The aim was to compare the data collected from the questionnaire with that available from official records. Unfortunately, despite the large number of individuals contacted for information, the participation level was very low. At this point the authors turned to translation of articles and information websites in the local languages, and going through the published papers in English as well as the online records of the universities in each country. Additionally, *WHO-AIMS Report on Mental Health System* (WHO, 2006, 2008, 2009) was used to check the validity of the collected information in some countries.

The following sections appear in the order of the amount of information gathered for this study. Each section starts with the recent historical state of the country and general information on psychology as an academic field of study, followed by specific information about psychological assessment. Wherever available, data related to the pioneers in the field, the current status of psychological assessment as a branch of higher education, and the contributions of the psychological assessment experts to the advancement of psychology in that country is included. The final portion of each section focuses on the future direction of psychological assessment in that country.

11.2   Iran

Psychological concepts had long been mentioned and discussed in the writings of Persian philosophers and polymaths. The term *nafs* (Arabic word meaning "self," "soul," and "psyche") was used to address mental state in the early writings in the region. Deriving from the philosophy of Plato and Aristotle, the Persian thinkers had presented modified notions of self and soul compatible with the social and religious contexts of their time. Early pre-Islamic and Islamic treatises on soul and interpretations of the Ancient Greeks' works by Arab polymaths, namely Abu Yusuf Ya'qub ibn Ishaq al-Kindi (c. 801–873), had also influenced the Persian philosophers. Abu Nasr al-Farabi (c. 872–950) had written extensively on intellect and human imaginative faculty, namely in *Opinions of the Inhabitants of the Virtuous City* (Fakhry, 2002). However, the significance of psychological assessment and the role of mental stability in human well-being were first mentioned in the writings of Muhammad ibn Zakariya al-Razi (also known as Rhazes; c. 854–925), and Ibn Sina (also known as Avicenna; c. 980–1037). Rhazes and Avicenna were pioneers in clinical observations of mental disorders and introducing an experimental aspect in the study of *nafs*. After Avicenna, the studies of soul had adopted a more Islamist tone, with a stronger emphasis on God. There were also attempts to dismiss the teachings of the Ancient Greek philosophers and replace them with Islamic approaches, as was the case in Abu Hamid al-Ghazali's (c. 1058–1111) *Tahafut al-Falasifa* (Raju, 2016).

Rhazes believed it to be crucial to consider the mood and mental state of patients when treating them for any physical ailments. He argued that there were instances where the causes of certain physical pains and illnesses were solely traceable in the patients' mental and emotional states. He had documented his psychiatric and psychological observations and findings in *Al-Hawi*, one of his many influential texts on medicine, along with other medical documentations and detailed case histories (Iskandar, 2016). Decades later, Avicenna extensively examined human soul (*nafs*) and intellect theoretically in *Kitab al-Shifa* and *Kitab al-Najat*. The sixth chapter of the second book of *Kitab al-Najat* (translated into English by Fazlur Rahman in 1952) is dedicated to soul, intuition, intellect, and active intelligence along with evidences in support of Avicenna's arguments (Rahman, 1981). These early contributions to classical psychology and assessment have been substantial to the development of future texts and treatises both within the Persian territory and in the West. It should be noted that since modern-day Central Asian countries were all part of Persia at the time of the early contributions, the impact of the writings and discoveries of the early scholars has always been present throughout the region, even after several territorial modifications, and has not been limited to modern-day Iran.

Psychology in its modern sense made its debut in contemporary Iranian academic circles in the 1950s as part of the curriculum for philosophy and educational sciences (Ghasemzadeh & Hamidpour, 2011). Shortly after the establishment of psychology as an independent field of study at the University of Tehran in the country's capital, the leading psychologists, all graduates of psychology doctoral programs abroad, began organizing more scientific course material with the aim of strengthening the program there, and establishing more psychology programs at a small number of other universities in other cities. The initial texts were translations of works being taught at universities in Europe and Northern America at that time. Of the earliest texts verifying psychology as a scientific field were *Ilm-un-Nafs or Psychology from the Education Perspective* by Ali Akbar Siasi (1895–1990), and *Assessing Intelligence or Practical Psychology* by Mohammad Bagher Hooshyar (1905–1957) (Ghasemzadeh & Hamidpour, 2011).

The establishment of psychological assessment and psychometrics as academic concentrations in psychology in Iran dates back to the 1960s. With psychology growing as an academic field, there was a need to provide the scholars with the necessary tools to make their studies and findings scientifically valid. For that matter, psychometric references of the West were translated and standardized to become applicable to the Iranian populations/samples and studies. Two of the pioneers in introducing psychometrics in the Iranian psychology community were Heidar Ali

Hooman (1932–2012) and Mohammad Naghi Baraheni (1932–2002). Hooman took on the task of standardizing the Tehran–Stanford–Binet Intelligence Scale, the first example of such standardization in Iran. Around the same time, Baraheni provided the Iranian researchers with the first translations of the 1954 book *Psychological Assessment* by Anne Anastasi, and the 1967 book *Test Theory* by David Magnusson. Hooman has been referred to as the "father of psychometrics" while Baraheni is known as the "father of psychological assessment" in Iran. Amir Houshang Mehryar was another figure who contributed to the early preparation of texts in psychological assessment and psychometrics by publishing a book entitled *Statistical Methods in Behavioral Sciences* at Shiraz University in 1970.

With the growing number of psychologists training in psychological assessment and psychometrics, more tests and scales were being standardized in Iran. However, the 1979 Iranian Revolution was followed by closing the universities as part of a cultural readjustment plan called the Cultural Revolution, which lasted from 1980 to 1983 and halted scientific research in all fields. During that period, psychology researchers focused their attention on writing and translating new materials for the time the universities would reopen. The year 1980 also marked the beginning of the Iran–Iraq war, which lasted until 1988. Although academic efforts in universities were going on to a degree during the war, academia faced significant setbacks. The already new and understrength field of psychological assessment, which was in its early phases of development and was adjusting itself to the international standards, had to deal with the challenges of war that would directly affect the Iranian populations and demographic data. Nevertheless, studies at the academic facilities, mainly in Tehran, were being conducted. Parirokh Dadsetan (1933–2010) was a prominent psychologist who mainly conducted research from a developmental perspective. Starting in 1984, a number of tests were being standardized under her supervision in Tehran. After the war, psychological assessment research gradually gained momentum. In 1992, Hamzeh Ganji published a Persian translation of *Psychologie de l'évaluation scolaire* by Georges Noizet and Jean-Paul Caverni. In 1995, Dadsetan authored a book entitled *Personality Assessment in Children Using Drawing Tests*.[2]

Currently, three universities offer programs in psychometrics as an independent field at graduate level under the title of Assessment and Measurement. All located in Tehran, the universities are the University

---

[2] Biography of Dr. Parirokh Dadsetan. Retrieved from https://psyedu.ut.ac.ir/.

of Tehran (doctoral program),[3] Allameh Tabataba'i University (master's and doctoral programs), and Islamic Azad University Central Tehran Branch (master's program). The programs cover a variety of fundamental courses including advanced measurement theories, nonparametric statistics, multivariate statistics, item response theory, factor analysis, structural equation modeling, and assessment tool design. In addition to the specialized programs in Tehran, psychometrics and assessment are among the mandatory courses for all psychology students in Iran. Moreover, students and researchers all over the country are encouraged to regularly participate in psychometrics training courses and workshops to gain knowledge, and in psychology conferences to share their findings with fellow researchers. During the past three decades, many psychological researchers from various universities in the country have contributed to the advancements of psychological assessment and psychometrics. Nevertheless, home to the three universities offering assessment and measurement programs, Tehran remains the scientific center for advancements in psychological assessment.

At present, Hasan Pasha Sharifi and Ali Delavar are two of the main forerunners in the field. Sharifi, who published his first book on psychological and educational assessment in the late 1960s, has been regularly authoring, coauthoring, and translating books on psychological assessment and psychometrics. Delavar has chiefly focused on applied statistics in psychology in his books. The main Iranian scholarly journal dedicated solely to psychological assessment and psychometrics is the *Quarterly of Educational Measurement* for which Delavar and Sharifi serve as the editor in chief and an editorial board member respectively.[4] Moreover, the *Psychometry Quarterly* of the Islamic Azad University Roudehen Branch publishes papers on assessment and psychometrics.[5] In addition to these specialized publications, there are over 40 Iranian psychology journals certified by the Ministry of Science, Research, and Technology that regularly publish psychological assessment papers among other studies. *International Journal of Psychology*, *Journal of Applied Psychological Research*, and *Journal of Psychological Achievements* are three of the well-known publications.[6]

---

[3] General information and lesson plan for assessment and measurement doctorate program. Retrieved from https://psyedu.ut.ac.ir/41
[4] Quarterly of Educational Measurement, http://jem.atu.ac.ir/?lang=en.
[5] Psychometry Quarterly, https://jpsy.riau.ac.ir/.
[6] International Journal of Psychology, www.ijpb.ir/; Journal of Applied Psychological Research, https://japr.ut.ac.ir/; Journal of Psychological Achievements, http://psychac.scu.ac.ir/.

Fortunately, Iranian psychological researchers have been able to maintain the progress in psychological assessment on a national level. In addition to the more experienced generation of researchers who contributed to the early flourishment of psychological research in Iran, several younger psychologists have been actively conducting new research according to the current needs of the society, updating and reevaluating the previous research to match the existing population, and translating the mainly computer-based new resources to keep up with the international trends in psychometrics. Data related to tests and assessment tools are usually archived in online databases and accessible to researchers. Moreover, the advancements in the other fields of science and engineering, especially neuroscience and software engineering, have facilitated the development and production of software programs and assessment devices in Iran.

In recent years, psychological testing and assessment have increasingly become a part of life on different levels. A growing number of Iranian public and private organizations are implementing psychological assessment tools as decisive factors in hiring and employee performance evaluation processes. Efforts to raise public awareness with regard to the significance of psychological studies and testing in enhancing the quality of life have proven to be effective, even though sometimes at a slow pace. The emphasis put on scientific testing and assessment tools in psychological research and practice by the State Welfare Organization of Iran and the Psychology and Counseling Organization of Iran has resulted in meticulous assessment implementations and more rigorous treatment plans (see PCOIRI, 2020). This national emphasis has also led to using current assessment techniques in categorizing students with special needs in the educational system. Iranian psychology students on both undergraduate and graduate levels have been able to update the overall quality of research. To that end, on graduate level, there has been a gradual shift from analysis of covariance to modeling, and from studying the effectiveness to meta-analysis or more complex patterns of analysis.

11.3   Pakistan

Up until the 1960s, psychology was being taught among the courses required for philosophy programs in Pakistan. Psychology as an independent academic discipline was established at the Government College, Lahore (GC now the Government College University, Lahore) in 1962 (Zadeh, 2017). Makhdum Muhammad Ajmal (1919–1994), who had studied philosophy at GC, obtained his Ph.D. in psychology from University College London. Upon graduation, Ajmal returned to GC to teach psychology at the department of philosophy. His efforts to help recognize psychology as an independent branch of study resulted in the establishment of the first department of psychology in Pakistan.

Independence from Britain in 1947 was the turning point in the history of psychology, and many other disciplines, in Pakistan. Prior to independence, when Pakistan was a part of the British India, Western and mainly British psychiatric and psychological methods were being implemented in the study, assessment, and treatment of mental health issues (Sohail et al., 2017). After independence, the Western approaches remained predominant, and psychological research was still highly influenced by the Western notions common in British India well into the 1960s. When Pakistan became an Islamic Republic in 1956, the scientific research underwent further change. A tendency to introduce Islamic doctrine into the psychological methods was becoming popular. After the establishment of the first psychology department in Pakistan, Ajmal (1968) started encouraging the move toward infusing Islamic tradition in psychotherapy.

One significant issue to be considered here is that, due to the British rule in the region and the presence of schools and colleges where lessons and lectures were provided in English, a large number of the local scholars were familiar with English. Therefore, the initial approach seemed to be not direct translation of foreign texts into Urdu, but preparing new texts modified in accordance with the Pakistani and Islamic tradition. Although Western tests have been regularly adapted to study intelligence, personality, and aptitude in the Pakistani population (Suhail, 2004), there have been attempts to develop assessment tools and inventories specific to the Pakistani culture. One of the earliest attempts was the Ghazali Personality Inventory (Rizvi, 1978), developed based on the teachings of Al-Ghazali with three scales determining the degree of normality with reference to bodily needs, social behavior, and divine force (Suhail, 2004). A more recent example of an attempt to include religiosity as a crucial indicator for personality is the Multi Dimensional Personality Inventory (Zeb et al., 2013), which considers religion as the most influential aspect of personality.

Previous information on the psychological research has shown that between 1980 and 1986, testing and assessment were the main topics of research in Pakistani psychology papers (Ansari, 1982; Suhail, 2004). The statistical analysis in the studies published before 1987 was mainly on a basic level, and only a small portion of studies used inferential statistics.

Suhail (2004) has reported improvements in the statistical analysis in the following decade; however, she has pointed out that the cases of advanced research methods such as multivariate, regression models, and discriminant analysis were still low in number.

Psychological testing and assessment along with psychometrics have been crucial to the structure of academic psychology programs from the beginning. Initially, introductory classes were taught in undergraduate programs in addition to several other courses. The establishment of graduate programs in Pakistan provided a chance to include advanced courses of assessment, statistics, and psychometrics in the curriculum. According to the department information for psychology programs available on university websites, Pakistani universities currently do not offer a program solely focused on and under the name of psychological assessment or psychometrics. However, the applied psychology master's and doctoral programs at the Institute of Applied Psychology (IAP),[7] University of the Punjab, are heavily focused on teaching psychological assessment methods and psychometrics. Similarly, the psychology graduate program at the National Institute of Psychology (NIP),[8] Quaid-i-Azam University, provides the students with comprehensive courses on psychological assessment and statistics. A third research facility called the Institute of Clinical Psychology (ICP),[9] University of Karachi, has also been contributing to assessment research in Pakistan since its inception in 1983. All three institutes have been conducting extensive research on assessment tools, standardization of psychological tests, and developing and validating indigenous psychological tests and scales in the Pakistani community.

A large body of standardized and randomized tests have been archived at all three institutes. The Testing Laboratory at IAP and the Test Resource Centre at NIP are the two main nationally recognized and trusted academic facilities for international and indigenous assessment. Several assessment tools and tests are being studied and randomized in the form of student theses and community projects annually. Two of the pioneering figures under whose supervision an ongoing number of assessment tools are being standardized or developed in the form of student theses are Farah

---

[7] Institute of Applied Psychology, http://pu.edu.pk/home/department/39.
[8] National Institute of Psychology, https://nip.edu.pk/.
[9] Institute of Clinical Psychology, Institute general information page, www.uok.edu.pk/research_institutes/icp/index.php.

Malik at IAP and Anila Kamal at NIP.[10] In addition, the research wing of ICP has been listing its master's and doctorate degree research topics since the 1980s. Farrukh Z. Ahmad, former professor and founder director of the institute, was an early leading figure in standardization and development of assessment tools.

The validation reports of these tests and scales are published in Pakistani journals. The authors were not able to locate any academic journals dedicated exclusively to psychological assessment and psychometrics. However, *Pakistan Journal of Psychological Research* and *Journal of Pakistan Psychiatric Society* are among the national scholarly journals publishing test validation papers on a regular basis. Moreover, *Pakistan Journal of Psychology*, the official publication of ICP, publishes assessment research among other topics.

Psychological assessment has been a valuable asset in employment processes in military and civil service (Suhail, 2004). Nevertheless, with mental health issues growing in Pakistan in past years (Sohail et al., 2017), there is an increasing need for more scientific research and systematic psychological assessment initiatives to tackle the psychological needs of the country. Advancement in psychological assessment and testing research is listed among the objectives of the Pakistani psychology departments (see IAP, 2019).

11.4   Afghanistan

The unrest that has been going on for the past 30 years has resulted in major setbacks in the academic and scientific development of Afghanistan. Apart from foreign invasions, domestic Islamic extremism has immensely hindered the social, cultural, economic, and academic achievements in the country. Academic progress has been interrupted by consecutive political and social conflicts that include, but are not limited to, the Saur Revolution in 1978, the Soviet–Afghan War between 1979 and 1989, two periods of Afghan Civil War (the first between 1992 and 1996, and the second between 1996 and 2001), and the current war in Afghanistan initiated by the invasion of the United States in 2001. This long-running instability has forced many of the researchers to move to other countries in search of a better life. Therefore, the study of the progression of

---

[10] List of scales/measures translated/adopted by Dr. Farah Malik. Retrieved from http://pu.edu.pk/images/image/Departments/appsy/Psychological_Translated-2018.pdf; Dr. Anila Kamal's faculty profile. Retrieved from https://nip.edu.pk/Facultyrpofiles/drAnilaKamal.html.

psychological assessment in Afghanistan is intertwined with the other branches of psychology. Moreover, because of the unique circumstances in Afghanistan, psychological research in general and psychological assessment in particular have been carried out on two levels: the continuation of the studies designed and funded by international organizations that have been in place since the 1990s; and the efforts made by the local psychology community members who have returned home after graduating from psychology programs abroad.

Psychology as a university program in Afghanistan has its roots in the field of education. The Education Faculty of Kabul University,[11] established in 1962, changed its name to Psychology and Educational Science Faculty years later. However, the main focus of the psychology teachings at the Faculty has remained educational due to the expertise of its professors (Ahmadi, online communication, February 15, 2020). Throughout the gradual recovery process of the academic system in Afghanistan, which began after the removal of the Taliban from power in late 2001, attempts have been made to strengthen the psychology programs at universities. Prior to strengthening the university programs, in 2007, periodic training courses of psychological assessment, diagnosis, and treatment for nurses and mental health workers began in Herat. The same year, the first undergraduate clinical psychology program was established at Eshraq Private University in Herat (Ahmadi, 2020).[12] The curriculum design followed the models of the Iranian universities since a number of professors involved in the process were graduates of psychology programs in Iran, and were familiar with the structure. In 2008, the first group of students was admitted into the program. Persian textbooks taught at the Iranian universities were used as teaching resources (Ahmadi, 2020).

For many years, a large portion of the reports and statistical information on psychology has come from the international organizations with foreign funding, usually with the help of local people and students in data collection and field work. A study entitled "The Afghan Symptom Checklist: A Culturally Grounded Approach to Mental Health Assessment in a Conflict Zone" is one of the most cited field analyses conducted in Kabul with the aim of identifying the indicators of distress. Released in 2006, the study was carried out under the supervision of Kenneth E. Miller, a psychologist, and Patricia A. Omidian, a medical anthropologist, by a group of local researchers. Miller and Omidian, both

---

[11] Kabul University, History. Retrieved from http://ku.edu.af/en/page/social-science/884/history.
[12] Eshraq Private University, http://eshraq.edu.af/.

experts in refugee studies and based outside of Afghanistan, have also done research on women's psychosocial well-being (2006), war experience (2008), and PTSD in Afghanistan (2009).

Psychological research and assessment made considerable progress in the 2010s. Comprehensive training programs were conducted by foreign agencies with the aim of professionally training mental health workers in Afghanistan. One such program was conducted under the supervision of Yousuf Rahimi, a psychiatrist from Wokingham, UK in 2013. Another important project with a stronger academic approach and a larger scope was the University Support and Workplace Development Program (USWDP), which was funded by the US Agency for International Development (USAID). With the goal of promoting the scientific potential at the universities of Afghanistan, in addition to other disciplines, USWDP recruited local psychologists to work with researchers outside Afghanistan on projects involving mental health.

Two significant steps were taken to enhance the state of psychological research, assessment, and practice on a national level. The first project involved dispatching researchers to provinces (*wilayats*) to gather information on the counseling needs of the society and the training needs of the mental health counselors. Data gathered from five provinces during six months was used to design a counseling university program, and the proposed design was handed to the Ministry of Education to be put into practice (Bragin & Akesson, 2018; Bragin et al., 2018). The second project involved determining how locals perceived "mental well-being" and defined the notion. Data for the culturally focused study was collected from five provinces. At the time of writing, the results of this study have not been published yet (Ahmadi, 2020). In addition to these two studies, USWDP facilitated a two-year training program for the psychologists in Kabul and Herat that included teachings by American, Canadian, and Indian professors, educational tours to India and Egypt, as well as field trips to various places in Afghanistan to gain practical knowledge (Ahmadi, 2020).

Considering the gradual advancements in psychological training and research in Afghanistan, the country has not been able to broadly implement psychological assessment in organizational settings with the aim of improving workplace productivity. The persistence of armed conflicts in Afghanistan seems to have focused the domestic and international attention on military settings to a greater degree compared to the other fractions of government and society. The foreign military forces deployed to Afghanistan have long included psychological assessments and interventions for their troops. In a sense, Afghanistan has become one of the ideal places for conducting assessment studies in military psychology for the foreign deployed troops (see Martinez-Sanchez, 2019). However, when it comes to domestic assessment research, studies are scant. Nevertheless, a larger portion of the available research is focused on the Afghan police force. The dire need for stability and security in the country justifies prioritizing police assessments for the time being. A number of foreign-funded researches have included psychological aspects in their studies, and have pinpointed some of the requirements to enhance performance with both general and gender-focused perspectives (see Kubota et al., 2016; Royal United Services Institute & Foreign Policy Research Institute, 2009). Meanwhile, Afghan researchers have been more active in assessment studies in civilian settings. They have taken steps to optimize mental health workforce and assessment tools as prerequisites to comprehensive assessment research (Ahmadi, 2020; Bragin et al., 2018) while getting help from the statistical information provided by a few international organizations such as the World Health Organization (WHO) and the International Psycho-Social Organization (IPSO).

Currently, the suboptimal condition of educational facilities and the lack of psychology professors with specialized expertise have made it difficult to design and organize systematic psychological assessment research or establish an independent psychometrics university program in Afghanistan. The analysis of the papers published by the professors and their commentaries on the necessary steps to improve psychological research and practice in Afghanistan indicates that enhancing the state of counseling and clinical psychology takes precedent over other aspects of psychological research at the moment (Ahmadi, 2020; Ayubi & Noori, 2018). In recent years, the professors at Kabul Education University of Rabbani, Kabul University, and Eshraq Private University have been addressing the psychological needs of the country more seriously and have published papers on them (see Ahmadi et al., 2018; Ayubi, 2018). In spite of the shortcomings in research and practice, the psychological research community of Afghanistan is making progress.

The group of psychologists who had taken part in the two-year training course by USWDP have shown better academic and practical competence (Ahmadi, 2020). This is why the current psychologist training approach in Afghanistan involves funding students' graduate studies at a number of prominent Iranian universities in Tehran, Mashhad, and Shiraz, and providing them with extra training courses in clinical assessment, research techniques, and statistics. The Persian textbooks of Iranian authors and Persian translations of international authors by Iranian translators are used in education and training. In addition to the ongoing research at universities in Kabul and Herat, a number of psychology professors have gathered at Behrawan Institute of Psychological Research and Services in Kabul with the aim of designing research projects, training mental health workers, building assessment tool archives, and counseling. Sayed Jafar Ahmadi, a professor at the University of Rabbani and the founder of Behrawan, has authored two books on research methods and statistics and a clinical interview pamphlet that is taught in Behrawan training courses. Apart from Ahmadi, Mohammadbaqir Rezaie, Seyed Rouhollah Rezvani, and Hossein Kaviani are active in clinical assessment research in Afghanistan. Kaviani, an Iranian clinical psychologist (nationality) at the University of Bedfordshire, UK, supervises collaborative research with Behrawan (Ahmadi, 2020).

11.5 Kazakhstan, Kyrgyzstan, Tajikistan, Turkmenistan, and Uzbekistan

Previously Soviet Socialist Republics, Kazakhstan, Kyrgyzstan, Tajikistan, Turkmenistan, and Uzbekistan declared their independence in the early 1990s. The rebuilding process after independence has been slow and rather similar for all of these countries. In addition to the economic and social strains instigated by the declaration of independence, the educational system suffered major setbacks mainly because of the funding cuts that were once in place while being part of the Soviet Union. The information retrieved from online sources and university websites show that many of the universities offering psychology programs, whether independently or jointly with another discipline, have been established after independence.

Unfortunately, the smallest amount of data could be gathered for this section. Based on the available research records at some of the universities, on an academic level, psychology is mainly imbedded in pedagogical and social science – such as the programs at Tashkent State Pedagogical University (Uzbekistan), or the programs offered by the Social Work and Practical Psychology Department at Bishkek State University (Kyrgyzstan). Although there are a number of departments focusing solely on psychology, psychological research and assessment has been carried out mainly in the form of educational studies (Qarshieva, 2019). Considering the age of the psychology departments and the low number of psychology professors with assessment and psychometrics expertise in these countries, advancement in psychological assessment and psychometrics will be a gradual process. This will require designing and offering university training courses focused on tests and assessments, implementing the assessment and analysis knowledge in the society while considering the specific ethnic and cultural issues, and increasing the level of data sharing with other countries, especially the neighboring ones, among other things.

In recent years, there have been cases of standardizing tests in the local communities. Such studies will gradually enrich the tests and assessments archives in these countries. As with the test and assessment resources, despite Russian not being the official language in these countries, it is vastly used in all of them. This makes it possible for the researchers of any field to use Russian texts whenever enough material is not available in their own language. Moreover, because of the existing sociocultural similarities, the scientifically reliable original psychology texts and assessment archives in Russia provide the researchers of these five countries with strong theoretical and applied bases which can expedite the development and refinement of country-specific psychological notions and researches.

11.6   Conclusion

Psychological assessment is a specialized branch of psychological science which requires systematic training and continuous test modifications according to international scientific standards along with culture-based features and needs of the demographics. Despite the ongoing efforts in the region to standardize the internationally valid psychological tests and assessment tools, the rate at which the Central Asian countries are making progress might not be satisfactory. As it has been mentioned throughout the chapter, a combination of factors has been curtailing the regional progress in the field. The ongoing conflicts in Central Asia throughout the past decades have weakened the efforts made by the researchers in each country in contributing to the advancement of psychological science in general and psychological assessment in particular. Each nation in the region has dealt with wars, famine, geopolitical challenges, sociocultural uprisings, and drastic shifts in social structure at some point in its recent history. Additionally, the existing stigma associated with mental health issues and seeking help from psychologists contributes to the generally slow pace of psychological research. The situation is even more challenging in the areas with lower rates of literacy, the areas adhering to more traditional and religious values, the areas lacking mental health professionals and facilities, and the areas involved in territorial disputes.

There are certain steps that would enhance the overall state of psychological research in the Central Asian countries, which would subsequently boost psychological assessment and psychometrics. These steps require the participation of various members of a society, from legislature to ordinary citizens. Firstly, effective measures should be taken to clarify the significance of mental health research. Secondly, capable mental health workers should be adequately trained to take on the tasks at theoretical and practical levels. In societies with skepticism toward mental health studies and services, only highly trained professionals with regards to techniques, potentials, culture, and ethnic needs would be able to gain public trust. Thirdly, all branches of psychological science should cooperate in and contribute to planning and executing researches. Finally, the collaborative research should go beyond borders to build comprehensive archives of assessment tools and research histories in the region with respect to cultural similarities and differences. Cultural and linguistic commonality in the region could expedite the advancements in the various branches of psychology. Hopefully, once the more general milestones are achieved in assessment and testing research, it will become possible to scientifically assess more sensitive topics, which have not been explored due to cultural limitations, on a large scale.

Despite the efforts to get local researchers from the countries mentioned in this chapter involved in the development of the material, little to no information was shared by the contacted researchers. Except for section 11.2 dedicated to Iran, the information for the other sections inevitably remained at a general level due to the lack of resources. The authors are hopeful that this chapter will encourage Central Asian psychological researchers to take steps toward discussing the state of psychological assessment and its future in their countries on an international level.

REFERENCES

Ahmadi, S. J. (2020, February 15), Personal online interview.

Ahmadi, S. J., Kajbaf, M. B., Neshat Doost, H. T., Dalgleish, T., Jobson, L., & Mosavi, Z. (2018). The efficacy of memory specificity training in improving symptoms of post-traumatic stress disorder in bereaved Afghan adolescents. *Intervention 16*(3), 243–248.

Ajmal, M. (1968). An introduction to Muslim tradition in psychotherapy. *Psychology Quarterly, 2*(4), 28–33.

Allameh Tabataba'i University. (n.d). Programs offered in psychometrics department. Retrieved from https://ped.atu.ac.ir/?fkeyid=&siteid=2&pageid=6065.

Ansari, Z. A. (1982). *Psychological research in Pakistan.* Islamabad: National Institute of Psychology.

Ayubi, B. (2018). Reflecting the potential role of family counseling in addressing emotional issues in Afghan youth. *Intervention 16*(3), 269–270.

Ayubi, B. & Noori, H. (2018). Addressing the mental health needs of many people with few resources: An interview with Dr. Rohullah Amin. *Intervention 16*(3), 202–206.

Barfield, T. (2010). *Afghanistan: A cultural and political history.* Princeton, NJ: Princeton University Press.

Behrawan Institute of Psychological Research and Services. (n.d.). Retrieved from https://behrawan.com/.

Bragin, M., Akesson, B. (2018). Towards an Afghan counseling psychology: A partnership to integrate psychological counselling into the university curriculum at Afghanistan's flagship public universities. *Intervention 16*(3), 261–268.

Bragin, M., Akesson, B., Ahmady, M., Akbari, S., Ayubi, B., Faqiri, R., Faiq, Z., Oriya, S., Karimi, B. A., Azizi, B. A., Barakzai, F., Noori, H., Sharifi, K., Rasooli, M. H., Ahmadi, S. J., Wolfson, H., & Seddiqi, S. (2018). Developing a culturally relevant counseling psychology degree programme in Afghanistan: Results from a DACUM study. *Intervention 16*(3), 231–242.

Dadabaev, T. (2017). Evaluations of perestroika in post-Soviet Central Asia: Public views in contemporary Uzbekistan, Kazakhstan and Kyrgyzstan. In T. Dadabaev & H. Komatsu (eds.), *Kazakhstan, Kyrgyzstan, and Uzbekistan: Life and politics during the Soviet era* (pp. 103–139). London: Palgrave Macmillan.

Fakhry, M. (2002). *Al-Farabi, founder of Islamic Neoplatonism: His life, work, and influence.* London: Oneworld.

Ghasemzadeh, H. & Hamidpour, H. (2011). *Selection of the works by the pioneers of scientific psychology in Iran.* Tehran: Arjmand.

Hiro, D. (2009). *Inside Central Asia: A political and cultural history of Uzbekistan, Turkmenistan, Kazakhstan, Kyrgyzstan, Tajikistan, Turkey, and Iran.* London: Duckworth Books.

IAP (2019). Prospectus IPA university of the Punjab. Retrieved from: http://pu .edu.pk/images/file/Prospectuses/Prospectus-APPSY-2019.pdf.

Iskandar, A. Z. (2016). Al-Razi. In H. Selin (ed.), *Encyclopedia of the history of science, technology, and medicine in non-Western cultures* (3rd ed., pp. 274–276). London: Springer.

Kubota, M., Takashi, N., Alam, M., Applebaum, A., & Mawby, B. (2016). *Strengthening the Afghan national police: Recruitment and retention of women officers.* Japan International Cooperation Agency & Georgetown Institute for Women, Peace and Security. Retrieved from: www.jica.go.jp/jica-ri/publica tion/booksandreports/l75nbg00000697z9-att/Case_Study_on_Afghanistan.pdf.

Lee, J. L. (2018). *Afghanistan: A history from 1260 to the present.* London: Reaktion Books.

Martinez-Sanchez, J. A. (2019). Spanish military psychology in international operations: Lessons learned in Afghanistan. *Psychologist Papers, 40*(2), 141–148.

Miller, K. E., Omidian, P., Kulkarni, M., Yaqubi, A., Daudzai, H., & Rasmussen, A. (2009). The validity and clinical utility of Post-traumatic Stress Disorder in Afghanistan. *Transcultural Psychiatry, 46*(2), 219–237.

Miller, K. E., Omidian, P., Quarashy, A. S., Quarshy, N., Nasiry, M. N., Nasiry, S., Karyar, N. M., & Yaqubi, A. A. (2006). The Afghan Symptom Checklist: A culturally grounded approach to mental health assessment in a conflict zone. *American Journal of Orthopsychiatry, 76*(4), 423–433.

Miller, K. E., Omidian, P., Rasmussen, A., Yaqubi, A., Daudzai, H. (2008). Daily stressors, war experience, and mental health in Afghanistan. *Transcultural Psychiatry, 45*(4), 611–639.

PCOIRI (Psychology and Counseling Organization of I.R. Iran). (n.d.). Specialty and professional scope of psychometrics. Retrieved from: www.pcoiran.ir/fa/commissions/ravansanji.

Qarshieva, D. S. (2019). Occupational stress in teachers and their psychological factors. *Central Asian Journal of Education, 3*(1), Article 5.

Rahman, F. (1981). *Avicenna's psychology: An English translation of Kitab al-Najat, book ii, chapter vi with historico-philosophical notes and textual improvement on the Cairo edition.* Westport, CT: Hyperion Press.

Raju, C. K. (2016). Logic. In H. Selin (ed.), *Encyclopedia of the history of science, technology, and medicine in non-Western cultures* (3rd ed., pp. 2564–2570). London: Springer.

Rizvi, A. A. (1978). Construction and development of Ghazali Personality Inventory. *Psychology Quarterly, 11*, 11–14.

Royal United Services Institute & Foreign Policy Research Institute (2009). *Reforming the Afghan National Police.* Retrieved from: www.fpri.org/docs/ReformingAfghanNationalPolice.pdf.

Sohail, S. A., Syed, A. A., & Rahman, A. (2017). Mental health in Pakistan: Yesterday, today and tomorrow. In H. Minas & M. Lewis (eds.), *Mental health in Asia and the Pacific: historical and cultural perspectives* (pp. 17–38). London: Springer.

Suhail, K. (2004). Psychology in Pakistan. *The Psychologist, 17*(11), 632–634.

Wahab, S., & Youngerman, B. (2010). *A brief history of Afghanistan* (2nd ed.). New York: Facts on File.

WHO. (2006). *WHO-AIMS report on mental health system in Afghanistan.* Retrieved from www.who.int/mental_health/evidence/Afghanistan_WHO_AIMS_Report.pdf.

(2008). *WHO-AIMS report on mental health system in the Kyrgyz republic.* Retrieved from www.who.int/mental_health/Kyrgyzstan_who_aims_report.pdf?ua=1.

(2009). *WHO-AIMS report on mental health system in the republic of Tajikistan.* Retrieved from www.who.int/mental_health/tajikistan_who_aims_report.pdf.

Zadeh, Z. F. (2017). Clinical psychology in Pakistan: past, present and future. *International Journal of Humanities and Social Science, 7*(11), 26–28.

Zeb, R., Riaz, M. H., & Jahangir, F. (2013). Development and validation of multidimensional personality inventory. *FWU Journal of Social Sciences, 7* (2), 113–123.

CHAPTER 12

History of Psychological Assessment in Southern Asia

Suresh Sundaram, Suresh Arumugam, and Asoke Kumar Saha

12.1 Introduction

The South Asian countries are said to be the psychological storehouse (Srivastava, 2012) in the form of ancient Indian literature that includes *Vedas*, the *Ramayana*, the *Mahabharata*, and the *Puranas*. The "Bhagavad Gita," the most famous section of the great ancient Indian epic the *Mahabharata*, mentions that India, Pakistan, Afghanistan, Nepal, Bhutan, Bangladesh, and Sri Lanka were kingdoms of the Indian subcontinent. The Indian subcontinent had a rich cultural heritage that is the birthplace of four major world religions, Hinduism, Buddhism, Jainism, and Sikhism. Unity in diversity is the essence of South Asian culture. The very diverse languages and language families of South Asia have made enormous contributions to world literature from ancient to modern times. As the largest country in South Asia, the historical continuity of India is stretching back thousands of years (Narayanan, 2014).

The chapter narrates the history of psychological assessment, both in ancient and modern times, highlighting how assessment is done in various settings in India, Sri Lanka, Bangladesh, Nepal, and Bhutan. As mentioned in the epics, the South Asian countries, excluding Maldives, were almost together as a single land with diversified kingdoms under the banner of an Indian subcontinent. The political boundaries of South Asia have changed dramatically, at various points, particularly after emergence and withdrawal of the British rule. Hence the principal areas of South Asia show a number of similarities and differences that make various overlapping divisions into social and cultural types (Tichelman, 1980). When compared with developed nations, psychology as a scientific field has underdeveloped in this region. Hence locating the distinctive history of psychological assessment from the general history of psychology was found challenging by the authors. This chapter begins by providing a brief account of assessment in the region during pre-colonialism. Secondly, the history of assessment in India is presented, followed by Sri Lanka, Bangladesh, Nepal, and Bhutan. The chapter ends with a brief conclusion.

12.2 Assessment in South Asia Pre-colonialism

In ancient days, kings and emperors practiced rudimentary methods of applying psychological knowledge for selection and placement. The methods of selection varied from arbitrary and quick to detailed and lengthy procedures. The selection of monks and priests through dreams and selection of kings by the method of garlanding by elephants were the examples of arbitrary selection (Kaur et al., 2016). The "Swayamvara" was a system of choosing the bridegroom on the spot based on a quick assessment of skills possessed by them. With the passage of time, with improved education and enlightened public opinion, a need for replacing arbitrary selection with more objective criteria was felt. Appointment by ancestry lost its popularity, and people craved a system for evaluation of suitability based on capability. This paved the way for evolution of scientific selection procedures and tests.

12.3 Psychological Assessment in India

India occupies the greater part of South Asia. It has 1.3 billion people, 28 states, nine union territories, 1,652 spoken languages, and at least nine recognized religions yet still stands united. India is the second largest country in the world in terms of population with roughly 17% of the world's population despite occupying just 2.4% of the world's land area. India is one of the oldest civilizations in the world with a diversified and rich cultural heritage. Of the South Asian countries included in the region, India is possibly the most developed with regards to psychological assessment. Hence, for this chapter the history of assessment is described within the various sectors where it has historically been used. The narrative begins with psychological assessment in educational settings followed by clinical, social, workplace, and military settings.

12.4 Assessment in Educational Settings

In ancient times India had the Gurukula system of education in which children were trained under a Guru (Sanskrit term for a teacher, guide, expert, or master). Under this system, the students stay with the Guru until they acquire maximum knowledge and competence. This system is based on experiential learning rather than formal classroom teaching. The knowledge and competence of the pupil is evaluated by the Guru under whom they reside, by making them perform tasks and targets given by the Guru. This form of assessment is well explained in the *Mahabharata* where the supreme Guru of Kauravas and Pandavas, Shri Dronacharya, assigned weapons to his *shishyas* ("students" or "disciples") based on their talents. Observation was the basic mode of assessment to get through *Upanayana*, which means acceptance of a pupil by a Guru to bestow knowledge through education (Kane, 1941).

Takshashila, the ancient world's first international University (c. 400–500 BCE to 550 CE) in ancient northern India, and Nalanda University, an ancient center of higher learning in Bihar, India established in the fifth century CE, are the two famous ancient universities of India and the oldest universities in the world. The University of Takshashila was especially famous for its instructions in medicine. Panini, Chanakaya, and famous physician Jivaka were students of this university (Rajkhowa, 2005). Nalanda University offered a choice of many subjects for study, though it specialized in Mahayana Buddhism. Instructions were imparted in logic, grammar, philosophy, astronomy, literature, Buddhism, and Hinduism. The method of discussion was used in the classrooms. This center of learning was destroyed toward the end of the twelfth century. The university had helped to spread Indian culture in foreign countries such as Tibet, China, and Central Asia and also in South East Asian countries. The students were admitted to these universities after a kind of entrance test to assess their capabilities to undergo the course of study. Admission was so difficult to achieve that only two or three out of ten were selected (Pinto & Myall 2006).

The rise of industrial revolution in the West (Inglehart, 1990) not only gave the world a flood of new inventions but also a new kind of education. The new model of education was brought to India by the British during colonial rule. They introduced a change in the educational system by bringing uniformity in curriculum to all students leading the Gurukula system of education to lose its importance. The intention of the British colonial education policy, which started in India during 1813, was to promote both Oriental culture and Western science (Whitehead, 2005). Historically, it is seen that up to 1921 the missionaries engaged in providing education were the first to use, construct, and validate tests in India (Sinha, 1983). The schools established by Christian missionaries are not in favor of caste distinctions and gave opportunity to lower caste students. Mental testing figured prominently in this process because it promised to disentangle innate capacities from the advantages of upbringing and education. The British officials collaborated with the missionaries of America to replicate US Army experiments and adopt the Stanford–Binet test for Indian school children. The meeting of the Central Advisory Board of Education (CABE) held at Simla in 1921 proposed to study the uses of mental tests in India (Linstrum, 2016). But in 1923, during a time of financial stress, the board was abolished without even a reference to provincial governments as to the advisability of its continuance. Later, in 1935, the board was revived (Mukerji, 1974).

The British educational system continued and evolved to become the Indian educational system. The children in the British system had to learn two or more languages, one of which was English. The sociocultural context of the West had a negative effect on the mental health of children but significant assessment tests in the area of child mental health were lacking (Shyam & Khan, 2009). Later on, initiatives were taken by healthcare professionals for the development of standardized tools and assessment procedures. Various tests of intelligence, maturity, curiosity, personality and temperaments, study habits, adjustment problems, development screening, parent–child relationships, and so on were imported from the West and used for diagnosis in schools (Shyam & Khan, 2009). One of the most prominent tests used in India after independence was Bhatia's Battery of Performance Tests. Bhatia (1955) devised these tests to serve as part of a test battery for testing school children in India. The Pattern Drawing Test, or Patterns Test, appeared to show some promise in the field of mental measurement. Bhatia's examiners found they had to exercise caution when children were tested. The inhabitants of the villages were reluctant to allow a child to be tested by a stranger. Hence the examiners usually tested the subjects outdoors to show the villagers that no harm came to the child (Frost, 1957).

Academic and research psychology were introduced in India with the establishment of psychology departments and laboratories at universities. In the beginning, psychology programs were started as a part of philosophy departments. Psychology training for Indian students at graduate level was not very intense, instead they were given heavy doses of philosophy and history. Hence, even at master's level, students had little idea about psychological experiments and were ill-prepared for any advanced work (Barnette, 1955). Gradual emergence of independent psychology departments took place. At that time, the field of psychology that was taught and practiced in India was predominantly Western in its contents and models. Some psychologists went abroad for higher studies in psychology and established departments and laboratories after their return to India. In the beginning, there were tests and apparatuses imported from other countries for assessment. Subsequently, the tests were mimicked for Indian context. At the same time, there is much good work done in India but mostly on intelligence and IQ testing and there are attempts made to adapt foreign materials to Indian context. This raised concerns that tests transposed from Western cultures rarely work out satisfactorily (Prakash, 1952). Dayal (1951) has urged more centralized research in the construction of psychological tests in India and has complained about the overlapping or unnecessary duplication in psychometric research.

The Institute of Psychological Research and Services (IPRS) – a postgraduate wing of the Patna University – emerged in 1945. The institute used clinical tests (especially projective tests) for their research, guidance, and counseling services. The interesting contribution of the institute was the development of a test battery for Home Guard selection. This consists of a verbal intelligence test, a psychomotor test of speed, digit-symbol test, TAT (local adaptation), and a group discussion situation. Around 1,700 candidates were tested from four districts of Bihar. The summary of test data was submitted to the Home Guard Board for the final selection of candidates (Barnette, 1955).

Parsi Panchayet Vocational Guidance Bureau, established in 1947 at Mumbai (operated by the Parsi Panchayet Trust is a private agency), and Vocational Guidance Bureau, Bombay State, established in 1950, used aptitude tests as part of their vocational guidance program. Most of the aptitude tests utilized are originally American, but they have been restandardized on local samples. In general, American norms have proven too "high" or else it was necessary to extend the time limits. A follow-up study conducted among the students using the battery consisting of the DAT Abstract Reasoning, Bennett Mechanical, and Revised Paper Form Board gave a promising result (Barnette, 1955). In 1949 at the request of the Government of Madras (later renamed as Tamil Nadu, a south Indian state), E. W. Menzel acted as consultant and advisor on aptitude test development for use in Madras (presently Chennai) schools (Barnette, 1955).

Menzel wrote the first book on tests and measurements in India in 1956, and perhaps Rice was the first person to attempt a standardization of the Binet–Simon tests in India (Adaval, 1968). After Rice, Kamat adapted, in the 1930s, the 1917 Stanford revision of the Binet tests in Marathi and Kannada. Shukla, in the 1940s, translated Kamat's version into Gujarati. Mahalanobis and G.C. Chatterji had developed separate intelligence tests in Bengali. Dr. A. Edwin Harper, Jr. made revisions to the Iowa Aptitude Tests for the suitability of Indian uses. The tests are so designed so that the material involving reading comprehension can be easily translated into the language of the region where it is being used (Harper, 1952).

In 1954, India's Ministry of Education established the Central Bureau of Educational and Vocational Guidance, which was one of the milestones in the development of psychological services to initiate guidance services in schools by counselors and teachers for the assessment of students' interests and abilities. The Examination and Evaluation Unit of National Council of Educational Research and Training (NCERT) was established in 1958, and this unit has conducted several studies with all-India character and practical nature. NCERT released a catalog that provides a reference guide comprising 2,000 tests in education, psychology, and allied areas. This is available in the National Library of Educational and Psychological Tests (NLEPT, 2019), located in the Department of Educational Psychology & Foundations of Education, NCERT, New Delhi. The NLEPT is a library-cum-depository of a rare collection of specimen sets of published and unpublished Indian and foreign tests. It caters to the reference needs of test users and test developers in the country. The tests cover most of the important areas of concern such as intelligence, ability and aptitude, interest, values, personality, achievement, creativity, learning, guidance and counseling, industrial psychology, and so on.

12.5 Assessment in Clinical Settings

The natural and holistic philosophy of Ayurveda (a system of medicine with historical roots in the Indian subcontinent) classifies innate qualities of human beings into three different categories known as trigunas, the complementary triad (*Sattva*, *Rajas*, and *Tamas*), and *Tridoshas* (*Vaata*, *Kapha*, and *Pitta*), the biological elements that represent dimensions of personality and constitution (Gupta, 1977). Food and diet were also classified according to this system to indicate foods that facilitate or inhibit the *gunas* or *doshas*. Ayurveda has eight branches, one of which, *Graha Chikitsa*, deals with the prevention, diagnosis, and treatment of mental disorders and marks the earliest traceable attempt at clinical assessment in India (Varma, 1965). Many disorders like depression, mood elevation, diminution, elongation, and so on show that the psychology of a person is encoded according to the bodily birthmarks of the person in *Samudrika Shastra* (a Sanskrit term that roughly translates as "knowledge of body features"), which is not scientific but a part of Vedic tradition. The somatotypes introduced by Sheldon's typology can be compared with *Samudrika Shastra* (Defouw & Svoboda, 1996).

Later in the modern era, around 1920, the European Mental Hospital (pre Central Institute of Psychiatry) at Ranchi was the first to recognize the importance of associating psychologists in clinical assessment and treating the mentally ill. This was developed by Dr. Girindrasekhar Bose as a vibrant profession, covering academic, research, and clinical work since the early 1920s (Prabhu, 2004). Bose significantly contributed to the development of the first psychology laboratory in India and stressed the necessity for objective quantification of psychological constructs (Mukherjee, 2017). During his tenure in the department of psychology, University of Calcutta, several psychological tests were devised by him and his associates. Among the tests were Word Association Tests (with M. N. Banerjee and N. N. Chatterjee, 1953), Group Matching Tests (with M. Deb, 1940), Sand Motor Test (1927), Group Pass Along (1933), Big Muscle Ergograph (1949), Dotting Test (1949), and the Neurotic Questionnaire (1950). Not only were these tests devised and standardize but norms of usage were also constructed. Christiane Hartnack (2001), in her publication *Psychoanalysis in Colonial India*, argues for Bose that he had propounded an original theory that didn't flourish due to the overpowering dominance of the British Empire in colonial India (Mukherjee, 2017).

Adorno's F Scale, Bernreuter's Personality Inventory, Eysenck's Personality Inventory, Allport's A-S Reaction Study and Apperception tests, the Rogers Test of Personality Adjustment, and the California Personal and Social Adjustment inventories are the most popular adaptations by Indian scientists in clinical settings. The questionnaires prepared by Dr. G. C. Pati on insecurity, aggression, and inferiority, the generalized conformity test by Narayana Rao, and the Fear checklist by Usha Rani Sidana are some of the other instruments developed during 1960s and 1970s (Pareek & Rao, 1992).

Dr. M. V. Gopalaswamy as Head of the Department of All India Institute of Mental Health (later the National Institute of Mental Health and Neuro Sciences – NIMHANS), Bangalore laid a solid foundation of psychological training as part of postgraduate programs and encouraged work in personality, psychological measurement, animal behavior, psychokinesis, and Indian psychology. Presently NIMHANS uses many psychological tests including neuropsychological batteries and clinical observations. NIMHANS's Neuropsychology Battery, based on Luria's method, was the first neuropsychology battery developed in the country. NIMHANS's Neuropsychology Battery – 2004, Neuropsychological

Battery for Children, Neuropsychological Battery for Intractable Epilepsy, Indian standardization of Wechsler Memory Scale-III, and Neuropsychological Battery for Spinocerebellar Ataxia are recent developments in the arena of neuropsychological assessment measures (NIMHANS, n.d.).

The first electroencephalogram (EEG) lab to examine the electrophysiological correlates was set up in the NIMHANS neuropsychology unit in the 1970s. The laboratory has kept pace with international trends and has grown from the initial four-channel recordings to high-density 128-channel recordings. Brain dysfunctions in neurological, neurosurgical, and psychiatric conditions have been identified with the EEG and event-related potential (ERP) techniques and topographic brain mapping has been used to understand the dysfunctions. Later the neuropsychology unit has acquired EEG neurofeedback equipment (NIMHANS, n.d.).

12.6   Assessment in Social Settings

Unlike the West, India is a collectivist society that emphasizes family unity and integrity, for an average Indian, family is an integral part of oneself as they are included in the "we" and "circle of intimacy" (Avasthi, 2011). As the family is almost inseparable from the individual, addressing an individual's psychological issues without taking the family into account is virtually impossible. Hence understanding and assessing an individual should always be considered in light of an individual's sociocultural milieu (Avasthi, 2011). Family, community, and caste are woven into the essential social fabric of Indian society. These institutions have molded the social, political, or economic interrelations. Slow changes have taken place as a result of English education, the Western judicial, administrative, and political systems introduced during colonial period, and greater democratization in the political and social spears after independence (Ahluwalia, 2019).

Historically, the Indian caste system is one of the main dimensions where people in India are socially differentiated. The other dimensions are class, religion, region, tribe, gender, and language. The caste system emerged in the early Vedic period and classified people into four hierarchically ranked castes called Varnas. By the end of the later Vedic period, the caste system had become rigid and hereditary. New subcastes emerged as new occupations came into existence (Bhashini, 2018). The caste system had been a problem for the British since their arrival in India. Coming from a society that was divided by class, the British attempted to equate the caste system to the class system. It was felt that the British systematically purged India's riches, destroyed its institutions, and created further divisions among its peoples. Hence there were rebellions against British rule, including the Indian Rebellion of 1857 (also called the Sepoy Rebellion) (Bruce, 2016).

The Spoy Mutiny of 1857–1858 constitutes a turning point in Anglo–Indian relations. Its most important fundamental cause was British interference in native religious beliefs and customs (Shafeeq, 1970). The episode of the greased cartridge provided the crucial element of psychological overstimulation, transforming perception into action. The mutinies thus expressed a collective mentality of opposition that embodied in it a whole matrix of panic, anxiety, and hope (Mukherjee, 1984).

Girindrashekar Bose, who founded a psychoanalytical society in (then) Calcutta in 1922, carried on a long correspondence with Freud and boldly questioned whether the master's theories such as the Oedipus complex applied to Bengali families as well as they did to Viennese families. In this sense, the "globalization" of psychoanalysis promised to unsettle the racial assumptions built into its European origins (Sharma, 2018).

As psychoanalysis attracted increasing interest among British intellectuals, some of them began to ask whether its methods could travel across cultural and racial boundaries. In the 1920s and 1930s, unlocking the secrets of the so-called "native mind" acquired new political urgency. Collecting the dreams of colonial subjects and analyzing them offered a way to explore the inner world of emotions and fantasies that were otherwise inaccessible to British rulers (Sharma, 2018).

The biggest network of imperial dream collectors, organized by an anthropologist named Charles Gabriel Seligman, set out with more modest ambitions. Seligman initially wanted to know whether Freudian concepts like repression and the Oedipus complex were universal for all human beings or culturally determined instead. So, he asked his contacts in far-flung locales across the British Empire to get people to describe their dreams in detail and then probe for clues about their emotional lives that might help to interpret them. As it happens, these dreams seemed to show that many of Freud's assumptions did hold true for other cultures (Sharma, 2018).

Psychologists in India started exploring sociopsychological variables for their research, one of the earliest experimental investigations was on group effects on performance by Sengupta and Singh (1926). Although it was modeled on experiments first carried out by Allport and his colleagues, it did lay the foundation for experimental social psychology in India.

Another notable early research contribution was conducted by Prasad (1935, 1950) and D. Sinha (1952) on rumor studies. Prasad (1935) examined the responses to the devastating earthquake in Bihar in 1934. Later, he published a comparative analysis of many earthquake rumors (Prasad 1950). D. Sinha (1952) studied rumors and behavior of people in catastrophic situations. These three early studies were used by Leon Festinger (1957) in the formulation of his theory of cognitive dissonance.

Adinarayan's (1941) research on color prejudice published in the *British Journal of Psychology* laid the foundation for later work in the area of attitude and prejudice. Group influence on behavior has been a concern of Indian social psychologists since the early period of development of the discipline. N. P. Mukerji (1940) examined ability differentials in work in group and isolation situations and Dr. S. K. Chatterji's (1943) "Languages and Linguistic Problems" was published in *Oxford Pamphlets on Indian Affairs*. Mohsin (1954) analyzed the effects of individual and group frustrations on problem-solving behaviors. Kuppusamy (1951) modified the Bogardus Social Distance Scale to suit Indian conditions and measured the social distance exhibited by college students in the Madras State toward various castes and religious groups.

After independence, communal violence erupted in India. Prime Minister Jawaharlal Nehru sought the help of UNESCO to conduct a large-scale investigation on the reasons behind increased hatred projected in terms of communal and social violence. As part of the UNESCO team, Gardner Murphy came to India and assisted in understanding the social consequences and establishment of necessary direction and support including for other social issues (Murphy, 1953). Murphy's psychological studies were conducted at six different sites in India by six teams. All of the studies deal with some aspect of group relations, the groups being differentiated along caste, religious, ethnic, or class lines. The method used is primarily that of interviewing a selected sample (Davis, 1954). The data acquired quantitatively through the psychological tests in the various sites lost their significance due to the smallness of the samples from which they were taken (Sarma, 1955). The results of the studies gave considerable insight into the status of group relations in India (Davis, 1954).

12.7 Assessment in Workplace Settings

In the time of kingdoms and empires, the king or emperor was the person considered to be superior and the head of the territory who looked after the welfare of the people. The satisfaction of the people about the king was assessed through the interview method, which was conducted with the help of agents or scholars in the king's chamber. Palace employees were also tested for their competence during selection, for example, while appointing ministers the kings followed proper mode of selection. The appointment of ministers is solely based on their qualifications – before being given responsible duties, their characters were tested by secret agents. Those who failed in one or more tests, but were otherwise qualified, were appointed in accordance with the ascertained degree of purity (as per Kautilya's view, mentioned by Majumdar, 1977).

According to *Arthashastra* (a celebrated ancient Indian work on polity, authored by Kautilya, also known as *Vishnugupta* and Chanakya, was the counselor of Chandragupta Maurya, the founder of the Maurya Empire, in the fourth century B.C.E), the Counselor-Chaplain's appointed are based on the assessment of certain exemplary qualities such as insightfulness, intelligence, keen memory, boldness, articulation, honesty, friendliness and loyalty, and so on. Someone who lacks a quarter of these qualities is mid-ranked, and someone who lacks half of them is low ranked. These aspects are assessed through the experts by the same branches of knowledge or their way of interacting with others is assessed through direct observation (Olivelle, 2013).

The large number of Indian scriptures contain references to and analyses of mental status and the content of human beings' mental activities over millennia. These ancient expositions are mostly based on the experiences of sages and seers (i.e., wise men) and self-verification by them. It is not easy to consider this psychological knowledge as scientific in the strict and modern sense of the term (Bryan, 2007).

In India, the study of industrial psychology started as a master's degree program in 1916 at the Calcutta University under N. N. Sengupta who acquired his doctorate under Dr. Munsterberg at Harvard University. Later in 1920, an undergraduate course was started in Calcutta, which was followed by the University of Mysore in 1924. During World War II many assessments were done to find out the reasons for decrease in production. W. T. V. Adiseshiah observes thus: "one of the first things to suffer when fatigue sets in is the accuracy in the timing of responses by the skilled operator" (Adinarayan, 1964). A large-scale survey on motivation in a large industrial organization was conducted by Kamla Chowdhury in 1950 (Chowdhury, 1953).

The rapid industrialization of the 1950s and 1960s created the need for better under understanding of the psychology of the workplace.

Areas that received attention at this time were job attitudes, work incentives, absenteeism, and job satisfaction (Ganguli, 1961). One of the major centers for psychological research was the Ahmedabad Textile Industry Research Association (ATIRA), which was established in 1950. Well-known psychologists such as Erik Erikson, David McClelland, and A. K. Rice were frequent visitors to this institute where several large-scale surveys were conducted to study psychological issues related to the textile industry (Bryan, 2007). As mentioned earlier in this chapter, the series of studies conducted by Murphy as a UNESCO consultant in India during 1949–1950 includes a study of the attitude of textile mill workers in Ahmedabad (Davis, 1954), where the tension between workers and supervisors are explored with the help of attitude questionnaire to understand how tension lead to aggression and violence (Sarma, 1955).

The introduction of railways is one of the legacies of the British rule in India. The need for a railway system was felt by British administrators because of many reasons like commerce, troop movements, and so on; and the Indian Railways became one of the largest rail networks in the world. The scientific approach and concept of psychotechnology and psychotechnological analysis was introduced in Indian Railways during 1964 and a unit was set up in the Railway Board's office, New Delhi. This unit was subsequently transferred to Research Design and Standards Organisation (RDSO) in 1970 and was given the status of a full-fledged Directorate in 1990. Since its inception, the Psycho-Technical Unit has been instrumental in development and standardization of behavioral intervention programs and their implementation, effectively addressing the safety concern of Indian Railways (RDSO, 2019).

The banking sector in India is one of the major employers in the country. After nationalization of banks in India 1969 there was a radical change in recruitment policy in the sector. The Institute of Banking Personnel Selection (IBPS) plays an important role in testing, selection, assessment, and management of human resources in India's banking industry. It was established in 1975 as Personnel Selection Service (PSS) and became an independent entity with the name of IBPS in 1984. Since then, IBPS has been involved in developing ability and aptitude test batteries. It serves public sector, regional, and rural banks. It designs and develops assessment tools for highly specialized jobs. Besides engaging in research in the area of testing, it serves the country by evolving and applying psychometric tools for personnel selection (Bhushan, 2017).

12.8   Assessment in Military Settings

The bewildering range of human capabilities varies widely from individual to individual, making it imperative to use the psychological principles to a great extent in the selection of armed forces personnel. In India, World War II added momentum to the research efforts in this area. During that war there was a provisional selection board, which screened military aspirants throughout the country and forwarded names of recommended candidates to a central interview board. The first military selection board, called the War Office Selection Board (WOSB), emerged in Dehradun in 1943 for the purpose of selection of officers through psychological techniques. This scientific system of personnel selection is based on temperament and character of individuals, which was later developed into an assessment and research wing as the Service Selection Boards (SSBs) and the Psychological Research Wing (PRW). The PRW was renamed the Directorate of Psychological Research (DPR) in 1962 with the expansion in its scope of work. Finally, it was designated as the full-fledged Defence Institute of Psychological Institute (DIPR) in 1982 (Mukerji et al., 2009).

The DIPR is actively engaging in psychological research in the area of testing technology where more than 80 psychologists work under one umbrella. The organization provides continuous psychological support and services to the armed forces in personnel selection, training, and human–machine interface for optimizing operational efficiency and well-being of service personnel (Mukherjee et al., 2009).

Introduction to hi-tech systems in the armed forces and changing war scenarios have changed the functioning of the armed forces personnel in general. Psychological research plays a vital role in coping with these newly emerging issues through its research activities and training modules. The importance of psychology was adequately appreciated by the Ministry of Defence. During the period, DIPR has emerged as a center of national importance in military psychology dealing with research activities pertaining to personnel selection, placement, and trade allocation.

The personnel selection department conducts research on problems pertaining to various psychological tests and techniques for development of intelligence, personality, and aptitude tests for the selection of effective personnel into the armed forces. It also imparts training to assessors in personnel selection and validates the selection system through follow-up studies. There is another important cell that works on human engineering research. This group works on problems related to psychological effect of extreme environment conditions on the operational efficiency of soldiers, psychological testing of the selection of efficient pilots, and human factors in human–machine interface (DIPR, 2007). A computerized pilot selection system (DIPR, 2005) has been developed that assesses various cognitive and psychomotor abilities required by pilot aspirants.

12.9   Psychological Assessment in Sri Lanka

Sri Lanka (formerly called Ceylon) is an island country in South Asia, located in the Indian Ocean just off the south eastern coast of India. The island is geographically separated from the Indian subcontinent by the Gulf of Mannar and the Palk Strait. Sri Lanka has a population of about 20 million people. The island's history of immigration, trade, and colonial invasion has led to the formation of a variety of ethnic groups, each with its own language and religious traditions. The two most prominent ethnicities are the Sinhalese and the Sri Lankan Tamils. The Sinhalese are predominantly Buddhist, and thus it is the major religion in the country, followed by Hinduism, which is actively practiced by the Tamils. The next most popular religion is Christianity, especially among the Burgher population. Although the members of these groups share many cultural practices, beliefs, and values, ethnic differences have become especially marked since the nation's independence in 1948. English was introduced during British rule and continues to be the language of commerce and the higher levels of both public and private sector administration.

   Given that Sri Lanka forms part of the South Asian regions that were not separated other than by kingdoms before colonialism, it shares much of the history of assessment with India. Hence there is a shared history as pertains to clinical diagnosis, employee selection in kingdoms, and the Gurukala education system. As a neighboring country, Sri Lanka is very socioculturally similar to India. The etiological factors and treatments of ethnic mental health care have roots in Ayurveda and Unani (system of medicine) concepts (Weerackody & Fernando, 2014). Unani medicine, which was practiced by the Muslims of Sri Lanka, has a long history going back to the twelfth century CE (Institute of Indigenous Medicine 2019). The basic theory of the Unani system is based upon the well-known four-humor theory of Hippocrates. This presupposes the presence in the body of four humors: blood, phlegm, yellow bile, and black bile. The concept of *Mizaj* (temperament) is one of the fundamentals of Unani medicine. Ancient physicians have discussed this in detail and defined it to the best of their knowledge in Unani classical literature. Mizaj is the amalgam of a person's physical characteristics and his or her psychological and emotional attributes (Glynn, 2003).

The country's experiences with Western psychology began in the 1800s through British rule, which stretched significantly from 1930 to 1970. Early development of the public mental health system occurred during the period of British rule in the late 1800s and was based on then dominant Western conceptualizations of mental health and illness (De Silva, 2002). During earlier days the laws available for insanity were designed only in terms of contracts and maintenance (De Alwis, 2017). Mentally ill individuals were imprisoned along with criminals and later institutionalized with leprosy patients (Carpenter et al., 1988). In 1939, an outpatient clinic was started in the general hospital, Colombo and this progressed to commencement of psychotherapy and follow-up clinics in 1941 and neuropsychiatric clinics in 1943. Treatment of mental illness was revolutionized after 1950s with the use of psychotropic drugs (Carpenter et al., 1988). The Mulleriyawa Mental Hospital was opened in 1958. Later, to cater to the growing need for psychological treatment methods, several private organizations were formed and trained the professionals.

Compared with other countries in South Asia, the prominence of psychology in Sri Lanka has to be given special attention due to its 30 years of suffering from internal armed conflict as well as the devastation caused by natural disasters like the tsunami in 2004. These events have necessitated psychological assessment and counseling on a large scale. Psychiatrists, counselors, nurses, and teachers hold the responsibility of educating citizens regarding psychological well-being (Kathriarachchi et al., 2019). All medical faculties teach medical undergraduates in the assessment and management of psychiatric disorders (Kathriarachchi, 2009). There are only a few scales that have been translated and validated in Sri Lankan populations. The General Health Questionnaire (GHQ-30 and GHQ-12), Kessler's psychological distress scale, Ways of Coping – Revised Scale (WOCS – R), Beck Depression Inventory (BDI), Patient Health Questionnaire-9 (PHQ-9), and Sri Lankan Index of Psychosocial Status - Adult Version (SLIPPS-A) are a few of the rating scales validated for Sri Lanka (Suraweera et al., 2013). A high suicide rate has been a challenge faced by Sri Lanka for several decades. The kinds of tools used in the assessment of maternal suicide and depression in Sri Lanka include the Psychological Autopsy Tool for Maternal Suicides, which is used preferably within 14 days of maternal suicide by a team of mental health professionals (Isuru et al., 2016). As a measure to detect and treat depression among vulnerable groups, the Edinburgh Postnatal Depression Scale validated in Sinhala was used with postnatal women (Agampodi et al., 2014).

12.10 Psychological Assessment in Bangladesh

Bangladesh is the world's eighth most populous country with nearly 163 million people, and is the 92nd largest country in land area, spanning 147,570 KM², making it one of the most densely populated countries in the world. Bangladesh shares land borders with India to the west, north, and east, Myanmar to the southeast, and the Bay of Bengal to the south. It is narrowly separated from Nepal and Bhutan by India's Siliguri Corridor in the north and from China by the Indian state of Sikkim in the northeast. Dhaka, the capital and largest city, is the nation's economic, political, and cultural hub. The predominant language of Bangladesh is Bengali (also known as Bangla). Bengali is the one of the easternmost branches of the Indo-European language family. It is a part of the Eastern Indo-Aryan languages in South Asia, which developed between the tenth and thirteenth centuries. In ancient Bengal, Sanskrit was the language of written communication, especially by priests. During the Islamic period, Sanskrit was replaced by Bengali as the vernacular language. Under British rule, Bengali was significantly modernized by Europeans. Bangladesh has a rich, diverse culture. Its deeply rooted heritage is thoroughly reflected in its architecture, dance, literature, music, painting, and clothing. The three primary religions of Bangladesh (Hinduism, Buddhism, and Islam) have had a great influence on its culture and history.

In Bangladesh teaching and research in psychology at University level started in 1956 at Rajshahi University and later, in 1965, the psychology department was established at the University of Dhaka, followed by Jagannath University (former Jagannath College) and Chittagong University.

Since 1984, the Bangladesh Protibondhi Foundation (BPF) has been a key institution in standardizing techniques of early screening identification and assessment of disabilities in children. The BPF uses tests in different capacities, such as Denver Developmental Screening Test (DDST), Stanford–Binet Intelligence Scale, Bayley Scales of Infant development, and the Wechsler scales among others. Similar psychological assessments were also used in other institutes, namely, the Institute of Pediatric Neuro-disorder and Autism (IPNA) and Bangabandhu Sheikh Mujib Medical University (BSMMU) (Akhtar, 1991).

The National Curriculum and Text Book (NCTB) Board of Bangladesh, Bangladesh Inter Service Selection Board (Army-ISSB),

Bangladesh Naval Service, Bangladesh Police, Primary Teachers Training Institute (PTI), Bachelor of Education (B.Ed.), Master's in Education (M.Ed.), Teacher Training Colleges, and Bangladesh Public Service Commission (BPSC) are all using psychological assessment for training of teachers and selection of civil servant candidates and their training, particularly to measure the mental ability of the candidates. Specifically, intelligence, achievement, attitude, and personality tests are used in the context of Bangladesh (Akhtar, 1991).

There is significant psychological testing and measurement is used in Bangladesh by psychologists at different universities, as can be seen in the edited volume *The First Two Decades of Psychological Research in Bangladesh: Some Selected Studies* by Akhtar (1991). Generally, four kinds of tests are used in Bangladesh:

1. Newly developed or constructed psychological tests.
2. Bengali adapted psychological tests.
3. Bengali translated psychological tests.
4. English version of psychological tests.

The traditional psychological tests used in Bangladesh are evidenced from the compilation of Hamida Akhter Begum and Chowdhury's *Bangladesh Psychological Abstracts* (1972–1989). These tests include MPI, MMPI, EPQ, WISC, and EPPS according to CPSRT (1990). Psychologists in Bangladesh are mostly using their Western and Eastern experience and are trying to use those tests to solve the behavioral problems particularly in the Bangladesh Army, Bangladesh Navy, and Bangladesh Police Academy.

12.11 Psychological Assessment in Nepal

Nepal is a landlocked country situated between China and India that sits at a high elevation in the Himalayan mountain range. The population is about 30 million people. Kathmandu is the capital of Nepal and the country's largest metropolis. Nepal is considered a multilinguistic country, Nepali being the official language. The country's diverse heritage evolved from four major language groups: Indo-Aryan, Tibeto-Burman, Mongolian, and various indigenous languages. Religion is a very important part of Nepali culture. Nepal occupies a special place in both Hindu and Buddhist traditions. Hinduism is the dominant religion, though Nepal was the birthplace of Buddha.

The history of psychology in Nepal can be traced back to 1947 when it was introduced at Tri-Chandra College, Kathmandu (Dangol, 2018). At that time Tri-Chandra was the only college in Nepal and was affiliated to Patna University in India. Psychology was introduced at the intermediate level as part of philosophy. When Tribhuvan University was established in 1959, other colleges also came into existence. By 1966, four more colleges had introduced psychology as an academic subject at either the intermediate or bachelor's degree level. The first generation of psychology teachers were educated at Indian universities. As a relatively new discipline with a small number of qualified individuals, psychology grew slowly (Subba, 1999).

With regard to assessment tools there were many unadapted standardized psychological tests and inventories taught in academic and applied sectors of Nepal, the majority of which are found irrelevant to the Nepalese setting (Subba, 1999). In 1961, Pandey prepared and standardized a group test of intelligence for school children in Nepal. The standardization was done on 2,674 Nepalese students of classes VIII to X representing different social strata of Nepal. The test had good psychometric properties. There are famous Western tools that are adapted for Nepal such as BDI (Kohrt et al., 2002), Beck Anxiety Inventory (Kohrt et al., 2003), Depression Self-Rating Scale and Child PTSD Symptom Scale (Kohrt et al., 2011), and Enhancing Assessment of Common Therapeutic Factors (ENACT) Scale (Kohrt et al., 2015).

PHQ-9, a shorter screening tool for depression, was adapted for use in Nepal by Kohrt et al. (2016). In order to adapt it, Kohrt et al. attempted to integrate the Nepali concepts of the heart–mind (responsible for affect and memory) and the brain–mind (responsible for cognition, rationality, and social behavior). The Nepali concept of depression differs significantly from the Western concept. There is no one word in Nepali that corresponds to the term depression, while some terms that on the surface may seem to be accurate translations, such as *mannasik rog* (mental illness) and *mannasik samasya* (mental problems), refer specifically to the brain–mind, and are highly stigmatizing. However, Kohrt et al. implemented an extensive translation and vetting process, including the removal of all English idioms and medical jargon, replacing them with local idioms, and the use of representative focus groups to assess the acceptability of each item. Burkey et al. (2016) explored the overlap between local categories of problematic behavior and Western diagnostic criteria as reflected in the Disruptive Behavior International Scale-Nepal version (DBIS-N). In Nepal the tool adaptions faced certain challenges, a large study identified a distinct factor structure for the Conners Scale (Pendergast et al., 2014) and another study documented an unsuccessful attempt to translate ADHD symptoms into Nepali due to lack of coherence of symptoms in the local context (Folmar & Palmes, 2009). Hence there is a strong need for the development of indigenous psychological instruments for the Nepalese context.

12.12 Psychological Assessment in Bhutan

Bhutan is located in the northern area of South Asia and is also in the eastern Himalayan mountain area. It is bordered in the north by China and to the south, east, and west by India. Geographically, Bhutan is divided into three zones: the southern zone, which has low foothills that are covered with dense tropical forests, and the central and northern zones, which consist of fertile valleys. The northern section forms part of the Himalayas with its high peak along the Tibetan borders. The largest percentage of the population lives in the central zone. The federal capital of Thimphu is a small, charming city sandwiched in the heart of the Himalayas. The population is about 600 million people. Bhutan's national language is Dzongkha. Approximately three-fourths of Bhutan's population follows Buddhism, primarily of the Tibetan variety; formerly the official state religion, it is described in the 2008 Constitution as the "spiritual heritage" of the country. The three main ethnic groups of Bhutan – the Bhutia, the Nepalese, and the Sharchop – display considerable variety in their cultures and lifestyles.

Development of psychology in Bhutan was much slower when compared to other South Asian countries. Bhutan was the least influenced by Western systems and is one of the few countries that have been independent and never colonized or governed by an outside power (Mathou, 2000). Traditional medicine in Bhutan is known as *Sowa Rigpa* (*gSo-ba Rig-pa*) and is one of the oldest surviving medical traditions in the world. Other medical systems – such as Chinese medicine, Indian Ayurvedic medicine, Unani medicine, and Greco-Roman medicine – and the country's rich cultures and traditions have greatly influenced the way traditional Bhutanese medicine evolved. However, Buddhist philosophy remains the mainstream of this medical system. *gSo-ba Rig-pa*'s principles are based on the perception that the human body is composed of three main elements: *rLung* (air), *mKhris-pa* (bile), and *Bad-kan* (phlegm). When these three elements are balanced in the body a person is said to be healthy (Wangchuk et al., 2007).

The first mental health program in Bhutan was started in 1997 in a hospital in Thimpu. Dr. Chencho Dorji was hired as Bhutan's first, and for a long time only, psychiatrist after leaving Bhutan to get his degree in Sri Lanka. Initially driven by a desire to treat his brother, a Buddhist monk who suffers from schizophrenia, he single-handedly spearheaded the creation of his country's first psychiatric ward in Thimphu. Later he began training doctors at the district level in basic mental health assessment and treatment (Johnson, 2018).

Today, Bhutan has additional native-born psychiatrists and a few visiting psychiatrists. But there is a dearth of psychologists, excepting some psychological counselors, and the university-level psychology programs are taught by non-native psychologists and others with a background in philosophy.

Gross National Happiness (GNH) is a famous concept that guides the government of Bhutan. It includes an index that is used to measure the collective happiness and well-being of a population. The phrase GNH was first coined by the fourth king of Bhutan, King Jigme Singye Wangchuck, in 1972 when he declared that "Gross National Happiness is more important than Gross Domestic Product." The concept implies that sustainable development should take a holistic approach toward notions of progress and give equal importance to noneconomic aspects of well-being (Ura et al., 2012).

Since then, the idea of GNH has influenced Bhutan's economic and social policy, and also captured the imagination of others far beyond its borders. In creating the GNH Index, Bhutan sought to create a measurement tool that would be useful for policymaking and create policy incentives for the government, NGOs, and businesses of Bhutan to increase GNH. The GNH Index includes both traditional areas of socioeconomic concern such as living standards, health, and education and less traditional aspects of culture and psychological well-being. It is a holistic reflection of the general well-being of the Bhutanese population rather than a subjective psychological ranking of "happiness" alone.

The GNH Index includes nine domains: psychological well-being, health, education, time use, cultural diversity and resilience, good governance, community vitality, ecological diversity and resilience, and living standards. The indicators and domains aim to emphasize different aspects of well-being, and different ways of meeting underlying human needs. The Government of Bhutan's Centre for Bhutan Studies revised and released an updated GNH Index in 2011. There are 33 indicators in the aforementioned nine domains and the Index seeks to measure the nation's well-being directly by starting with each person's achievements in each indicator. The GNH Index is based on the Alkire–Foster method of multidimensional measurement, which has been adapted for this purpose. It identifies four groups of people: unhappy, narrowly happy, extensively happy, and deeply happy (Ura et al., 2012).

12.13 Conclusion

Though the psychology of southern Asia has its distinctive past, the uses of psychological assessments are relatively less widespread when compared with developed nations. The collectivistic nature of South Asian societies contributes to this, where people depend on each other and accept the tradition as a norm. The unique feature of the joint family system is one in which the parents and the sons with their families live under one roof, and where informal counseling is given by elders to the children by way of ancient epics, strong traditional values, and firm spiritual beliefs. Further, although unity in diversity is the essence of South Asian culture, the perception of people toward change varies, and this has played an important role in the acceptance of psychology and psychological assessment in this region. However, a number of industrial organizations and government bodies are increasingly using tests imported from the West and psychological assessments are receiving greater acceptance. Hence, due to cultural differences between the Western and South Asian region, there is a definite need for the development of culturally sensitive and appropriate tools with sound psychometric properties.

REFERENCES

Adaval, S. B. (ed.). (1968). *Third Indian year book of education: Educational research*. New Delhi: National Council of Educational Research and Training.

Adinarayan, S. P. (1941). A research in colour prejudice. *British Journal of Psychology*, *31*(3), 217–229.

(1964). *Social psychology – with special reference to Indian conditions*. New Delhi: Allied Publishers Private Limited.

Agampodi, S., Wickramage, K., Agampodi, T., Thennakoon, U., Jayathilaka, N., Karunarathna, D., & Alagiyawanna, S. (2014). Maternal mortality revisited: The application of the new ICD-MM classification system in reference to maternal deaths in Sri Lanka. *Reproductive Health*, *11*, 17.

Ahluwalia, H. S. (2019). *Imaging Malgudi: R.K Narayan's fictive town and its people*. Cambridge: Cambridge Scholars Publishing.

Akhtar, K. (1991). *The first two decades of psychological research in Bangladesh: Some selected studies*. Dhaka: University Press Limited..

Avasthi, A. (2011). Indianizing psychiatry – is there a case enough? *Indian Journal of Psychiatry*, *53*(2), 111–120. https://doi.org/10.4103/0019-5545.82534.

Barnette, W.L. (1955). Survey of research with psychological tests in India. *Psychological Bulletin*, *52*(2), 105–121.

Begum, H.A. & Chowdhury, M.S. (1990). *Bangladesh Psychological Abstract* (1972–1989 2nd ed.). Centre for Psycho-Social Research and Training. Dhaka: Fah-Ra Printing and Publications.

Bhashini, M. (2018). *My book of history and civics*. New Delhi: New Saraswati House (India) Private Limited.

Bhatia, C. M. (1955). *Performance tests of intelligence under Indian conditions*. London: Oxford University Press.

Bhushan, B. (2017). Centenary year of psychology in India: A brief review. In Bhushan, B. (eds.), *Eminent Indian psychologists: 100 years of psychology in India*. New Delhi: Sage Publications.

Bruce, O. (2016). What were the advantages and disadvantages for British people living in India? *eNotes Editorial*, March 8, 2016. www.enotes.com/home work-help/what-advantages-disadvantages-british-people-646808.

Bryan, L. K. (2007). History of industrial/organizational psychology in other parts of the world. In S. G. Rogelberg (ed.), *Encyclopedia of industrial and organizational psychology*, (Vol. 1, pp. 317–321). Thousand Oaks, CA: Sage Publications.

Burkey, M. D., Ghimire, L., Adhikari, R. P, Kohrt, B. A., Jordans, M. J. D., Haroz, E. E., & Wissow, L. S. (2016). Development process of an assessment tool for disruptive behavior problems in cross-cultural settings: The Disruptive Behavior International Scale – Nepal version (DBIS-N). *International Journal of Culture and Mental Health*, *9*(4), 387–398.

Carpenter, J., Mendis, M., & Samarasinghe, D. (1988). *The history of mental health care in Sri Lanka*. Colombo: Marga Publications.

Chatterji, S. K. (1943). *Languages and the linguistic problem*. London: Oxford University Press.

Chowdhry, K. (1953). *An analysis of the attitudes of textile workers and the effect of those attitudes on work efficiency*. Ahmedabad: ATIRA Research Note.

CPSRT. (1990). *Psychosocial studies*. Dhaka: Centre for Psycho-Social Research and Training..

Dangol, A. K. (2018). *History of counselling in Nepal*. [Blog post]. Retrieved from http://sciencenpsychology.blogspot.com/2018/03/history-of-counselling-in-nepal.html.

Davis, K. (1954). Book reviews [Review of the book *In the minds of men: The study of human behavior and social tensions in India* by Gardner Murphy]. *American Sociological Review 19*(4), 486–488.

Dayal, I. (1951). A note on psychological tests in India. *Journal of Educational Psychology Baroda*, *8*, 195–197.

De Alwis, L. A. (2017). Development of civil commitment statutes (laws of involuntary detention and treatment) in Sri Lanka: A historical review. *Medico-Legal Journal of Sri Lanka, Colombo, 5*(1), 23.

De Silva, D. (2002). Psychiatric service delivery in an Asian country: The experience of Sri Lanka. *International Review of Psychiatry, 14*(1), 66–70.

Defence Institute of Psychological Research. (2005). *Development of computerised pilot selection system* (DIPR Technical Report). Delhi: DIPR.

(2007). *Human factors and man-machine interface for the Army: Human factor evaluation in driver selection* (DIPR Technical Report). Delhi: DIPR.

Defouw, H. & Svoboda, R. (1996). *Light on life: An introduction to the astrology of India*. New Delhi: Penguin Books.

Festinger, L. A. (1957). *A theory of cognitive dissonance*. Stanford, CA: Stanford University Press.

Folmar, S. & Palmes G. K. (2009). Cross-cultural psychiatry in the field: Collaborating with anthropology. *Journal of the American Academy of Child and Adolescent Psychiatry, 48*(9), 873–876.

Frost, R. E. (1957). *The relationship between Bhatia's patterns test, porteus maze test, grade scores and a group measure of Achievement.* (Unpublished Master's Thesis, The University of British Columbia).

Ganguli, H. C. (1961). *Industrial productivity and motivation: A Psychological analysis*. Bombay: Asia Publishing House.

Glynn, J. P. (2003). Temperament revisited – new interest in an old concept, *Journal of Islamic Medical Association of South Africa, 10*, 82–84.

Gupta, S. P. (1977). *Psychopathology in Indian medicine – Ayurveda*. 1. Aligarh: Ajay Publishers (1st ed.).

Harper, A. E., Jr. (1952). Adaptation of Iowa aptitude tests. *Teaching.* (25, 45–46) Bombay: Oxford University Press.

Hartnack, C. (2001). *Psychoanalysis in colonial India*. Delhi: Oxford University Press.

Inglehart, R. (1990). *Culture shift in advance industrial society*. Princeton, NJ: Princeton University Press.

Institute of Indigenous Medicine. (2019). *By-laws, regulations and curriculum of the bachelor of unani medicine and surgery (bums) degree programme.* Curriculum Development and Evaluation Committee of the Unani Section, University of Colombo.

Isuru, L. L. A., Gunathillaka, K. D. K., & Kathriarachchi, S. T. (2016). Reducing maternal suicide in Sri Lanka: Closing the gap. *Sri Lanka Journal of Psychiatry, 7*(1), 1–3.

Johnson, E. (2018). *Bhutan, known for its Gross National Happiness Index, comes to terms with mental health crisis.* PRI's The World. Retrieved from www.pri .org/stories/2018-05-07.

Kane, P. V. (1941). Upanayana, Chapter VII, *History of Dharmasastras*, Vol. II, Part I (pp. 268–287). Bhandarkar Oriental Research Institute.

Kathriarachchi, S. T. (2009). A review of trends in suicide and deliberate self-harm in Sri Lanka. *Vidyodaya Journal of Humanities and Social Sciences,* Joint Golden Jubilee Issue (pp. 171–184).

Kathriarachchi, S. T., Seneviratne, V. L., & Amarakoon, L. (2019). Development of mental health care in Sri Lanka: Lessons learned. *Taiwanese Journal of Psychiatry*, *33*(2), 55.

Kaur, G., Anand, D., & Awasthy, S. (2016). Intelligence and aptitude testing. In N. Maheshwari & V. V. Kumar (eds.), *Military psychology: Concepts, trends and interventions* (pp. 33–35). New Delhi: Sage Publications.

Kohrt, B. A., Jordans, M. J, Tol, W. A., Luitel, N. P., Maharjan, S. M., & Upadhaya, N. (2011). Validation of cross-cultural child mental health and psychosocial research instruments: Adapting the Depression Self-Rating Scale and Child PTSD Symptom Scale in Nepal. *BMC Psychiatry*, *11*(17), 1–17.

Kohrt, B. A., Kunz, R. D., Koirala, N. R., & Sharma, V. D. (2003). Validation of the Nepali version of Beck Anxiety Inventory. *Journal of Institute of Medicine* *25*(1), 1–4.

Kohrt, B. A., Kunz, R. D., Koirala, N. R., Sharma, V. D., & Nepal, M. K. (2002). Validation of a Nepali version of the Beck depression inventory. *Nepalese Journal of Psychiatry*, *2*(4), 123–130.

Kohrt, B. A., Luitel, N. P., Acharya, P., & Jordans, M. J. D. (2016). Detection of depression in low resource settings: validation of the Patient Health Questionnaire (PHQ-9) and cultural concepts of distress in Nepal. *BMC Psychiatry*, *16*(38), 1–14.

Kohrt, B. A., Ramaiya, M. K., Rai, S., Bhardwaj, A., & Jordans, M. J. D. (2015). Development of a scoring system for non-specialist ratings of clinical competence in global mental health: a qualitative process evaluation of the Enhancing Assessment of Common Therapeutic Factors (ENACT) scale. *Global Mental Health*, 2, e23.

Kuppusamy, B. (1951). *The social distance scale*; Manasayan, 32, Netaji Subash Marg, Delhi-6.

Linstrum, E. (2016). *Ruling minds: Psychology in the British empire*. Cambridge, MA: Harvard University Press.

Majumdar, R. C. (1977). *Ancient India*. New Delhi: Motilal Banarsidass Publishers Pvt. Ltd.

Mathou, T. (2000). The politics of Bhutan: Change in continuity. *Journal of Bhutan Studies*, *2*(2), 250–262.

Menzel, E. W. (1956). *The use of new type tests in India* (4th ed.). London: Oxford University Press.

Mohsin, S. M. (1954). Effect of frustration on problem solving behaviour. *Journal of Abnormal and Social Psychology*, *49*(1), 152–155.

Mukherjee, D. G. (2017). Girindrasekhar Bose. In Bhushan, B. (eds.), *Eminent Indian psychologists: 100 years of psychology in India*. New Delhi: Sage Publications.

Mukherjee, S., Kumar, U., & Mandal, M. K. (2009). Status of military psychology in India: A review. *Journal of the Indian Academy of Applied Psychology*, *35*(2), 181–194.

Mukerji, N. P. (1940). An investigation of ability in work in groups and in isolation. *British Journal of Psychology*, *30*(4), 352–356.

Mukherjee, R. (1984). *Awadh in revolt, 1857–1858: A study of popular resistance.* New Delhi: Oxford University Press.

Mukherji, S. N. (1974). *History of education in India (modern period).* Baroda: Acharya Book Depot.

Murphy, G. (1953). *In the minds of men.* New York: Basic Books.

Narayanan, R. (2014). Review essay "India and South Asian Security Issues: Problems Aplenty," *Solutions Hazy, Prospects Unsettling Journal of International and Global Studies* (Linden Wood University, Missouri), 5 (2), 114–118.

National Institute of Mental Health and Neurosciences (n.d.). *Clinical psychology – neuropsychology.* http://nimhans.ac.in/clinical-psychology/clinical-psychol ogy-neuropsychology/.

NLEPT. (2019). *Catalogue of Tests.* Aurobindo Marg, New Delhi: NCERT, Sr. – 110016.

Olivelle, P. (2013). *King, governance, and law in ancient India: Kautilya's Arthasastra.* New York: Oxford University Press.

Pandey, R. E., (1961). *The preparation and standardised group test of general mental ability for school-going students in Nepal.* Ph.D., Psychology, Banaras Hindu University.

Pareek, U. & Rao, T. V. (1992). *First handbook of psychological and social instruments* (Vol. 25). New Delhi: Concept Publishing Company.

Pendergast L. L. Vandiver, B. J., Schaefer, B. A., Cole, P. M., Murray-Kolb. L. M., & Christian, P. (2014). Factor Structure of Scores from the Conners' Rating Scales-Revised Among Nepali Children. *International Journal of School & Educational Psychology*, *24*, 261–270.

Pinto, X. & Myall, E. G., (2006). *New ICSE history and vivics – Part I for class IX.* New Delhi: Frank Bros. & Co. (Publishers) Ltd.

Prabhu, G. G. (2004). Therapeutic role of the clinical psychologists: Progress and problems. *India Journal of Clinical Psychology*, *31*(1), 42–47.

Prakash, R. (1952). Difficulties in adapting and translating mental tests in other cultures. *Indian Journal of Educational Research*, *3*, 299–307.

Prasad, J. (1935). The psychology of rumour: A study relating to the great Indian earthquake of 1934. *British Journal of Psychology*, *26*(1), 1–15.

(1950). A comparative study of rumours and reports in earthquakes. *British Journal of Psychology*, *41*(3–4), 129–144.

Rajkhowa, S. C. (2005). Ancient European and Indian Universities. In Sharma & Sharma (eds.), *Encyclopaedia of higher education: The Indian perspective* (Vol. 1, pp. 1–6) New Delhi: Mittal Publications.

Research Design and Standards Organisation (RDSO). (2019). Retrieved from: https://rdso.indianrailways.gov.in/view_section.jsp?lang=0&id=0,2,456,506.

Sarma, J. (1955). In the minds of men: The study of human behavior and social tensions in India. *Gardner Murphy, American Journal of Sociology*, *60*(4), 407–408.

Sengupta, N. N. & Singh, C. P. N. (1926). Mental work in isolation and in group. *Indian Journal of Psychology, 1*, 106–110.

Shafeeq, S. (1970). *British reaction to the sepoy mutiny, 1857–1858*. (Unpublished master's thesis,. North Texas State University, Denton, Texas).

Sharma, M. (2018). *What Sigmund Freud, psychoanalysis had to do with the British Empire's hold over India, colonies*. Retrieved from www.firstpost.com/living/what-sigmund-freud-psychoanalysis-had-to-do-with-the-british-empires-hold-over-india-colonies-4308917.html

Shyam, R. & Khan, A. (2009). *Clinical child psychology*. New Delhi: Kalpaz Publishing House.

Sinha, D. (1952). Behaviour in a catastrophic situation: A psychological study of reports and rumours. *British Journal of Psychology, 43*(3), 200–209.

(1983). Human Assessment in the Indian Context. In S. H. Irvine & J. W. Berry (eds.), *Human assessment and cultural factors* (pp. 17–34). New York: Plenum Press.

Srivastava, K. (2012). Concept of personality: Indian perspective. *Industrial Psychiatry Journal, 21*(2), 89–93. https://doi.org/10.4103/0972-6748.119586

Subba, (1999). *NASA Newsletter*, No. 7, Department of History of Religions, Artillerivej 86, DK – 2300 Copenhagen S, Denmark.

Suraweera, C., Hanwella, R., Sivayokan, S., & De Silva, V. (2013). Rating scales validated for Sri Lankan populations. *Sri Lanka Journal of Psychiatry, 4*(2), 16–24.

Tichelman, F. (1980). *Social evolution of Indonesia. The Asiatic mode of production and its legacy*. Studies in Social History, Issued by International Institute of Social History. Amsterdam: Martinus Nijhoff Publishers.

Ura, K., Alkire, S., Zangmo, T., & Wangdi, K. (2012) *An extensive analysis of GNH index*. Thimphu: Centre for Bhutan Studies.

Varma, L. P. (1965). Psychiatry in Ayurveda. *Indian Journal of Psychiatry, 7*(4), 292.

Wangchuk, P., Wangchuk, D., & Hansen, J. A., (2007). Traditional Bhutanese medicine (gSo-ba-Rig-pa): An integrated part of the formal health care services. *South East Asian Journal of Tropical Medicine and Public Health 38* (1), 161–167.

Weerackody, C. & Fernando, S. (2014). Mental health services in Sri Lanka. In R. Moodley & M. Ocampo (eds.), *Critical psychiatry and mental health*. East Sussex: Routledge.

Whitehead, C. (2005). The historiography of British imperial education policy, Part I: India. *History of Education, 34*(3), 315–329.

CHAPTER 13

The History of Psychological Testing in East Asia

Fei Huang and Mingjie Zhou

13.1 Introduction

China, Japan, and South Korea as three representative countries in East Asia, all have their own historical and cultural traditions, but they are closely related. In particular Chinese culture has a great influence on Japan and Korea. The history of psychological testing in East Asia can be traced back to the ancient Chinese talent selection system. For example, an important content of the system of selecting officials in ancient China, the imperial examinations not only penetrated the middle and late stages of Chinese feudal society but also had a particularly profound impact on the entire East Asian civilization (Liu, 2007). However, despite some similarities in culture, the three countries have maintained their own ways of living. In this chapter we discuss the histories of psychological assessment of the three countries. We were unable, however, to locate collaborators to contribute to the Japanese and South Korean histories. Hence the systematic review method was used to create a narrative of the history of assessment across those two countries.

In recent decades, researchers have conducted an increasing number of studies on psychological assessment in indigenous East Asian samples (China, Japan, and South Korea). Cheung, Leong, and Ben-Porath (2003) systematically reviewed psychological assessment in Asia from 1971 to 2000. Drawing on their approach, we chose to search in all databases on the EBSCO host platform (including PsycINFO) and specified the name of a list of East Asian regions or ethnic groups (China/Chinese/Taiwan/Hong Kong, Japan/Japanese, Korea/Korean) as the search terms for the three most popular English language journals on psychological assessment – *Psychological Assessment*, *Assessment*, and *Journal of Personality*, respectively.

We thank Ms. Guo Wei and Ms. SooJung Ro for their assistance in providing relevant psychological testing information for Japan and Korea.

Table 13.1. *Number of articles identified in assessment journals*

		Chinese (mainland China, Taiwan, Hong Kong)	Korea/ Korean	Japan/ Japanese
Assessment[a]	1991–2000	2	0	1[c]
	2001–2010	0	0	0
	2011–2020	30[c]	2[c]	6[c]
Journal of personality assessment	1971–1980	1	0	3
	1981–1990	1	1	0
	1991–2000	3	1	3
	2001–2010	11[c]	1	2
	2011–2020	14[c]	3[c]	4[c]
Psychological assessment[b]	1981–1990	2	0	0
	1991–2000	10	1	0
	2001–2010	6[c]	2[c]	0
	2011–2020	24[c]	3[c]	4[c]

[a]First published in 1994. [b]First published in 1989. [c]One or more articles contain more than one ethnic group.

The period was limited from 2001 to 2020. We perused the titles and abstracts to delete items that were not directly relevant to indigenous East Asian samples and read the actual article when the abstract information was ambiguous. Reviews, meta-analyses, a case discussion, and critical articles were excluded. Only those articles in which the specified ethnic group was the focus or was identified as a distinct group were included. Studies focusing on immigrants, descendants of immigrants, or international students were not included, such as Japanese sojourners and immigrants to the United States, Chinese American, and North Korean refugees. Articles in which an ethnic group was mentioned only as part of a larger sample's composition were also not included. Finally, we divided the period into two groups: 2001–2010 and 2011–2020. Table 13.1 lists the number of articles identified in these two time periods in the three assessment journals combined with table 1 of Cheung et al. (2003) in which the articles were from 1971 to 2000 in the same three assessment journals and included Asian American.

In the chapter to follow we present the history of psychological assessment in China first. Then the development of psychological testing in these decades in China, Japan, and South Korea is introduced respectively.

13.2   The History of Psychological Testing in China

The People's Republic of China (PRC) is located in the east of Asia and on the west coast of the Pacific, with a population of around 1.4 billion in 2019. The official language of China is Chinese.

13.2.1   The Idea and Practice of Psychological Testing in Ancient China

It is believed that tests and testing programs first came into being in China as early as 2200 BCE (DuBois, 1966, 1970). That was the time of Three Sovereigns and Five Emperors according to Chinese classical literature such as the *Records of the Grand Historian* and the *Bamboo Annuals*. It is traditionally believed that Chinese civilization originates from the era of Huang Di and Yan Di, and we Chinese call ourselves the descendants of Yan and Huang. Hundreds of years after the time of Yan Di and Huang Di, Chinese ancient society developed into the age of abdication. Abdication is a system for generating a new chieftain. At that time, two famous examples of abdication were from Yao to Shun and from Shun to Yu. Yao, one of the Five Emperors and chief of the tribal alliance on the central plain, had been on the throne since 2168 BCE. As he grew old, he selected Shun, another one of the Five Emperors, as his successor after careful observation. With the consent of all chieftains, Shun (the last one of the Five Emperors) came to the throne. Following similar procedures, Shun passed the throne to Yu. From a historical perspective, abdication is a traditional election system in the time of tribal commune, yet from a psychological perspective, this is a procedure of psychological testing or assessment. Hence China can be viewed to be among the first places to employ psychological testing (see *the Book of Document,* 尚书)

Contributions of ancient China to psychological testing are not limited to legends but also manifested in several particular aspects (Jin, 2005). Firstly, individual differences were perceived and treated seriously, and psychological properties were believed to be measurable. As early as 2,500 years ago, Confucius proposed the theory of individual differences in the *Analects of Confucius*, which said that human's natures are much the same, but their habits become widely different. He also differentiated between upper wise people and lower fool people according to a person's intelligence and said we could discuss complex and abstruse knowledge with people at or above the medium level, but not with people below medium. Another famous Confucian representative, Mencius, expressed the thought that psychological properties can be measured just like physical properties in the following quote:

> we know the weight by weighing; we know the length by measuring; and we can get to know the psychological properties just like the way we understand physical properties.

Secondly, there were some emergent but concrete psychological assessment practices, especially in the domain of personnel assessment and selection. One good example was the imperial examination system, which germinated in Shang and Zhou Dynasties, flourished in Sui and Tang Dynasties, and reached its zenith in Ming Dynasty. This examination system lasted about 1,300 years until 1905 when the Qing Dynasty faced its demise. Testing was instituted as a means of selecting who, of many applicants, would be competent for government positions. To some extent, psychological testing promoted social progress significantly. Before the implementation of the examination system, there were various kinds of recommendatory systems for personnel selection, including the nine-grade "*zhongzheng*" system (九品中正制), which was initiated in the Western Han Dynasty and annulled in the Sui Dynasty. In such a system, candidates were recommended for the nine-grade feudal official positions by appointed gentlemen and officials. In this system, a person's social position was determined solely by the family he or she was born into. The emergence and operation of the national examination system implied that one could improve one's situation by performing excellently on an examination, which offered opportunities to some talented and diligent people from low-status families.

As might be expected, the contents and formats of the examination changed over time with the cultural expectations and the values of the ruling dynasty. During Shang and Zhou dynasties, six skills of rites and ceremonies, music, archery, driving, writing, and arithmetic were emphasized and tested. All these arts served sacrifices and wars. During Han Dynasty, contents related to the Five Classics were tested, including law, military, agriculture, taxing, and geography. During Tang Dynasty, the examination system improved gradually and became the main official selection procedure, and the formats of testing were increasingly complex and diverse. During the Song and Ming dynasties, tests emphasized the understanding of classical literature. Test takers who demonstrated their mastery of the classics were perceived to have acquired the wisdom of the past and were therefore entitled to a government position. In dynasties with state-sponsored examinations for official positions (referred to as *the imperial examination*), privileges that candidates obtained were dependent on the grade achieved. During some periods, those who passed the examination were entitled to a government job.

Besides practices of state-sponsored examinations, there were a variety of nongovernment self-sponsored measurement activities. *Record on the Subject of Education* was a book edited by an apprentice of Mencius about 2,000 years ago. It was the first book to combine teaching and testing. Some puzzle games like the Tangram puzzle and the Chinese ring originated in China, and these games could be used to train and enhance intelligence and eventually evolved into standardized tests.

Thirdly, with the increasing diversity of test contents, different methods of measurement emerged one after another. Zhuge Liang proposed seven methods to explore human nature in his book (*Jiang Yuan – Zhi Ren Xing*, 将苑-知人性篇). Another book written by Liu Shao in the Three Kingdoms time (220–280 CE), the *Records of Personage* (人物志), could be seen as a monograph on ability and personality, which was translated by an American man, J. K. Shryock, in 1937. Liu categorized people's abilities into 12 kinds, and personality was also divided into 12 kinds via the approaches of eight observations and five inspections. He thought that we could not observe all the behavior of a human, yet we could observe an individual's regular responses in particular situations to know their quality.

In general, ideas and practices of testing in ancient China contributed and inspired a lot of modern-day psychological testing in the region.

13.2.2   Development of Modern Psychological Testing in China (1915–1948)

In the late Qing Dynasty, Western psychology was introduced into China, including modern theories and methods of psychological testing. The first recorded psychological testing was conducted on 500 children in Guangzhou in 1915 by Creighton. In 1916, Fan Bingqing introduced and evaluated the Binet–Simon Scale. He was the first person to introduce Western testing into China formally and systemically. In 1918, Walcott used a revised version of the Stanford–Binet Scale by Terman on students at Tsinghua University. At the same time, Chinese scholars started to develop tests by themselves, among which the Chinese Calligraphy Scales of Elementary School by Yu Ziyi in 1918 was the first native psychological test. In 1920, Liao Shicheng and Chen Heqin began to teach testing courses in Nanjing Higher Normal School. One year later, they published a book named *Methods of Testing* to formally introduce scientific psychological testing.

In 1922, Liao and Chen translated the Binet–Simon Scale manual into Chinese and added several new scales. Then they applied it to a sample of 1,400 persons aged from 3 to 20 in several cities. But the Binet–Simon Scale was first translated into Chinese by Jia Peijie and used in Zhejiang and Jiangsu provinces in 1922. Also in this year, Zhang Yaoxiang published an article about psychological measurement and new examination methods in a journal of educational series. In the autumn of 1922, a psychological and educational testing task group was founded in the Chinese Association for Education Promotion, and an American expert on psychometrics, W. A. McCall, was invited to China to lecture. With the help and supervision of McCall, more than 50 standardized tests were constructed. In 1923, a nationwide large-scale (102,000 in total) general intelligence and educational test was conducted in cooperation with McCall. Age norms, grade norms, and some other statistical indications between the third and the eighth grades were computed. It attracted the attention of many educators. Since 1926, Ai Wei had been working on educational tests and developed a lot of tests for different grades and subjects for elementary schools and high schools under the sponsorship of the China Foundation for the Promotion of Education and Culture. In 1928, a division of scientific testing was founded in the China Vocational Education Association, and a general clerk test was developed under the hosting of Chen Xuanshan. In the same year, a testing section office was founded in the Central Training Department as a committee to develop standardized tests and train professional testing clerks. The Bureau of Children's Intelligence Test was founded in Jiangxi province in 1928, and more than 4,000 children in Nanchang and Jiujiang were tested.

This period from 1915 to 1928 saw the rapid development of psychological testing in China. Unfortunately, because of misuse and exaggeration by some scholars, the development of psychological testing fell sharply during 1929 and 1930. To turn the tables, some psychological scholars like Ai Wei suggested uniting to discuss theories of testing and establish an organization. Then, in 1931, the Chinese Association of Testing was established. There were only three annual meetings: first in 1931, second in 1933, and third in 1936. The journal *Testing* came out in 1932. It published nine issues and 97 articles and ceased after the July 7 Marco Polo Bridge Incident of 1937 (a minor clash between Japanese and Chinese troops near Beiping). From 1931 to 1937, many test programs were planned and progressed. For example, together with Zhang Yaoxiang, Ai Wei devoted himself to tests for learning Chinese characters and assessing children's interest in reading – he eventually developed a Reading Scale. In 1939, the Chinese Association of Testing published an article to show that testing was pervasive in domains of administration management, military, education, industry and commerce, justice, and communication. After the war of resistance against Japan broke out, the work of the association continued and progressed. However, its development was impeded by the war (Zhang & Yu, 2012). In the journal *Research on Educational Psychology*, founded by Ai Wei in 1940, there were still many articles about psychological testing even during the hard period of war (Fan, 1994).

We have introduced much progress on ability testing. In the domain of personality testing, there were also some events worth noting (Dai et al., 2010). Woodworth's personal data sheet was revised by Xiao Xiaorong, who developed norms for people aged from 9 to 15. Some Chinese scholars used personality scales from the West to investigate Chinese students. For example, in 1935, Shen Youqian adopted the personality inventory to conduct cross-cultural comparisons between Chinese and American students and, in 1937, Zhou Xiangeng used Thurstone's emotional stability scale to measure Chinese students. In 1943, Lin Chuanding used the Pressey X-O Test on Chinese adolescents.

13.2.3   Development of Psychological Testing in China after 1949

The PRC was established in 1949. At the time, under the influence of the Soviet Union and later the Cultural Revolution, psychological testing was taboo in China. Psychological measurement and statistics courses had been closed in normal colleges and universities, and the research and practical applications in this field had accordingly ceased.

In the late 1970s, the Cultural Revolution ended. People recognized the role of psychological measurement and various tests again, and realized the importance of understanding individual differences in real life. Since then, psychological test has gradually recovered its status and developed again in China. The third national academic congress of psychology was held in 1979, and a psychological testing task group was founded in the Division of Medical Psychology. Lin Chuanding, Wu Tianmin, and Zhang Houcan organized a national psychological testing training course, which could be seen as the recovery of psychological testing. In 1980, a psychological testing course was first set up in Beijing Normal University, and then more and more universities followed. On the fifth national academic congress of psychology held in 1984, the division of psychological testing under the Chinese Psychological Society (CPS) was established. The first academic conference of this division was held in 1990. In this year, Professor Zhang Houcan attended the conference of the International Test Commission (ITC) and was elected onto the board of directors. Regulations of psychological testing and ethical principles of researchers and practitioners of psychological testing were developed and issued first in 1992, then revised in 2008, and finally published in *Acta Psychologica Sinica* in 2015 (CPS, 2015).

During this period, intelligence testing in China progressed a lot. From 1979 to 1982, WAIS-R was revised under the hosting of Gong Yaoxian for medical diagnosis, and similar work was hosted by Zhang Houcan from 1982 to 1986. WPPSI, WISC-R, and the Binet–Simon Scale were also revised in the 1980s. WISC-IV was revised as a Chinese version under the hosting of Zhang Houcan in 2007 (Zhang, 2009). WPPSI-IV and WAIS-IV were also revised into a Chinese version in recent years (Li, 2012; Wang et al., 2013). Group intelligence tests like Raven's Progressive Matrices were revised and standardized too. Some revised popular personality inventories were also introduced into China, such as Minnesota Multiphasic Personality Inventory (MMPI), Sixteen Personality Factor Questionnaire (16PF), Eysenck Personality Questionnaire (EPQ), and so on. MMPI was first formally revised into a Chinese version in 1980 under the hosting of Song from the Institute of Psychology, Chinese Academy of Sciences (Song, 1985). And in 1991, MMPI-2 was revised and introduced into mainland China and Hong Kong (Zhang et al., 1999). Cattell's 16PF inventory was first revised in 1981 by the Institute of Educational Sciences of Liaoning Province, and a norm was established in this province. Then, in 1985, national norms based on a sample of 2,034 people were constructed (Zhu & Dai, 1988). EPQ was first tested and revised into Chinese in 1981 under the hosting of Chen Zhonggeng (1983), and adult and children norms were obtained under the hosting of Gong Yaoxian (1984). A short version of EPQ-R was revised and validated by Qian Mingyi et al. (2000) and Chinese norms were made.

Beyond the battery of intelligence testing and personality inventory, some individual personality scales were also revised into Chinese, for example, Rosenberg's self-esteem scale, the internal–external locus of control scale, the self-description questionnaire (Wang et al., 1999) and the self-efficacy scale (Zhang & Schwarzer, 1995). Some general or special aptitude tests were also introduced into China, for example, the

Hiskey-Nebraska test of learning aptitude (Qu et al., 1996) and the pupil rating scale revised screening for learning disabilities (Jing et al., 1995). Some scales or questionnaires used in the career domain were introduced and revised by industrial and organizational psychologists, such as Holland's vocational preference inventory, Holland's self-direct search test, Strong–Campbell Interest Inventory, and so on (Zhang et al., 2004).

Many scales were also developed by psychologists from various fields, for example, the mechanical aptitude test battery (Zhang & Tian, 1988), the Chinese Personality Assessment Inventory (CPAI; Song et al., 1993), and other indigenous Chinese personality scales (Wang & Cui, 2003).

Regarding psychometric theories, the classical testing theory is the most popular theory that was widely used in the research and practice of psychological testing (e.g., Jin, 2005), and the item response theory (e.g., Yu, 1992) and the generalizability theory (e.g., Yang & Zhang, 2003) were also introduced and applied.

13.2.4   CPAI: One Representative Personality Test

The goal of the CPAI was to construct an inventory that is relevant to the Chinese cultural context, and would also meet the scientific psychometric standard expected of established assessment instruments, in order to provide the Chinese society with a reliable, valid, and useful personality measure. CPAI was initiated in the early 1990s (Cheung et al., 1996), and has being continuing its development in Hong Kong and Mainland China. Professor F. Cheung and colleagues led the research to work out a second version of CPAI (Cheung et al., 2001).

The CPAI was constructed by adopting a combined etic–emic approach – an approach that takes into account both universal and culture-specific aspects of Chinese personality. CPAI included four normal personality dimensions: social potency, dependability, accommodation, and interpersonal relatedness. What is worth mentioning is that "interpersonal relatedness (IR)" contained many indigenous personality constructs, it showed the pattern of behavior and the cultural connotation of how Chinese people "conduct themselves" in society, such as caring about relationship orientation, avoiding face-to-face conflicts, and maintaining surface harmony, while everyone is able to maintain "face". Interestingly enough, the joint factor analysis of CPAI and Five Factor Model showed that while the four CPAI factors overlap with the Big Five, the IR factor from CPAI stood out as an independent factor in addition to the Big Five Personality Model, which constitute a "Big Six" structure that can be used to describe and explain Chinese personality and behavior (Cheung et al., 2001). Up to now, CPAI-2 has been translated into English, Japanese, Korean, Vietnamese, Dutch, and Romanian. After applying the translated versions into corresponding cultural groups, the IR factor can still be retrieved in some non-Chinese samples (Zhang & Zhou, 2006). The utility of the IR factor has obtained noticeable empirical support and application validity.

Though the CPAI is aimed at applying it to other cultural backgrounds, the effective use of IR inventory in both Chinese and Western cultural backgrounds indicated that it could reveal some deficiencies in Western personality theory and evaluation, which is inclined to focus on intrapsychic and individual traits related to heredity, thereby ignoring the important fields involving social culture and interpersonal relations. These findings prompted the CPAI team to consider the cross-cultural applicability of CPAI-2, and to later rename the CPAI as the "Cross-cultural (Chinese) Personality Assessment Inventory." The CPAI-2 is widely recognized to be a useful personality measure that covers culturally relevant dimensions of the Chinese personality and demonstrates incremental validity beyond Western models of personality.

13.3 Psychological Testing in Japan

Japan is located in East Asia and the Pacific Northwest. The territory consists of the four major islands of Honshu, Shikoku, Kyushu, and Hokkaido, and more than 7,000 small islands. The main ethnic group is the Japanese, and the total population is about 126 million in 2019. Japanese is the common Japanese language.

From the literature it was evident that modern psychological testing in Japan started early in the 1900s and has been studied since the 1930s. Tsujioka (1989) reviewed the development of psychological testing in Japan in these decades. The development can be reflected specifically from the following aspects:

1. A series of standardized foreign scales such as MMPI, Yatabe–Guilford Personality Inventory, WISC, TAT, State–Trait Anxiety Inventory for Children (STAIC), and so on. Based on the original version, some improvements of scaling have been made, for example, three Japanese versions of the Binet-type test and a Japanese version of WISC were scaled by an improved method of scaling.

2. A series of scales and tests were developed independently. Ikuzawa (1954), for example, published the Kyoto Scale of Mental Development for Pre-school Children. In 1982, Ikuzawa and others revised the scale (the Kyoto Scale of Psychological Development, KSPD) and extended the age range up to 13 years old. Meanwhile, it should be noted that the establishment of the National Center for University Entrance Examination (NCUEE) in Tokyo in 1970 encouraged Japanese psychologists to work on evaluative studies of entrance examinations.

3. Some new methods have long been used by Japanese psychologists in developing new measurements, such as item response theory (Indow & Samejima, 1962, 1966) and latent structure analysis (Ikuzawa, 1982, 1984).

4. The new method has been developed to explore examining the cultural similarities and differences in psychological variables. For example, a cultural-link method was used in a large-scale survey over 30 years of a statistical study of the Japanese national character (Hayashi, 1982, 1988).

Besides the research itself, psychological assessment is also widely used in Japan. Anzi (2007) collected and sorted out the application and development of psychological measurement in clinical psychology in Japan. She found that since World War II psychological assessment has been beneficial to the reform of education, medical care, and welfare of the people. In the postwar clinical psychological practice of children's psychological counseling and the juvenile correctional institutions, the psychological measurement must be carried out first.

Hori (2018) collated and analyzed the psychometric scales used from 1990 to 2010. The criteria for the selection and collation were as follows: (a) Japanese question forms (including translation), (b) reliability and feasibility of the two or one party inspection, (c) more than 50 samples are used to test the validity of the scale (the more the better), (d) the subjects of middle school students and above (the fourth book mainly takes infant and children as the main sample), (e) it is still useful now and in the future, and (f) whether it is commercialized. Based on obtaining the reprint permission of the copyright owner and the scales' research results before 1990, about 300 psychometric scales were used in the end. Considering the large quantity and the convenience of users, six sets of scales about the psychological measurement were categorized. From 1990 to 2000, the research on psychological measurement was concentrated in the first to the fourth books, which were organized, discussed, and analyzed from four aspects: individual, individual and society, mental health, and the parent–child relationship. The research on psychometrics after 2000 was concluded in the fifth and sixth books and excluded the psychometric scales introduced before 2000.

13.4 Psychological Testing in South Korea

South Korea is located in East Asia, on the southern half of the Korean Peninsula located out from the far east of the Asian landmass. South Korea's 2020 population is estimated at more than 50 million people at mid-year according to UN data. Korean is the official language of South Korea; Seoul dialect is the standard version that is used on news reports. And there are also five more different dialects from different districts.

The modern psychological testing in South Korea is mostly taking in the counseling scene. It was the 1950s when counseling first started in South Korea. Kim and Kim (2001) described the current situation of the use of psychological tests in adolescent counseling in South Korea, which was very similar to those in foreign countries and sentence completion test (SCT), MMPI, intelligence tests, and painting tests are mostly used. Lee's findings (2010) are very similar to those in the United States in 1982 (Lubin et al. 1984). Except for some aptitude tests, the top 10 psychological test models used in South Korea are almost consistent with those used in the United States.

In addition to counseling scenarios, there were also some psychiatric studies that were related to psychological testing. Research showed that the most commonly used psychological tests in South Korea could be divided into self-report tests, observation methods, intelligence tests, projection tests, and others (Zhang et al.,1989).

As shown in Table 13.2, research on psychological tests in South Korea can be divided into several types according to the fields, but most of them focused on analyzing the frequency of using these tests, so it is not easy to assess the real practicability of these tests. Moreover, most of the research on psychological tests in South Korea is only limited to the field of psychological counseling and has not been extended to other fields. To ensure that these psychological tests can be applied to a variety of scenarios, standardized work is needed for Koreans, and they need to be tested in both the normal population and clinical samples. It is worth mentioning that, as a specialized institution, Korea Institute for Psychological Test Standardization standardized many measurement instruments/psychological tests in Korea, such as the Kaufman Assessment Battery for Korean

Table 13.2. *Research on the current situation of psychological tests in South Korea*

Research	Field	Tests
Zhang et al., (1989)	Psychiatric research	Self-report test, observation, intelligence test, projection test, others
Kim & Kim (2001)	Youth counseling	MBTI, SCT, MMPI, Vocational Aptitude Test, Drawing Test, Intelligence Test, and Academic Test
Lee (2010)	Personal consultation	SCT, MMPI, MBTI, Drawing Test (HTP & KFD), Intelligence Test (WAIS/WISC), Vocational Exploration Test, Aptitude Test

Children (KABC, KABC-II), Detroit Tests of Visual Aptitude (DTVP-II, DTVP-III), Korean Kaufman Brief Intelligence Test, Second Edition (KBIT- II), and so on.

13.5 Challenges and Future Directions of Psychological Testing in East Asia

Psychological testing and assessment are important tools for psychologists in their research and practice. With the rapid development of the global economy, psychologists face many challenges in testing and assessment in the East Asian region. These challenges include the development of psychological measurements (the lack of scientific tools relevant to the local context), shortage of qualified professionals, problems in test translation, high costs of standardized tests, big data protection issues, and copyright violations in test use, among others. ITC guidelines are helpful in promoting the standards of testing and assessment in China. However, it is necessary for the divisions of psychological testing in each of the countries to establish local codes and rules for research and practice related to psychological testing and promote progress in this field. Journals related to this division should be re-established, which would play an important role as a platform for academic publishing, idea exchanging, and promotion of the development of this discipline.

REFERENCES

Anzi, J. (2007). A history of Japanese TAT studies. *The Proceedings of the Annual Convention of the Japanese Psychological Association, 71,* 1AM001 (in Japanese).

Chen, Z. G. (1983). Item analysis of Eysenck Personality Questionnaire tested in Beijing-District. *Acta Psychologica Sinica, 15*(2), 85–92.

Cheung, F. M., Leong, F. T. L., & Ben-Porath, Y. S. (2003). Psychological assessment in Asia: introduction to the special section. *Psychological Assessment, 15*(3), 243–247.

Cheung, F. M., Leung, K., Fan, R. M., Song, W. Z., Zhang, J. X., & Zhang, J. P. (1996). Development of the Chinese Personality Assessment Inventory. *Journal of Cross-Cultural Psychology, 27*(2), 181–199.

Cheung, F. M., Leung, K., Zhang, J. X., Sun, H. F., Gan, Y. Q., Song, W. Z., & Xie, D. (2001). Indigenous Chinese personality constructs: Is the five-factor model complete? *Journal of Cross-Cultural Psychology, 32*, 407–433.

CPS. (2015). Regulations on the Administration of Psychological Tests[心理测验管理条例] *Acta Psychologica Sinica, 47*, 1415–1418.

Dai, H. Q., Zhang, F., & Chen, X. F. (2010). *Psychological and educational measurement* (revised ed.). Guangzhou: Jinan University Press.

DuBois, P. H. (1966). A test-dominated society: China 1115 B. C. E–1905 A. D. In A. Anastasi (ed.), *Testing problems in perspective* (pp. 29–36). Washington, DC: American Council on Education.

(1970). *A history of psychological testing*. Boston, MA: Allyn & Bacon.

Fan, Z. (1994). Chinese association of testing in the period of Republic of China. *Republican Archives*, (1), 140–143.

Gong, Y. X. (1984). Eysenck Personality Questionnaire Revised in China. *Journal of Psychological Science, 4*, 13–20.

Hayashi, C. (1982). *The study of Japanese in three decades*. Tokyo: Shiseido (in Japanese).

Hayashi. C. (1988). *Measuring Japanese minds*. Tokyo: Asahi Sinbun Sha (in Japanese).

Hori, Y. (2018). Psychometric scale set (electronic version). Tokyo Katsuma society (in Japanese).

Ikuzawa, M. (1954). A report on the construction of Kyoto scale of mental development for preschool children. *Studies in the Humanities, Osokn City University, 5*, 58–75 (in Japanese).

(1982). Latent class analysis of revised Kyoto scale of psychological development: From 0 to 13 year old children. *Bulletin of the Faculty of Literature, Osaka City University, 34*, 629–657 (in Japanese).

(1984). Latent class analysis of Kyoto scale of psychological development: Correspondence of chronological age groups with latent classes. *Bulletin of the Faculty of Literature, Osaka City University, 36*, 313–336 (in Japanese).

Indow, T. & Samejima, F. (1962). *LIS measurement scale of reasoning ability.* Tokyo: Nippon Bunka Kagaku-sha (in Japanese).

Indow. T. & Samejima, F. (1966). On the results obtained by the absolute scale model and the Lord model in the field of intelligence. *The third report from the Psychological Laboratory on the Hiyoshi campus, Keio University* (in Japanese).

Jin, Y. (2005). *Psychological measurement* (2nd ed.). Shanghai: East China Normal University Press.

Jing, J., Yu, M., & Deng, G. F. (1995). Development of the revised PRS and the application to pupils. *Psychological Development and Education, 11*(2), 24–29.

Kim, Y. B. & Kim, K. H. (2001). Use of psychological tests in youth counseling. *The Korean Journal of Counseling and Psychotherapy, 13*(3), 149–162 (in Korean).

Lee, H. (2010). *Choice and use of psychological tests in personal counseling. Master Dissertation.* (Master's dissertation, Sungkyunkwan University, Seoul, South Korea) (in Korean).

Li, Y. Q. (2012). *The new development of the Wechsler preschool and primary scale of intelligence.* Abstracts of the 15th national conference on psychology

Liu, H. (2007). Influence of China's imperial examinations on Japan, Korea and Vietnam, *Frontiers of History in China, 2*(4), 493–512.

Lubin, B., Larsen, R. M., & Matarazzo, J. D. (1984). Patterns of psychological test usage in the United States: 1935–1982. *American Psychologist, 39*(4), 451–454.

Qian, M. Y., Wu, G. C., Zhu, R. C., & Zhang, X. (2000). Development of the revised Eysenck Personality Questionnaire short scale for Chinese. *Acta Psychologica Sinica, 32*(3), 317–323.

Qu, C. Y., Sun, X. B., & Zhang, P. Y. (1996). The Chinese Norms of H-NTLA for Deaf Children and Adolescents. *Chinese Journal of Clinical Psychology, 4* (4), 202–205.

Song, W. Z. (1985). Analysis of results of MMPI of normal Chinese subjects. *Acta Psychologica Sinica, 17*(4), 10–19.

Song, W. Z., Zhang, J. X., Zhang, J. P., Cheung, F. M., & Leung, K. (1993). The significance and process of developing Chinese Personality Assessment Inventory (CPAI). *Acta Psychologica Sinica, 25*(4), 400–407.

Tsujioka, B. (1989). Psychological assessment in Japan in these decades. *Applied Psychology, 38*(4), 353–372.

Wang, D. F. & Cui, H. (2003). Processes and preliminary results in the construction of the Chinese Personality Scale (QZPS). *Acta Psychologica Sinica, 35*(1), 127–136.

Wang, J., Zou, Y. Z., Cui, J. F., Fan, H. Z., Chen, N ... & Jiang. X. (2013). Reliability and construct validity of the Chinese version of the Wechsler Adult Intelligence Scale-Fourth Edition. *Chinese Mental Health Journal, 27* (9), 692–697.

Wang, X. D., Wang, C. L., & Ma, H. (1999). *Handbook of mental health assessment scales.* Beijing: Chinese Mental Health Press.

Yang, Z. M. & Zhang, L. (2003). *Generalizability theory and its applications.* Beijing: Educational Science Publishing House.

Yu, J. Y. (1992). *Item response theory and its applications.* Nanjing: Jiangsu Education Press.

Zhang, H. C. (2009). The revision of WISC-IV Chinese version. *Journal of Psychological Science, 32*(5), 1177–1179.

Zhang, H. C. & Tian, G. Z. (1988). Introducing the Mechanical Aptitude Test Battery. *Acta Psychologica Sinica, 20*(2), 24–31.

Zhang, H. C., & Yu, J. Y. (2012). The history of psychological testing development in China. *Journal of Psychological Science, 35*(3), 514–521.

Zhang, H. C., Feng, B. L., & Yuan, K. (2004). Characteristics of vocational interest of Chinese high school students and the development of interest Scale for their college entrance and career guidance. *Acta Psychologica Sinica, 36*(1), 89–95.

Zhang, H., Ban, G., Kim, K., & Yum, T. (1989). A review on the psychological test instruments used for psychiatric research in Korea. *Journal of Korean Neuropsychiatric Association, 28*, 697–704 (in Korean).

Zhang, J. X. & Schwarzer, R. (1995). Measuring optimistic self-beliefs: A Chinese adaptation of the general self-efficacy scale. *Psychologia, 38*(3), 174–181.

Zhang, J. X. & Zhou, M. J. (2006). Searching for a Personality Structure of Chinese: A Theoretical Hypothesis of a Six Factor Model of Personality Traits. *Advances in Psychological Science, 14*(4), 574–585.

Zhang, J. X., Song, W. Z., & Cheung, F. M. (1999). Introduction to the new Minnesota Multiphasic Personality Inventory (MMPI-2) and its standardization process in mainland China and Hong Kong. *Chinese Mental Health Journal, 13*(1), 20–23.

Zhu, B. L. & Dai, Z. H. (1988). Norm of 16 PF constructed with Chinese subjects. *Journal of Psychological Science, 11*(6), 16–20.

CHAPTER 14

Psychological Assessment and Testing in Malaysia and Singapore

Ivan M. H. Lee and N. Sheereen Zulkefly

14.1 Introduction

This chapter reviews the history and development of psychological assessment and testing in the region of Southeast Asia. Malaysia and Singapore are the focus of this chapter as both countries share similar yet significant historical, racial, and cultural backgrounds. Given that the field of psychological testing is more prominent in Western countries, it is natural for countries within Southeast Asia, or in this chapter Malaysia and Singapore, to adapt to Western cultures. The major question will then be pointing toward the validity and reliability of most psychological assessment and testing if they are used within Southeast Asia, with various native languages cohabiting within the societies. Thus, the aim of this review is to provide an update regarding the cross-cultural validity of psychological assessment in Southeast Asia, as well as to introduce instruments that are appropriately and culturally adapted and developed.

14.2 Contextualizing Malaysia

Malaysia is a multiracial federation situated in Southeast AsiaIt is composed of two noncontiguous regions – that is, Peninsular Malaysia and East Malaysia – which are divided by the South China Sea. Peninsular Malaysia, situated on the southernmost section of the Malay Peninsula, is neighbors with south of Thailand, north of Singapore, and east of the Indonesian island of Sumatra. Peninsular Malaysia can be further categorized into four regions: Northern, Southern, Central, and East Coast. Each region consists of several states and some have federal territories. In total, Peninsular Malaysia has 11 states and two federal territories. East Malaysia, on the other hand, is situated mostly on the northern part of Borneo island. It comprises of the two largest states and one federal territory in Malaysia – Sabah and Sarawak – and has land bordering with Brunei to the north and Indonesian Borneo to the south. In terms of the country's total area including approximately 265 square miles (690km^2) of inland water, Peninsular Malaysia covers 40% of the country's land, whereas East Malaysia constitutes about 60% (Lockard et al., 2020).

The population of Malaysia as of the second quarter of 2019 is estimated to be 32.58 million with an annual population growth rate of 1.1% (Department of Statistics Malaysia, 2019). Out of the total population, approximately 25.7 million Malaysians live in the Peninsular Malaysia, while 6.7 million live in East Malaysia. As a country that has been colonized by Portugal and Britain (1500s–1800s) and occupied by Japan (1941–1945), Malaysia is proof that colonization has significant influences on the psychology of individuals regarding race and culture (Okazaki et al., 2008). Malaysia, known as Malaya pre-colonization, was dominated by the indigenous population but evolved into a multi-ethnic, multicultural, and multireligious country due to the migration of individuals from different countries during the colonization. The colonial administrators started to define the diverse population by racial categories based on the individual's original countries. Today, the Malaysian citizens are divided along ethnic groups, with the majority (69.3%) being Malays, followed by Chinese (22.8%), and Indians (6.9%). Out of the total population, 66.7% practices Islam, 17.9% Buddhism, 9.0% Christianity, 5.1% Hinduism, and 1.3% traditional Chinese religion. The remainder are accounted by other faiths and belief systems (Department of Statistics Malaysia, 2010). The national language of Malaysia is *Bahasa Malaysia* known as Malaysian language or Malay language. Malay language is spoken by most of the country and is the official language use in the government and public education system. Malaysian English derived from the British English remains as the second most commonly spoken language in Malaysia (Lockard et al., 2020). It is often used in education and at times allowed for some official government purposes under the National Language Act of 1967. In addition to these two languages, there are other languages spoken by Malaysians. The Chinese predominantly speak Mandarin, which is widely used in schools and business, while the Tamil language is predominantly spoken by Indian Malaysian. The indigenous tribes in Malaysia have their own unique and distinct ancestral language heritage including subdialects. On the Malaysian Peninsular, the major language groupings are Negrito, Senoi, and Malayic. Meanwhile in East Malaysia, the native people in Sarawak commonly speak Iban, while those in Sabah mainly speak Dusun or Kadazan.

In terms of economy, Malaysia is at present an upper-middle income country. Since its independence from the United Kingdom in 1957, Malaysia has seen rapid changes in its economy from agriculture to manufacturing and services (Yusof & Bhattasali, 2008). Since 2010, Malaysia's economy has been soaring upward with an average growth of 5.4% and is expected to achieve a high-income economy by 2024 (Hill, 2010). In 2018, Malaysia's economy grew 4.7%, with a value of Gross Domestic Product (GDP) recorded at RM1.23 trillion (USD3 billion) at constant prices and MYR1.43 trillion (USD3.49 billion) at current prices. For the year 2019, the Malaysian economy expanded moderately by 4.3% (Central Bank of Malaysia, 2020) mainly due to private sector spending. It is expected that for the year 2020, Malaysia's economy will remain stable despite the affect from the coronavirus outbreak (Central Bank of Malaysia, 2020). It is likely that the support from private sector activity, household spending, and higher sector capital spending will help with the economic growth despite the overall impact of the COVID-19 virus on the Malaysian economy (Central Bank of Malaysia, 2020). In line with the objectives of Shared Prosperity Vision 2030, Malaysia will be restructuring the economy by developing new economic areas and creating business opportunities and high-paying jobs (Ministry of Economic Affairs, 2019). This move by the government will require an inclusive, sustainable, and meaningful economic development to provide a decent standard of living for all Malaysians.

14.3   History of Psychology in Malaysia

The field of psychology in Malaysia first started in the early 1960s as a service subject offered by several departments (e.g., anthropology, sociology, medicine, and education) at Universiti Malaya, the oldest university in Malaysia (Rahman, 2005). Psychology as a discipline became prominent with the establishment of several local universities such as Universiti Kebangsaan Malaysia (UKM), Universiti Pertanian (now known as Putra) Malaysia (UPM), International Islamic University Malaysia (IIUM), Universiti Malaysia Sabah (UMS), and Universiti Teknologi Malaysia (UTM). With the establishment of these universities, Malaysia became the fifth country in Asia after Bangladesh, India, China, and Taiwan to introduce psychology as a subject or program offered in the local universities (Rahman, 2005).

Psychology grew in importance with the establishment of the first Department of Psychology at UKM in 1979, which was upgraded to the

Center of Psychological Studies and Human Development in 2002, and the first Faculty of Psychology in UMS known as the School of Psychology and Social Work in 1995 (Rahman, 2005). In 1987, a Psychology Colloquium was organized by Dewan Bahasa dan Pustaka where a meeting for psychologists in Malaysia was held. Subsequently, in the following year, the first psychology association, the Malaysian Psychological Association (PSIMA), was founded. Along with the Department of Psychology at UKM, PSIMA played an important role in promoting psychology. Series of seminars and workshops were organized to provide a platform for psychologists across Malaysia to discuss issues related to the psychology discipline.

Another important milestone that has marked the growth of psychology in Malaysia is the establishment of the Department of Psychology in the Kuliyyah of Islamic Revealed Knowledge and Humane Science, IIUM in 1990. This department provided a platform for psychology students to examine systematically and critically the role of modern-day Western psychological theories and how Islam contributed to the knowledge (Rahman, 2005).

With the increasing demand for psychology in society, the numbers of students, faculties, and departments offering psychology both at undergraduate and postgraduate levels have surged. Recent years have seen the growth of new public universities such as Universiti Malaysia Sarawak (UNIMAS), Universiti Utara Malaysia (UUM), Universiti Teknologi Mara (UiTM), and Sultan Idris Education University (UPSI). Psychological courses and programs are now offered at private universities as well. HELP University College through the Faculty of Behavioral Sciences was the first private university to offer a degree in psychology in Malaysia in the mid-1990s. Psychology at this university started as a service center to offer counseling and psychological services to the students. As the university employed more counselors and psychologists, the psychological services offered grew, and culminated in the establishment of programs and degrees, and a specialized Faculty of Psychology and Behavioral Sciences. In the following years, undergraduate and postgraduate psychology programs have been offered by the International Medical University (IMU), Sunway University, UNISEL-Universiti Selangor, Universiti Tunku Abdul Rahman (UTAR), Monash University Malaysia, University of Nottingham Malaysia Campus, Cyberjaya University of College Medical Sciences (CUCMS), UCSI University Malaysia, Taylor's University, and University College of Islam Melaka (KUIM).

New psychological associations have been established to support and promote psychology to the nation. In the early 2000s, a handful of clinical psychologists worked together toward creating a professional association for clinical psychologists. This association, later known as the Malaysian Society of Clinical Psychology (MSCP), became the professional voice and registration body to protect professional integrity as well as public interest. By December 2009, a meeting of around 40 clinical psychologists elected a pro tem committee who later then worked on registering the Society with the Registrar of Societies. Among the objectives of the MSCP was to promote and improve research in psychology, and to disseminate psychological knowledge through meetings, lectures, professional contacts, discussion, and publications.

14.4   The Development of Psychological Assessments in Malaysia

Psychological assessment is undoubtedly an essential feature in the profession of psychology. It is common practice among professional psychologists to use scientific tools in a variety of settings such as clinical and counseling work, personnel selection, and program evaluation. Furthermore, the use of psychological tools strengthens the professional capability of psychologists, provides objectives measures for decision-making, and enhances the professional profiles of psychologists (Fauzaman et al., 2005). In the past, most psychological assessments were related to industrial and counseling psychology. A study by Fauzaman, Ansari, and Khan (2005) on the patterns of psychological assessments in Malaysia indicated that despite the number of professionals interested in the area of psychological assessments, the field was not yet fully developed. That study further reported that psychological assessments were mostly translations of English tests into Malay or Chinese, whereas work on original test development and adaptation was still lacking. Fauzaman and colleagues also stated that among the major factors that hindered the professional development of psychological tests in Malaysia were lack of research, lack of or unavailability of training in specialized tests, poor documentation, and absence of infrastructure (Fauzaman et al., 2005).

As most psychological assessment tools used by professional psychologists in Asia are a direct translation of their Western counterparts, there has been a great need for a more culturally relevant and sensitive psychological test for Asian populations (Cheung et al., 2003). Earlier studies have documented research of test use in various countries throughout different periods. Particularly, in the early years of the 2000s, studies (i.e., Butcher et al., 2003; Cheung et al., 2003; Chan et al., 2003) emphasized the current status and problems of psychological tools in the Asian context.

Despite most Western tools being commonly translated into Asian context, the quality and translation of the adaptation varies (Cheung et al., 2003), and the tools were interpreted under the assumption that they were equivalent to the original version (Cheung et al., 2003). Similarly, Fowler (2002) emphasized that the direct translation and adaptation of Western tools create doubts on the adequacy and suitability in a non-Western context as most of the translated tools were not standardized for the non-Western population. Therefore, having psychological tests that are more culturally suited for the population at hand would be beneficial to clients in a non-Western context.

Studies on psychological assessments in Asia could be traced back to the early 2000s. Past studies (Butcher et al., 2003; Cheung et al., 2003; Chan et al., 2003) reviewed cognitive and neuropsychological assessment as well as the MMPI-2 with the Asian population. These studies reported the development and utilization of psychological tools in Asian countries such China, Hong Kong, Japan, Korea, Taiwan, Thailand, and Vietnam. However, Malaysia was not reported.

The earliest documentation found on the development of tests and measurements in Malaysia was a study by Maznah and Lah in 1987. In their study, they mentioned research involving the Mooney Problem Checklist, Tennessee Self-Concept Scale, School-Anxiety Scale, Holland Vocational Interest Blank, Work Values Inventory, Test of General Aptitude, and Repertory Grid Technique. These tests as reported by Maznah and Lah (1987) were mostly use in the context of counseling. In 2005, Fauzaman et al. (2005) conducted a study to examine the current development of psychological testing in Malaysia including nature of testing (i.e., translation and adaptation) and further recommendations for future usage. The respondents of their study were 65 potential users of psychological tests in Malaysia comprising clinical and industrial/organizational psychologists, psychiatrists, counselors, and educators in various sectors. Fauzaman et al. (2005) reported that less than half of the respondents of their study has received professional training in testing at local or overseas higher education institutions. The most common psychological tests used for cognitive ability measures are the Wechsler Intelligence Scale for Children (WISC; Wechsler, 1955, 1974), Wechsler Adult Intelligence Scale (WAIS; Wechsler, 1955, 1974), and Progressive Matrices Test. For the personality test, the most frequently used are the Beck Depression Inventory, Eysenck Personality Inventory/Questionnaire (EPI/Q) and General Health Questionnaire. Another personality test that was often used in clinical settings is the Minnesota Multiphasic Personality Inventory (MMPI; Hathaway & McKinley, 1967). Other tests that were less popularly used included Rorschach, Millon Clinical Multiaxial Inventory, Halstead–Rietan Neuropsychological Inventory, and Luria–Nebraska Neuropsychological Battery.

As the psychological tools commonly used by psychologists in Malaysia originated from the West, professionals have been found to either conduct a test in English or translate it into Malay or Mandarin. Since the majority of Malaysians are Malay, psychological tests are most often found to be directly translated into the Malay language. Among the earlier translated tests popularly used are the Child Behaviour Checklist, EPI, General Health Questionnaire, MMPI, and Strait-Trait Anxiety Inventory (Fauzaman et al., 2005). However, as there are various translation versions of these psychological assessments done by different researchers, the quality of translation and adaptation to the Malaysian culture has raised concerns.

In the past years, a database known as the Malaysian Questionnaire Database (MQDB) was developed by the Mental Health Information and Research Center (Ramli, 2019). The MQDB contained a listing of psychological assessments that have been translated to Malay. Based on the database, there are 141 assessments related to the field of psychology. Out of this number, 103 measurements are validated, five are undergoing validation, and only 26 are translated without any validation documentation. Among some of the examples of psychological tools that have been translated and validated are the Automatic Thought Questionnaire (Oei & Mukhtar, 2008), Dysfunctional Attitude Scale Malay (Mukhtar & Oei, 2010), Beck Anxiety Inventory for Malays (BAI-Malay; Mukhtar & Zulkefly, 2011), Amsterdam Preoperative Anxiety and Information Scale (APAIS; Lai & Loh, 2015), and Depression, Anxiety, and Stress Scale (DASS; Musa et al., 2011). It is important to note that this database is built upon the contribution of researchers on the effort in translating and validating assessments. Further, for the MQDB to be updated, researchers all over Malaysia would need to contribute to recent publications on any psychological assessment tools.

Based on the MQDB, there are a few indigenous comprehensive personality inventories developed for the Malaysian population. Some of these native instruments are adaptations of Western measures developed by local researchers to suit the cultural sensitivity of the Malaysian population. As an example, the International Index of Erectile Function (IIEF-15; Rosen et al., 1997) has been adapted and validated from its original version for use in Malaysia (Lim et al., 2003). On the other hand, there are some local instruments developed by cross-cultural psychologists with theoretical interests in indigenous personality constructs. For instance, the Muslim Religiosity Personality Inventory (MRPI; Krauss et al., 2005) was developed to examine the application of Islamic teaching in everyday life in a sample of Muslim youth in Malaysia.

Although the number of psychological assessments has increased, there is still a paucity of empirical data on the translation and validation of world-known assessment batteries such as the Wechsler tests and MMPI. As both Wechsler's tests and MMPI are the primary tools to measure overall cognitive functioning and personality among the clinical psychologists, a translated and validated version suitable to the Malaysian culture is needed. It is important to note that cross-cultural comparisons, local standardization, and validation studies are required in order to prevent presumptuous interpretation of test results according to the original tests. Furthermore, an accurate translation from the original version of an assessment is insufficient to ensure cross-cultural equivalence.

14.5   Contextualizing Singapore

"Little Red Dot" is often used in casual conversation and/or in the media as a reference to Singapore. The city-state has a total land area of no more than 718.3km^2 and, compared to Malaysia or any other Southeast Asia neighbors, it is significantly smaller. As of June 2018, Singapore has a population of approximately 5.64 million and a large percentage of this number are non-residents. It is the second densest city-state in the world after Monaco. Similar to Malaysia, Singapore is a multiracial and multicultural country with the citizen population percentage breakdown of 76.2% (Chinese), 15% (Malay), and 7.4% (Indian), making up the majority of the population (National Population and Talent Division, 2014).

The city-state is recognized as a global city with its primary node in the global economic network. Singapore is a highly developed country, and it is the only country in Asia with an AAA sovereign rating. It is also ranked ninth on the UN Human Development Index and with the seventh highest GDP per capita in the world. Singapore is placed highly in key social indicators including health care, quality of life, personal safety and housing, and education (UN Development Programme, 2019).

Singapore has four official languages: English, Chinese, Malay, and Tamil – with English as the nation's lingua franca and Malay as the national language. English is used as the language of business and government, and in schools. All subjects are taught and assessed in

English except for other language papers, also known as the mother tongue subjects (Dixon, 2009).

14.6   History of Psychology in Singapore

According to Long (1983, 1987), one of the pioneer psychologists in Singapore, during its early development psychology focused on clinical and medical services. The teaching of psychology in Singapore started in the King Edward VII College of Medicine (previously known as the Straits Settlement and Federated Malay States Government Medical School) in 1914. It was the first clinical course in psychological medicine being taught to the medical students. However, despite psychology being offered as early as 1914, the growth of this field was stunted. Psychology did not have its own recognized program nor its own separate department until several decades later. It was implemented as part of the social work curriculum in 1952. Only in 1976 was a sociology/psychology program offered as a standalone degree under the Faculty of Arts of Nanyang University, which unfortunately was discontinued after the merger of the Nanyang University and the University of Singapore into the National University of Singapore (Blowers & Turtle, 1987).

Psychological services in Singapore started in the medical field in 1956 when Australian psychologist V. W. Wilson was appointed to the Colonial Medical Service. He was tasked with incorporating a full psychological service within a mental health program based at the Woodbridge (Mental) Hospital (currently known as the Institute of Mental Health). He established a framework of psychological services that included four major functions: (1) providing psychological and clinical services in medial, social welfare, and educational fields; (2) planning a program of basic psychological research on social and cultural influences; (3) organizing formal courses in psychology for psychiatric nurses and other professional staff working with psychological problems; and (4) making available professional advice to government bodies (Tan, 2002).

The growth of the field was relatively slow and stunted in the 1960s and even the 1970s. It has been long reported that "psychology, re-implanted as a psychiatry-based service was hardly seen as relevant to Singapore's drive towards industrialization. As an academic subject, psychology was regarded as a 'soft' science involving experiments with rats and the like. The pressing need of Singapore was a technocrat in a factory, not a rat in a Skinner box." (cited in Blowers & Turtle, 1987, 232). Two reasons were identified that could explain the slow progression of the field: (1) resistance to foreign interference to Singapore's socio-political policies after independence in 1965; and (2) the establishment of psychological services in psychiatric services. Within psychiatric services, applied psychological services were gradually being accepted and in fact provided major contributions to the governmental sector. More psychologists were employed in the ministries and public services, including the Ministry of Health under the Department of Psychology, the Armed Forces' Education Department, Ministry of Defence, Ministry of Education (MOE), Institute of Education, and Ministry of Home Affairs, which provided services to Juvenile Court Probation and Aftercare Service and the Prisons Department.

On January 11, 1979, the Singapore Psychological Society (SPS) was officially established and listed as a registered society (Supplement of the Republic of Singapore Government Gazette, 1979). On January 20, 1979, the SPS was inaugurated with 40 founding members with the aim to advance psychology as a science and a profession in Singapore (Long, 1983). It was set to promote psychological knowledge and its application for the benefit of the people. The formation of this society showed an acceptance of psychologists by other professionals as a distinct professional group (Long, 1983). To date, the membership of the SPS has increased from 40 to more than 1,000. The SPS continues to serve as a central body of institution to promote ethical psychological practices to the people (Lim, 2000).

The advancement of psychology as an independent discipline and profession lies heavily on its teaching at higher education institutions. In 1986, a more comprehensive program of psychology was offered to undergraduates at the Department of Social Work and Psychology, National University of Singapore (NUS) and this establishment marked the beginning of a systemic study of psychology (Tan, 2002). Half a decade later, the then Division of Psychological Studies (currently known as the Psychological Studies Academic Group) of the National Institute of Education (NIE, 1997–1998) played a major role in teaching psychology to student teachers of the diploma, degree, and postgraduate programs. The modules are structures according to the MOE's policies and initiatives. Various institutions then introduced psychology into their programs and the discipline started to grow exponentially. These included the Singapore Management University, Nanyang Polytechnic (offering an integrated program for nursing), and Ngee Ann Polytechnic (offering an early childhood education program). There was also a growth in psychology graduate programs by the late 1990s.

14.7   The Development of Psychological Assessment in Singapore

It has always been the role of the psychologist to conduct psychological assessment involving the use of various psychological tests and measures in the study and understanding of human behavior.

Due to the nature of how psychology was introduced in Singapore, psychological assessment and testing were mainly conducted in clinical settings. Psychological assessment and testing were part of the framework for psychological services at the Woodbridge (Mental) Hospital laid by Wilson and Wong Man Kee (another pioneer psychologist) in 1956. This appears to be the earliest evidence of the use of psychological testing in Singapore. The purpose of psychological assessment and testing was essentially to facilitate the clinical diagnosis of psychiatric patients at the Woodbridge (Mental) Hospital as well as the classification of young residents at several welfare homes. During the late 1950, Wilson had used psychological tests for the study of juvenile prostitutes as well as evaluating the responses of Asian people on the Rorschach test. A psychological testing program, which included the Stanford–Binet Intelligence Scale, WISC, Bender Visual Motor Gestalt Test (abbreviated as Bender-Gestalt test), and Vineland Social Maturity Scale, was already well established for children at the Singapore General Hospital's Pediatrics Department in 1968. Long (2019) reported that the purpose was to assist the pediatricians and doctors to gage the developmental milestones of the young patients there.

The tests commonly used by psychologists at the Woodbridge (Mental) Hospital (during the 1960s–1980s) included tests of intelligence (e.g., WAIS, WISC, Stanford–Binet Intelligence Scale, Raven's Progressive Matrices, etc.), cognitive functions (e.g., Bender–Gestalt test, Graham and Kendall's Memory-for-Designs Test), personality (Rorschach inkblot test, Thematic Apperception Test – TAT, Children's Apperception Test – CAT, EPI, Sixteen Personality Factor Questionnaire – 16PF, MMPI), achievement (e.g., Schonell Reading and Spelling tests), aptitude and vocational interests (e.g., Study of Values – SOV, Rothwell–Miller Vocational Interest Blank). Some of these tests were in all likelihood also used in the Singapore Armed Forces and MOE. For the selection of Public Service Commission (PSC) scholarship candidates, a battery of tests (intellectual ability, personality, critical thinking, values, etc.) was administered to applicants by psychologists.

By the late 1960s and early 1970s there were several psychology graduate officers in the Singapore Armed Forces as well as the MOE who conducted psychological testing in their respective fields. In the Singapore Armed Forces and Ministry of Defence, with the setting up of the Personnel Research Department (later PRED then ABSD), testing was used for selection and classification of military personnel. At the MOE, an active vocational guidance program was established in the mid-1960s. Later, in 1984, the Gifted Education Program (GEP) was launched to identify the top 1% of pupils of each year's cohort by means of psychometric testing. In the 1970s, the Renal Unit established the hemodialysis and kidney transplant program at Singapore General Hospital. Psychological assessment was included in the selection of suitable candidates for such treatment. During the late 1970s and early 1980s, the PSC required psychological testing as an important aspect of the selection of PSC scholarship applicants.

Those aforementioned psychological tests were essentially used by trained psychologists and officers who were graduates in psychology employed at other government ministries or institutions. There were also guidance and educational officers who were trained in the use of achievement and vocational tests. At the then University of Singapore, the serving student physician, Dr. Kadri (1971) had used the MMPI on the student population. His study was recorded as the first and only MMPI study in Singapore at that time that depicted a profile of Singapore university students using the original English MMPI, but no data on cross-validation with the Chinese MMPI were given (Kadri, 1971). Results of his study showed that the test–retest reliability of the Chinese MMPI (N = 144, male = 52, female = 92) was good with an average of 0.83 across scales.

The Myers–Briggs Type Indicator (MBTI) was also used in Singapore and its first published usage was dated back in 1990s (Tan & Tan, 2000). The article focuses on the use of the MBTI in Singapore and builds on previous findings based on a group of managers between 1997 and 1999 where MBTI scores were also compared with those of students from local universities. This research attempted to provide a validation of the instrument by comparing the Singaporean respondents' scores on the MBTI with the EPQ and the California Personality Inventory (CPI).

The main criterion for the use of psychological tools was that the user must have the proper training and qualification for their use. This guideline was in accordance with the sales condition stipulated by the test publishers (e.g., National Foundation for Educational Research, ACER Psychological Assessment Services, Psychological Corporation) of the time. Also, the psychological tests were selected for use on the basis of having adequate psychometric properties (validity, reliability, etc.). By the 1980s, there were management consultants and human resource specialists who purportedly also used "psychological tools" for their profiling work. In general, psychologists had refrained from using tests that had questionable or unknown psychometric properties.

Apart from making modifications to certain test items on tests such as the WAIS and WISC to suit our cultural context, making translations of the EPI, 16PF, and MMPI into Chinese and Malay, and establishing local norms for several tests (e.g., Raven's Progressive Matrices, 16PF, etc.), there were hardly any original psychological tests developed locally. In the year 2000, the Wechsler Objective Reading and Language Dimensions (WORLD) – which was a representation of children aged 6 to 12 years old – was adapted, validated, and standardized in Singapore (Rust, 2000).

In 1987, an effort was made to validate the EPQ for Singapore use. Later, in the early 1990s, the psychologists at the Institute of Mental Health (previously known as the Woodbridge Hospital) developed the SCOPE-I (Stress Coping Inventory) for its own mental health program. Careful attempts were made to ensure its validity and reliability and other psychometric properties. In the late 1990s, the Rape Trauma Questionnaire was developed for a pilot study in identifying and differentiating rape victims from false complainants. However, no further continuation of said questionnaire and its date were being recorded.

Over the years, psychological assessment and testing have been evolving. In the 1950s and 1960s, psychologists were perceived as mental testers. During the early years in the mental health and medical settings, psychological testing was treated by the medical personnel as akin to laboratory testing (e.g., blood, urine, etc.). Psychologists were regarded somewhat like laboratory technicians who carried out certain tests as requested by the doctors. It took some time to convince the medical fraternity that psychologists were professionals in their own rights, and that psychological assessments were used as scientific measures in the study of behavior. In the medico-legal field, psychologists were required to conduct psychological assessment on persons charged for various criminal offenses, especially capital offenses. In his experience as a pioneer psychologist in Singapore, Long (2019) shared that psychologists at that time would be called upon as expert witnesses in their own right to present their findings to the court after assessing the accused's mental state when the question of "abnormality of mind" was raised.

In the early 1980s the syndrome approach (versus unitary concept) was applied in clinical neuropsychological assessment of cognitive dysfunctions, differential diagnoses, lateralization and localization of lesions, and so on by using a battery of short psychological measures and tests. Long (2019) further added that this approach replaced the previous practice of single testing (e.g., Bender–Gestalt Test, Graham and Kendall's Memory-for-Designs Test, etc.) to assess "brain damage."

Since 1980, to the present day, psychological assessment has extended even to the political domain. Singapore was probably one of the few countries in the world that employed a comprehensive psychological evaluation of their future national leaders. At the behest of the governing authority, psychological assessment was conducted on political candidates earmarked for election and appointment to public office. Beginning in the late 1980s and into the 1990s, the assessment center method was vigorously used for selection purposes by the Singapore Police Force, MOE (selection of principals), MINDEF, and other organizations. By the late 1980s and 1990s, a number of psychologists had set up their own consultancies or companies providing occupational/industrial–organizational psychological services in the corporate world.

14.8   Conclusion

Overall there has been an improvement in the field of psychological assessment and testing within Asian countries as there is now more attention and focus on assuring the quality of instruments with regards to cultural relevance and the cross-cultural validity of adapted instruments, as well as translations (Lonner & Berry, 1986; Paunonen & Ashton, 1998). It is also evident in both Malaysia and Singapore that there is an observable growth in the number of researchers and research studies in the field of psychology typically on the usage of psychological and testing, and this phenomenon signifies the growth of the profession. Despite a slow start for both countries, the usage and adaptability of psychological tests have shown to be helpful in contributing to the countries beyond just the mental health field, with assessments being conducted in other contexts such as education, government departments, and organizational settings. The continual growth of psychological assessment and testing in both the public service bodies and private sector organizations as essential inputs for their respective missions can be attributed to and influenced by the high standard of professionalism of well-trained psychologists as scientist-practitioners in their contributions to nation-building in both Malaysia and Singapore.

REFERENCES

Blowers, G. H., & Turtle, A. M. (eds.). (1987). *A Westview special study. Psychology moving East: The status of Western psychology in Asia and Oceania.* Boulder, CO/Sydney: Westview Press/Sydney University Press.

Butcher, J. N., Cheung, F. M., & Lim, J. (2003). Use of the MMPI-2 with Asian populations. *Psychological Assessment, 15*(3), 248–256.

Camara, W. J., Nathan, J. S. & Puente, A. E. (2000). Psychological test usage: Implications in professional psychology. *Professional Psychology Research and Practice, 31*(2), 141–154.

Central Bank of Malaysia. (2020). Economics and Financial Development in Malaysia in the Fourth Quarter of 2019. *First Quarter 2019 Report* (pp. 5–25).

Chan, A. S., Shum, D., & Cheung, R. W. Y. (2003). Recent development of cognitive and neuropsychological assessment in Asian countries. *Psychological Assessment, 3*(15), 257–267.

Cheung, F. M., Leong, F. T. L., & Ben-Porath, Y. S. (2003). Psychological assessment in Asia: Introduction to the special section. *Psychological Assessment, 3*(15), 243–247.

Department of Statistics Malaysia. (2010). Population Distribution and Basic Demographic Characteristics.

(2019). Demographic Statistics Second Quarter 2019.

Dixon, L. Q. (2009). Assumptions behind Singapore's language-in-education policy: Implications for language planning and second language acquisition. *Language Policy, 8*(2), 117–137. doi:10.1007/s10993-009-9124-0

Fauzaman, J., Ansari, Z. A., & Khan, R. (2005). Patterns of psychological test usage in Malaysia. In Z. A. Ansari, N. M. Noor, & A. Haque (eds.), *Contemporary Issues in Malaysian Psychology* (pp. 265–284). Singapore: Thompson Learning.

Fowler, R. D. (2002). Regional psychology conference in India. *International Clinical Psychologist: Newsletter of the International Society of Clinical Psychology, 4*(1), 5–6.

Hambleton, R. K., & Patsula, L. (1999). Increasing the validity of adapted tests: Myths to be avoided and guidelines for improving test adaptation practices. *Journal of Applied Testing Technology, 1*, 1–12.

Hathaway, S. R., & McKinley, J. C. (1967). *The MMPI manual.* New York: Psychological Corporation.

Hill, H. (2010). *Malaysian economic development: Looking backwards and forward in working papers in trade and development.* Canberra: The Australian National University.

Kadri, Z. N. (1971). The use of the MMPI for personality study of Singapore students. *British Journal of Social and Clinical Psychology, 10*, 90–91.

Krauss, S., Hamzah, A., Rumaya, J., & Hamid, J. (2005). The Muslim Religiosity-Personality Inventory (MRPI): Towards Understanding Differences in the Islamic Religiosity among the Malaysian Youth.

Lai, L. L. & Loh, P. S. (2015). Validation of the Malay version of the Amsterdam preoperative anxiety and information scale (APAIS). *The Medical Journal of Malaysia, 70*(4),243–248.

Lim, K. K. (2000). Vital who administers IQ tests. *Forum, The Straits Times, November,* (18), 34.

Lim, T. O., Das, A., Rampal, S., Zaki, M., Sahabudin, R. M., Rohan, M. J., & Isaacs, S. (2003). Cross-cultural adaptation and validation of the English version of the International Index of Erectile Function (IIEF) for use in Malaysia. *Int J Impot Res, 15*(5), 329–336. doi:10.1038/sj.ijir.3901009

Lockard, C. A., Ahmad, Z., Leinbach, T. R., & Ooi, J. B. (2020). *Malaysia.* Retrieved from www.britannica.com/place/Malaysia

Long, F. Y. (1983). Psychology in Singapore: Its roots, contexts and growth, *Singapore Psychologist, 1*(2), 5–15.

(1987). Psychology in Singapore: Its roots, contexts and growth. In G. H. Blowers & A. M. Turtle (eds.), *Psychology moving east* (pp. 223–248). Boulder, CO/London: Westview Press.

(1987). Personal communication (15 September).

Lonner, W. J., & Berry, J. W. (1986). *Field methods in cross-cultural research.* Beverly Hills, CA: Sage.

Maznah, I. & Lah, K. P. (1987). A survey of tests/measurement instruments in counselling [in Bahasa Malaysia]. *Journal Perkama, 1*, 105–121.

Ministry of Economic Affairs. (2019). *Shared prosperity vision 2030: Restructuring the priorities of Malaysia's development.* Kuala Lumpur: Percetakan Nasional Malaysia Berhad.

Mukhtar, F. & Oei, T. P. S. (2010). Exploratory and confirmatory factor validation of the dysfunctional attitude scale for Malays (DAS-Malay) in Malaysia. *Asian Journal of Psychiatry, 3*(3): 145–151.

Mukhtar, F. & Zulkefly, N. S. (2011). The beck anxiety inventory for Malays (BAI-Malay): A preliminary study on psychometric properties. *Malaysian Journal of Medical Health Science, 7*(1): 739.

Musa, R. (n.d.). The Mental Health Information and Research Centre. Retrieved from www.ramlimusa.com/.

Ramli, M. (2019). Mental Health Information & Research Center (June 11). Retrieved from www.ramlimusa.com/about/mahir/.

Musa, R., Ramli, R., Abdullah, K., & Sarkarsi, R. (2011). Concurrent validity of the depression and anxiety components in the Bahasa Malaysia version of the Depression Anxiety and Stress Scales (DASS). *ASEAN Journal of Psychiatry, 12*(1), 66–70.

National Institute of Education. (1997–1998). *Prospectus for graduate programmes* (pp. 15–16).

National Population and Talent Division. (2014). *2014 population in brief.* Retrieved from https://web.archive.org/web/20150513031121/http://www.nptd.gov.sg/portals/0/news/population-in-brief-2014.pdf

Oei, T. P. S. & Mukhtar, F. (2008). Exploratory and confirmatory factor validation and psychometric properties of the automatic thoughts questionnaire for Malays (ATQ-Malay) in Malaysia. *Hong Kong Journal of Psychiatry, 18*(3), 92–100.

Okazaki, S., David, E. J. R., and Abelmann, N. (2008). Colonialism and psychology of culture. *Social and Personality Psychology Compass, 2*(1), 90–106. doi: 10.1111/j.1751-9004.2007.00046.x.

Paunonen, S. V. & Ashton, M. C. (1998). The structured assessment of personality across cultures. *Journal of Cross-Cultural Psychology, 29*(1), 150–170.

Rahman, W. R. A. (2005). History of psychology in Malaysia. In Z. A. Ansari, N. M. Noor, & A. Haque (eds.), *Contemporary Issues in Malaysian Psychology* (pp. 1–17). Kuala Lumpur: Thompson Learning.

Rosen, R., Riley, A., Wagner, G., Osterloh, H., Kirkpatrick, J., & Mishra, A. (1997). The international index of erectile function (IIEF): A multidimensional scale for assessment of erectile dysfunction. *Urology*, *49*, 822–830.

Rust, J. (2000). *Singapore Wechsler objective reading and language dimensions manual.* London: The Psychological Corporation.

Supplement of the Republic of Singapore Government Gazette. (July 20, 1979). List of registered societies in the Republic of Singapore, published in accordance with the provisions of section 5 of the Societies Act, as on April 1, 1979, no. 18/79, p. 85.

Tan, A. G. (2002). Development of psychology in Singapore: Some perspectives. In A. G. Tan & M. Goh (eds.), *Psychology in Singapore: Issues of an emerging discipline* (pp. 3–19). Singapore: McGraw-Hill Education (Asia).

Tan, V. L. M. & Tan N.T. (2000). *Personality and effective management: MBTI profiles of Singapore managers.* Singapore: Singapore Institute of Management.

United Nations Development Programme. (2019). *Human development report 2019: Inequalities in human development in the 21st century.* Retrieved from http://hdr.undp.org/sites/all/themes/hdr_theme/country-notes/SGP.pdf.

Rahman, W. R. A. (2005). History of psychology in Malaysia. In Z. A. Ansari, N. M. Noor, & A. Haque (eds.), *Contemporary issues in Malaysian psychology* (pp. 265–284). Singapore: Thompson Learning.

Wechsler, D. (1955). *The Wechsler adult intelligence scale.* New York: Psychological Corp.

(1974). *Wechsler intelligence scale for children – revised.* New York: Psychological Corp.

Yusof, Z. A. & Bhattasali, D. (2008). *Economic growth and development in Malaysia: Policy making and leadership.* Washington, DC: The World Bank.

CHAPTER 15

A Brief History of Testing and Assessment in Oceania

John O'Gorman, Ross St George, and Peter Macqueen

15.1 Introduction

Oceania comprises those islands scattered through the Pacific Ocean bounded by Australia and Papua New Guinea to the west, the Hawaiian Islands to the north, New Zealand to the south, and Easter Island to the east.[1] The geographical spread of Oceania is matched by the range of its cultural and language groups, with culturally distinct regions of Melanesia, Micronesia, Polynesia, and Australasia recognized. Separate migrations from Borneo (about 50,000 years ago) and Taiwan (about 5,000 years ago) were responsible for original settlement of the islands, and European exploration from the sixteenth century brought Portuguese, British, Dutch, French, German, and later American influences to the region. Today, many of the island groups are self-governing, but the French influence remains in New Caledonia and French Polynesia. Hawaii has been a state of the United States since 1959 and American Samoa is one of its unincorporated territories. There is a loose alliance of 26 island territories, currently known as the Pacific Community, to promote economic development. The largest islands of Australia, New Zealand, and Papua New Guinea (PNG) contain three-quarters of the total population of Oceania, which is about 47 million people. Fiji and the Solomon Islands are the next most populated but eight of the states contain fewer than 20,000 people (United Nations, 2019). Although there are many cultures and nations in Oceania, psychological assessment as practiced today developed mainly in Australia and New Zealand. Hence this chapter provides a

---

[1] In referring to the indigenous peoples of the various islands, the authors have sought to use terms most acceptable to those peoples. In Australia, the term Aboriginal and Torres Strait Islander peoples is gradually being replaced by First Nations peoples. In Aotearoa/New Zealand, Māori is the appropriate term and Pakeha is used to refer to non-Māori (usually, but not exclusively, those of European descent). The term Pasifika is used in Australia and Aotearoa/New Zealand to refer to peoples from the Pacific Islands.

history of psychological assessment across these two countries. A brief history is also presented for PNG and the Pacific Islands.

15.2 Australia: Beginnings at the Turn of the Twentieth Century

In the early 1850s, Australia's first universities were founded in Sydney and Melbourne. From 1890, mental philosophy was taught first at Sydney and then at Melbourne in the British empiricist tradition, from which psychology was to emerge early in the next century and with it the use of psychological tests (Buchanan, 2012; O'Neil, 1987). The Education Acts in each of the Australian states were legislated during the 1870s to the 1890s and it was in education that testing was to be first employed, notably in the assessment of student performance and in vocational guidance.

As early as 1895, a committee of the Australasian Association for the Advancement of Science was corresponding with E. B. Titchener at Cornell and Francis Galton in London. It was chaired by the professor of philosophy at Melbourne University, Henry Laurie, supported by the professor of philosophy at Sydney University, Francis Anderson. Their purpose was "to devise a scheme of statistical inquiries, of theoretical and practical value, in connection with the State school systems of the Australasian colonies" (Laurie, 1966, 40).

In 1898, the first recorded use of tests with First Nations people occurred when the Cambridge Anthropological Expedition to the Torres Strait tested people living on the most easterly of the Strait islands, as well as in Queensland and PNG. Richards (2010) provides a brief critical account of the psychological work, which concentrated on sensory and psychomotor functions. In 1901, a dictation test was used to determine entry of migrants to Australia. It was administered in one of the main European languages chosen at the discretion of the immigration official, and served to maintain a White Australia, a practice that was to last until 1957 (Kendall, 2008).

15.3 World War I and the Interwar Years

The influences on psychological testing in Australia in the second, third, and fourth decades of the twentieth century continued to be predominantly British. World War I, although it had a major impact on Australia, did not have an impact on psychological testing, certainly not the impact that World War II was to have on psychology and its practical application. Models for Australian education and public administration came from Great Britain. Ideas of merit and efficiency had wide currency in public policy and to these were added the ideas of individual differences, educational backwardness, and person–job fit to support the application of testing in schools and industry.

Systematic work on mental and achievement tests began at Melbourne Teachers College in 1910, and in 1921 H. T. Parker published a revision of the Binet–Simon Scale (Clark, 1958). There had also been work at Sydney Teachers College for almost as long and in 1924 Phillips, who had worked with Spearman, published an Australian version of Goddard's version of the Binet Scale. In 1913, Stanley Porteus was appointed head of a school for intellectually handicapped children in Melbourne. Dissatisfied with the Binet test, he developed his own pencil-and-paper maze test based on the layout of streets in the Melbourne district of Fitzroy. The test was subsequently used because of its nonverbal character to test First Nations people in central Australia and still has some use in neuropsychology.

In 1926, the Vocational Guidance Bureau (VGB) was formed in New South Wales (NSW; Naylor et al., 1985; Rose, 1976). Traits were assessed initially using interviews and input from parents and school sources, where available. Subsequently, intelligence tests were employed. In 1928, A. H. Martin established the Australian Institute of Industrial Psychology (AIIP; Clark, 1958), which had ties with the National Institute of Industrial Psychology (NIIP) in the United Kingdom. Martin followed Thorndike's multiple abilities approach to the structure of intelligence, and is credited with a number of adaptations of tests for use in Australia, including a form of the Army Alpha test, a spatial aptitude test, a clerical speed and accuracy test, and a version of the Stenquist Mechanical Aptitude Test (O'Neil, 1987). Vocational guidance was the Institute's main business (Bucklow, 1977), but approximately 100 firms sought advice on staff selection, fatigue, and working conditions, directed to maximizing efficiency.

A major stimulus to work using educational and psychological tests came in 1930 with the establishment of the Australian Council for Educational Research (ACER), with funds from the American Carnegie Corporation (Connell, 1980). One of its first tasks was the standardization of scholastic and mental tests for use in Australia. Subtests for identifying deficiencies in pupils' reading and arithmetic followed and then verbal and nonverbal tests of intelligence.

15.4   World War II and the Postwar Years

When Australia entered World War II, ACER put its experience in test development at the federal government's disposal, first with selection testing for the Department of Army and later for the Department of Labour and National Service. Informed by the success of testing during the war years, the army moved in 1952 to establish a uniformed psychological service in the form of a specialized corps named the Australian Army Psychology Corps, or AA Psych Corps (Owens, 1977). For many years its role was to advise on selection and allocation. Psychologists controlled testing and no arrangements were to be made for testing by civilians or other army members without the approval of AA Psych Corps. There was also a research unit, with norming and validation of tests as its major concern. Psychology in the Royal Australian Air Force (RAAF) began in 1942 with George Naylor's work on aircrew selection (Want, 1970). Naylor had worked with Martin at the AIIP. His brief was to determine a minimum cut-off score for success in training and to do this in minimum time, a brief he met with a battery of aptitude tests, without an interview. The interview was standard practice at AIIP and subsequently in the other armed services.

In 1958, the Public Service Selection Test was introduced to establish an order of merit for entry (White, 1977). Using educational qualifications to establish the order of merit had proved difficult, with different Australian states and territories having different curricula and different systems of final examination. The Clerical Selection Test (CST) was developed by ACER for this purpose and introduced in 1961. Other selection tests followed, and a program of validation studies was completed over the next decade. The CST, for example, showed a validity coefficient against supervisors' ratings of 0.25 and against promotion rate of 0.28 (O'Gorman & Carstairs, 1988). There was no evidence of bias in terms of age, gender, or language background.

15.5   Testing in Australia: 1960–1990

The army work was extended to selection testing for the Pacific Island Regiment in PNG by Ord (1977) and this led to development of the Queensland Test for use with First Nations peoples in Australia (Kearney, 1966; McElwain et al., 1967; McElwain & Kearney, 1970). The test took about an hour to complete and consisted of five subtests: Knox Cube Imitation Test, Beads Test, Alexander Passalong Test, Form Assembly

Test, and Pattern Matching Test. None of the subtests included pictures or objects with common uses and all were presented by mime, making language use unnecessary. Scoring used the Rasch model. Degree of acculturation was found to affect test scores, with higher scores being obtained by those living in communities closer to European culture (Kearney & McElwain, 1976).

Recently the test has been republished in a slightly amended form as the Q Test, with advice from Kearney, for the assessment of "trainability" in indigenous communities in Australia and South Asia (Davidson & Macfarlane, 2009). Validity was reported as 0.6 against supervisors' ratings for 100 indigenous employees of a mining company in West Papua (Value Edge, 2017). The test is one of those recommended for use with First Nations peoples by Adams, Drew, and Walker (2014) as a "culturally validated assessment tool." It has high acceptability by those working with First Nations peoples, and has been used by mining companies for job selection in PNG, New Zealand, and some Pacific islands (Pearson, 2012).

Up to the 1960s, the role of the clinical psychologist in Australia was essentially that of mental tester or, once the projective techniques were introduced, psychological assessor (Birnbrauer, 1996). The Wechsler tests were used in combination with the Minnesota Multiphasic Personality Inventory (MMPI) and the projectives (commonly the Rorschach or TAT). An important exception to the use of overseas tests in clinical work is the Depression Anxiety Stress Scale (DASS) developed by Lovibond and Lovibond (1995) to assess changes in these states over relatively short periods of time. Test construction maximized the discrimination of measures of the three constructs and norms are available for a number of groups. The DASS is one of the most commonly used self-report measures in Australian health research and clinical practice (Bibb et al., 2016). The area of clinical work that has been most innovative in test development is neuropsychology. This is well-reviewed by Ponsford (2016).

Private consultant psychologists operated in the large Australian cities of Sydney and Melbourne in the post-World War II years (Young, 1977). Howe and Craig (1970) undertook a survey of use of tests in government and industry, and found that group tests of intelligence were the most used, including the Otis Higher Tests, the ACER B40, and Raven's Standard Progressive Matrices (SPM). Tests of spatial and clerical ability were next most used, such as the Minnesota Paper Form Board Test and tests of clerical speed and accuracy. Vocational interest tests such as the Kuder, the Phillips, and the Rothwell-Miller were also used and, less frequently, personality tests such as the 16PF (Sixteen Personality Factor

Questionnaire). Patrickson and Haydon (1988) estimated an increase in the use of psychological tests in selection over the period 1954 to 1973 from 3% to 61%. In a later survey, Hartshorne and Kirby (1998) reported that the use of testing had increased from about one-third of companies surveyed in 1972 to two-thirds in 1998, with the major increase being in the use of personality testing.

15.6   Changes with the Coming of the Twenty-First Century

The VGB closed in 1997. The world of work had changed considerably since individuals were first matched with jobs that would remain the same during their lifetimes, and everyone it seemed had a story to tell about a failure of vocational guidance (Naylor et al., 1985). Carl Rogers and humanistic psychology influenced counseling practice greatly, making norm-referenced test scores redundant. Centralized government services, such as the VGB and the Commonwealth Employment Service, gave way to outsourcing to private providers.

The rise of psychological therapies changed the role of clinical psychologists from that of assessor to therapist. Once the national health insurance system (Medicare) was opened to psychologists in 2006, assessment (which was not funded) was reduced to symptom checklists and intake interviews. In education, teachers' unions took aim at high-stakes testing such as ACER's NAPLAN that was an extension of its earlier work on assessing specific abilities. Australia had not seen the anti-testing movement such as in the United States in the 1960s (Hicks, 1991), but teachers had long been suspicious of intelligence tests (e.g., O'Neil, 1984). Opposition to certain assessment activities has extended to very recent times, with the NSW Teachers Federation blocking the introduction of automated essay scoring for NSW students in 2018.[2]

Testing initially played a role in the development of psychology as a profession in Australia, with testing being a competence that only psychologists could claim. Cooke (2000) made the point in his history of the Australian Psychological Society (APS) that psychologists saw themselves as custodians of testing. Some support for this was provided by the first legislation in Australia that served to register the profession, The Victorian Psychological Practices Act 1965. ACER seems to have accepted this too by restricting the sale of many of its tests to psychologists. Jenkinson (2006) described the difficulties remedial and special education teachers

---

[2] See https://www.nswtf.org.au/news/2017/08/01/online-naplan.html.

had with ACER in gaining access to tests for their work. The privileged role of psychologists was not sustainable, however, as more test distributors entered the market and the role of psychologist changed from that of assessor to that of therapist.

The argument that there has been a power shift in the use of tests is compelling, with test publishers and distributors able to bypass the psychologist, increasingly, and advances in technology are abetting this clear trend. However, the rapid ascension of technology in testing has enabled the development of new tests, including My Potentia, an Android tablet version of the Q Test that is an updated version of the Queensland Test. My Potentia has been used extensively in PNG in recent years. Further, game-based assessments, developed from the ground up, show promise in providing an effective and valid means of assessing general cognitive ability (Hawkes et al., 2018; Quiroga et al., 2015). Australia is now in the process of "exporting" such test developments, including joint venturing with major global organizations.

A survey of approximately 300 human resource practitioners in Australia and New Zealand by Saville and Holdsworth (SHL) in 2017 indicated that of firms using tests for hiring over 90% conducted the testing online, and 22% made use of mobile-based assessment. Both of these were the highest percentages recorded globally, as was the 79% for testing of senior managers or executives (Kantrowitz et al., 2018).

Testing was also initially an important aspect of university research in departments of psychology. Until the 1950s, psychology research consisted mainly of the measurement of individual differences (Taft & Day, 1988). From then on, other aspects of psychology became the focus and psychological assessment declined in research importance. Keats and Keats (1988) in their review of psychological assessment in Australia noted that a number of Australians had made contributions to test theory.

Australia has been actively involved with the International Test Commission (ITC) since its foundation, with the APS being the second full member. John Keats was a former ITC president and APS president, and Barry McGaw a former ITC Council member and APS president. For a number of years, the APS supported a highly credentialed Committee on Psychological Tests and Testing. Disbanded in the mid-1990s, it was reformed in 2011 as the Tests and Testing Reference (now Expert) Group.

15.7   Recognizing Cultural Differences in Test Use

Possibly the most significant change for psychological testing in Australia with the coming of the twenty-first century, although one yet to be fully worked through, has to do with its unfortunate legacy for First Nations peoples. The work of the Cambridge Expedition and Porteus has been touched on briefly, and later in the century the more sophisticated approach of constructors of the Queensland Test. From the First Nations' viewpoint (Dudgeon et al., 2014), however, this narrative is yet another aspect of colonization, in which the dominant white culture used testing to validate indigenous primitiveness and inferiority and assist in social control and marginalization. It is only relatively recently that mainstream Australia has acknowledged the harm done by dispossession and years of social policy with respect to First Nations peoples.

An Australian psychologist, Graham Davidson, has argued that the cultural bias of commonly used cognitive tests compromises their use with those from non-Western cultures. According to Davidson (1995), the differences between white and First Nations cultures is such that, with very few exceptions, psychological testing of First Nations peoples should be abandoned in favor of individualized forms of assessment. In its place, a multi-axial model of assessment should be adopted, which according to the qualitative research of Dingwall, Pinkerton, and Lindeman (2013) is much closer to the actual practice of those undertaking assessment in First Nations communities.

The APS has been working to dispel the deep suspicion that psychology and psychological testing has engendered and has partnered with the Australian Indigenous Psychologists Association (AIPA) to address this.[3] Attempts at assessing mental illness have likewise been viewed with suspicion because of cultural differences in the meaning of symptoms. For First Nations communities, mental health involves recognition of the close connection between land, kin, and spirit. Social and emotional well-being is the concept now most frequently used when assessing mental health and requires a holistic and qualitative approach to assessment. Western methods are being adapted by First Nations psychologists (e.g., Adams et al., 2014) to provide more culturally authentic assessment to the benefit of all Australians. This progress will be enhanced by Australia's endorsement and adoption of the International Declaration of Competences in Professional Psychology (International Project on Core Competences, 2016), leading to a much greater focus on cultural matters for psychology students, practitioners, and researchers.

---

[3] See http://www.indigenouspsychology.com.au/.

15.8   Aotearoa/New Zealand: The Early Years

The history of psychology in New Zealand is essentially a history in two parts, the history of academic or experimental psychology and the history of applied and professional psychology (Haig & Marie, 2012).[4] The history of testing and assessment lies largely with the second of these. The bifurcation is due largely to the development of departments of philosophy, which taught moral and mental science, and education, with a focus on learning and teaching. It was education departments rather than psychology departments, when they emerged, that were largely responsible for the development of applied and professional psychology in New Zealand.

Thomas Hunter is credited with establishing psychology as a separate discipline in New Zealand when he was appointed to a professorship at Victoria College, Wellington, in 1907. Hunter was a proponent of laboratory methods having been strongly influenced by Titchener at Cornell, and is credited with setting up the first psychological laboratory in Australasia in 1907. He was also impressed by Witmer's clinic at Pennsylvania State University and sought in 1926 to establish a similar one at Victoria College. Ivan Sutherland provided the psychometric testing in the clinic, although he was cautious in its use. He spoke publicly about the risks inherent in psychometric testing and the limited value it held when conducted mechanically and without understanding of the child's social world (*Evening Post*, 1931, cited in Berliner, 2014). Witmer's case conference approach, as practiced in the Victoria clinic, was a useful corrective.

A similar clinic was established at Canterbury University College under the directorship of Clarence Beeby who worked closely with the professor of education, James Shirley. Beeby had completed his Ph.D. under Spearman at London and had met Lewis Terman and valued his test. Like Witmer's Clinic, it was essentially a child guidance clinic but took referrals from schools on a wide range of educational and behavioral problems, from speech and reading to vocational choice and juvenile delinquency. The Clinic was deemed successful and Beeby went on to become the first director of the New Zealand Council for Educational Research (NZCER) and subsequently New Zealand's director general of education.

---

[4] As well as this reference, the St. George (1979) collection has been drawn on heavily in writing this section. The theses prepared by Jackson (1998) and Berliner (2014) have also proved useful.

A clinic was established at Otago in 1934 to "examine children who were in need of psychological treatment and guidance (especially in such matters as backwardness, intellectual assessment ... and also to train students of Education practically in the principles of child guidance) as part of the work prescribed for Education Stage III" (Connor, 1959, 202). Intelligence tests were regularly administered, often more than one. The Binet was the most widely employed followed by the SPM. Social history taking was extensive and tests were interpreted against the background of school reports (Connor, 1959; Mitchell, 1954, 1956).

15.9 Testing in Education, Industry, and the Clinics: 1940 Onwards

The clinics associated with the colleges continued and by 1950 there were five providing education and diagnostic services (Berliner, 2014), but expanding government services saw these replaced (Besley, 2002; Furbish, 2012; Winterbourn, 1974). From the 1960s, rising unemployment led to adults being given access to these services. The central commitment to career services remained until the 1980s when a user-pays approach to government services, followed by a share market crash, led to its curtailment.

An expansion of services in the 1990s saw the sorts of changes in theory experienced in other parts of the Anglosphere (Furbish, 2012). The trait and factor approach to guidance, with individuals being matched to jobs, was displaced by approaches that recognized the increased complexity of the labor market and the changing meaning of jobs and, with these changes, the need for career counselors to help clients manage their life circumstances rather than predict their futures. Although Holland's theory of careers is still widely used and with it the need for psychometric testing, postmodern approaches, such as that advocated by Savickas (e.g., 2005), suited the more holistic approach recommended by Ministry of Education guidelines (Furbish, 2012).

An important development for testing, particularly for testing in education, was the establishment of the NZCER in 1934. It was funded initially through grants from the Carnegie Corporation, but from 1972 operated as an independent research organization under its own act of parliament. Its role is to conduct educational research and offer advice to teachers and others concerned with education. As part of its current operations it provides Psychological Test Services, which supply psychometric tests (most of overseas origin) and advice about them for use in education, clinical psychology, and human resources. The NZCER's major focus is, however, education and its testing work is principally in the area of educational assessment.

New Zealand had widespread general intelligence/mental ability testing at the entrance to secondary school from 1924 through to the late 1960s.[5] Initially, the Terman Group Test of Mental Ability was used but this was superseded by the Otis Test of Mental Abilities. NZCER developed the Test of Scholastic Abilities (TOSCA) in about 1971 to replace the Otis. There was considerable debate in educational circles as to its cultural suitability and the effects of streaming in schools, and TOSCA was withdrawn in the late 1990s.

New Zealand does not now have mandatory national ability assessment in primary or secondary schools and has attempted to avoid the disadvantages seen in large-scale high-stakes testing (Willis, 1993). The emphasis has been on diagnostic assessment rather than on ranking students based on standardized summative assessment. A novel approach has been the development of Assessment Resource Banks (e.g., Croft, 2002). Teachers can design their own items or select items from an online "bank" sorted by curriculum level.

In the early 1980s, the Tests and Standards Committee of the New Zealand Psychological Society undertook a survey of psychological and educational measurement course content at New Zealand universities and in-service training by agencies using tests in their day to day work (Reid & St. George, 1982). There was some suggestion in the survey responses that university departments were lessening their psychological measurement course offerings in the light of controversies relating to psychometrics – it was a time when the "race and intelligence debate" was prominent in social sciences literature.

Industrial psychology had begun with the Canterbury clinic but by 1938 there was little if any being practiced (Hearnshaw, 1948). It was, however, to become the focus of a small unit formed within the Department of Industrial and Scientific Research in 1942. Its establishment was prompted by a need to increase productivity as part of the war effort and by a view that personnel managers were not adequately trained. It had only a small staff but provided consultancy services in vocational selection for firms and the armed services. It was wound up after World War II, but a new unit was established in 1948.

Although the war proved a major stimulus to applied psychology in Britain, the United States, and Australia, this was not so in New Zealand,

---

[5] See https/nzhistory.govt.nz/intelligence-tests-arrive-new-zealand-schools.

where psychology was little used outside the Royal New Zealand Air Force (RNZAF). There it was used for aircrew selection as well as with other occupational groups. The Army relied on personnel selection officers who came from the Education and Welfare Corps and were not psychologists. They were involved in initial selection of recruits, trade classification, and officer selection.

Toulson and Williams (1979), in their report on the use of psychological testing in the New Zealand Armed Services, noted that the tests used in the RNZAF were based on those developed for similar work in Canada, Britain, and the United States. General mental ability was assessed using the Royal Canadian Air Force General Classification Test. There was a space perception test developed by the NIIP, and a test of motor coordination and reaction time that employed apparatus built to British specifications.

Inkson (1987; Inkson & Paterson, 1993) reviewed the literature on industrial-organizational psychology in New Zealand published between 1970 and 1990. Among the trends noted over that period was an increase in research on selection methods and the psychometrics of techniques used in the workplace. The review indicated, however, that the measures and the issues addressed were largely of overseas origin, although there was recognition of the importance of the multicultural nature of New Zealand society.

15.10   Testing in New Zealand: The Current Climate

Testing continues to be part of the repertoire of the applied psychologist. Dugdale and Dunn (2002) from the NZCER reported on patterns of test use in New Zealand based on a survey of test users. Their major finding was that there were few differences in the tests used in New Zealand compared with those used in the United States, with the exception that there was little use of projective tests. Almost 50% of the sample spent less than 10% of their time using tests. The top five tests used once a month or more were the Beck Depression Inventory-II, followed by Wechsler Adult Intelligence Scale-III (WAIS-III), Wechsler Intelligence Scale for Children-III (WISC-III), SPM, and Myers-Briggs Type Indicator. Dugdale and Dunn (2002) noted that previous studies in New Zealand had indicated much the same ordering of tests in use.

Worthy of mention is the work of James Flynn at the University of Otago and his finding of large gains in IQ over time (e.g., Flynn, 1987). Such an increase, from 1956 to 1984, was reported in the review of work on standardization of the SPM in New Zealand (Reid & Gilmore, 1989).

Little information has been formally reported on the use of psychological tests in the clinical and psychotherapeutic fields. Ross-McAlpine, Leathem, and Flett (2018) reported that the WISC-V and ABAS-II-Parent were the most frequently used measures for cognitive and neurological assessments with children.

In the human resources field, Taylor, Keelty, and McDonnell (2002) examined the selection procedures employed by 100 organizations with 200 or more employees in two of the six major business regions in the country, Auckland and Hamilton. Interviews, personal history information, and reference checks were widely used by organizations and recruiting firms. Occupational testing was more likely to be used by recruiting firms than by organizations, with 64% of recruiting firms reporting the use of cognitive tests and 89% the use of personality tests. The SHL numerical and verbal tests were the most frequently employed cognitive tests and the SHL Occupational Personality Questionnaire was the most often used of the personality tests. The authors compared their findings with those of an earlier survey they had conducted (Taylor et al., 1993) and noted that the use of cognitive tests for selection had more than doubled in frequency over the decade and that use of personality tests had increased by 20%. This placed New Zealand in the top five countries for use of occupational tests in terms of the Ryan, McFarland, Baron, and Pages (1999) survey of 18 countries.

Historically, psychological test sales in New Zealand (and hence use by appropriately qualified persons) have been controlled by test marketing agencies – principally NZCER and Pearson Clinical, both of which market an extensive range of psychological assessment products from across the world. NZCER and Pearson Clinical categorize psychological tests according to user competency requirements that are evaluated prior to purchase and use. The New Zealand Psychological Society (NZPsS) for many years had a Tests Standards Committee to give guidance on psychological test matters to its governing council and members. This ceased in 1999. However, the Society has published guidance and advisory material that is in the public domain. In 2016, the NZPsS published *Professional Practice of Psychology Aotearoa* containing a paper by Eatwell and Wilson (2016) on the effective use of psychometric tests in decision-making.

15.11   Recognition of Cultural Differences

For the greater part of the nineteenth and twentieth centuries, prohibitions on the use of Māori language in schools and prohibitions on Māori cultural practices such as Māori healing had negative impacts on Māori identity, health, education, and welfare. Developments in the late twentieth century sought to turn this around and recognize and honor cultural difference (Spoonley, 2018). This change is now having some influence on testing and assessment.

Possible differences in performance on psychological and educational tests of abilities have been examined for some time, although the wider implications of culture for psychological assessment have taken longer to recognize, which is not a situation peculiar to New Zealand. St. George (1983a) summarized his review of 24 studies up to that time comparing Māori and Pakeha abilities. He noted that the weight of evidence did not support a proposition that Māori performed less well than Pakeha and that the more recent studies showed smaller differences than the older studies. Further, he noted that any differences were not necessarily reduced by the use of non-verbal scales, and that there was very little effort devoted to ensuring the comparability of scales in the two ethnic groups by, for example, examination of the psychometric properties of the scales.

The establishment of the University of Waikato in 1964 and the appointment of James Ritchie as the foundation professor of psychology saw the blossoming of cross-cultural psychological research, including psychometric studies. Central influences were the work of Don McElwain and George Kearney from the University of Queensland and the appointment of Geoff Ord from PNG. They fostered cross-cultural studies based upon their Australian and PNG experiences, and collectively spurred the cross-cultural work of Brooks (1976), A. St George (1972) and R. St George (1970, 1983a, 1983b).

More recent studies have indicated that on some tests there are no important differences between cultural groups, while on others Māori participants may score higher or lower than Pakeha. Where differences are found these have been attributed to differences in the English language curriculum of schools, the greater diversity of language background in parents of the Māori children, and socioeconomic differences (e.g., Guenhole et al., 2003; Haitana et al., 2010; Ogden & McFarlane-Nathan, 1997). The authors noted the importance of engaging the children in the task and of answering in culturally appropriate ways the questions of the children's caretakers about the research.

As well as affecting the use of psychological tests, cultural differences affect psychological assessment more broadly. Milne (2005) consulted with Māori communities, on behalf of the New Zealand Psychologists Board, to better understand the point of view of Māori on Pakeha psychology and psychological services. The resulting report indicated the (then) levels of distrust and dissatisfaction with a Western world view and way of doing things as expressed in current psychological knowledge and practices. Fundamental differences about psyche and self meant that there were profound differences in styles of thinking about behavior and the way it is understood.

In seeking to respond to these concerns, if not the specific report, *The Code of Ethics for Psychologists Working in Aotearoa/New Zealan*d (NZPsS, 2002) now includes a value statement that encourages psychologists to apply the principles of Te Tiriti of Waitangi to their work and "seek advice and undertake training in the appropriate way to show respect for the dignity and needs of Māori in their practice" (6). Pitama et al. (2017) have developed a clinical guide that includes recognition of the components of the Māori worldview, including evaluation of the impact of colonization, racism, migration, and marginalization in the life situation of the Māori client. So too, Macfarlane, Blampied, and Macfarlane (2011) proposed a framework for assessment that recognizes that an evidence-based approach to assessment must include both scientific and indigenous knowledge. The latter, they noted, may require the assistance of a senior member of the Māori community who can assist and importantly challenge the Pakeha professional, and this challenge needs to be respected.

In tandem with the contemporary emphasis on a multicultural perspective to psychological testing and assessment practice in New Zealand, there is dearth of core reliability, validity, and normative data supporting the majority of "off the shelf" test tools. While Annan (2011) appears optimistic in her view that in New Zealand standardized testing, at least in educational settings, typically occurs as part of contextualized assessment incorporating multiple methods, the broader picture suggests otherwise. Inevitably psychologists are having to use the assessment tool of choice assuming construct transportability and technical data relevance. This is an international concern and not just one for psychologists in Aotearoa/New Zealand. Nevertheless, Aotearoa/New Zealand seems well served given that two members of the small work group on the International Project on Competence in Psychology are involved actively in Aotearoa/New Zealand psychology.

15.12 PNG and the Pacific Islands

Work on testing in PNG commenced in the early 1960s and is well-described by Ord (1966, 1977), who played a key role in organizing and supervising this work. It was directed to selection testing for the public service and the army but was extended in time to educational selection. The work was undertaken by expatriate, chiefly Australian, psychologists, with AA Psych Corps playing a significant role. Independence in 1975 led to different political priorities to those set during Australia's administration of the territory and, in the view of indigenous psychologist Marai (1997), to stagnation of research and development in psychological testing. There has been some improvement subsequently, with increasing numbers of native Papua New Guineans graduating from the university program in organizational psychology.

Price (1984) noted concerns with the extent of psychological test use in the PNG public service and the state of the conceptual and technical underpinnings, and pointed to the issue of quality of criterion data when trying to establish criterion-related validity. Faith in psychological testing was also called into question by Bau and Dyck (1992) who reviewed officer selection in the PNG Defence Force (PNGDF). The results from Public Service Commission tests and assessments similar to War Office Selection Boards were assessed against subsequent Officer Evaluation Reports (OERs). Correlations with OERs were notably low or inverse leading the authors to conclude that "There is no evidence that officer selection procedures in the PNGDF are valid: indeed, there is evidence that they may be counterproductive" (Bau and Dyck 1992, 89).

The work in Fiji, granted independence in 1970, was largely an extension of the work in PNG. There had been the early research of Mann (1935, 1939) on a general ability test but the major measurement work in Fiji was undertaken by the Psychological Assessment Unit of the University of the South Pacific (USP) in the 1970s. This work was stimulated by the recommendations of Ord who drew on the models developed in PNG. Later, advice was sought from ACER on the development of a scholastic aptitude test for university selection. The Test Development Unit provided services and advice to a number of island territories, including Vanuatu, Samoa, and Tonga. Other extension work in the Pacific islands was undertaken from PNG to the Solomon Islands by Hicks (1969) and from New Zealand to the Cook Islands by St. George and St. George (1975).

In Kiribati and Tuvalu, the earliest reference to testing was a small-scale feasibility study of the Queensland Test by McElwain (1965). In 1972, Bennett (n.d.) authored an advisory report on psychological test use for educational selection purposes and suggested that the USP General Ability Test could be adopted.

In Vanuatu, there was reference to an unspecified general ability test being used in conjunction with school assessments for selection (Hong Tiy &

Beveridge, 1978). Chandra (1977) as a consultant from Fiji recommended the use of a battery of verbal and nonverbal tests in Nauru for educational selection and overseas scholarship purposes. In the Solomon Islands, Hicks (1969) and Harwood and Thomas (1973) trialed reasoning and scholastic aptitude tests from PNG for use in secondary school selection.

As early as the 1930s, intelligence tests (unspecified), Haggerty Tests, Thorndike-McCall reading Scales, and the Knox Cube Test were in use in the Cook Islands (Binsted, 1931). Beaglehole (1957) reported on the use of the SPM, the Kohs Block Design and the Goodenough Draw a Man Tests with Aitutakian children aged between 7 and 15 years. Taylor (1966) began work on norming ACER scholastic tests, but it was not completed. At this time, Taylor (1967) was also investigating the Culture Fair Scales and others for secondary school selection purposes. In 1971–1972 the USP General Ability Test was administered to all Form 1 and 2 level students across the island group.

Suitability of the Queensland Test was examined as part of the work of the University of Waikato in the 1970s. Use of the Pacific Infants Performance Scale (PIPS) in educational contexts was extended to the Cook Islands (St. George & St. George, 1975). The PIPS was robust in its psychometric characteristics but, as with the Queensland Test, there were marked gender differences at the subtest level favoring males. It raised the question of gender-based role differences in the competitive task of test taking. There was also work on cognitive ability assessment with young children by Perry (Perry, personal communication to R. St. George, December 16, 1971).

In Western Samoa, early use of psychological testing reflected the prejudices of the day. Rutherford (1931) was scathing of Samoan character on the basis of Rorschach interpretations and Cook (1942) made equally negative judgments regarding cognition. Beaglehole (1957) also postulated a race-genetic effect with the SPM when comparing test results of European, "mixed-race," and "pure-Samoan" children. By the early 1960s, secondary school selection was an issue. Ma'ai'a (1958) had compared the use of an English language version of the Otis test with a Samoan language version for Samoan overseas students. Not surprisingly they performed better on the English language version, being the language in which they were immersed. With educational selection and placement in mind, the mid-1960s to 1970s was a period of influence from the USP and local (expatriate) education personnel trialed a range of tests (see Rapson, 1967; McMahon, 1968).

Tonga has also made use of quasi-psychological and educational assessment approaches in education. Ford (1957) noted the use of an arithmetic and "best-reasons" test. In the early 1970s, Bennett (n.d.) administered the USP General Ability Test to primary school children. At the secondary school level, he administered the Pacific Reasoning Series, a Word Knowledge Test, the SPM, and a numerical speed test. Tongan norms were derived, and a call made for the use of these tests in educational settings. In Niue and the Tokelau Islands, St. George (1981) noted small scale studies of reading interests, handedness, parental expectations of schooling, and a survey of psychosocial issues associated with out-migration.

A major criticism of the work in the Pacific was voiced by St. George and Preston (1980) directed to the work of the PNG PSB. They observed that some 20 tests had been developed for use in the territory but that the bulk of these had not been developed to the test standards recognized for the time. St. George's subsequent evaluation was that most of the work was characterized by what might be termed dustbowl empiricism. He wrote:

> in the majority of cases the use of standard ability scales has either been to address the issue of comparative performances of European and other South Pacific samples, or for the very pragmatic ends of assisting educational and, to a lesser extent, job selection. In both cases, studies to support a test's utility in a new set of cultural circumstances have been limited. (St George, 1983b, 73)

His perspective was challenged by Hicks (1981) and Hutton (1981) who saw the work in a good deal more positive light than St. George and Preston. Marai (2016), however, argued that a major limitation of the work was the lack of any indigenous psychology. Techniques and models for test development were appropriated from Anglo-American literature, with the easy or unrecognized assumption that these are universal in their application and there is no need for deeper analysis.

15.13   Conclusion

The history of testing and assessment in Oceania up until the 1970s had been largely derivative of Anglo-American practice. From the mid-1960s, social changes in Aotearoa/New Zealand have driven both Māori and increasingly multicultural perspectives into most facets of society including the application of psychology. In Australia, "multiculturalism" was born in the early 1970s, although recognition of the culture of the First Nations people and its implications was slower in coming and has yet to be worked through. In the islands of the Pacific, independence movements beginning in Fiji and PNG in the early 1970s have seen a growing assertion of the importance of their cultures. Constructs from the Anglosphere are being modified and adapted to reflect cultural diversity and this includes psychological assessment methods and practices. While "off-the-shelf" assessment tools will continue to be called upon, interpretation in cultural context is a contemporary consideration. Equally there is a need to innovate. In Aotearoa/New Zealand the renewed emphasis in the society on a shared partnership with Māori and the migration of Pasifika people has meant a more considered understanding of culture in the process of assessment and testing and this is likely to lead in future to greater indigenization of assessment methods and possibly a genuine cultural mix of approaches.

Although agreeing in hindsight that there was insufficient recognition of the cultural context in which test development was undertaken, it would be unfair not to acknowledge the exigencies under which the research was conducted and the tests used. In Australia, for example, the numerical dominance of migration from the United Kingdom hid realization of an emerging multicultural society and of First Nations people within it. In the Pacific, former colonies of European powers were moving rapidly to independence, with a need for talented public servants and an educated middle class from which they could be drawn. Indigenization of psychological assessment processes takes time and social and political support at various levels from professional associations to government. There are now clear guidelines (ITC, 2018) for translating and adapting tests that provide a reference point for test developers and their critics, and following these should provide better recognition of cultural differences in Oceania than has been the case to date.

REFERENCES

Adams, Y., Drew, N., & Walker, R. (2014). Principles of practice in mental health assessment with Aboriginal Australians. In P. Dudgeon, H. Milroy, & R. Walker (eds.), *Working together: Aboriginal and Torres Strait Islander mental health and wellbeing principles and practice* (pp. 271–288). Canberra: Commonwealth of Australia.

Annan, J. (2011). Test use by educational psychologists in New Zealand. *The IAAP Bulletin*, 23(October), 4–6. Retrieved 21 August 2019 from https://iaapsy.org/site/assets/documents/october2011.pdf.

Bau, L. P. & Dyck, M. J. (1992). Predicting the peacetime performance of military officers: Officer selection in the Papua New Guinea defence force, *South Pacific Journal of Psychology*, 5, 27–37.

Beaglehole, E. (1957). *Social change in the South Pacific*. London: Allan and Unwin.

Bennett, M. (n.d.). *Psychological testing for educational selection in the Gilbert and Ellice Islands colony*. Psychological Assessment Unit: University of the South Pacific.

Berliner, A. (2014). *A history of psychology in New Zealand: Early beginnings 1869–1929*. (Master of Arts thesis, University of Canterbury, Christchurch, New Zealand). Retrieved from https://ir.canterbury.ac.nz/handle/10092/10579" https://ir.canterbury.ac.nz/handle/10092/10579.

Besley, T. (2002). Over 40 years of guidance counselling: Specialist teachers in New Zealand schools 1959–2001. *New Zealand Annual Review of Education, 11*, 276–302.

Bibb, J., Baker, F. A., & M Ferran, K. S. (2016). A critical interpretive synthesis of the most commonly used self-report measures in Australian mental health research. *Australasian Psychiatry, 24*(5), 453–458.

Binsted, R. (1931). Education in the Cook Islands. In Jackson, P. M. (ed.) *Māori and education* (pp. 357–389). New Plymouth: Avery..

Birnbrauer, J. (1996). Development of clinical psychology in Australia. In P. R. Martin & J. S Birnbrauer (eds.), *Clinical psychology: Profession and practice in Australia* (pp. 21–51). Melbourne: Macmillan Education Australia.

Brooks, I. R. (1976). Cognitive ability assessment with two New Zealand ethnic groups. *Journal of Cross-Cultural Psychology, 7*(3), 347–356.

Bryson, J. & Hosken, C. (2005). What does it mean to be a culturally competent i/o psychologist in New Zealand? *New Zealand Journal of Psychology, 34*(2), 69–76.

Buchanan, R. (2012). Australia. In D. B. Baker (ed.), *Oxford handbook of the history of psychology* (pp. 18–33). Oxford: Oxford University Press.

Bucklow, M. (1977). Applied psychology in Australia – the history. In M. Nixon & R. Taft (eds.), *Psychology in Australia: Achievements and prospects.* (pp. 23–34). Sydney: Pergamon.

Chandra, S. (1977). *Consultants report: Scholarship selection in the Republic of Nauru*. Suva: Institute of Education: University of the South Pacific.

Clark, J. F. (1958). Psychology in the public service, business, and industry. *Australian Journal of Psychology, 10*(1), 30–41.

Connell, W. F. (1980). *The Australian Council for Educational Research 1930 – 1980*. Melbourne: ACER.

Connor, D. V. (1959). A child guidance clinic in a university setting. *Australian Journal of Psychology, 11*(2), 202–208.

Cook, P. H. (1942). Mental structure and the psychological field: Some Samoan observations. Character and Personality, *10*, 296–308.

Cooke, S. (2000). *A meeting of minds: The Australian Psychological Society and Australian Psychologists 1944–1994*. Melbourne: The Australian Psychological Society.

Croft, C., (2002). The Assessment Resource Banks: From national testing to a school-based resource. *New Zealand Annual Review of Education, 11*, 229–243.

Davidson, G. (1995). Cognitive assessment of Indigenous Australians: Toward a multiaxial model. *Australian Psychologist, 30*(1), 30–34.

Davidson, P. & MacFarlane, D. (2009). Optimise the training outcomes of Indigenous prisoners through the valid, reliable, culture-fair assessment of their training potential with the Q Test. Retrieved from https://acea.org.au/wpcontent/uploads/2015/04/davidson-peter.pdf.

Dingwall, K. M., Pinkerton, J., & Lindeman, M. A. (2013). "People like numbers": A descriptive study of cognitive assessment methods in clinical practice for Aboriginal Australians in the Northern Territory. *BMC Psychiatry, 13*, 42. http://www.biomedcentral.com/1471-244X/13/42.

Dudgeon, P., Rickwood, D., Garvey, D., & Gridley, H. (2014). A history of Indigenous psychology. In P. Dudgeon, H. Milroy, & R. Walker (eds.), *Working together: Aboriginal and Torres Strait Islander mental health and wellbeing principles and practice* (pp. 39–54). Canberra: Commonwealth of Australia.

Dugdale, J. & Dunn, K. (2002). Patterns of use of psychological tests in New Zealand. Paper presented at the Inaugural International Test Users' conference, Sydney, July3–5. https://www.nzcer.org.nz/system/files/12579.pdf.

Eatwell, J. & Wilson, I. (2016). The effective use of psychometric assessments in decision-making. In W. W. Waitoki, N. R. Roberstson, J. S. Feather, & J. J. Rucklidge (eds.). *Professional practice of psychology in Aotearoa New Zealand* (pp. 405–419). Wellington: New Zealand Psychological Society.

Flynn, J. R. (1987). Massive IQ gains in fourteen nations: What IQ tests really measure. *Psychological Bulletin, 101*(2), 171–191.

Ford, C. T. (1957). *Report on an investigation into the selection of pupils for secondary schools in the Kingdom of Tonga.* Dunedin: University of Otago.

Furbish, D. (2012). An overview of New Zealand career development services. *Australian Journal of Career Development, 21*(2), 14–24.

Guenhole, N., Englert, P., & Taylor, P. J. (2003). Ethnic group differences in cognitive ability test scores with a New Zealand applicant sample. *New Zealand Journal of Psychology, 32*(1), 49–54.

Haig, B. D. & Marie, D. (2012). New Zealand. In D. B. Baker (ed.), *The Oxford handbook of the history of psychology: Global perspectives* (pp. 1–32). Oxford: Oxford University Press.

Haitana, T., Pitama, S., & Rucklidge, J. J. (2010). Cultural biases in the Peabody picture vocabulary test-III: Testing Tamariki in a New Zealand. *New Zealand Journal of Psychology, 39*(3), 24–33.

Hartshorne, M. & Kirby, N. (1998). Australian personnel managers and organisational psychology: An update. *Australian Psychologist, 33*(2), 148–154.

Harwood, T. B. & Thomas, E. A. (1973). Findings on the form 2 school selection test: British Solomon Islands protectorate. *New Guinea Psychologist, 5*(3), 90–95.

Hawkes, B., Cek, I., & Handler, C. (2018). The gamification of employee selection tools: An exploration of viability, utility, and future directions. In J. C. Scott, D. Bartram, & D. H. Reynolds (eds.), *Next generation technology-*

enhanced assessment: Global perspectives on occupational and workplace testing (pp. 288–313). Cambridge: Cambridge University Press.

Hearnshaw, L. S. (1948). Industrial psychology in New Zealand. *Occupational Psychology*, 22, 1–6. In St. George, R. (1979). *Beginnings of psychology in New Zealand: A collection of historical documents and recollections.* Delta research monograph, no. 2. Palmerston, North: Dept. of Education, Massey University..

Hicks, R. E. (1969). Psychological tests in the British Solomons: A trial run, December 1968. *New Guinea Psychologist*, 1, 32–34.

(1981). Comments in St George and Preston's "Psychological Testing in Papua and New Guinea: A critical appraisal of the work of the Psychological Services Branch." *Australian Psychologist*, 2(16), 275–277.

(1991). Psychological testing in Australia in the 1990s. *Asia Pacific Human Resource Management*, 29(1), 94–101.

Hong Tiy, F. & Beveridge, P. (1978). *Report on an Investigation into the establishment of the South Pacific board for educational cooperation.* Suva: Department of Education.

Howe, M. A. & Craig, J. D. (1970). Survey of psychological tests as predictors of training and job success. *Personnel Practice Bulletin*, 26(4), 246–252.

Hutton, M. A. (1981). Letter to the Editor. *Australian Psychologist*, 16(2)281.

Inkson, K. (1987). Organisational behaviour: A review of the New Zealand research. *New Zealand Journal of Psychology*, 16(1), 9–27.

Inkson, K. & Paterson, J. (1993). Organisational behaviour in New Zealand 1987–92: A review. *New Zealand Journal of Psychology*, 22(1), 54–66.

International Project on Core Competences. (2016). International Declaration on Core Competences in Professional Psychology. Retrieved from https://www.psykologforeningen.no/foreningen/english/ipcp.

International Test Commission. (2018). ITC guidelines for translating and adapting tests (2nf ed.) *International Journal of Testing*, 18(2), 101–134.

Jackson, P. M. (1998). The mind of a nation: A philosophical and historical critique of psychology in New Zealand (Ph.D. thesis, Massey University, Palmerston North, New Zealand). https://mro.massey.ac.nz/bitstream/handle/10179/1308/02_whole.pdf;sequence=1.

Jenkinson, J. C. (2006). A history of Learning Difficulties Australia: Part 1. *Australian Journal of Learning Difficulties*, 11(1), 45–53.

Kantrowitz, T. M., Tuzinski, K. A., & Raines, J. M. (2018). *2018 Global assessment trends.* New York: SHL.

Kearney, G. E. (1966). *Some aspects of the general cognitive ability of various groups of Aboriginal Australians as assessed by the Queensland test* (Doctoral dissertation, Brisbane: University of Queensland).

Kearney, G. E. & McElwain, D. W. (1976). *Aboriginal cognition: Retrospect and prospect.* Canberra, Australia: Institute of Aboriginal Affairs.

Keats, J. & Keats, D. (1988). Human assessment in Australia. In S, H, Irvine & J. W. Berry (eds.), *Human abilities in cultural context* (pp. 283–297). New York: Cambridge University Press.

Kendall, T. (2008). *Within China's orbit? China through the eyes of the Australian parliament.* Commonwealth of Australia. Canberra: Australian Parliament House. https://www.aph.gov.au/About_Parliament/Parliamentary_Departments ./Parliamentary_Library/pubs/APF/monographs/Within_Chinas_Orbit/ Chapterone

Laurie, H. (1966). Out of the past. *Australian Psychologist, 1*(1), 39–40.

Lovibond S. H. & Lovibond, P. F. (1995). *Manual for the depression, anxiety, stress scales* (2nd ed.). Sydney: Psychological Foundation.

Ma'ai'a, F. (1958). An examination of the practicability of adapting the Otis Intelligence Tests for use in selecting Samoan students for Post-Primary study (Dip. Ed. paper, Wellington: Victoria University of Wellington).

Macfarlane, A. H., Blampied, N. M., & Macfarlane, S. H. (2011). Blending the clinical and cultural: A framework for conducting formal psychological assessment in bicultural settings. *New Zealand Journal of Psychology, 40*(2), 5–15.

Mann, C. W. (1935). *Fiji test of general ability and handbook.* Suva: Fiji Government Printer. Cited in Ord, I. G. (1977). Australian psychology and Australia's neighbours. In M. Nixon & R. Taft (eds.) *Psychology in Australia: Achievements and prospects* (pp. 252–285). Sydney: Pergamon.

(1939). A test of general ability in Fiji. *Journal of Genetic Psychology, 54,* 435–454. In M. Nixon & R. Taft (eds.) *Psychology in Australia: Achievements and prospects* (pp. 252–285). Sydney: Pergamon.

Marai, L. (1997). The development of psychology in Papua New Guinea: A brief review. *South Pacific Journal of Psychology, 9,* 1–6.

(2016). Industrial and organizational psychology in Papua New Guinea. *TIP: The Industrial-Organizational Psychologist.* Retrieved from http://www.siop .org/tip/Apr13/16_Spotlight.aspx.

McElwain, D. W. (1965). *Field study in the Gilbert and Ellice Islands.* Brisbane: University of Queensland.

McElwain, D. W. & Kearney, G. E. (1970). *Queensland test handbook.* Melbourne: ACER

McElwain, D. W., Kearney, G. E., & Ord, I., (1967). *The Queensland test.* Melbourne: ACER.

McMahon, D. J. (1968). *The ACER arithmetic tests: Western Samoan standardization.* Apia: Teachers' Training College.

Milne, M. (2005). Māori perspectives on Kaupapa Māori and psychology: A discussion paper. Report to the NZ Psychologists Board. Retrieved from http://www.pbanz.org.nz/docs/KAUPAPA%20MĀORI%20AND% 20PSYCHOLOGY1%20Moe%20Milnes%20Report_doc1.pdf.

Mitchell, F. W. (1954). A note on the university of Otago child guidance clinic. *Australian Journal of Psychology, 6*(1), 94–96.

(1956) A study of 90 cases of delinquency. *Australian Journal of Psychology, 8* (1), 47–60.

Naylor, F. D., Elsworth, G. R., & Day, N. A. (1985). *Careers guidance and counselling in Australia, Canberra: Commonwealth department of education monograph.* Canberra: Australian Government Publishing Service.

NZPsS. (2002). *The code of ethics for psychologists working in Aotearoa/New Zealand.* Wellington: NZPsS.

Ogden, J. A. & McFarlane-Nathan, G. (1997). Cultural bias in the neuropsychological assessment of young Māori men. *New Zealand Journal of Psychology, 26*(2), 2–12.

O'Gorman, J. G. & Carstairs, J. (1988). Selection practices in the Australian Public Service. Paper presented in the Symposium on Staff Selection Practices in Large organisations, XXIV Congress of Psychology, Sydney, September.

O'Neil, W. M. (1987). *A century of psychology in Australia.* Sydney: Sydney University Press.

  (1984). Recent criticisms of group ability testing in the schools. *Australian Psychologist, 19*(3), 271–274.

Opoliner, A., Blacker, D., Fitzmaurice, G., & Becker, A. (2014). Challenges in assessing depressive symptoms in Fiji: a psychometric evaluation of the CES-D. *International Journal of Social Psychiatry, 60*(4), 367–376.

Ord, I. G. (1966). Psychological Services in Papua New Guinea. *Australian Psychologist, 1*(2), 100–105.

  (1977). Australian psychology and Australia's neighbours. In M. Nixon & R. Taft (eds.), *Psychology in Australia: Achievements and prospects.* (pp. 252–284). Sydney: Pergamon.

Owens, A. G. (1977). Psychology in the Armed Services. In M. Nixon & R. Taft (eds.), *Psychology in Australia: Achievements and prospects* (pp. 202–215). Sydney: Pergamon.

Patrickson, M. & Haydon, D. (1988). Management selection practices in South Australia. *Human Resource Management in Australia, 26*(4), 96–104.

Pearson, C. (2012). Recruitment of Indigenous Australians with linguistic and numeric disadvantages. *Research and Practice in Human Resource Management, 20*(1), 66–80.

Pitama, S. G., Bennett, S. T., Waitoki, W., Haitana, T. N., Valentine, H., Pahina, J., Taylor, J. E., Tassell-Matamua, N., Rowe, L., Beckett, L., Palmer, S., C., Huria, T. M., Lacey, C. J., & McLachlan, A. (2017). A proposed Hauora Māori clinical guide for psychologists: using the hui process and Meihana model in clinical assessment and formal evaluation. *New Zealand Journal of Psychology, 46*(3), 7–19.

Ponsford, J. (2016). The practice of clinical neuropsychology in Australia. *The Clinical Neuropsychologist, 30*(8), 1179–1192.

Price, J. (1984). A look at psychology in Papua New Guinea since independence. *South Pacific Journal of Psychology,* 1, 1–15.

Quiroga, M. Á, Escorial, S., Román, F. J., Morillo, D., Jarabo, A., Privado, J., Hernandez, M., Gallego, B., & Colom, R. (2015). Can we reliably measure the general factor of intelligence (g) through commercial video games? Yes, we can! *Intelligence, 53* (November–December), 1–7.

Rapson, T. H. (1967). *Testing and selection procedures.* Apia: Department of Education.

Reid, N. & St George, R. (1982). Psychological and educational test-training in New Zealand. *A report of a national survey. Newsletter of the International Test Commission,* (16), 10–16.

Reid, N. & Gilmore, A. (1989) The Raven's Standard Progressive Matrices in New Zealand. *Psychological Test Bulletin 2*(2), 25–35.

Richards, G. (2010). Loss of innocence in the Torres Straits. *The Psychologist, 23* (12), 982–983.

Rose, D. E. (1976). Trait measurement and prediction of success. In Department of Labour & Industry (ed.), *Critical issues in vocational guidance: Commemorating 50 years of vocational guidance services in NSW.* Sydney: Division of Vocational Guidance Services, NSW. Department of Labour and Industry.

Ross-McAlpine, K. S., Leathem, J. M., & Flett, R. A. (2018). A survey of psychologists administering cognitive and neuropsychological assessments with New Zealand children. *New Zealand Journal of Psychology, 47*(1), 13–22.

Rutherford, D. A. J. (1931) Education in Western Samoa. In P. M. Jackson(ed), *Māori and education* (pp. 331–353). New Plymouth: Avery.

Ryan, A. M., McFarland, L., Baron, H., & Page, R. (1999). An international look at selection practices: Nation and culture as explanation for variability in practice. *Personnel Psychology, 52*(2), 359–392.

Savickas, M. L. (2005). The theory and practice of career construction. In S. D. Brown & R. W. Lent (eds.), *Career development and counseling: Putting theory and research to work* (pp. 42–70). Hoboken, NJ: Wiley.

Spoonley, P. (2018). Ethnic and religious intolerance – Intolerance towards Māori, *Te Ara - the Encyclopedia of New Zealand.* Retrieved from http://www.TeAra .govt.nz/en/ethnic-and-religious-intolerance/page-1, accessed 17 May 2021.

St George, A. (1972). *The Pacific infants performance scale: Some preliminary and comparative New Zealand studies* (B.Phil. thesis, University of Waikato).

St George, R. (1970). The psycholinguistic abilities of children from different ethnic backgrounds. *Australian Journal of Psychology, 22*(1), 85–89.

(1979). *Beginnings of psychology in New Zealand: A collection of historical documents and recollections.* Delta research monograph, no. 2. Dept. of Education, Massey University. Palmerston, North, N.Z.

(1983a). Some psychometric properties of the Queensland Test of cognitive abilities with New Zealand European and Māori children. *New Zealand Journal of Psychology, 12*(2), 57–68.

(1983b). The assessment of psychological abilities and psychologists' inabilities in the South Pacific. In S. H. Irvine & J. W. Berry (eds.), *Human assessment and cultural factors.* New York, NY: Plenum.

St George, R. & St George, A. (1975). *The measurement of cognitive abilities in the Cook Islands: A research report.* Psychology Research Paper no. 4, Hamilton: University of Waikato.

St George, R. & Preston, R. (1980). Psychological testing in Papua New Guinea: A critical appraisal of the work of the Psychological Services Branch. *Australian Psychologist, 15*(1), 57–71.

Stone, R. J. (1985). Personality tests in executive selection. *Human Resource Management Australia*, November, 10–14.

Taft, R. & Day, R. (1988). Psychology in Australia. *Annual Review of Psychology, 39*, 375–400.

Taylor, J. W. (1966). *The ACER arithmetic tests: Cook Islands standardization*. Rarotonga: Department of Education.

(1967). *Selection and promotion in the Cook Islands*. Paper to Technical Meeting on Selection and Assessment of Pupils for Promotion or Vocational Guidance. Noumea, New Caledonia: South Pacific Commission.

Taylor, P., Keelty, Y., & McDonnell, B. (2002). Evolving personnel selection practices in New Zealand organisations and recruiting firms. *New Zealand Journal of Psychology, 31*(1), 8–18.

Taylor, P., Mills, A., & O'Driscoll, M. P. (1993). Personnel selection methods used by New Zealand organisations and personnel consulting firms. *New Zealand Journal of Psychology, 22*(1), 19–31.

Toulson, P. K. & Williams, W. C. J. (1979). History of personnel research and psychological services in the New Zealand Armed Forces. In St. George, R. (1979). *Beginnings of psychology in New Zealand: A collection of historical documents and recollections*. Delta research monograph, no. 2. Dept. of Education, Massey University. Palmerston, North, N.Z.

United Nations, Department of Economic and Social Affairs, Population Division (2019). *World Population Prospects 2019: Data Booklet. ST/ESA/ SER.A/424.*

Value Edge (2017). Submission to the Royal Commission into the protection and detention of children in the Northern Territory. Retrieved from http:// pandora.nla.gov.au/pan/160243/20180522-0124/childdetentionnt .royalcommission.gov.au/submissions/Pages/default.html#top.

Want, R. L. (1970). The history of psychology in the Royal Australian Air Force. *Australian Psychologist, 5*(1), 2–8.

White, S. J. (1977). The history and future of the C.S.T. Psychological Research Report 4/77. Selection Techniques Section, Office of the Public Service Board, Canberra, Australia.

Willis, D. (1993). Assessment trends in 1992: Future directions handicapped by a legacy from the past? *New Zealand Annual Review of Education, 2*, 245–262.

Winterbourn. R. (1974). *Guidance services in New Zealand education*. Wellington: NZCER.

Young, J. P. (1977). Private practice of occupational psychology. In M. Nixon & R. Taft (eds.), *Psychology in Australia: Achievements and prospects*. (pp. 216–222). Sydney: Pergamon.

CHAPTER 16

Psychological Assessment in South America
Perspectives from Brazil, Bolivia, Chile, and Peru

Solange Muglia Wechsler, Marion K. Schulmeyer, Eugenia V. Vinet, and José Livia

16.1 Introduction

Test development and the use of psychological instruments constitute one of the most important activities of applied psychology. However, these activities have to be considered within the reality of various cultural contexts. Therefore, the purpose of this chapter is to describe and compare the realities of four South American countries: Brazil, Bolivia, Chile, and Peru. Although three of these countries share similarities in the Spanish Language (Brazil is the only nation that speaks Portuguese), they have undergone different historical moments that influenced the training and practice of psychological assessment in their countries. The goal of this chapter is to contrast the most important points of their history of psychological tests with the challenges perceived for their full use of psychological assessment in these countries.

16.2 Brazil

In order to understand the history of testing in Brazil, it is important to explain Brazilian demographic and economic characteristics. Brazil is the largest country in South America with a population estimated to be 190 million habitants on the 2010 census. There is considerable ethnic variety in Brazil, comprised of different populations who came to Brazil during its history, such as Portuguese (who brought their language), Italians, Spanish, Chinese, and Koreans. Presently the racial proportions include whites (57% – mainly European descendants), blacks (6% – descendants from Africa), Asians (9% – mainly from Japan and Korea), Indians (3% – the original habitants), and mulattos (38% – from mixed marriage between whites and blacks). Gender is balanced in the population, with 51.5% women (Instituto Brasileiro de Geografia e Estatística-IBGE]/Brazilian Institute of Geography and Statistics, 2019a).

Although Brazil has the tenth largest economy in the world, its extreme income inequality contributes to problems of social exclusion and economic growth. An estimated 84% of the population live in urban areas, and its distribution is irregular, as the north and northeast states have fewer people whereas the south and southeast are largely populated and are wealthier states.

Brazil's basic educational system includes elementary grades (ages 6–15) and high schools (ages 15–17). Elementary education is mandatory for all children and has a 98% registration rate. Approximately 70% of children attend public schools, mainly from low-income communities, whereas others, usually from more affluent families, attend private schools. The illiteracy rate for those above 15 years old reaches 10% of the population (IBGE, 2019b.). Although there are diverse types of behavior and achievement problems encountered in Brazilian schools, there are no federal or state regulations requiring the presence of psychologists in schools.

In order to understand the practice of psychological assessment in Brazil it is important to present an overview of its history and the influences of other countries on its development. The current stage of test development in Brazil reflects how much growth was achieved by the sustained efforts of researchers and professional associations, as will be discussed.

16.2.1   Historical Aspects of Test Use in Brazil

Tests were introduced to Brazil in the late nineteenth century, mainly influenced by the worldwide movement in the area of individual assessment by Wundt in Germany (Angelini, 1995). Two centers of applied psychology, known as laboratories, were founded in 1906 and 1914; these were mainly dedicated to learning research, using mental development and learning tests of reading and writing (Pasquali, 2016).

By 1914, a psychological laboratory was organized in São Paulo and later affiliated with the first educational and psychological undergraduate programs offered by the University of São Paulo. The importance of tests in educational, clinical, and personnel assessment was widely recognized by the late 1940s (Pasquali, 2010) and an infrastructure to support their use was forming. For example, an institute for vocational guidance was established in Rio de Janeiro. A scientific society was formed, the Sociedade Brasileira de Psicotécnica, later renamed the Sociedade Brasileira de Psicologia Aplicada (Brazilian Society of Applied Psychology). The first scientific journal, *Arquivos Brasileiros de Psicotécnica* (*Brazilian Psychometric Archives*), published research on test use and was later renamed the *Arquivos Brasileiros de Psicologia* (*Brazilian Psychological Archives*) (Pessoti, 1988).

The period between 1950 and 1960 was very productive for those interested in testing. Funds from industrial agencies (Servico Nacional de Aprendizagem Comercial, Servico Nacional de Aprendizagem Industrial/ National Service of Commercial Learning, National Service on Industrial Learning—SESI, SENAI) were invested into developing tests for personnel assessment, along with the development of group intelligence tests (e.g., General Intelligence – G36, Non-Verbal Intelligence Test – INV) and aptitude batteries (e.g., Bateria Fatorial CEPA/Intelligence Factor Battery). These tests were used for many years. Moreover, the use of several psychological tests (e.g., general intelligence, personality, aptitude) to obtain a driver's license became legally required, thus acknowledging the importance of testing and expanding the market for psychological services as well as for test development – and these requirements last still to date (Wechsler, 2009).

Shortly after 1960, a second period, lasting approximately 20 years, began in which tests were not considered sufficiently important to warrant financial and professional investments. Because of negative attitudes toward testing, work on test development or revisions largely halted. As a result, Brazilian norms or other test adaptations were not available for a long time, which led to greater use of theory-driven projective measures to assess psychological dysfunction (Wechsler et al., 2019).

Criticisms of test use during this period came from both scientific and political sources. Scientists criticized tests for not being constructed or adapted in light of Brazilian culture, leading to the belief that such tests could not effectively measure Brazilians' cognitive and personality qualities. Prevailing political views also did not favor test use. Tests highlighted individual and group differences and were viewed as being antithetical to prevailing socialist and collectivist views. Considering Brazil's huge socioeconomic differences, test use was seen as favoring the more privileged individuals and groups while overlooking the needs of the less privileged ones.

These negative views had a deleterious effect on test production as well as on psychology students' interest in taking testing courses (Alves, 2009). Classes promoting psychotherapy skills were seen as more relevant to preparation for a professional career than classes dedicated to assessment. Students at this time preferred qualitative methods that emphasized an understanding of the entire person to quantitative methods that seemingly led to more narrow views (Hutz, 2009, 2010).

16.2.2   The Development of Psychological Assessment

Concerns about the quality of psychological assessment in Brazil began to arise as early as the 1980s. The first meeting to address these concerns was organized by the Federal Council of Psychology (CFP) (Wechsler et al., 2019). Several actions were proposed, which did not have major impact. Therefore, psychology professors decided to organize university-based laboratories for constructing and validating tests for the Brazilian population as well as to adapt and validate etic tests.

The first laboratory formed was in Brasilia, Brazil's national capital (Federal University of Brasilia), followed by three others in the state of São Paulo (State University of São Paulo, Pontifical Catholic University, and University of São Francisco) and one in the south in Rio Grande do Sul (Federal University of Porto Alegre). Today there are approximately 60 groups of laboratories, hosted in universities, dedicated to the construction and development of Brazilian tests, as well as to developing and validate etic tests for Brazil (Wechsler et al., 2010, 2014).

An increased interest in the scientific qualities related to testing led to the founding of the Brazilian Institute of Psychological Assessment – IBAP (IBAP, 2020). In 2002, IBAP created the scientific journal *Psychological Assessment* to promote and disseminate research in this area. Since then, the IBAP has been promoting biennial congresses on psychological assessment, and the last one in 2019 attracted 1,000 delegates including students, professors, and professionals in psychology. The IBAP creation can be considered the foundation for the growth of psychological assessment in Brazil. Two other associations devoted to psychological assessment were also founded since then: the Brazilian Society for Rorschach and Projective Methods (SBRo) and the Society for Assessment and Psychological Measurement for Minas Gerais state (SAPSI-MG). The existence of three professional associations in the country for psychological assessment indicates the importance currently accorded to assessment in Brazil (Wechsler et al., 2019).

16.2.3   Professional Regulations and Training

National standards for test development, quality, and use were developed by the CFP and the Brazilian Institute of Psychological Assessment. Guidelines on test use approved in 2000 by the International Test Commission (ITC) helped form the basis of these standards. In 2003, the CFP adopted federal regulations that require that all tests used in the country have empirical evidence of their validity, reliability, and norms relevant to Brazil. This regulation emphasizes the need to adapt tests in light of the Brazilian environment before using tests originally developed elsewhere.

According to the CFP regulations, all existing and new psychological tests must be evaluated under these new rules, and a national commission was convened to evaluate tests in light of the new standards. The titles of approved tests are listed on the CFP's website as the System for Evaluating Psychological – SATEPSI (SATEPSI, 2019) to inform psychologists and the public which tests produce scientific quality and can be used by professionals. Psychologists whose practices disregard the requirement to use only approved tests may face sanctions under the profession's ethics code (CFP, 2003). Tests not listed may be used only for research. In addition, currently approved tests need norms reviewed every 15 years and new evidence of validity established for the Brazilian population (CFP, 2010) every 20 years. This commission has 15 years of successful experience, which contributed to the high evaluation that psychological tests now have in the country, as they are recognized as assuring scientific quality to make assessments in various contexts (Reppold & Noronha, 2019).

16.2.4   Increase of Research Groups and Production

The great improvement of psychological instruments was due to the considerable increase in numbers of Brazilian researchers interested in psychological evaluation. This fact can be observed when we notice the growth of task force groups in psychological assessment created at the National Association of Graduate Psychology and Research Programs – ANPEPP (ANPEPP, 2019).

The first task group at ANPEPP was created in 1989, namely "Perspectives in Psychological Assessment and Diagnosis." Currently this group has five subgroups: Research in Psychological Assessment, Projective Methods in the Context of Psychological Assessment, Cognitive and Neuropsychological Assessment, Assessment in Positive Psychology and Creativity, and Personality and Psychopathology.

Undoubtedly the expansion of these task force groups exemplifies the growth of the area of psychological assessment in the country. The organization of these groups can be considered not only as scientific but also as a space to debate policies, as they have produced documents with positions on specific professional issues that are sent to the CFP. From a scientific and academic perspective, these groups are producing articles and books, making a major contribution to improve the training and performance in the areas of psychological evaluation. The 20 books produced by these groups to date are being used as textbooks in most undergraduate and graduate courses.

16.2.5   Challenges and Vision of the Future

Psychological assessment in Brazil has seen great development in the last two decades. However, much remains to be done. Most tests currently used in Brazil are designed for typically developing children between ages 6 and 12 years. Additional tests are needed for children with special needs as well as for younger and older children (e.g., preschool and adolescent populations). Moreover, industrial and commercial organizations need more tests for use in personnel assessment, including assessment of skills and personality characteristics related to work productivity in Brazilian business contexts (Wechsler et al., 2010).

Tests that assess intelligence and attention are the most predominant in the list of tests approved in SATEPSI, thus requiring investigation of other areas of mental functioning and personality (Reppold et al., 2017). In addition, there is a need for advancement of the criteria for the approval of projective tests as they are more subjective in scoring and interpretation (Primi et al., 2009). Moreover, there is an abundance of paper-and-pencil tests, and scarcity of tests that can be administered and scored online, which is a necessity for large-scale testing for educational purposes as well for selecting personnel for organizations.

The training of psychologists to work in the area of psychological assessment is another area of great concern (Noronha et al., 2013; Mendes et al., 2013). There is much emphasis on theory and testing techniques, while other content such as test design and psychometrics principles are largely left unchallenged. Continuing education could solve the problems and minimize the existing prejudices in this area (Borsa, 2016), although few programs in the country offer the possibility of e-learning or specialized courses on psychological assessment.

The growth in the number of graduate programs with a research focus on psychological evaluation is noteworthy. Universities must continue their efforts to improve their research infrastructure leading to test development and evaluation as well as the preparation of those who will develop and use the next generation of tests. Companies that publish and distribute tests will have to collaborate with the increasing number of university-based test development and research laboratories and increase their liaison with this scientific community to be able to publish tests developed in

Brazil. Finally, the three professional associations devoted to psychological assessment in the country should continue their efforts to develop more tests to address different needs of the Brazilian population as well as to combine programs to better train psychologists to provide quality services to the country.

16.3 Bolivia

Political, economic, and social realities in Latin America vary from one country to another and so does the history of psychology. There are countries with a long tradition in psychology and others with a more recent one. For example, the first psychology program in a Latin American university was created in 1928 in Mexico, and more than 40 years later, the last country to begin a psychology program in the region was Bolivia, where the first university program started in 1971 (Alonso & Eagly, 1999). In the 1970s there were three psychology programs in the country, the programs that came after that decade have around 20 years of existence. Psychology in Bolivia therefore has a relatively short history (Ministry of Education, 2012).

To understand the context in which psychology developed in Bolivia, we must consider the country's political, economic, and social reality. Its political history has always been one of instability. Since it was founded there have been 88 different governments (De Mesa, 2001). This situation interrupted the functioning of universities, forcing them to close every now and then. The country has always had around the lowest Human Development Index of the 12 South American countries and the highest percentage of people living below the income poverty line (Human Development Index, 2019). The country's social composition is diverse. Bolivia has around 11 million people from 36 different ethnic groups and cultures. Until recently it was thought that most of the population was indigenous, but the census conducted in 2012, showed that only 31% of Bolivians identify themselves as belonging to one of the indigenous groups. While UNESCO (2017) says that the national level of literacy rate is 92.3%, it is lower among people whose first language is indigenous (88.96%), and even lower among rural indigenous women, where the literacy rate is 64.37%.

16.3.1 History of Psychological Assessment

The political, economic, and social aspects mentioned affected the development of psychology in different ways. The closing of universities resulted in people studying abroad. Hence most psychologists over 50 years of age did not study in Bolivia. There is a strong presence of psychoanalytic psychologists since most psychologists went to study in neighboring countries like Argentina, Uruguay, and Brazil. The economic situation ensures that psychologists have low wages, which in turn reduces their possibilities to access better educational opportunities – continuous education, postgraduate courses, international congresses, and so on (Datax, 2019). The social context presents psychologists with a diversity in cultures and reading proficiency. Many people are illiterate or have limited reading comprehension and generally lack test wiseness. Hence, when psychologists assess individuals, they encounter people who have little experience using pen and paper, and less experience drawing. When interviews are conducted, culturally embedded explanations and names for psychological symptoms and life experiences that are not necessarily recognized by the urban psychologist are used (Gabriel, 2005; Schulmeyer, 2015; Schulmeyer & Piotrowsky, 2017).

16.3.2   Professional Training in Psychology

Currently there are five public universities and 13 private universities that have psychology programs in Bolivia (Ministry of Education, 2012). The analysis of psychology programs' content found that 9% of the courses were related to methodology, 10% were assessment courses, 25% were dedicated to different psychological theories, and 29% focused on applied psychology. This is very similar at least to what Puche (2003) found in Colombia (Schulmeyer, 2015).

The first years of the psychology program at the Catholic University San Pablo of La Paz, came with changes every year. The 1971 program lasted only one year and proposed clinical and educational training. In 1972 and 1973 still more changes were made to the program dividing it into two branches, one on Clinical Psychology and the second, on Educational Psychology. In 1974, Social Psychology was added, and the University created a two-and-a-half-year Psychometry program to train educational counselors, but after a first group of students graduated, the program was discontinued (Via, 2000). This experience ensured psychometry as a subject was perceived as being of little importance in psychological training.

Currently psychological assessment training in undergraduate programs in Bolivian universities, gives emphases to projective techniques over objective tests, and only three programs (of 28) include test theory. As a rule, psychoanalytic theory is prevalent in syllabi and bibliographies for assessment courses (Schulmeyer, 2016). Even though the country has a diverse population, little is done to create, adapt, or validate tests. Few specialized articles can be found in national and international journals (only seven by 2013; a few more have been added to the list in recent years). Six years ago, we could only identify 11 psychologists working in the adaptation and validation of instruments in different universities. Their research only makes up 2% of pre-graduate theses (Schulmeyer et al., 2013). This is important because research in psychology is greatly limited to the under-graduate level. Master's degree programs in the country are scarce, and there has only been one doctorate program (Schulmeyer, 2015).

16.3.3 Assessment Practice

Due to time, cost, availability, and perceived validity, health professionals base their psychological assessment mainly on the clinical interviews and then on different projective tests. The Draw-a-Person-in-the-Rain Test is the most popular test, followed by Machover's HTP (House TreePerson). The use of TAT (Thematic Apperception Test) and Rorschach tests is less frequent, mainly because these two are difficult to source in Bolivia and there is not much training in them (Schulmeyer & Piotrowsky, 2017). Objective tests, on the other hand, are used to corroborate information obtained through the interview and projective tests. The most commonly used instruments are the Beck Depression Inventory (BDI) and Beck Anxiety Inventory (BAI), which are short and widely accessible.

In general, psychologists find both projective and objective assessment useful. They recognize the need for instruments that are adapted to our population's characteristics and want more and better educational oppor-tunities to improve their evaluation skills. However, we have to find some way to disseminate the work that is accomplished in creating and adapting instruments, since it is hard to access because it stays in the libraries of the universities. The answer might sound simple when the normal channel is doing this through specialized journals. However, Bolivian professionals make little use of modern digital communication technology and very few know of the importance of publishing their research in journals or know how to accesses international and national research in order to stay updated (Gainsborg, 2013; Sainz, 2009).

16.3.4 Challenges

The challenges of psychological evaluation in Bolivia have much in com-mon with those of neighboring countries. However, its particular history and context makes limitations greater. Information and tests in universities are over 20 years old. Accessibility and costs determine the books that are used, and the instruments taught (Schulmeyer, 2013, 2016).

The economic limitations affect the professional practice as well. In the clinical and health system, projective tests (which do not have costs per administration) and objective photocopied tests are mostly used. Moreover, in the public services, the demand outnumbers the psychologists available, which does not give them the time they need to make an appropriate evaluation. The economic situation even affects organizational psychology since companies find it hard to pay for online tests for their selection processes or other assessment needs and psychologists use whatever they have at hand.

An important limitation faced by psychological practice in general is the lack of entities that supervise and protect the profession. This situation affects assessment practices as well, since no organization regulates the instruments used or the professionals that use them. This absence allows other professionals, besides psychologists, to test people for different purposes. The existing psychology associations have started to work together over the last four years. One of their goals is to pass a bill of professional practice but there has been resistance in different governments to accept one. In 2020, the psychology associations of Bolivia presented a project to the central government, but it was rejected. At the time this chapter was being written, the associations were working on a second proposal that would give the official national College of Psychologists tuition to certify psychologists and regulate the psychological practice in the country.

16.4 Chile

Chile is a South American country occupying a long, narrow strip of land between the Andes mountains to the east and the Pacific Ocean to the west. It borders Peru to the north, Bolivia to the northeast, and Argentina to the east and far south. Chile's 2017 census reported a population of 17,574,003, with a population decrease since 1990 due to a declining birth rate. About 85% of the population lives in urban areas, with 40% living in Greater Santiago. Chilean education is segregated by wealth in a three-tiered system where quality of schooling received is associated with socio-economic backgrounds. Today, Chile is one of South America's most stable and prosperous nations, leading Latin American nations in human development, competitiveness, income per capita, globalization, and economic freedom, but with a high level of social inequality. Recently,

Chile has become attractive for immigrants, mostly from neighboring Venezuela, Peru, Haiti, Colombia, Bolivia, and Argentina.

16.4.1   Initial Historical Context

In a concise historical synthesis, Salas and Lizama (2009) place the start of psychology in Chile in 1889, closely linked to the improvements in education and the creation of the Pedagogical Institute. Then, in 1908, the first Experimental Psychology Laboratory was created under the influence of German experimental psychology. In 1941, the Institute of Psychology was created at the University of Chile, and in 1947 this university offered the first special course in psychology. Finally, in 1954, the School of Psychology was created at the Catholic University.

In this initial period, psychological assessment was marked by measurement in psychology. Between 1925 and 1928, the Ministry of Public Instruction, today the Ministry of Education, entrusted Luis Tirapegui with applying the Binet–Simon method to measure the intelligence of Chilean children on a massive scale (Salas et al., 2018). In 1944, Grassau's studies on the Binet test and Bernales's on the Terman intelligence test were among the first studies conducted by the Institute of Psychology at the University of Chile. In addition, the first special course in psychology at the University of Chile had a chair in test construction and application (Nassar, 1955). Later, the Catholic University adapted and standardized Wechsler's intelligence tests (Bravo, 2004). These studies reflect the importance of psychometrics at the beginning of Chilean psychology, where new psychologists needed valid instruments with which to work.

For about 25 years, the only two existing schools of psychology in the country marked different trends: the University of Chile had an experimental and positivist orientation, whereas the Catholic University had a phenomenological, psychoanalytical, and subsequently behaviorist trend, balancing the initial training of Chilean psychologists (Bravo, 2004, 2013). In addition, psychology as a profession was officially validated in 1968 with the formal establishment of the College of Psychologists of Chile, which had legal powers to control the practice of the field.

The breakdown of Chile's institutionality, which occurred in 1973, and the period of military dictatorship that followed (1973–1981) caused academic activity to stagnate, affecting psychology and psychological assessment. At the end of the dictatorship in 1981, among the "mooring laws" of the military regime, the General Law of Chilean Universities currently in force was enacted, which restructured the existing eight universities in the country and allowed the creation of new private universities (Moyano & Ramos, 2013). A process of accelerated proliferation of psychology programs in various regions of the country began, with a significant increase in enrollment. Also, in the 1980s, Chilean professional associations lost their legal powers to supervise professions. This generated a deregulation in training and in the professional practice of psychology. In psychological assessment, the rigor in training and professional practice that had characterized Chilean psychological assessment since its inception was lost.

16.4.2   Deregulation and Attempts at Regulation

In the last 35 years there has been a considerable increase in the number of psychologists, which is estimated to be 60,000 practicing psychologists (Superintendencia de Salud/Health Administration, 2019) for a population of 19 million people (Instituto Nacional de Estadística/National Statistics Institute, 2019). The following is an overview of the current situation of psychological assessment in Chile focused on efforts to overcome deregulation in training and professional practice and to develop research in psychological assessment.

16.4.2.1   Training

The sustained growth of enrollment in psychology became a problem due to the low quality of the programs offered and the difficulties new psychologists have integrating into the labor market (Villegas et al., 2003). At state level, the situation was addressed by creating accrediting institutions of universities, programs, and curricula, which analyzed whether the proposed program profile that each university offered its students effectively matched the service it offered, without really involving a quality certification system that considered the assessment of important contents for the profession (Moyano & Ramos, 2013). The current accreditation system arose from this initiative and is the responsibility of the National Accreditation Commission (CNA, Chile) under the Ministry of Education.

In this context, in 2006 seven directors of psychology schools belonging to the Consortium of State Universities of Chile (CUECh) self-convened to agree on the common requirements, considered minimum or fundamental for granting the professional title of psychologist in the country. This led to the creation of the CUECh Schools of Psychology Network (CUECh Psychology Network), currently comprised of the 10 CUECh universities that have accredited psychology programs. One of the results of the CUECh Psychology Network was the creation of a graduation profile with cross-sectional and professional skills for a psychologist, which has been implemented gradually in different partner schools (Calderón, et al., 2007; Moyano & Ramos, 2013).

In the graduate profile of the psychologist trained in the Network, competences linked to psychological evaluation were established in specific overall competence three (out of seven), described as competences to "evaluate and diagnose phenomena and psychological processes in individuals, groups and organizations with procedures validated by the discipline, for decision-making and to critically examine their consequences" (Moyano & Ramos, 2013). However, the CUECh Psychology Network can only influence its partner schools.

16.4.2.2 Professional Practice

The current situation is precarious because the certification and control of the profession has not been regulated since 1981. Although the College of Psychologists has ethical and behavioral regulations for professional practice, and specific ones for the management of tests (College of Psychologists, 2008), it has no legal powers of control (Winkler et al., 2007). In addition, its influence is very low because only 6,000 of the nearly 60,000 psychologists practicing in the country are registered members.

As in other countries, there is no national register of authorized tests for professional work, nor an explicit affiliation to international standards governing the use of tests and adaptation and standardization procedures. The results of a survey on attitudes toward and the use of tests in Latin American countries illustrate this situation. According to Vinet, Rodríguez-Cancino, and Sandoval (2019), Chilean psychologists report a great diversity and heterogeneity of tests used, with the intensive use of projective techniques (55% of the total of the 20 most frequently used tests). In addition, of the aforementioned tests, 91% have not registered psychometric studies (reliability, validity, and/or standards) in the last 10 years in the country.

16.4.2.3 Research

With the increase of postgraduates in psychology, coming mostly from foreign programs, research has been strengthened in various areas. Among the initiatives that have contributed to this development are the following.

The CUECh Psychology Network has held annually since 2006 a congress of psychology at the headquarters of the programs attached to the Network. These conferences have invigorated research, enhancing various areas, among them the "Methodology, Measurement, and Assessment" area. However, beyond presentations at conferences, these studies have been published only occasionally in scientific journals, as noted by Vinet and González (2013) in a 10-year review (2002–2012), which recorded only 41 items on psychological testing in the country's three most prestigious psychology journals.

Regarding the development of tests, in 2011 the CUECh Psychology Network formed a working group to promote the development of psychometric instruments with high quality standards, adapted and standardized to the Chilean reality; however, its formalization through the universities belonging to the CUECh Psychology Network posed challenges to its continuity (Vinet & González, 2013). Later, at the 2015 Chilean Congress of Psychology, the CUECh Psychology Network supported the creation of the ACMME,[1] a group of national researchers oriented to interdisciplinary exchange and the promotion of scientific knowledge currently in force in four subdisciplines: research methodology, data analysis, psychometrics, and applied assessment procedures.

There are also two research and development centers at the Catholic University of Chile, which have favored the development of psychological evaluation tools. They are MIDE UC,[2] a research, development, and services center, oriented to the measurement and applied evaluation in fields such as education, public entities, business and society, and CEDETI UC,[3] aimed at developing and promoting technological tools to help improve the quality of life of people with disabilities and in the educational field, which is responsible today for the national adaptation of the Wechsler Intelligence Tests.

Finally, internationally, thanks to an initiative by the Interamerican Psychological Society, Iberoamerican researchers, including some Chileans, decided to render a diagnosis regarding attitudes and practices in the use of tests in their countries, in order to subsequently propose plans for joint development under international standards led by the ITC.

16.4.3   Conclusions and Challenges for Assessment in Chile

It is perceived that the critical situation in the national psychological evaluation is a result of the university and professional deregulation arising in the military regime (1973–1981). In addition, it is perceived that the

---

[1] See http://acmme.cl/.   [2] See www.mideuc.cl/.   [3] See www.cedeti.cl/.

necessary changes are aligned with the three challenges already posed by Vinet and González (2013).

Consequently, today the following three aspects need to be addressed: (1) regulation in professional training that incorporates topics of psychological evaluation to enable the appropriate use of tests in all psychology programs; (2) evaluation and determination of psychological instruments that comply with international standards for the appropriate use of tests nationally; and (3) development and strengthening of research groups able to provide the country with tools and instruments to carry out suitable evaluation practices with valid and culturally relevant instruments.

Finally, this review calls for coordination between training in psychological assessment, professional practice, and research in psychological tests. Ideally, a national approach to psychological assessment should be aligned with international standards. In this way, the Chileans could benefit from a fair assessment, developed with ethical and scientific support. Each area has evolved separately in the last 35 to 40 years and joint objectives are required to overcome the current deregulation.

16.5 Peru

Peru is located in the central and western part of South America. According to the 2017 census, its population reached over 31 inhabitants. The National Institute of Statistics and Informatics (INEI) suggests that life expectancy at birth is 76.5 years (INEI, 2019) and as reported by the United Nations Development Program (INEI, 2017) the Development Human Index is 0.74 at a high level, surpassed in the Latin American context by Chile (0.84), Argentina (0.82), Uruguay (0.79), and Brazil (0.75). In recent years, Peru has made great efforts to reduce poverty, which indicates that 21.7% of the population is poor (INEI, 2017)

16.5.1 History of Psychological Assessment in Peru

Psychological assessment may be perceived as occurring in three periods. The first stage, lasting from 1920 to 1940, was termed the "individual phase." The Binet–Simon Scale, Otis Intelligence Test, and Terman Collective Test were used, with Luis Miro-Quesada often recognized as the promoter of psychometry in Peru at the time (Alarcón, 1968). The development of psychology in Peru at the beginning of the 20th century had a spiritual-philosophical tendency, and later developed into the scientific-experimental line and another one of psychoanalytic tendency, as described by Alarcón (1968). It has been pointed out that this first stage served as the basis for the development of a phenomenological, existential, and humanistic current (Anicama, 1999).

The second phase of development for assessment in Peru (1940–1960) is called systematic. It was established under the leadership of Walter Blumenfeld (1882–1967), a German psychologist, who arrived in Peru in 1935 to lead the Institute of Psychology and Psychotechnics at the Faculty of Letters of the San Marcos University. The function of his lab was to develop psychotechnical examinations for businesses and educational institutions and to perform psychometric research. Blumenfeld conceived psychology as a natural science that studies the behavior of living beings, focused the subject of psychic measurement, and adhered to the principles of Gestalt psychology applying them to the pedagogy. This period was one of great scientific productivity, in terms of books and articles, developing experimental and psychometric research, even transcending the country's borders (Alarcón, 1994; 2000).

Finally, a third phase defines assessment in Peru from 1970 to the present day, which is called nonsystematic because there is no structured policy for the construction and adaptation of instruments. These assessments are developed through the thesis of the faculties of psychology and the individual efforts of researchers. The third trend, in this foundational stage of Peruvian psychology, was shaped by psychoanalysis and developed primarily by psychiatrists. Therefore, psychological assessment in Peru received influence reflected by clinical psychology, mainly from the Rorschach technique

16.5.2   Training

The professionalization of psychology in Peru began in 1955 when the Section of Psychology was created at the National University of San Marcos. After the creation of the specialty of psychology at San Marcos University, the psychology section was founded in 1958 at the Pontifical Catholic University of Peru, and spread later to other universities, such as San Agustin National University of Arequipa in 1964, and then other higher learning institutions, both public and private. There are psychology programs in almost all regions of Peru nowadays, most of them located outside Lima, 87% of which are private, and they came out between the 1990s and 2000s.

In relation to user training, it can be pointed out that all undergraduate psychology programs include compulsory courses of psychological evaluation, as part of the curriculum to get the degree in psychology (psychological diagnosis, personality and intelligence tests, performance testing, psychological report writing, techniques of observation, and interview), as well as subjects related to the methodological aspects of the tests such as construction of tests or psychometrics, together with statistics. The central problem lies in the teaching of the tests; these are not properly selected; they are not necessarily taught with original tests and updated standards, being scarce postgraduate user training policies, either from universities or from the College of Psychologists of Peru.

Regarding the professional practice of psychology in Peru, it is protected by Law 29369 (Law of the Labor of the Psychologist) promulgated on October 27, 2004 and its regulations given by Supreme Decree 007 on August 2, 2007, which allows professional psychologists to perform activities of their professional competence in the various areas of their specialty. In relation to organized psychology, there is the College of Psychologists of Peru, created by Law 23019 on April 30, 1980 and modified by Law 30702 on December 21, 2017. It is an internal, autonomous, and regulatory public law body of the profession of psychology that requires registration as a psychologist in this entity to practice as a psychologist. The College has a code of ethics and deontology, which highlights aspects related to the psychological evaluation, especially in the use of psychological tests and the issuance of psychological certificates. In the 2010–2012 Biennium, the board of directors held the first international symposium entitled "The Psychological Tests: Development, Methodology and Ethical Aspects," and as a consequence of this activity the National Psychological Tests Committee was formed.

There is no policy for the organization of professional academic bodies as federations, associations, or societies; within the latter, some institutions have emerged such as the Peruvian Association of Neuropsychology, the Peruvian Society of Emergency and Disasters, the Positive Psychology Peruvian Society, the Psycho-oncology Peruvian Society, and the Psychological Assessment Peruvian Society.

16.5.3   Research

The first contributions to psychological research were given by psychiatry and pedagogy. Studies on psychological tests were also Valdizan's interest. He created the test of attention and translated the Binet–Simon Metrics Scale. Izcue (1920) also performed work on memory. Chueca (1920) compared Lima school students with French students through Binet–

Simon tests. There was a great interest in the Rorschach test, which was applied to various groups: aphasic (Majluf, 1949), epileptics (Sal & Rosas, 1950, 1954), and Aguaruna Indians (Sánchez, 1958). The TAT was also of interest; profiles were made in Mestizo population (García, 1961). The Bender test (Bambarén, 1956), the Wartegg test (Luza, 1959), the Tzedek test (Bazán, 1955), and the Szondi test (Donayre, 1955) were also used.

On the other hand, Miro-Quesada (1945) offered a pedagogy seminar where the study of psychological and pedagogical value of testing was addressed. Other researchers applied tests to students, as the Terman collective test (Rodríguez and Coz, 1934), and a construction manual for objective exams was edited (Coz, 1947). The National Psychopedagogy Institute, which is dependent of the Ministry of Education, conducted psychopedagogical research focusing on personality, intelligence, and cognitive processes of children and adolescents between 1942 and 1962 (Alarcón, 1994). The Psychopedagogical Institute of the Faculty of Education of San Marcos University, created in 1955 and directed by Blumenfeld, also contributed to the psychological research, emphasizing themes of cognitive variables, personality and adjustment, vocational interests, and the use of collective tests.

Meza, Quintana, and Lostaunau (1999) conducted a review of Peruvian psychological production. The authors point out that the predominant approach is cognitive with 34.10%, followed by psychometrics with 29%, and psychodynamic with 24%; most of them are theoretical works (54%) over the factual ones – by subject area, general psychology dominates (25%), then developmental psychology (10%), psychometrics, social and experimental processes (9.5% each), and educational psychology (8.3%). In the diverse studies, psychometric tests were used such as inventory (40.1%) and scales (26%), projective tests had little use (8%) as well as interviews (16%).

16.5.4   Challenges

The development of psychological evaluation in Peru faces a serious problem. There is no standardized evidence of emic psychological tests. Further, there is a lack of a control policy that regulates the proper use of psychological tests. Peruvian psychologists apply tests without analyzing their origin or making use of ethic norms. Within this perspective, it is necessary to have adapted psychological tests that suit the Peruvian context (Thorne, 1993).

Livia and Ortiz (1996) found the most commonly used objective tests in Lima were the Wechsler Scale of Intelligence tests, the Bender test, the

Raven test, the Eysenck Personality Questionnaire (EPQ), and the Benton Visual Retention Test. The more used projective techniques were the Machover (86%) followed by Rorschach (71%) tests. In another survey with 153 psychologists in Lima (Livia and Ortiz, 2008), a prevalence in the use of Wechsler scales and Cattell test (Factor G) was found, while 8% stated that they did not use any psychological tests. Regarding the personality tests, the most used tests were the EPQ, the Machover test, the Minnesota Multiphasic Personality Inventory (MMPI), the Rorschach test, and the Sixteen Personality Factor Questionnaire (16PF).

Another aspect that attracts attention in the psychological evaluation is that referring to the use of the test manuals; 42% reported using original manuals from recognized publishing companies, while the other 58% used photocopies or manuals edited informally. Photocopies were used by 90% to reproduce the protocol sheet. Some 57% stated that tests were acquired in universities, but it must be emphasized that no higher education institution publishes any edition authorized by the formal providers of tests.

In relation to teaching, Noronha (2003) found that 26% of the 75 university professors surveyed were teaching psychological evaluation. Paula, Pereira, and Nascimento (2007) concluded that universities do not offer adequate training for the practice of psychological evaluation. On the other hand, Hutz and Bandeira (2003) recommended that some strategies for continuing education and specialization must be developed, programs for the training of professors as well as providing support for the creation, development, and integration of evaluation laboratories must be organized, these aspects could also be applied to Peru

The production of books about psychological evaluation written by Peruvian authors and about construction of psychological instruments are scarce, however, some relevant and useful psychological material must be highlighted: Scales of Psychological Tests in Peru by Aliaga and Giove (1993), Measurement in Psychology and Education by Delgado, Escurra, and Torres (2006), Achenbach Inventory of Behavioral Problems and Social Skills by Livia and Ortiz (1993), and Construction of Psychometric Tests: Applications to Social Sciences and Health by Livia and Ortiz (2014).

Noting the organized development of the psychological assessment in countries such as the United States, Spain, and Brazil, it is recommended that one professional academic organization should bring together specialists, such as the Psychological Assessment Peruvian Society, which was founded in 2015 and adopted the Declaration of Lima with the purpose of promoting good practices, under the principles of the ITC. Likewise, it should issue a scientific publication such as the *Peruvian Journal of Psychometrics*. Additionally, it should organize training events as well as a specialized congress. It also should play a main role in the publishing, construction, and trading of tests and a strong role at universities for researching.

16.6   Conclusion

The development and use of standardized tests constitute one of the most important technical contributions of psychologists to society. The value of tests, when grounded on scientific bases can help any society to take decisions for diverse objectives, such as psychodiagnosis, counseling children and parents, vocational guidance, job selection, assisting judges to make decisions, diagnosing disabling disorders, retaining or promoting individuals, and so on. The histories of the four countries in South America reflect the importance of test use and development to help their citizens to make decisions. The trajectory of test development in these countries, as presented, usually followed one of two paths: preferences for theory, often based on psychoanalysis, or great reliance on test adaptation. However, the experience with tests constructed in other nations has not been satisfactory as reported by psychologists from these countries, thus a general feeling of dissatisfaction with etic tests not valid within their own countries. Therefore, professionals and researchers are trying to change this situation, mostly accomplished by Brazil, which has now one national institute of psychological assessment, the IBAP, and two professional associations – Peru just founded its professional association, Chile is making progress in this direction, and Bolivia is still trying to gather efforts to build its professional association. The existence of strong professional associations in each country can provide guidelines for best practices on psychological assessment as well as to develop national tests to be used in their own (Oakland, 2004).

An interesting characteristic of the trajectory of test development in Latin America is the existence of political and financial influences on the test movement. While the political influences had strong impact on Chile's history and delay somewhat the development of the test movement, financial difficulties for professional training and access to tests were the greatest barriers mentioned by these countries, especially in Bolivia.

Among the countries discussed in this chapter, Brazil is the one that has achieved the highest organization of the test development movement. It must be emphasized that the Brazilian movement received great support not only from the CFP but also from the ITC, which sent members to visit

Brazil and assist researchers on their discussions to construct a strong and scientific movement. Moreover, the highest standards of tests use in Brazil were based on ITC guidelines, thus indicating the importance of ITC support to developing nations to attain high scientific standards to psychological services rendered to society.

Some limitations have to be considered in this chapter since it describes only four countries in South America. Other nations should be included in this discussion of test movement, in the future, in order to allow a better panorama of the test movement in this region. Furthermore, there is also the need to conduct research with professionals in these countries in order to compare their attitudes, difficulties, and instruments most used.

REFERENCES

Angelini, A. (1995). Abertura do encontro de Técnicas de Exame Psicológico, Ensino, Pesquisa e Aplicações [Lecture at the First Convention of Psychological Examination: Teaching, Research and Applications]. *Boletín de Psicología/Psychology Bulletin, 45,* 9–18.

Alonso, M. M. & Eagly, A. H. (eds.). (1999). *Psicología en las Américas [Psychology in Americas]*. Buenos Aires: Sociedad Interamericana de Psicología.

Alves, I. C. B. (2009). Reflexões sobre o ensino da avaliação psicológica na formação do psicólogo [Reflections on psychological assessment teaching for psychologists]. In C. S. Hutz (ed.), *Avanços e polêmicas em avaliação psicológica [Questions and issues and progress in psychological assessment]* (pp. 217–246). São Paulo: Casa do Psicologo.

ANPEPP (2019). Grupos de Trabalho [Working groups]. Retrieved from www .anpepp.org.br/grupos-de-trabalho

Alarcón, R. (1968). *Panorama de la psicología en el Perú [Overview of psychology in Peru]*. Lima: San Marcos.

(1994). *El pensamiento psicológico de Walter Blumenfeld [Walter Blumenfels's psychological thinking]*. Lima: CONCYTEC.

(2000). *Historia de la Psicología en el Perú. De la Colonia a la República [History of psychology in Peru]*. Lima: Universidad Ricardo Palma.

Aliaga, J. & Giove, A. (1993). *Baremos de tests psicológicos utilizados en el Perú [Norms for psychological tests in Peru]*. Lima: Amauta.

Anastasi, A. (1987). What test users should know about the interpretation of test scores. *Keynote address at Joint Committee on Testing Practices Second Test Publishers Conference*, Rockville, Maryland.

Anastasio, A. & Urbina, S. (1998). *Los testes psicológicos [Psychological tests]*. México: Prentice Hall.

Anicama, J. (1999). La Psicología en el Perú [Psychology in Peru]. In Alonso & Eagly (eds.), *Psicología en las Américas [Psychology in the Americas]*. Buenos Aires: Edit. SIP.

Araujo, M. (2007). Estratégias de diagnóstico e avaliação psicológica. *Psicologia. Teoria e pratica*, *9*(2),126–141.

Borsa, J. C. (2016). Considerações sobre a Formação e a Prática em Avaliação Psicológica no Brasil [Considerations on the training and practice of psychological assessment]. *Temas em Psicologia/Topics in Psychology*, *24*(1), 131–143. doi: 10.9788/TP2016.1-09.

Bravo, L. (2004). Cincuenta años de psicología en la Universidad Católica [Fifty years of psychology at the Catholic University]. *Psykhe*, *13*(1), 197–204. https://dx.doi.org/10.4067/S0718-22282004000100016.

(2013). Cincuenta años de la psicología en Chile: Una perspectiva personal [Fifty years of psychology in Chile: A personal account]. *Psykhe*, 22(1), 125–137. https://dx.doi.org/10.7764/psykhe.22.1.631.

Bambarén, C. (1956). *La prueba de la Gestalt de Bender en esquizofrénicos. Evaluación cuantitativa según Pascal y Sutell* (Tesis de Bachiller Inédita) [The Gestalt Bender Test for schizophrenics: Quantitative system by Pascal and Sutell (undergraduate report)]. Faculty of Medicine, National University of San Marcos, Lima, Peru.

Bazán, E. (1955). *Prueba de Tzaedek en esquizofrénicos*. (Tesis de Bachiller Inédita). Faculty of Medicine, National University of san Marcos, Lima, Peru.

Buela-Casal, G., Sierra, J. C., Carretero-Dios, H. & De los Santos-Roig, M. (2002). Situación actual de la evaluación psicológica en lengua castellana [Current perspective of psychological assessment in Spanish]. *Papeles del Psicólogo/Psychologists' Papers*, *83*, 27–33.

Calderón, C., Cuadra, A., Denegri, M., González, S., Juliá, M. T., Moyano Díaz, E., & Redondo, J. (2007). *Mejoramiento de la formación general y específica de los profesionales psicólogos del Consorcio de Universidades del Estado mediante el diseño e implementación de un marco curricular común basado en competencias* [Improvement of general and specific training of professional psychologists of the Consortium of Universities of the State through the design and implementation of a common curriculum framework based on competencies]. Proyecto Fondos Innovación Académica, Programa MECESUP 2, Ministry of Education, Chile.

Census. (2012). El 69% de los bolivianos dice no pertenecer a ninguno de los 36 pueblos indígenas reconocidos por la Consitución (2013, 31 de julio). [2012 Census: 69% of Bolivians say they don't belong to any of the 36 indigenous groups recognized by the Constitution] La Razón Digital. http:77www.la-razon.com/index.php.

Chueca, F. (1920). Estudio sobre la capacidad intelectual de los niños en las escuelas de Lima [Studies on school children's intellectual abilities]. *Anales de la Facultad de Medicina de Lima*, 6, 46–57.

CFP (2003). *Caderno especial de resoluções: Resolução CFP002/2003* [*Special compendium of legal decisions: Resolution CFP002/2003*]. Brasília: CFP.

(2010). *Avaliação Psicológica: Diretrizes na regulamentação da profissão.* [*Psychological assessment: Resolution for professional regulation*] Brasília: CFP.

College of Psychologists. (2008). *Código de Etica Profesional.* [Code of Professional Ethics]. Retrieved from http://colegiopsicologos.cl/web_cpc/wp-content/uploads/2014/10/CODIGO-DE-ETICA-PROFESIONAL-VIGENTE.pdf.

Cortada de Kohan, N. (2001). Importancia del avance en la Investigación Psicométrica. Publicación virtual de la Facultad de Psicología y Psicopedagogía de la USAL Año II N° 7 setiembre 2001 [Importance of the psychometric advances. Online publication of Psychology and Psychopedagogie department of the USAL]. Retrieved from www.salvador.edu.ar/psic/ua1-9pub02-7- 01.htm.

Coz, F. (1947). *Exámenes objetivos: su construcción y calificación* [Objective assessment: construct and qualification]. Lima: Stylo.

Dawes, R. M. (1988). *Rational choice in an uncertain world.* San Diego, CA: Hartcourt and Brace.

Datax. (2019). *Datax. Toda la información estadística de Bolivia.* [Datax. All the statistical information of Bolivia.] Retrieved from www.datax.com.bo/.

Delgado, A., Escurra, L., & Torres, W. (2006). *La medición en psicología y educación: Teoría y aplicaciones* [*Measurement in Psychology and Education: Theory and Applications*]. Lima: Editorial Hozlo.

De Mesa, J. (2001). *Historia de Bolivia* [*History of Bolivia*]. La Paz: Gisbert y Cia.

Donayre, J. (1955). *El test de Szondi en los esquizofrénicos* (Tesis de Bachiller Inédita) [*Szondi test for schizophrenics* (undergraduate psychology paper)]. Faculty of Medicine, National University of San Marcos, Lima.

Etzkowitz, H. (2008). *The triple helix: university-industry-government innovation in action.* New York: Routledge.

Fernández-Ballesteros, R. (2004). *Evaluación psicológica [Psychological assesment].* Madrid: Pirámide.

(1998). *Introducción a la evaluación psicológica [Introduction to psychological assessment].* Madrid: Pirámide.

Ferrezuelo, P. (1985). Definición del psicólogo clínico y funciones que desempeña [Definition and functions of clinical psychologists]. *Papeles del Colegio de Psicólogos/Papers of the College of Psychology, 20,* 3–6.

Gabriel, M. (2005). *Hacia una psicobiología antropológica. Aspectos biopsicopatológicos culturales* [*Towards an anthropological psychobiology. Cultural biopsychopathological aspects*]. Santa Cruz: Editorial Santa Cruz.

Gainsborg, C. (2013). *Modelo de alfabetización digital para profesores universitarios a partir de un estudioempírico: Caso Universidad Privada de Santa Cruz de la Sierra* [*Digital literacy model for university faculty based on an empirical study: Private University of Santa Cruz de la Sierra*]. Unpublished work. Faculty of Education, Departamento de Teoría e Historia de la Educación, University of Salamanca.

García, C. (1961). Rasgos culturales de un grupo de mestizos serranos a través de la prueba de apercepción temática (TAT) [Cultural traits on the Thematic Aperception Test (TAT) of montain mestizos]. *Revista Psiquiátrica Peruana/Peruvian Psychiatric Magazine, 47,*130–135.

Human Development Index by Country Population. (September 20, 2019). Retrieved from http://worldpopulationreview.com/countries/human-devel opment-index-(hdi)-by-country/.

Hutz, C. S. (ed.). (2009). *Avanços e polêmicas em avaliação psicológica* [*Questions and progress in psychological assessment*]. São Paulo: Casa do Psicólogo.

(ed.). (2010). *Avanços em avaliação psicológica e neuropsicológica de crianças e adolescentes* [*Progress in psychological and neuropsychological assessment for children and adolescents*]. São Paulo, Brazil: Casa do Psicólogo.

Hutz, C. S. (ed.), *Avanços e polêmicas em avaliação psicológica* [*Advances and debates in psychological assessment*] (pp. 243–265). São Paulo: Casa do Psicólogo.

Hutz, C. S. & Bandeira, D. R. (2003). Avaliação psicológica no Brasil: Situação atual e desafios para o futuro [Psychological assessment in Brazil: Current situation and future challenges]. In O. H. Yamamoto & V. V. Gouveia (eds.), *Construindo a psicologia brasileira: Desafios da ciência e prática psicológica* [*Building Brazilian psychology: Challenges for sicence and practice*] (pp. 261–275). São Paulo: Casa do Psicólogo.

IBAP. (2020). IBAP-Home. Instituto Brasileiro de Avaliação Psicológica [Brazilian Institute of Psychological Assessment]. Retrieved from www .ibapnet.org.br/index.php.

Instituto Brasileiro de Geografia e Estatística. (2019a). Sistema IBGE de recuperação automática-SIDRA [IBGE system of automatic recuperation-SIDRA]. Retrieved from https://sidra.ibge.gov.br/pesquisa/censo demogra fico/demografico-2010/universo-caracteristicas-da-populacao-e-dos-domicilios.

(2019b). Brasil: em síntese [Brazil: a synthetic view]. Retrieved from https:// brasilemsintese.ibge.gov.br/educacao.html.

Instituto Nacional de Estadística (2018). Bolivia cuenta con más de 11 millones de habitantes a 2018 [Bolivia counts with more than 11 million inhabitants by 2018]. Retrieved from www.ine.gob.bo/index.php/convocatorias-de-bienes-y-ser vicios/item/3170-bolivia-cuenta-con-mas-de-11-millones-de-habitantes-a-2018.

INEI. (2019). *Día Mundial de la Población: 11 de julio 2019 [World population day: 11 July 2019]*. Lima: Autor.

(2017). *Informe Técnico: Evolución de la Pobreza Monetaria 2007–2016* [*Technical report on the evolution of monetary poverty 2007–2016*]. Lima: Autor.

Instituto Nacional de Estadistica. (2019) *Población total: Proyección al 30 de Junio de 2019* [Total population: Projection as of 30 June 2019]. Retrieved from www.ine.cl/estadisticas/demograficas-y vitales?categoria=proyecciones%20de %20poblaci%C3%B3n.

Izcue, V. (1920). Asociaciones experimentales en cien niños con palabras corre-spondientes a las fracciones [Experimental associations with 100 children with words and fractions]. *Revista de Psiquiatría y Disciplinas Conexas/Journal of Psychiatry and Related Disciplines, 3,* 5–8.

León, R. (1982). Dos psicólogos peruanos: Walter Blumenfeld y Honorio Delgado [Peruvian psychologists: Walter Blumenfeld and Honorio Delgado]. *Acta Psiquiátrica y Psicológica de América Latina/ Psychiatric and Psychological Act of Latin America, 28,* 310–318.

(1983). Un pionero de la Psicología en América Latina: Walter Blumenfeld [Psychology pioneer in Latin American: Walter Blumenfeld]. *Revista Latinoamericana de Psicología/Latin American Journal of Psychology, 15,* 433–452.

(1993a). Contribuciones a la historia de la Psicología en el Perú [*Contributions to the history of Psychology in Peru*]. Lima, Perú: CONCYTEC.

(1993b). Walter Blumenfeld a veinticinco años de su muerte [Walter Blumenfeld: twenty-five years after his death]. *Revista de Psicología/Journal of Psychology, 11,* 182–194.

Livia, J. & Ortiz, M. (1993). *Inventario de problemas conductuales y destrezas sociales de T. Achenbach* [T. Achenbach's inventory of behavior problems and social abilities]. Lima: PSIDE.

(1996). Los test psicológicos en el Perú investigación, uso y abuso. Rev. [Psychological tests in Peru].*Psicología Actual/Current Psychology, 18,* 23–32.

(2014). *Construcción de pruebas psicométricas: aplicaciones a las ciencias sociales y de la salud [Construction of psychometric tests: applications to social and health sciences].* Lima: Editorial Universitaria.

Livia, J., Ortiz, M., & Salazar, G. (2008). El empoderamiento de la psicometría en el Perú [The empowerment of Psychometry in Perú]. Comunicaciones libres. VI Congreso Iberoamericano de Psicología [Free communications. VI Ibero-American Congress of Psychology] (July), Lima Peru.

Luza, S. (1959). La prueba Wartegg y los brotes agudos de esquizofrenia*/Warteg's test and acute schizophrenic symptoms]. Revista de Neuropsiquiatría/ Journal of Neuropsychiatry, 17,* 488–493.

Majluf, E. (1949). La prueba de Rorschach en la afasia [Rorschach's test in aphasia]. *Revista de Neuropsiquiatría/ Journal of Neuropsychiatry, 12,* 56–74.

Marín, G. (1986). Metodología de la investigación psicológica [Methodology of psychological research]. *Acta Psiquiátrica y Psicológica de América Latina/ Psychiatric and Psychological Act of Latin America, 32,* 3.

Mendes, L. S., Nakano, T. C., Silva, I. B., & Sampaio, M. J. (2013). Conceitos de Avaliação Psicológica: Conhecimento de Estudantes e Profissionais [Concepts of psychological assessment: Students and professionals's knowledge]. *Psicologia, ciência e profissão, 33*(2), 428–445

Meza, A., Quintana, A. & Lastanau, G. (1999). La producción psicológica en el Perú [Psychological production in Peru]. *Revista de Psicología, volumen extraordinario.*

Minbela, C., Urbano, V., & Vargas, J. (2002). *Psicólogos sanmarquinos ilustres [Famous Sanmarquinos psychologists].* Lima: Colegio de Psicólogos del Perú.

Ministry of Education (2012). Guía de Universidades del estado Plurinacional de Bolivia 2012 [Guide of Universities of the Plurinational State of Bolivia 2012]. La Paz: Ministry of Education.

(2019). *Dónde y qué estudiar. Buscador de carreras* [Where and what to study. Career finder]. Retrieved from www.mifuturo.cl/buscador-de carreras/?tipo= carrera.

Miró Quesada, O. (1945). *Ideas y realizaciones pedagógicas* [*Ideas and pedagogical transformations*]. Lima: Librería e Imprenta Gil.

Moyano, E. & Ramos, N. (2013). Transformaciones en la formación de psicólogos en universidades del Estado de Chile [Transformations in the training of psychologists in universities of the State of Chile]. *Integración Académica en Psicología, 1*(2), 29–37.

Muñiz, J., & Fernández-Hermida (2000). Utilización de los test en España [Utilization of tests in Spain]. *Rev. Papeles del Psicólogo, 76*(1), 41–49.

Muñiz, J., Prieto, G., Almeida, L., & Bartram, D. (1999). Test use in Spain, Portugal and Latin American countries. *European Journal of Psychological Assessment, 15*(2), 151–157.

Nassar, C. (1955). Experiencias recogidas en torno a la preparación profesional del psicólogo en Chile [Experiences from around the professional training of psychologists in Chile]. In *Actas del Primer Congreso Interamericano de Psicología, Sociedad Interamericana de Psicología* (pp. 585). Ciudad Trujillo: Editora del Caribe.

Noronha, A. P. P. (2003). Docentes de psicologia: Formação profissional [Psychology professors: Professional background]. *Estudos de Psicologia (Natal), 8*(1), 169–173.

Noronha, A. P. P., Castro, N. R., Ottati, M. V., C., Barros, M. V. C., & Santana, P. R. (2013) Conteúdos e Metodologias de Ensino de Avaliação Psicológica: um Estudo com professores [Contents and methologies on teaching psychological assessment: a study with professors]. *Paideia, 23*(54), 129–139.

Oakland, T. (2004). Use of educational and psychological tests internationally. *Applied Psychology, 53*, 157–172. doi:10.1111/j.1464-0597.2004.00166.x.

Parakh, M., Mehta, V., & Ghosh, D. (2014). Web based assessment: New avenues in psychological testing. *Indian Journal of Health and Wellbeing, 5* (4), 504–506.

Pasquali, L. (2016). Os testes psicológicos no Brasil [Psychological tests in Brazil]. In L. Pasquali (ed.) *TEP- Tecnicas de Exame Psicológico: Os fundamentos [TECP – Techniques of Psychological Assessment]* (pp. 201-220). São Paulo: Vetor Editora.

(ed.). (2010). *Instrumentação psicológica: Fundamentos e práticas* [Psychological instruments: Foundations and practical issues]. Porto Alegre: Artes Médicas.

Paula, A. V., Pereira, A. S., & Nascimento, E. (2007). Opinião de alunos de psicologia sobre o ensino em Avaliação Psicológica [Students' opinions on psychologists' training on psychological assesment]. *Psico-USF, 12*(1), 33–43.

Perales, A. (1987). Problemática de la investigación psiquiátrica y salud mental en el Perú [Problems on psychiatric research and mental health in Peru]. *Anales de Salud Mental, 3*, 55–68.

Pessoti, I. (1988). Notas para uma historia da psicologia brasileira [Notes on the history of Brazilian psychology]. In CFP (ed.), *Quem é o psicólogo brasileiro* [Who is the Brazilian psychologist?] (pp. 17–31). São Paulo: Edicon.

Pfromm Netto, S. (1996). Pioneiros da psicologia escolar: Mira y Lópes (1886–1996) [School psychology pioneers: Myra and Lópes: 1886–1996]. *Psicologia Escolar e Educacional*, *1*, 87–88. doi:10.1590/S1413-85571996000100015.

Primi, R., Muniz, M., & Nunes, C. H. S. S. (2009). Definições contemporâneas de validade de testes psicológicos [Current definitions of validity for psychological tests]. Em C. S.

Prieto, G. & Muñiz, J. (2000). Un modelo para evaluar la calidad de los tests utilizados en España [A model for evaluating the quality of psychological tests in Spain]. In C, S. Hutz (ed). *Avanços e polemicas em avalia;áo psicológica* (pp. 243–265). Sao Paulo: Casa do Psicologo.

Programa de las Naciones Unidas para el Desarrollo. (2007). *Desarrollo Humano 2007–2008. La lucha contra el cambio climático: solidaridad frente a un mundo dividido* [Human development 2007–2008: The fight against climate change: solidarity against a divided world]. New York: ONU.

Puche, R. (2003). *Elementos relevantes para pensar un "estado del arte de la psicología académica" en Colombia* [Relevant elements to think of a "state of the art of academic psychology" in Colombia]. *Memorias del proyecto ECAES de Psicología*. ASCOFAPSI-ICFES

Reppold, C., Serafini, A. J., Gurgel, L. G., & Kaiser, V. (2017). Avaliação de aspectos cognitivos em adultos: análise de manuais de instrumentos aprovados [Assessment of adults' cognitive aspects: análisis of manuals of approved instruments. *Avaliação Psicológica*, *16* (2), 133–144.

Reppold, C., Wechsler, S.M., Almeida, L. S., Hutz, C. S., & Elosua, P. (2019). Perfil dos psicólogos brasileiros que utilizam testes psicológicos: áreas de atuação e instrumentos mais utilizados [Brazilian psychologists' profile who use psychological tests: áreas of practices and instruments most used Psicologia: Ciência e Profissão 2020 v. 40, e201348, 1–14. https://doi.org/10.1590/1982-3703003201348.

Reppold, C. & Noronha, A. P. (2019). *O impacto de 15 anos do SATEPSI na avaliaçãopsicológica brasileira [15 years of SATEPSI impacto on Brazil's psychological assessment].* Psicologia: Ciencia e Profissão, *38*(n.esp), 6–15. Doi: esp.), 6-15. https://doi.org/10.1590/1982-3703000208638.

Robertson, G. & Eyde, L. (1993). Improving test use in the United States. *European Journal of Psychological Assessment*, *9*, 137–146.

Rodríguez, M. (1994). *Walter Blumenfeld y sus aportes a la Psicología como ciencia* [Walter Blumenfeld 's contributions to psychology as a science]. Lima: Universidad Nacional Mayor de San Marcos.

Rodríguez, N., & Coz, F. (1934). *Informe de la labor de algunos experimentos pedagógicos realizados en el Colegio Nacional de Ica, durante el año escolar de 1933* [Work report on pedagogical experiments at the National College of ICA, during the school year of 1933]. Lima: National College of Ica.

Salas, G. & Lizama, E. (2009). *Historia de la psicología en Chile. 1889–1981* [History of psychology in Chile. 1889–1981]. La Serena: University of La Serena Press.

Salas, G., Scholten, H., Norambuena, Y., Mardones, R., & Torres-Fernández, I. (2018). Psicología y educación en Chile: problemas, perspectivas y vías de investigación (1860–1930) [Psychology and education in Chile: Problems, perspectives, and lines of investigation (1860–1930)]. *Universitas Psychologica, 17*(5), 1–14. https://doi.org/10.11144/Javeriana.upsy17-5.pecp

Sal & Rosas, F. (1950). El psicodiagnóstico de Rorschach para estudiar la localización de respuestas con sistemas localizadores propios [Rorschach psychodiagnosis to study answers with proper locations]. *Revista de Neuropsiquiatría, 12*, 23–28.

(1954). Emplazamiento exterior e interior de las áreas de respuesta del test de Rorschach [External and internal answers localization to the Rorschach test]. *Revista de Neuropsiquiatría, 17*, 352-353.

Sainz, P. (2009). *Actitudes del Profesorado con Respecto al Uso de Tecnologías de la Información Comunicación en la Enseñanza Superior [Faculty attitudes toward information and communication technologies in higher education].* Tesis de Maestría del Máster TIC en Educación: Análisis y diseño de procesos, recursos y prácticas formativas. University of Salamanca.

Sánchez, J. (1958). Los indios aguarunas vistos a través del Rorschach [The aguarunas Indians on the Rorschach test]. *Boletín del Departamento de Higiene Mental, 1*, 10–37.

SATEPSI. (2019). Testes favoráveis [Tests approved]. Retrieved from http://satepsi.cfp.org.br/testesFavoraveis.cfm

Schulmeyer, M. K. (2015). La Psicología en Bolivia: formación y situación laboral [Psychology in Bolivia: training and employment]. *Informació psicologica, 109*, 3–18. doi: dx.medra.org/10.14635/IPSIC.2015.109.3.

Schulmeyer, M.K., López, G., & Ortuño, A. (2013). Formación e investigación psicométrica en Bolivia [Pschometric training and research in Bolivia]. *Psiciencia. Revista Latinoamericana de Ciencia Psicológica, 5*(2), 123–129. doi: 10.5872/psiciencia/5.2.101.

(2016). La formación en evaluación psicológica en carreras de Psicología de Bolivia [Assessment training in Psychology pregraduate programs in Bolivia]. *Revista Interamericana de Psicología/Interamerican Journal of Psychology, 50*(2), 288–300.

Schulmeyer, M. K. & Piotrowsky, C. (2017). Assessment practices of psychologists in the mental health system in Bolivia. *Journal of Projective Psychology & Mental Health, 24*(2), 109–115.

Superintendencia de Salud. (2019). *Estadísticas de Prestadores Individuales de Salud a Marzo de 2019* [Statistics of Individual Health Providers as of March 2019]. Retrieved from www.supersalud.gob.cl/documentacion/666/articles-18219_recurso_1.pdf.

Thorne, C. (1993). Variantes psicosociales y el usos e interpretación de pruebas psicológicas [Psychosocial variables, uses and interpretation of psychological tests]. *Revista de Psicología*, 11(1) 97–105.

UNESCO. (2017). *Indigenous knowledge and practices in education in Latin America: exploratory analysis of how indigenous cultural worldviews and concepts influence regional educational policy.* Santiago: Santiago and Regional Bureau for Education in Latin America and the Caribbean, UNESCO.

Via, F. (2000). Historia y formación del psicólogo en Bolivia [History and training of psychologist in Bolivia]. *Ajayu, 8,* 51–62.

Villegas, J., Marassi, P., & Toro, J. P. (2003). *Problemas centrales para la formación y el entrenamiento profesional del psicólogo en las Américas (vol. II)* [Central problems for professional training of psychologist in the Americas (vol. II)]. Santiago: Sociedad Interamericana de Psicología (SIP)/Interamerican Society of Psychology.

Vinet, E. & González, N. (2013). Desarrollos actuales y desafíos futuros en la evaluación psicológica en Chile [Current developments and future challenges in psychological assessment in Chile]. *Psiencia. Revista Latinoamericana de Ciencia Psicológica*, 134–138. http://dx.doi.org/10.5872/psiencia.v5i2.117.

Vinet, E., Rodríguez-Cancino, M., & Sandoval, A. (2019). *Ciencia y profesión: Evaluación psicológica en Chile* [Science and profession: Psychological assessment in Chile]. S. M. Wechsler (Chair), Evaluación psicológica en América Latina: Propuestas de colaboraciones intercultural. Symposium conducted at the XXXVII Interamerican Conference of Psychology (July), La Habana, Cuba.

Wechsler, S. M. (2009). Impact of test development movement in Brazil. *World*Go*Round, 36*(2), 7–8.

Wechsler, S. M., Hutz, C. S., & Primi, R. (2019). O desenvolvimento da avaliação psicológica no Brasil: Avanços históricos e desafios [The development of psychological assessment in Brazil: historical advances and challenges]. *Avaliação Psicológica/Psychological Assessment, 18*(2), 121–128. Doi: 10.15689/ap.2019.1802.15466.02.

Wechsler, S. M., Oakland, T., León, C., Vivas, E., Almeida, L., Franco, A., Solis, P., & Contini, N. (2014). Test development and use in five Iberian Latin American Countries. *International Journal of Psychology, 49*(4) 233–239. doi: 10.1002/ijop.12068.

Wechsler, S. M., Pérez-Solis, M., Ferreira, C., Magno, I., Contini, No., Bluemn, S., Vivas, E., & Viloria, C. L. (2010). Test movement in Iberian–Latin American countries. *Testing International*, (24), 7–8.

Winkler, M., Pasmanik, D., Alvear, K., & Reyes, M. (2007). Cuando el bienestar psicológico está en juego: La dimensión ética en la formación profesional de psicólogo [When psychological well-being is at stake: The ethical dimension in the professional training of psychologists in Chile]. *Terapia Psicológica, 25* (1), 5–24. https://dx.doi.org/10.4067/S0718–48082007000100001.

CHAPTER 17

Historical Development of Psychological Assessment in the Caribbean

Janelle N. Robinson and Michael Canute Lambert

17.1 Introduction

The Caribbean is a diverse, geographical region comprised of 7,000 islands, reefs, cays, and islets (Nicolas & Wheatley, 2013). This region has distinct nations and unique cultures with a growing population of approximately 44 million people (United Nations, 2019). The majority of its approximately 30 recognized territories, including sovereign states, are Spanish-speaking (over 50%), approximately 25% are English-speaking, 22% are French-speaking, and less than 2% are Dutch-speaking (Edwards, 2013; Nicolas & Wheatley, 2013).

Extensive diversity across the Caribbean makes it challenging to discuss the region as one unit in a meaningful way. People within the Hispanic Caribbean (e.g., Dominican Republic and Cuba) have more ties with Latin America. Puerto Rico and parts of the Virgin Islands are US territories. Aruba, Curacao, and Suriname are connected to the Netherlands, and Martinique and Guadeloupe associate with continental France. Jamaica, Barbados, The Bahamas, and Trinidad and Tobago, among others, form the English-speaking Caribbean, also called the British Caribbean, Anglophone Caribbean, or the West Indies (Beauburn, 1992; Edwards, 2013; Ward & Hickling, 2004).

This chapter includes regions within the Caribbean basin but focuses primarily on the British Caribbean and Spanish-speaking nations. Each country is highly influenced by ruling European political powers predating their independence. The Euro-American political power also shaped Caribbean psychological theories, assessment, and treatment. Focusing on historical use of psychological assessment in the Caribbean, this chapter highlights four historical periods: (1) pre-Columbian era (i.e., the period before the arrival of Christopher Columbus in 1492) and ending in the eighteenth century; (2) the beginning of slavery to the nineteenth century; (3) abolition of slavery to the twentieth century; and (4) the twenty-first century.

17.2 Pre-Columbian Era to the Eighteenth Century

The first inhabitants of the Caribbean were Arawak Indians and Caribs (Nicolas & Wheatley, 2013). Arawaks predominantly occupied smaller Caribbean islands while the Caribs lived in the larger islands and South America (Nicolas & Wheatley, 2013). The Arawak population described mentally ill people as "mind riven" (Hickling, 1988). They used direct observation to identify anomalous behavior and provided basic psychopharmacology during their time. They treated the mentally ill with lavings, unguents, and solvent herbs blended with food while singing. (Beaubrun, 1992; Hickling, 1988). Arawaks left blended mixtures of herbs and food hanging on fruit trees for wanderers deemed mentally ill. To the authors' knowledge, there is no documented account that the Caribs utilized similar approaches or had their own system of assessment and intervention.

Unfortunately, the indigenous system of assessment and treatment suffered dismantling with the arrival of the Spanish conquerors in the fifteenth century. These Europeans viewed the indigenous groups as uncivilized and in need of enslavement and eradication (Beaubrun, 1992; Hickling, 1988; Ward & Hickling, 2004). Because Europeans virtually eradicated native Caribbean people, the majority of the region's population is of European and African heritage (Nicolas & Wheatley, 2013). Thus, indigenous people's practices in assessment and healing of individuals with mental illness is extinct.

17.3 Slavery to the Nineteenth Century

Following the genocide of indigenous people, European practices replaced their assessment and treatment of the mentally ill. By the mid-seventeenth century, the British had captured most Caribbean islands, established transatlantic slave trade, and created a predominantly African population (Beaubrun, 1992; Edwards, 2013; Hickling, 1988). Europeans primarily ignored mental illness in Africans and indigenous people. They believed their brains were superior to that of Africans and Caribbean natives. European's racist viewpoints guided assessment of psychopathology among natives and Africans. For example, a diagnosis of "drapetomania" was given to slaves deemed to have an "uncontrollable urge to run away" (Hickling & Hutchinson, 1999, 257), and treatment involved whipping the devil out of them.

The negative consequences of slavery on Africans' physical and mental health created extensive need for mental health services. However, the

Europeans utilized solitary confinement, violence, and restraint for "treatment." Additionally, they erected buildings to house Europeans and others suffering from mental illness, which marked the commencement of institutionalization within the West Indies (Beaubrun, 1992; Hickling, 1988; Ward & Hickling, 2004).

It is important to note, during this era, that US independence of 1783, England's Industrial Revolution of 1760, the French Revolution of 1789, and the Haitian Revolution of 1791 marked a new economic, social, intellectual, and political awakening throughout the Caribbean (Bernal, 1985). These events facilitated international trade and free movement, which provided opportunities for development, modernization, and revitalization. With free movement and international trade came the introduction of European physicians in the Caribbean. For example, by 1833, there were 300 European-trained physicians in Jamaica, who provided medical attention only to the white local population and plantation slaves (Hickling, 1988). Medical attention to the slaves was inconsistent and as such the remaining population coped with mental illness by enlisting the services of traditional healers such as the black slave preachers, voodoo priests, and obeah men and women (Beaubrun, 1992; Ward & Hickling, 2004). These traditional healers were autonomous of colonial control and played a significant role in slaves' physical and psychological well-being.

17.4 Traditional Healers

Traditional healing practices have been and continue to be pervasive throughout the Caribbean, where people rely on the knowledge of herbs and plants to manage health care. This knowledge coupled with stealthily finding ways of using Christianity to conceal engaging in African cultural traditions and ceremonies led to the formation of several spiritual religions and healing practices such as espiritisme, maat, samtaeria, spiritism, voodoo, and obeah, among others (Moodley & Bertrand, 2011).

Assessment of physical and mental health challenges involved transmitting supernatural powers from the spirits of the ancestors to reconcile with problem-causing spirits. The ultimate aim was to regulate emotions and lifestyle. Two specific mediums guided assessment of such health problems: spiritual insights and physical or material mediums. Spiritual insights came in the form of visions, "knowing," intuition, or sudden feelings. Traditional healers referred to spiritual insight as the "third eye" used to connect to the ancestors, and/or the Holy Spirit to identify specific health challenges (Moodley & Bertrand, 2011). Assessment through physical and material medium occurred through the rhythmic sounds of drumming or divination over candlelight (Moodley & Bertrand, 2011). That is, these mediums called upon the spiritual realm to assist in understanding the presenting concerns of the clients. Subsequently, treatment occurred through direct or mediated spiritual interventions.

Traditional healers were so influential that the British sanctioned legislations banning indigenous healing practices across the Caribbean such as the Obeah Act passed as early as 1760 (Paton, 2009). The Obeah Act forbade individuals, enslaved or black, from carrying a weapon and congregating. Furthermore, it inflicted capital punishment to anyone who practiced obeah. Yet, research indicated that contrary to the belief that the intended use of religious practices such as obeah was to cause harm, the practice demonstrated a focus on assessment and healing. That is, gaining understanding of presenting health problems through the spiritual world, bringing healing, reconciling "evil" spirits, and thus resolving mental and physical health challenges. More recently, undercover operations by law enforcement in Jamaica found that the most common reasons for eliciting the services of these traditional healers were for health concerns, relationship problems, employment, and spiritual protection (Paton, 2009).

17.5   Emancipation to the Twentieth Century

Although the mid-nineteenth century marked emancipation for slaves, Caribbean people struggled to gain independence and national identities. The post-emancipation period did not result in more humane psychological assessment and treatment. Instead, behaviors considered as anomalous received punitive intervention (Hickling, 1988). The response was militarization and custodial institutionalization for apprehended offenders. Secure prisons, built in 1844, became housing for the "insane" (Beaubrun, 1992; Hickling, 1988). Due to overcrowding and inefficient resources, the prisons were unable to meet the demands. Governments therefore created larger and more secure "lunatic asylums." An asylum constructed in Antigua served all of the Leeward Islands and another in Grenada served the Windward Islands (Hickling, 1988). Within these "asylums," restraint was the main therapeutic tool and continued to be until the mid-twentieth century (Hickling, 1988; Ward & Hickling, 2004).

By the 1930s, the asylums began to collapse due to overcrowding and lack of supervision, as well as minimal and inadequately trained staff (Hickling, 2010; Ward & Hickling, 2004). All lunatic asylums were renamed mental health hospitals and given individual names to reduce stigma – for example, Bellevue in Jamaica, Black Rock in Barbados, Richmond Hill in Grenada, and St. Ann's in Trinidad (Beaubrun, 1992; Hickling, 1988).

A decade later marked the introduction of electroconvulsive therapy (ECT), insulin coma, and lobotomy, while the 1950s signaled the advent of phenothiazines and occupational therapy. Nonetheless, the largest segment of the population continued to receive assessment and treatment by traditional healers who survived the Europeans' attempts to cease their practice.

Compared to the previous five centuries, the twentieth century marked increased research, training, and clinical services (Ward & Hickling, 2004). For example, within the British Caribbean, the most critical action was the establishment of a Faculty of Medicine at the University of the West Indies in 1947 and the development of psychiatry in 1965 (Hickling, 1988; Ward & Hickling, 2004).

It is important to note that improvement in the psychological assessment and treatment of the mentally ill was disparate. Although exact dates are unknown, non-English-speaking Caribbean territories had an earlier start on incorporating psychological processes than the English-speaking Caribbean. For example, Cuba was the first to integrate mental health care at varying levels of society, (Bernal, 1985; Caldas de Almeida & Horvitz-Lennon, 2010; Javier et al., 2012; Edwards, 2013; Hickling, 2010; Ward & Hickling, 2004; Beaubrun, 1998). Guadeloupe, Martinique, and Haiti also utilized psychological services before the English-speaking Caribbean.

In Cuba, José Agustin Caballera (1760–1835) introduced associationism and the works of John Locke and Condillac. Associationism purports that simple and discrete ideas form the foundation of complex ideas. These concepts, sometimes referred to as "mental chemistry" provided the basis for scientific psychology. Based on this theory, Caballera introduced an experience-based model to define and understand reality, specifically with children (Bernal, 1985). Felix Varela (1788–1853), a Catholic priest in Cuba who extended the work of Caballera, was interested in the sensory development of children. Through direct observations, he examined how children used touch to identify distances, and combined sensory knowledge to form images and ideas (Bernal, 1985).

The twentieth century was also pivotal for Cuba as they achieved independence. However, a strong North American presence existed within this century that pervaded fields of social and natural sciences (Bernal, 1985). Nonetheless, this time marked Cuban psychology development rooted in national identity and the economic realities of Cuba. Yet,

North American culture leaked into this development. The struggle between those vying for Cuban psychology and those persisting on imitating and adapting North American psychological models was evident in the use of psychological testing. Many Cubans trained in North America returned in the twentieth century and introduced European and American psychological tests, mainly the Rorschach (Quevedo & Butcher, 2005), the Thematic Apperception Test, and assessment of hypnotic susceptibilities (Bernal, 1985).

Additionally, during the 1940s and 1950s, Alfonso Bernal del Riesgo (1902–1975), a trained psychologist in Vienna (1931–1933), returned to Cuba to establish a psychology research lab where he published a Spanish translation of the Minnesota Multiphasic Personality Inventory (MMPI) in 1951 (Bernal, 1985; Quevedo & Butler, 2005). The Spanish translation of the MMPI marked the first step in objective assessments in Cuba. This translation also permitted the use of the MMPI in the neighboring Latin American countries (Quevedo & Butcher, 2005). Professionals subsequently imported multiple psychological tests from North America and translated, published, and sold them with little attempt to adapt or validate them for the Cuban population. Despite a genuine interest in North American psychology, many Cuban psychologists regarded the blind application of such theories and psychological testing to Cuba as unrealistic and unethical (Bernal, 1985). Bernal del Riesgo warned that assessment and treatment should become culturally valid by integrating knowledge of the population's culture (Bernal, 1985; Quevedo & Butcher, 2005).

Following the Cuban Revolution period, Cuba began to reject the North American-based psychological models and guided psychological assessment and intervention using a Marxist approach. Cuban psychology emerged as action-oriented and pragmatic to resolve social and community needs (Bernal, 1985). Arguably, their interventions were innovative and reflected the needs of the people. For example, they introduced *psicoballet* (psychoballet), where they employed classical ballet as a method of psychotherapy to treat mental illness. Furthermore, television programs frequently educated parents on child development.

Similarly, between the 1940s and 1960s, there was an increase in trained mental health professionals at the doctoral level in other Caribbean nations, such as Jamaica, Trinidad and Tobago, and Barbados (Beaubrun, 1992; Ward & Hickling, 2004). However, affiliated Euro-American countries trained these professionals (psychologists, psychiatrists, anthropologists, and sociologists, among others) and predominantly taught them Euro-American assessment and intervention procedures.

Although psychology as a discipline emerged in the Caribbean in the late 1900s, early evidence points to European-trained professionals assessing behavior systematically through observation. One early attempt was by José Ramon Lopez (1866–1922) in the Dominican Republic (Edwards, 2013; Javier et al., 2012). Lopez's training was in sociology and he deduced through indirect observation that nutrition and proper diet played a significant role in psychological development and functioning. Specifically, the lack of a proper diet resulted in development of poor character, substandard cognitive ability, proneness to violence, and intellectual challenges. Lopez concluded that, in the Dominican Republic, the poor and disenfranchised resided in the rural communities, and as such, deemed them most susceptible to poor psychological conditions (Javier et al., 2012).

Lopez's methodology of assessing psychological functioning was criticized as lacking empirical validation. As a result, between 1945 and 1950, others such as exiled Spaniards Fernando Sainz and Antonio Ramon Duran attempted to remedy the deficits of Lopez's methodology (Javier et al., 2012). They grounded their approach in philosophy and medicine. They argued that individuals within society are more complex and myriad of factors (not just nutrition) influence psychological adjustment. Rodriguez Arias further suggested comparative assessments to describe the Dominican people. That is, since research inferences in the 1940s and 1950s emerged from studying people living in slums and not the entire population (Javier et al., 2012).

Concerned with the social factors occurring in the English-speaking Caribbean, specifically Jamaica, Edith Clarke (1876–1977) also employed systematic observation in the twentieth century. Clarke served as an anthropologist and advocate for social justice in Jamaica after her training in England in social anthropology. She aimed to describe human behavior by living in the communities she studied (Barrow, 1998). Clarke utilized her training in data collection intertwined with her intimate knowledge of the Jamaican community to create community surveys (Barrow, 1998). Her special interest was in Jamaica's lower-class communities. That is, in stability, cohesion, and overall dynamics of familial relationships within these communities. Through observing community members and gaining feedback via basic questionnaires and interviews, Clarke's research informed policy changes (Barrow, 1998). Noteworthy is that Clarke was not the first to conduct such studies. T. Simey preceded Clarke but because he painted the idiosyncrasies of Afro-Caribbean people in a negative light, other scholars criticized his work. Clarke attempted to avoid such biases (Barrow, 1998). Clarke recognized the importance of gaining input from people to make her research inferences. She reiterated in several of her books and even warned politicians that policies must incorporate the culture and knowledge of the people in their assessment, interpretation of research findings, and decision-making (Barrow, 1998).

17.6 The Twenty-First Century and Cross-cultural Issues of Euro-American Assessment Methods

The late twentieth century and the twenty-first century marked proliferation of published psychological research and practice in the Caribbean. Although their numbers are inadequate, the number of professionals providing psychological services and conducting research also increased. This resulted in an increasing need for psychological assessment tools to conduct clinical and industrial/organizational evaluations and research. Because few if any indigenous tools developed for and normed on Caribbean people exist, service providers and researchers rely heavily on assessment tools developed by and for members of the Western, educated, industrialized, rich, and democratic (WEIRD) societies (Henrich et al., 2010). Such Euro-American psychological tools do not match Caribbean people's language, cultural norms, and everyday realities. These tools might therefore possess questionable psychometric appropriateness for Caribbean people and could lead to inaccurate test-related research findings and implausible clinical inferences about Caribbean people (Edwards, 2013; Sutherland, 2011; Dudley-Grant, 2016).

To meet psychological assessment needs of Caribbean people, development of emic measures indigenous to the region is essential. For example, the Caribbean Symptom Checklist (Lambert et al., 2013) and the Behavioral and Emotional Assessment of Children of Caribbean Heritage (Lambert et al., 2016) assess psychological functioning of adults and children respectively who are of Caribbean heritage. These measures are both conceptually and culturally valid for English-speaking Caribbean countries.

17.7 Conclusion

The pre-Columbian era marked early efforts to develop psychology that reflects the uniqueness of Caribbean nations, but Europeans destroyed such practices. It is therefore not surprising that historical and contemporary Caribbean psychological testing continues to rely on tools developed in WEIRD nations. Yet, countries such as Cuba have fought to develop psychology that reflects their people's needs.

Caribbean psychologists have begun addressing psychometric issues of psychological assessment tools. Their tasks and that of others who collaborate with them is to increase development of psychological tools for Caribbean nationals. Test developers should include Caribbean traditional healers' input when creating these culturally valid assessment tools. Collaborating with traditional healers has proven to be more efficacious than relying solely on contemporary assessment and treatment (Khoury et al., 2012; Moodley & Bertrand, 2011).

To conclude we note that despite our call for developing more culturally appropriate psychological assessment tools, the professional resources required to address this need are sparse. We recommend that policymakers, educators, and practitioners form collaborative relationships between Caribbean psychologists who practice in the Caribbean and psychometricians of the Caribbean diaspora, as well as those of other cultural backgrounds. Such collaborations could focus on the desperate need to develop indigenous assessment tools for the Caribbean region.

REFERENCE

Barrow, C. (1998). Edith Clarke: Jamaican social reformer and anthropologist. *Caribbean Quarterly*, *44*(3/4), 15–34. Retrieved from www.jstor.org/stable/40654041.

Beaubrun, M. H. (1992). Caribbean psychiatry yesterday, today and tomorrow. *History of Psychiatry*, *3*(11), 371–382.

Bernal, G. (1985). A history of psychology in Cuba. *Journal of Community Psychology*, *13*(2), 222–235.

Caldas de Almeida, J. M. & Horvitz-Lennon, M. (2010). Mental health care reforms in Latin America: an overview of mental health care reforms in Latin America and the Caribbean. *Psychiatric Services*, *61*(3), 218–221.

Dudley-Grant, R. (2016). Innovations in clinical psychology with Caribbean peoples. In J. L. Roopnarine & D. Chadee (eds.), *Caribbean psychology: Indigenous contributions to a global discipline* (p. 357–386). American Psychological Association. Retrieved from https://doi.org/10.1037/14753-015.

Edwards, D. J. (2013). Psychology bridge building in the Caribbean: A proposal. *Interamerican Journal of Psychology*, *47*(2), 265–276

Henrich, J., Heine, S., & Norenzayan, A. (2010). The weirdest people in the world? *Behavioral and Brain Sciences*, *33*(2–3), 61–83. doi:10.1017/S0140525X0999152X.

Hickling, F. (2010). Psychiatry in Jamaica. *International Psychiatry*, *7*(1), 9-11. doi: 10.1192/S1749367600000928.

Hickling, F. W. (1988). Psychiatry in the Commonwealth Caribbean: A brief historical overview. *Bulletin of the Royal College of Psychiatrists*, *12*(10), 434–436.

Hickling, F. W. & Hutchinson, G. (1999). Roast breadfruit psychosis: disturbed racial identification in African–Caribbeans. *Psychiatric Bulletin, 23*(3), 132–134.

Javier, R. A., Orlievsky, D., Ruíz-Matuk, C. B., Diaz-Loving, R., & del Castillo, C. C. (2012). Latin America and the Caribbean, History of Psychology In R. W. Rieber (ed.), *Encyclopedia of the History of Psychological Theories* (1st ed., pp. 619–634). New York: Springer.

Khoury, N. M., Kaiser, B. N., Keys, H. M., Brewster, T., & Kohrt, B. A. (2012). Explanatory models and mental health treatment: Is vodou an obstacle to psychiatric treatment in rural Haiti. *Culture, Medicine and Psychiatry, 36*(3), 514–534. https://doi.org/10.1007/s11013-012-9270-2.

Lambert, M. C., Lambert, C. T. M., Hickling, F., Mount, D., Le Franc, E., Samms-Vaughan, M., . . . & Levitch, A. (2013). Two decades of quantitative research on Jamaican children and current empirical studies on Caribbean adult functioning. *Caribbean Journal of Psychology, 5*(1), 14–39. Retrieved from http://ez.lib.jjay.cuny.edu/login?url=http://search.ebscohost.com/login .aspx?direct=true&db=a9h&AN=95972941&site=ehost-live

Lambert, M. C., Sewell, W. C., & Levitch, A. H. (2016). Metamorphosing Euro American psychological assessment instruments to measures developed by and for English-Speaking Caribbean People. In J. L. Roopnarine & D. Chadee (eds.), *Caribbean psychology: Indigenous contributions to a global discipline* (pp. 327–355). Washington, DC: American Psychological Association.

Moodley, R. & Bertrand, M. (2011). Spirits of a drumbeat: African Caribbean traditional healers and their healing practices in Toronto. *International Journal of Health Promotion and Education, 49*(3), 79–89.

Nicolas, G. & Wheatley, A. (2013). Historical and socio-political perspectives of the Caribbean region on mental health. *Revista Interamericana de Psicologia/ Interamerican Journal of Psychology, 47*(2), 167–176.

Paton, D. (2009). Obeah acts: Producing and policing the boundaries of religion in the Caribbean. *Small Axe: A Caribbean Journal of Criticism, 13*(1), 1–18.

Quevedo, K. M. & Butcher, J. N. (2005). The use of the MMPI and MMPI-2 in Cuba: A historical overview from 1950 to the present. *International Journal of Clinical and Health Psychology, 5*(2), 335–347.

Roopnarine, J. L. & Chadee, D. E. (2016). *Caribbean psychology: Indigenous contributions to a global discipline.* Washington, DC: American Psychological Association.

Sutherland, M. E. (2011). Toward a Caribbean psychology: An African-centered approach. *Journal of Black Studies, 42*(8), 1175–1194. https://doi.org/10 .1177/0021934711410547.

United Nations. (2019). World Population Prospects 2019, Comprehensive Tables. Elaboration of data by United Nations, Department of Economic and Social Affairs, Population Division. Retrieved from https://population .un.org/wpp/Publications/Files/WPP2019_ComprehensiveTablesVol1.pdf.

Ward, T. & Hickling, F. W. (2004). Psychology in the English-speaking Caribbean. *Psychologist-Leicester, 17*(8), 442–444

CHAPTER 18

The History of Psychological Assessment in North America

Janet F. Carlson and Kurt F. Geisinger

18.1 Introduction

This chapter reviews the history of psychological testing in North America,[1] comprising more than 360 million people in Canada and the United States. Socioeconomic indicators suggest that residents of both countries have median per-capita incomes that are comparable to one another and are at least 50% higher than the worldwide median (Phelps & Crabtree, 2013). However, these figures obscure the reality of wide income disparities such that poverty and subsistence living are clearly present. Although English and French are the official languages of Canada, and English is the official language of the United States, hundreds of other languages are spoken within the two countries, as pockets of immigrants from countries across the globe have preserved many features of their home cultures, including languages.

British efforts to colonize North America began in the late sixteenth century, at about the same time that French colonies also appeared, primarily in what became Canada. Western civilization took root on the continent thereafter. Although the chapter authors found no evidence of assessments being used by indigenous tribes that inhabited North America before Europeans arrived, the use of assessments by Native Americans in pre-colonial times remains an open question. What is known about early inhabitants of the continent has been told almost entirely from a Western perspective that sought to instill European habits and values in indigenous peoples, while taking little notice of their culture, traditions, and practices. As Dana (1986) observed, "Native Americans have been treated with

---

[1] The histories of American and Canadian psychology are difficult to disentangle due to their overlap. For example, the American Psychological Association (APA) was founded in 1892 and served both Americans and Canadians. The Canadian Psychological Association (CPA) was not founded until 1938–1939 and both associations provide significant membership discounts to those who belong to both associations.

uncaring ambivalence as a conquered people with an implied demand for renunciation of tribal identities, values, and cultural history" (493). This perspective permeates testing practices, too, as recounted by Darou (1992), who provided numerous case examples of the incongruity between experiential backgrounds of native Canadians and task demands associated with specific intelligence test items. Assessment efforts are duly complicated by the heterogeneity of the continent's native groups, which represent more than 550 tribes and more than 250 languages (Saxton, 2001).

Relatively speaking, the history of psychological testing in North America is brief but dense. Given the similarities in language and culture of Canada and the United States, it is not surprising that many events in the history of psychological testing were shared by the two countries. Progress in academic and professional realms readily crosses the border, helping to sustain a stable and mutually beneficial relationship. The following sections describe milestone events in the shared history of these two countries that marked turning points in the development of instruments and testing practices. Activities by European scholars laid the foundation for further developments in North America. These activities are reviewed first, followed by discussions of events concerning the North American history of intellectual assessment, personality testing, and psychological testing used in employment contexts. Next, major impacts of the history of psychological testing in North American are described to demonstrate how they have helped to shape psychological testing in the larger international sphere.

18.2   Antecedents of Psychological Testing in North America

It is as clear as the so-called fact that Europeans "discovered" the North American continent that American and Canadian psychology has its roots in European psychology. Wundt's laboratory at the University of Leipzig spawned several of the earliest significant impacts on psychological testing in Canada and the United States. James McKeen Cattell was among the Americans who went to Europe to study psychology and earned his doctorate in 1886 having served as Wundt's assistant for some of his graduate student years. After receipt of his doctorate, he traveled to Great Britain where he worked in Galton's Anthropometric Laboratory for two years.

Both Wundt and Galton had great influence on Cattell: Wundt on the use of rigorous, standardized assessment procedures and Galton on the nature of the measures that he studied, which were mostly psychophysical in nature, but were thought to be measures of intelligence. Cattell became North America's first psychology professor at the University of Pennsylvania in 1888 where he established the first psychological laboratory on the continent. His laboratory focused primarily on the development of a battery of measures for general intelligence, at least 50 of them, which "were largely of sensory and motor functions, with related measures of perception, association, and memory beginning to appear ... scoring tended to be in terms of physical units, such as time, distance, pitch, temperature, and force" (DuBois, 1970, 22). Later in his career, Cattell founded the Psychological Corporation, which has probably served as the single most influential psychological testing company in the United States for much of its existence.

At nearly the same time, Alfred Binet had begun working to identify students who were not succeeding in the Parisian public schools. This work led to the development of the Binet–Simon scale in 1908 and the revised version in 1916. This test consisted of 30 subtests, each with items that increased in difficulty and were arranged by years of age. The test included rudimentary norms for children aged 3–11 years. Other scientists at the time were also working on the development of measures of intelligence, mostly with more limited success (Peterson, 1925). Around the same time in North America, Cattell (1890) identified the need for an empirically derived normative database for score interpretation and work by Thorndike (1904, 1920) on educational testing paralleled Binet's work closely.

18.3   Intellectual Assessment

18.3.1   Adaptations of the Binet Scales

A number of psychologists worked on translating the Binet scales into English (e.g., Goddard, 1908; Huey, 1910; Kuhlmann, 1911); however, the single scale that achieved prominence came from Lewis M. Terman at Stanford University in 1910 (Chapman, 1988; DuBois, 1970). Terman had earned his doctoral degree at Clark University in Massachusetts and had begun developing mental tests, aware of the fact that Galton's and Cattell's work had not achieved much success. Although others had translated and adapted versions of the Binet scales, Terman was responsible for making the Binet scale a recognized and accepted professional tool. Terman adapted, revised, and renormed the instrument a number of times (Becker, 2003; Terman, 1916; Terman & Merrill, 1937, 1960). As a result of Terman's research and development efforts, the original Binet–Simon scale eventually become the Stanford–Binet Intelligence Scale and was used widely throughout Canada and the United States.

18.3.2   Performance Scales

Around 1910, a number of American psychologists began work on using performance tasks as part of intelligence scales. Robert S. Woodworth (1910) tested individuals using performance tasks in a study where he collected data at the St. Louis World's Fair to consider racial differences. Howard Andrew Knox (Richardson, 2011) developed, administered, and utilized a number of performance tasks at Ellis Island to make determinations of whether individuals arriving to the United States could enter the country as immigrants. His measures required no language responses. Others developed various form boards in which individuals were timed to see how long it took them to place objects of varying sizes into places where those objects fit. Knox also developed a subtest whereby cubes with different colors on various sides could be arranged to replicate designs presented visually to test takers. Rudolf Pintner and Douglas Paterson (1917) developed the first test completely composed of performance tasks as a measure that did not require language. These measures stood on their own, but were found more useful when combined with tests of complex thinking generally using language, such as the Wechsler tests of intelligence, that appeared decades later.

18.3.3   The Wechsler Scales

Terman (1916) asserted that the Stanford–Binet had no rival in intelligence testing at that time. He was almost certainly correct (Thorndike & Lohman, 1990). However, the Stanford–Binet could not be used effectively with adults as the idea of mental age employed by the Binet tests did not make much sense when interpreting scores obtained by adults. David Wechsler, a staff psychologist at New York City's Bellevue Hospital, asserted that the Stanford–Binet lacked appropriate adult norms, the test materials were not appropriate for adults, and the test over-emphasized speed of performance. He therefore set about building an intelligence test, initially published in 1939 as the Wechsler–Bellevue and later as the Wechsler Adult Intelligence Scale (WAIS) in 1955. Instead of using mental age as a term for the assessment of adult intelligence, Wechsler employed deviation scores, where norms determined the scores assuming an underlying normal distribution of intelligence scores (Wechsler, 1939), a term first suggested by Otis. He set the mean to 100 as per convention, but set the standard deviation to 15, so that approximately 50% of the population would fall between 90 and 110. This method permitted an individual's score to retain its relative position in the distribution as he or she aged. A similarly major distinction from the Stanford–Binet was that Wechsler introduced separate subtests, thus permitting differential interpretations of specific abilities. After studying different intelligence tests for two years,

> [Eleven] tests were identified for inclusion. Five tests – Information, Comprehension, Memory Span for Digits, Similarities, and Arithmetic Reasoning (with Vocabulary as an alternate) – made up the Verbal Scale; Picture Arrangement, Picture Completion, Block Design, Object Assembly, and Digit Symbol composed the Performance Scale. The Verbal Scale and the Performance Scale were combined to yield a Full Scale score. (Thorndike & Lohman, 1990, 81)

The individual subtests were standardized to have means of 10 and standard deviations of 3. Verbal and Performance scales had means of 100 and standard deviations of 15, as did the full-scale intelligence scores. Thus, Wechsler imagined a multifaceted approach to intelligence, with multiple, highly correlated abilities contributing to a generalized intelligence.

The standardization samples of the original Wechsler tests for adults and for children were not geographically representative, as the samples were drawn almost entirely from Wechsler's work at Bellevue Hospital. Even so, the Wechsler tests became dominant over the Stanford–Binet tests as individual intelligence tests over a period of years (e.g., Benson et al., 2019). To this day, tests in the Wechsler series continue to be used widely in the United States, Canada, and other countries, especially in Europe (Elosua & Iliescu, 2012).

During World War I (1914–1918) intelligence testing generated considerable interest. A committee for the examination of recruits included many of the most active psychologists in testing to determine how to sort recruits for their best use in the US military. This group included, for example, Robert Yerkes (an experimental psychologist), Lewis Terman, G. M. Whipple, and Henry Goddard, who was active in the assessment of immigrants as well. DuBois (1970) and Yoakum and Yerkes (1920) provide considerable detail on the committee's activities. Ultimately, and largely because of Terman's presence on the committee, the prior work of one of his former students and later colleague, Arthur Otis, concerning a group test of intelligence, the committee recognized that it would be far more efficient to examine individuals with such a measure. Much of Otis's measure was adapted to become the Army Alpha, a group test of intelligence that could be taken by literate English language speakers. The committee met in May 1917, and in seven days had decided on the nature of the examination, with 10 types of items, and had generated enough items to develop 10 forms of the measure. One form was printed and administered to about 500 inmates, hospital patients, and individuals who had previously taken the Stanford–Binet and to 114 soldiers. It correlated 0.87 with the full Stanford–Binet and 0.81 with an abbreviated Stanford–Binet previously taken by some of the examinees. The test was revised, and several forms printed and studied in August of the same year by E. L. Thorndike, who declared it the best test ever built. During the war, more than 1.7 million recruits completed the Army Alpha. A second test, the Army Beta, was constructed for individuals who were illiterate or who were immigrants who were unable to read the Army Alpha well enough to yield valid scores. The Army Beta was developed using a model created by Pintner and Patterson (1915, 1917) for use with deaf students that included form boards and mazes. By the end of the war, examinations were performed in 35 camps administered by 120 officers and 350 enlisted soldiers, one of whom was Wechsler (DuBois, 1970).

The impact of the seeming success of the Army Alpha during World War I led to a plethora of testing after the war. In schools, group testing of intelligence and school subjects became commonplace. Otis published his intelligence test in 1918. It became common practice to follow an unusual intelligence score obtained on a group measure with the administration of an individual measure so that the examiner administering the test could record observations. The group testing of educational achievement is beyond the scope of this chapter; the testing for admissions to colleges, universities, and other educational opportunities is not, as follows later in this chapter.

18.3.4   *Batteries of Ability Tests*

Thurstone (1931) developed the Centroid method of factor analysis, by which one could determine (with judgment) how many dimensions were needed to explain a correlation matrix showing the relations among a group of tests (or test scores). Essentially, Thurstone demonstrated that factors could explain covariances or relationships among a group of tests. He applied this procedure in a monumental study to identify the structure of intelligence (Thurstone, 1935; 1938). He called the factors comprising intelligence primary mental abilities. The analyses, which could be done in seconds today on any microcomputer, took 20 individual computers (people) approximately six months to compute. Thurstone then developed techniques both for identifying the number of factors found in the factor analysis and for rotating the factors, once the number had been identified. He originated the concept of simple structure and of orthogonal and oblique rotations. He identified 12 primary mental abilities, "seven of which were defined with sufficient clarity for Thurstone to name them" (Thorndike & Lohman, 1990, 72): verbal comprehension, word fluency, number facility, spatial visualization, associative memory, perceptual speed, and reasoning. He then constructed a battery of tests so that each of these factors could be assessed. His work led to the construction of many other batteries of skills, even though there continued to be debate over the existence of such abilities or whether utilizing measures of general intelligence or "g" was the better approach to testing individuals. The development of the General Aptitude Test Battery would be but one example of such a battery.

During World War II, testing in the US military followed the lead of Thurstone in using batteries rather than solely simple intelligence tests such as the Army Alpha. The Army General Classification Test began as an intelligence scale but evolved into a measure of four constructs: arithmetic computation, arithmetic reasoning, reading and vocabulary, and spatial relations. It provided scores for each as well as an overall score (DuBois, 1970). The tests proved to be valid for many uses. The spatial relations test, for example, correlated 0.64 in an unselected sample with the pass/fail criterion in initial training of pilots (Thorndike & Lohman, 1990). The US military has continued testing recruits and has become one of the most advanced testing organizations in the world today, often using advanced computer-based testing batteries.

18.3.5   College Admissions Testing

Developed abilities have now been tested for college admissions for more than 50 years in North America. The College Entrance Examination Board began testing students for admission to mostly the Ivy League of prestigious colleges in the early 1900s and at that time most of the students came from exclusive private high schools. Their entrance examination, known as the "College Boards" was first administered in 1901. Those boards were essentially academic achievement measures and consisted of essay tests on English, French, German, Latin, Greek, history, mathematics, chemistry, and physics. One answered these essay examinations for five eight-hour days. These tests were replaced by a test called the Scholastic Aptitude Test (SAT) that was published by the College Entrance Examination Board. These tests comprised lengthy multiple-choice type examinations in 1926. That test initially consisted of seven verbal subtests (definitions, classification, artificial language, antonyms, analogies, logical inference, and paragraph reading) and two mathematical subtests (number series and arithmetic problems). Early versions of this test were highly speeded with 315 questions administered in 97 minutes. Beginning in 1930, the SAT was divided into two sections: Verbal Aptitude and Quantitative Aptitude (Lawrence et al., 2003). Many changes to the SAT were made over the years in both minor and major revisions (e.g., adding and removing analogies and antonyms). Slowly, the tests changed from being more like intelligence tests (Lemann, 1999) to being more related to the kinds of long-term academic skills learned in school to the extent that the current verbal test is a test of critical reading ability. The length of readings, for example, was extended in order to more closely resemble the types of materials that students might read in college, and the questions related to those selections thoroughly examined a student's ability to discern meaning.

18.4   Personality Testing

The term "personality testing" refers to various forms and methods of assessment – observational measures, self-reports, third-party reports or ratings, and projective (i.e., performance-based) techniques – employed to describe or evaluate emotional, motivational, interpersonal, and attitudinal characteristics and tendencies that remain relatively stable across time and situation. In short, personality testing seeks to provide information about what a person is like rather than his or her capabilities.

In North America, developments in personality testing followed closely on the heels of intellectual/cognitive assessment and many events and trends in personality testing paralleled those seen in cognitive testing. As noted earlier in relation to cognitive testing, ideas and methods that originated in Europe arrived in North America and were developed further by psychologists who had studied these trends under the tutelage of European theorists and scholars. Also of note, most personality measures developed in North America were designed for use with adults. Downward extensions of many of these measures occurred as needs for understanding children's abilities expanded beyond purely cognitive elements.

A commonly drawn distinction among personality tests is whether the test asks respondents to endorse a response from a set of alternatives provided or to produce a response by relying on features of their own personalities. The former tests are described as "objective" measures because responses may be scored and interpreted via objective means such as computer algorithms or, originally, with scoring templates. Results from objective measures may be compared to those from other test takers, as occurs when scores are interpreted using performance standards or norms. Self-report measures are valued as direct measures. However, they are also prone to response distortions, some of which may represent purposeful efforts to achieve a particular outcome (e.g., impression management by providing socially desirable answers). Tests that require respondents to construct responses are termed "performance-based" and scoring tends to be far more subjective compared to objective tests. To some extent, subjectivity of scoring may be mitigated by the adequacy and availability of coding guidelines and rubrics. Performance-based measures are valued as indirect measures that are "more likely than [self-report inventories] to elicit clues to personal characteristics and behavioral tendencies of which individuals are not fully aware or are reluctant to divulge" (Weiner, 2013, 154).

18.4.1   Self-report Measures

Personality testing in North America is barely 100 years old. It began with self-report inventories and later expanded to include performance-based measures (e.g., projective techniques) and observational approaches (e.g., behavior rating scales). The publication of Woodworth's Psychoneurotic Inventory (WPI) in 1920 marked the beginning of personality testing in North America. Shortly after its publication, Papurt (1930) described the measure as a "controlled, objective test for the presence, or lack of, emotional stability" (335). Woodworth's inventory developed out of a practical need that had surfaced a few years earlier during World War I. A number of soldiers experienced psychological symptoms later dubbed "shell shock," typically following their direct and gruesome experiences in battle. Some men suffered from heart palpitations, amnesia, nausea, or uncontrollable weepiness. Emotional instability was believed to be responsible for the appearance of these symptoms. The US military sought a method to identify emotionally unstable individuals whom they believed were prone to demonstrating symptoms of shell shock and to prevent them from serving in the military.

Woodworth worked to develop a measure of emotional stability that would identify enlistees who were unfit for service due to emotional instability. Ultimately, he produced a 116-item scale of psychoneurotic tendencies that was not completed in time to be put to its originally intended purpose. The scale had been developed, piloted, refined, and administered to hundreds of recruits as well as a small number of individuals with psychiatric diagnoses and was on the verge of being tried out as a preliminary screener of new recruits when the war ended.

Woodworth continued his work on the test and adapted it for non-military uses, primarily in industry. The test was renamed the Woodworth Personal Data Sheet (WPDS) and consisted of 75 yes/no items that addressed personal adjustment. In industry, the test was to be used to identify prospective workers whose maladjustment would be likely to cause disruption in the workplace. As with the WPI, examinees could complete the WPDS in 10–15 minutes. Questions answered in a direction judged to indicate maladaptive tendencies were counted. Answering many questions in an unfavorable direction suggested emotional instability. The measure also flagged unfavorable responses to certain items believed to be problematic regardless of the overall pattern of responses. The identification and inclusion of such critical items has become a mainstay of self-report inventories.

Additional unidimensional inventories appeared during the 1920s and 1930s, primarily targeted toward the assessment of personality via a single dimension such as maladjustment, or specific traits such as introversion, extraversion, and neuroticism. Two exceptions deserve mention – the Bernreuter Personality Inventory (BPI) and the Humm–Wadsworth Temperament Scale (HWTS). These inventories used a multidimensional framework to assess personality and results informed treatment efforts or hiring decisions. Both tests gained substantial followings in clinical and human resource contexts and sustained these followings for many years.

Robert Bernreuter developed the BPI while conducting his dissertation at Stanford University under the direction of Terman (Gibby & Zickar, 2008). Its initial publication in 1933 presented 125 yes/no items to evaluate four dimensions of personality – neurotic tendency, self-sufficiency, introversion–extroversion, and dominance–submission. By 1935, the test had been refined to assess six personality traits – the original four plus self-consciousness and solitariness. It was widely applied in vocational assessments, as suggested by a poll of American psychologists who endorsed the BPI as the best-known test from among the 53 other vocational tests included in the survey (Pallister, 1936, as cited in Gibby & Zickar, 2008).

The HWTS appeared in 1934, in response to an incident of workplace violence in which an employee killed his supervisor. The test marked the first effort to build a test that corresponded with a specific theoretical framework, in this case being the theory of personality put forth by Aaron Rosanoff, who identified four abnormal traits that characterize personality – antisocial, autistic, cyclothymic, and epileptic. The HWTS used responses to 165 questions, embedded with 153 filler items, to assess personality on seven dimensions aligned with Rosanoff's theory – normal, hysteroid, manic, depressive, autistic, paranoid, and epileptoid, as well as a response bias scale (Glennon, 1965). In North America today, developers of personality tests routinely build tests with a clear theoretical base and mechanisms to identify response distortions.

Self-report inventories that developed during the first half of the twentieth century focused on negative or maladaptive aspects of personality and their primary application was in industrial settings. Managers in industry believed that worker maladjustment accounted for many workplace problems, such as low morale and low productivity, as well as increased rates of workplace accidents and worker dissatisfaction (Gibby & Zickar, 2008). Business leaders and managers thought it important to root out the malcontents in order to boost productivity and workplace morale. As a result, they embraced tests like the WPDS, BPI, and the HWTS that were objective, structured, relatively brief, and affordable.

18.4.2   Performance-based Techniques

Meanwhile, the development of a much different type of assessment was underway in Europe – the Rorschach Inkblot Test appeared in Switzerland in 1921. In contrast to the objective, structured form of self-report inventories, nearly everything about the Rorschach technique was subjective and unstructured. In the late 1930s, North American clinicians worked extensively with the Rorschach blots to develop systems for scoring and interpreting responses. Among the most notable individuals were Bruno Klopfer, whose system gained and held prominence for several decades thereafter, and John Exner, whose comprehensive scoring system displaced Klopfer's around 1972 (Skadeland, 1986). In many ways, the Rorschach technique represented everything self-report inventories were not. It was, and still is, time-consuming to administer, score, and interpret, factors that contribute to its cost. Further adding to the per-participant cost is the unstructured nature of the task, which requires individual administration. All scoring/interpretive systems involve much subjectivity and evidence regarding reliability and validity has been mixed, at best (Lilienfeld et al., 2000). Nevertheless, the technique developed a substantial following, primarily among psychoanalytically oriented clinicians engaged in the delivery of individual psychotherapy. Its continued popularity among clinical and forensic practitioners has prompted numerous contributions to the professional literature, much of which examined the clinical utility of the technique or delved into the theoretical underpinnings of the method; articles in empirical journals have been rare (Lilienfeld et al., 2000; Meyer & Archer, 2001).

The basic premise of projective techniques invokes the projective hypothesis, which suggests that test takers presented with ambiguous stimuli and asked to organize (disambiguate) them, reveal (project) aspects of their personalities in doing so. According to psychoanalytic theory, the most powerful aspects of one's personality are unconscious and therefore unknown to the individual. Their existence surfaces now and then during unguarded moments, such as when dreaming, when anxiety levels are elevated to the point that anxiety overwhelms efforts to control or defend against it, or when engaged in tasks that penetrate the unconscious such as disambiguating Rorschach stimuli (Lilienfeld et al., 2000).

In addition to the development of some Rorschach-specific scoring and interpretive systems, several other types of projective techniques were developed in North America. For example, Henry Murray developed a storytelling task, the Thematic Apperception Test (TAT; Murray, 1943), which has been highly influential in the realm of personality testing and continues to enjoy widespread use. Butcher (2009) regards the TAT as one of the three major clinical personality assessment instruments of the twentieth century, with the Rorschach technique and the Minnesota Multiphasic Personality Inventory (MMPI) as the other two. Over the years, various efforts have sought to develop reliable scoring and interpretive systems for the TAT, but none have garnered wide acceptance. Instead, many clinicians use the TAT as a tool to generate hypotheses about a test taker's personality that may be helpful in formulating or advancing a clinical treatment plan.

Figure drawing techniques developed originally as nonverbal measures of intellectual ability. Their usage evolved to evaluate personality, especially with regard to emotional adjustment. The Draw-a-Man test was developed by Florence Goodenough who, as another of Terman's associates, helped Terman revise and validate the Stanford–Binet test. Goodenough sought to develop a measure of intelligence to use with young children and believed that children's drawings revealed aspects of how they made sense of their world, an undertaking that rested on intellectual development. In 1926, Goodenough described test administration and scoring, which involved 73 scorable items that emphasized observational accuracy and conceptual thinking more so than artistic ability. Later revisions of the Draw-a-Man test sought to assess personality, with minimal evidence of success. Correspondence of test scores from later revisions of the Draw-a-Man test with those of other intelligence tests vary widely, although the majority of coefficients exceed 0.50 (Abell et al., 2001; Anastasi & Urbina, 1997).

Another figure-drawing task aimed at assessing personality appeared in 1949 as the Draw-a-Person Test (D-A-P; Machover, 1949). In this test, the test giver provides pencil and paper and instructs the test taker simply to "draw a person." Afterwards, instructions to the test taker direct him or her to "draw a person of the opposite sex" or "of a different gender." An inquiry typically follows the production of the drawings, although exact scripts for these queries are scarce. The D-A-P uses qualitative scoring and projective analyses that vary considerably from one clinician to another. Even so, and somewhat surprisingly, the test remains in wide use in North America and elsewhere (Benson et al., 2019; Oakland et al., 2016), at least among school psychologists. Clinicians who use drawing tasks with children may find doing so enhances rapport or facilitates compliance. Children are familiar and usually quite comfortable drawing pictures; one seldom encounters fierce resistance when one asks a child to draw something.

18.4.3   Empirically Keyed Self-reports

The 1943 publication of the MMPI (Hathaway & McKinley, 1943) was a landmark event in the history of psychological testing in North America. The MMPI was born of a practical need to expedite the diagnosis of inpatients at the University of Minnesota Hospitals. Its authors, Starke Hathaway and Charnley McKinley, employed an innovative approach to personality test development in keying the inventory empirically rather than logically. Previous instruments, including the WPDS, used a rational (logical) approach to keying. In empirical (criterion) keying of the MMPI, responses made by participants in the standardization sample were compared to those made by groups of individuals with specific psychiatric diagnoses: hypochondriasis, depression, hysteria, psychopathic deviate, paranoia, psychasthenia, schizophrenia, and hypomania. These eight diagnoses comprised the original clinical scales. The original version of the MMPI also included four validity scales that were built to detect and correct for response biases, primarily false or distorted responses. Within a few years of publication, two additional scales were developed: masculinity/femininity and social introversion. Response patterns that aligned with those made by persons with specific diagnoses indicated personality maladjustments in the same domains.

The MMPI rapidly gained acceptance by clinical practitioners and researchers alike and, although the test fell short of its intended diagnostic application, clinicians continue to find its descriptions of personality features and functioning helpful in their work with individuals and organizations. Elevations on single scales do not connote a specific mental disorder and rarely meet the criterion that makes them worthy of interpretation. Rather, profile interpretation is the norm. This approach considers high scores in relation to all other scores and typically focuses on clear elevations on two or three scales.

By the latter part of the 1950s, the MMPI achieved the status of being the most widely used objective measure of personality and psychopathology (Butcher, 2009). It continues to enjoy favored status among testing professionals (Camara et al., 2000; Elosua & Iliescu, 2012; Wright et al., 2017). The MMPI underwent a substantial revision that culminated in a second edition, published as the MMPI-2 (Butcher et al., 1989). Thereafter, a shorter version of the inventory was offered as the MMPI-2-RF, where RF stands for restructured form (Ben-Porath & Tellegen, 2008). The MMPI and MMPI-2 spawned many other similar inventories, objectively scored, and often heavily researched. These include derivative measures designed for use with adolescents (e.g., Butcher et al., 1992; Archer et al., 2016) and for assessing symptoms associated with specific disorders, such as alcoholism (MacAndrew, 1965) and combat-related post-traumatic stress disorder (Keane et al., 1984). Still other test developers relied upon the MMPI to greater and lesser extents to produce other omnibus personality measures, many of which drew heavily upon the approach or items of the MMPI and the MMPI-2 and, themselves, enjoy wide use in clinical, vocational, and employment contexts.

18.5 Psychological Testing in Employment and Vocational Contexts

Given the brevity of this chapter, the authors focused coverage on developments in intelligence and personality testing. Nevertheless, two objective measures of vocational interests deserve mention, as does the use of psychological tests in the selection of public service personnel.

18.5.1   Assessing Vocational Interests

Edward K. Strong was another of Cattell's doctoral students at Columbia University, graduating in 1911. He subsequently also worked with the Committee on Classification of Personnel in the Army during World War I in 1917, where one of his jobs was to match US soldiers to appropriate positions within the military, and he trained examiners on the Army Alpha and Army Beta. In 1923, he took a position at Stanford University, where he remained for the rest of his career. He developed the Strong Vocational Interest Blank (SVIB; Strong, 1943) in 1927 using the same empirical keying approach as was applied to the MMPI (Hansen, 1987). As a criterion, he used the length of time that people spent in specific careers.

G. Frederick Kuder was a second psychologist to have performed critical work in career interests and choice. "He began his career as an editor for pioneering psychologist James McKeen Cattell's Science Press in New York City" (Hakel, 2000, 273). Using the kind of initially logical and model-based approach to test development rather than empirical keying, Kuder developed a number of career choice inventories, the most famous being the Kuder Preference Record – Vocational, first published in 1938. He later validated the measure using approaches not unlike those used with the SVIB. Both of these measures have been revised and renamed over the course of their existence. Many schoolchildren took one of these vocational interest inventories to help them decide on their vocational paths and pursuits.

18.5.2   Using Psychological Tests in the Selection of Public Servants

Like the US Civil Service Commission, Canada's Public Service Commission (PSC) "is responsible for promoting and safeguarding a merit-based, representative and non-partisan public service that serves all Canadians" (PSC, 2020). Both commissions in the United States and Canada have attempted to assure that positions are filled with competent individuals and not through political patronage. As such, the PSC of Canada recruits and evaluates candidates for non-elected, non-appointive governmental or civil service positions. The PSC has long had a testing program to aid this process. Its testing program offers a relatively full complement of civil service testing from initial screening measures, office skills assessments, and intelligence tests, through leadership assessments, in-basket measures, and executive simulations. All tests are available in both English and French, these being the two official languages of Canada. Historically, most if not all of the tests have been developed first in English and translated into French. In at least some of the cases, the French average scores are somewhat below those in English, very possibly due to translation/adaptation differences. Unique in North America, however, is the role of second language testing in Canada. Individuals who are bilingual French/English are awarded extra points in civil service evaluations due to their enhanced value of being able to speak, understand, write, and read both languages. Traditionally, many more of those who achieve this status are native French speakers. The United States provides no such official credit civil service tests, even though a host of languages are spoken in the country.

The Appointment Policy promulgated by the PSC includes several standards specific to the use of assessments in the hiring process, including the requirement to "obtain the PSC's approval prior to using psychological tests of intelligence, personality, integrity and aptitude tests and tests of mental health" (PSC, 2019). Approval is required for these types of tests, which may be used in an appointment process even though they do not evaluate job-relevant skills. The PSC calls for advance approval in order to ensure tests to be used in this capacity have been developed properly and in accordance with accepted international standards, such as the standards published by the American Psychological Association (APA) and its partner associations. The PSC notes that the Canadian Psychological Association (CPA) endorses these standards and also refers to guidelines developed by the Society for Industrial-Organizational Psychology, a division within APA. The PSC refers to the Standards for the Development and Use of Tests for Appointment Purposes (PSC, 2007) as the federal benchmark for standardized tests.

18.6   Impact of Events in the History of Psychological Testing in North America

Testing continues to be a mainstay of psychological practice in North America (Benson et al., 2019; Camara et al., 2000; Wright et al., 2017). In addition to the development and exportation of several specific tests that have been adopted or adapted in many countries beyond Canada and the United States, several impactful features of psychological testing history in North America are presented in what follows.

18.6.1   Test Evaluation

While a professor at Rutgers University, Oscar Krisen Buros founded the Institute of Mental Measurements and established a process for appraising commercially available tests and disseminating these evaluations. Buros's interest in doing so reflected a growing concern among statisticians and other observers of the burgeoning testing industry that emerged during the early twentieth century. In 1938, he published the first of what would become a series of reference books containing critical reviews of commercial tests. The *Nineteen Thirty Eight Mental Measurements Yearbook* (*MMY*; Buros, 1938) was born during a time when consumer protectionism was on the rise with growing sentiment that commercial products, including psychological and educational tests, must be held accountable for claims made about these products. In the foreword, Buros (1938) expressed his hope that the *MMY* would inform prospective test users and inspire test developers to publish better tests. Subsequently, Buros (1961) developed a second reference series, *Tests in Print* (*TIP*), which listed available measures and provided essential information about these published tests. In 2013, the Buros Center for Testing published *Pruebas Publicadas en Español* (*PPE*; Schlueter et al., 2013), a Spanish equivalent of *TIP*. In the largely continued absence of governmental regulation of testing in North America, the *MMY* (currently in its 21st edition), *TIP* (currently in its 9th edition), and *PPE* (currently in its 2nd edition), continue to serve an important mission that assists prospective test users in making informed test selection decisions and, ideally, inspires test developers to improve their tests.

18.6.2   Development of Standards for Test Development and Use

In 1954, the APA published the *Technical Recommendations for Psychological Tests and Diagnostic Techniques*. The document prescribed procedures to follow in developing psychological tests and testing practices. Revisions to the document followed and other stakeholder organizations joined the effort to establish standards to guide test development and use. The most recent set of testing standards, produced by the American Educational Research Association (AERA), APA, and National Council on Measurement in Education (NCME), appeared in 2014 as the *Standards for Educational and Psychological Testing* (hereafter referred to as the *Standards*; AERA, APA, & NCME, 2014). The *Standards* provide a frame of reference for test development and evaluation as well as criteria "for the development and evaluation of tests and testing practices and ... guidelines for assessing the validity of interpretations of test scores for the intended test uses" (1) and are updated approximately every 15 years. The CPA (2017) also endorses the use of the *Standards*, in lieu of updating standards developed previously for Canada. In addition, various guidelines exist to promote sound practices in specific testing applications, such as disability assessment (Canadian Academy of Psychologists in Disability Assessment, 2004).

18.6.3   Validity

The third important North American contribution to psychological testing worldwide relates to validity in terms of both the (a) incorporation of validity scales in personality tests, and (b) furtherance of the unitary view of validity. Validity scales were introduced with the publication of the MMPI; their inclusion in self-report measures of personality is now routine. "Although preventing the impact of response biases in self-report measures may be an ultimate goal, it is somewhat of a holy grail – an elusive quest that may or may not ever be fully reached" (Helmes et al., 2015, 38). In the interim, ongoing research and methods to mitigate these effects must suffice. Regarding point (b), more and more test authors, developers, and critics appreciate validity as a unitary construct, the evidence for which derives from recognizable sources and applies to the interpretation of test scores rather than the test itself (AERA et al.,, 2014; Cizek et al., 2008).

18.6.4   Test Theory

The development of classical test theory, or observed score theory, was developed by scholars from around the world. However, in the last century there is perhaps one individual, Frederic M. Lord, often referred to as the "father of modern test theory." Lord's volume in conjunction with co-author Melvin Novick (Lord et al., 1968) provides an elegant summary statement of classical psychometric theory, one in which it is hard to imagine a more complete description of this theory. Indeed, that same volume offered an appendix by Allen Birnbaum that many consider to mark the birth of the current test theory most in vogue, item response theory, previously known as latent trait theory. Today, item response theory underlies most large-scale testing programs and makes some of the processes of test delivery and scoring (e.g., test equating, computer-adaptive testing) possible, or at least much easier.

18.6.5   Differences in Testing

Together with what may be regarded as positive contributions in psycho-logical testing, it is important to acknowledge some less admirable features of North America's history. Colonialism has had a long arc in both Canada and the United States, owing to the European invasion of lands populated by indigenous peoples. In addition, slave traders captured and transported individuals from Africa and the Caribbean to the United States in order to advance the wealth and status of white slaveholders.

The savagery of slavery deeply wounded US society and its sequelae became apparent throughout American culture, including psychological testing. The dominance of white men over all other demographic groups accounted for what has been viewed by some as inappropriate testing practices. As recounted earlier, some major psychological tests were normed using non-representative samples comprised primarily or even entirely of whites, yet the tests were intended for use with individuals from all racial, ethnic, and gender groups. Thus, the performance of whites set a standard of performance for everyone else. Developments in psychometrics and in test development practices have helped to identify and remedy resultant differences. For example, differential item functioning (DIF) is useful during test development and for test evaluation purposes. Likewise, bias review panels often are employed to flag items suspected to cause problems for members of different racial, ethnic, or gender groups, so that these items may be sometimes revised or deleted.

Notably, the current edition of the *Standards* (AERA et al., 2014) elevates concerns about test fairness by expanding coverage and identifying fairness as a primary concern for test developers and users. In addition, fairness considerations are codified in several documents that guide psychological practice. For example, in industrial/organizational psychology, test developers work to ensure that hiring or promotion decisions emanating from their tests do not show adverse impact for members of underrepresented groups, as operationalized in the four-fifths rule. To demonstrate absence of adverse impact, US guidelines (Uniform Guidelines on Employee Selection Procedures, 1978) suggest the proportion of minority group members hired (or promoted) normally should equal or exceed 80% of the passing (or promotion) rate of majority group members.

18.7   Conclusion

Canada and the United States were colonized by Europeans around the same time and their histories and cultures evolved along highly similar lines, including their histories of psychological testing. Despite its relative brevity, several momentous events in psychological testing history took place in North America and the influence of tests, test development, and testing practices extends well beyond the continent. For example, Oakland et al. (2016) reported that of the 10 tests used internationally by school psychologists, nine were developed in North America. Likewise, Elosua and Iliescu (2012) reported that eight of the 10 most used psychological tests in Europe originated in North America. Currently, the testing industry flourishes in Canada and the United States. Both countries are home to major test publishers, several of which have offices or headquarters in both locations. These nations are exporting specific tests, test formats, and constructs to the rest of the world through the process of test adaptation and translation. Eminent scholars in both countries contribute to the knowledge base in testing and psychometrics through advancements in theory and practice. Psychologists in North America recognize that much of their work originated elsewhere and many early psychologists received their training from international testing pioneers. Some have been able to capitalize on these experiences and contribute something of value back to the international testing community.

REFERENCES

Abell, S. C., Wood W., & Liebman, S. J. (2001). Children's human figure drawings as measures of intelligence: The comparative validity of three scoring systems. *Journal of Psychoeducational Assessment, 19*(3), 204–215.

AERA, APA, & NCME. (2014). *Standards for educational and psychological testing.* Washington, DC: AERA.

APA. (1954). Technical recommendations for psychological tests and diagnostic techniques. *Psychological Bulletin, 51*(2, Pt.2), 1–38.

Anastasi, A. & Urbina, S. (1997). *Psychological testing* (7th ed.). Upper Saddle River, NJ: Prentice-Hall.

Archer, R. P., Handel, R. W., Ben-Porath, Y. S., & Tellegen, A. (2016). *Minnesota multiphasic personality inventory-adolescents-restructured form (MMPI-A-RF): Manual for administration and scoring.* Minneapolis, MN: University of Minnesota Press.

Becker, K. A. (2003). *History of the Stanford–Binet intelligence scales: Content and psychometrics.* Stanford-Binet Intelligence Scales, Fifth Edition Assessment Service Bulletin No. 1.

Ben-Porath, Y. S. & Tellegen, A. (2008). *Minnesota multiphasic personality inventory-2-restructured form (MMPI-2-RF): Manual for administration and scoring.* Minneapolis, MN: University of Minnesota Press.

Benson, N. F., Floyd, R. G., Kranzler, J. H., Eckert, T. L., Fefer, S. A., & Morgan, G. B. (2019). Test use and assessment practices of school psychologists in the United States: Findings from the 2017 National Survey. *Journal of School Psychology, 72*, 29–48.

Buros, O. K. (ed.). (1938). *The nineteen thirty eight mental measurements yearbook of the School of Education, Rutgers University.* New Brunswick, NJ: Rutgers University Press.

(ed.). (1961). *Tests in print.* Highland Park, NJ: The Gryphon Press.

Butcher, J. N. (2009). Clinical personality assessment: History, evolution, contemporary models, and practical applications. In J. N. Butcher (ed.), *Oxford handbook of personality assessment* (pp. 5–21). New York: Oxford University Press.

Butcher, J. N., Dahlstrom, W. G., Graham, J. R., Tellegen, A., & Kaemmer, B. (1989). *Minnesota multiphasic personality inventory-2 (MMPI-2): Manual for administration and scoring.* Minneapolis, MN: University of Minnesota Press.

Butcher, J. N., Williams, C. L., Graham, J. R., Archer, R., Tellegen, A., Ben-Porath, Y. S., & Kaemmer, B. (1992). *Minnesota multiphasic personality inventory-adolescent (MMPI-A): Manual for administration, scoring, and interpretation.* Minneapolis, MN: University of Minnesota Press.

Camara, W. J., Nathan, J. S., & Puente, A. E. (2000). Psychological test usage: Implications in professional psychology. *Professional Psychology: Research and Practice, 31*(2), 141–154.

Canadian Academy of Psychologists in Disability Assessment. (2004). Practice standards for the psychological assessment of disability and impairment. Retrieved from www.capda.ca.

CPA. (2017, February 1). CPA publications. Retrieved from https://cpa.ca/thecpastore/purchasecpapublications/.

Cattell, J. McK. (1890). Mental tests and measurements. *Mind, 15*(59), 373–381.

Chapman, P. B. (1988). *Schools as sorters: Lewis M. Terman, applied psychology, and the intelligence testing movement, 1890–1917.* New York: New York University Press.

Cizek, G J., Rosenberg, S. L., & Koons, H. H. (2008). Sources of validity evidence for educational and psychological tests. *Educational and Psychological Measurement, 68*(3), 397–412.

Dana, R. H. (1986). Personality assessment and Native Americans. *Journal of Personality Assessment, 50*(3), 480–500.

Darou, W. G. (1992). Native Canadians and intelligence testing. *Canadian Journal of Counselling, 26,* 96-99.

DuBois, P. H. (1970). *A history of psychological testing.* Boston, MA: Allyn & Bacon.

Elosua, P. & Iliescu, D. (2012). Tests in Europe: Where we are and where we should go. *International Journal of Testing, 12*(2), 157–175.

Gibby, R. E. & Zickar, M. J. (2008). A history of the early days of personality testing in American industry: An obsession with adjustment. *History of Psychology, 11*(3), 164–184.

Glennon, J. R. (1965). Test review of the Humm-Wadsworth Temperament Scale. In O. K. Buros (ed.), *The sixth mental measurements yearbook* (pp. 251–252). Highland Park, NJ: The Gryphon Press.

Goddard, H. H. (1908). The Binet and Simon tests of intellectual capacity. *The Training School Bulletin*, *5*(10), 3–9.

Hakel, M. D. (2000). Dr. G. Frederic Kuder 1903–2000. *Personnel Psychology*, *53* (2), 273–274.

Hansen, J. C. (1987). Edward Kellog Strong, Jr.: First author of the strong interest inventory. *Journal of Counseling & Development*, *66*(3), 119–125.

Hathaway, S. R. & McKinley, J. C. (1943). *The Minnesota multiphasic personality inventory*. Minneapolis, MN: University of Minnesota Press.

Helmes, E., Holden, R. R., & Ziegler, M. (2015). Response bias, malingering, and impression management. In G. J. Boyle, D. H. Saklofske, & G. Matthews (eds.), *Measures of personality and social psychological constructs* (pp. 16–43). San Diego, CA: Elsevier.

Huey, E. B. (1910). The Binet scale for measuring intelligence and retardation. *Journal of Educational Psychology*, *1*(8), 435–444.

Keane, T. M., Malloy, P. F., & Fairbank, J. A. (1984). Empirical development of an MMPI subscale for the assessment of combat-related post-traumatic stress disorder. *Journal of Consulting and Clinical Psychology*, *52*(5), 888–891.

Kuhlmann, F. (1911). Binet and Simon's system for measuring the intelligence of children. *Journal of Psycho-Asthenics*, *11*, 79–92.

Lawrence, I. M., Rigol, G. W., Van Essen, T., & Jackson, C. A. (2003). A historical perspective on the content of the SAT. *College Board Research Report No.* 2003-3.

Lemann, N. (1999). *The big test: The secret history of the American meritocracy*. New York: Farrar, Straus & Giroux.

Lilienfeld, S. O., Wood, J. M., & Garb, H. N. (2000). The scientific status of projective techniques. *Psychological Science in the Public Interest*, *1*, 27–66.

Lord, F. M., Novick, M. R., & Birnbaum, A. (1968*). Statistical theories of mental test scores*. Oxford: Addison-Wesley.

MacAndrew, C. (1965). The differentiation of male alcoholic outpatients from non-alcoholic psychiatric outpatients by means of the MMPI. *Quarterly Journal of Studies on Alcohol*, *26*(2), 238–246.

Machover, K. (1949). *Personality projection in the drawing of the human figure: A method of personality investigation*. Springfield, IL: Charles C. Thomas Press.

Meyer, G. J. & Archer, R. P. (2001). The hard science of Rorschach research: What do we know and where do we go? *Psychological Assessment*, *13*(2), 486-502.

Murray, H. A. & the staff of the Harvard Psychological Clinic. (1943). *Thematic apperception test: Manual*. Cambridge, MA: Harvard University Press.

Oakland, T., Douglas, S., & Kane, H. (2016). Top ten standardized tests used internationally with children and youth by school psychologists in 64 countries: A 24-year follow-up study. *Journal of Psychoeducational Assessment*, *34*(2), 166–176.

Papurt, M. (1930). A study of the Woodworth Psychoneurotic Inventory with suggested revision. *Journal of Abnormal and Social Psychology*, *25*(3), 335–352.

Peterson, J. (1925). *Early conceptions and tests of intelligence*. Yonkers, NY: World Book.

Phelps, G. & Crabtree, S. (2013, December 16). Worldwide, median household income about $10,000. Retrieved from https://news.gallup.com/poll/166211/worldwide-median-household-income-000.aspx.

Pintner, R. & Paterson, D. G. (1915). The Binet scale and the deaf child. *Journal of Educational Psychology, 6*(4), 201–210.

Pintner, R., & Paterson, D. G. (1917). *A scale of performance tests*. New York, NY: Appleton.

Public Service Commission of Canada. (2020, June). Public Service Commission. Retrieved from www.canada.ca/en/public-service-commission.html.

(2019, July). Appointment Policy. www.canada.ca/en/public-service-commission/services/appointment-framework/appointment-policy.html.

(2007, September). Standards for the Development and Use of Tests for Appointment Purposes. www.canada.ca/en/public-service-commission/services/public-service-hiring-guides/testing-public-service-canada.html#toc3.

Richardson, J. T. E. (2011). *Howard Andrew Knox: Pioneer of intelligence testing at Ellis Island*. New York: Columbia University Press.

Saxton, J. D. (2001). An introduction to cultural issues relevant to assessment with Native American youth. *The California School Psychologist, 6,* 31–38.

Schlueter, J., Carlson, J. F., Geisinger, K. F., & Murphy, L. L. (eds.). (2013). *Pruebas publicadas en Español [Tests published in Spanish]: An index of Spanish tests in print*. Lincoln, NE: Buros Center for Testing.

Skadeland, D. R. (1986). Bruno Klopfer: A Rorschach pioneer. *Journal of Personality Assessment, 50*(3), 358–361.

Strong, E. K., Jr. (1943). *Vocational interests of men and women*. Palo Alto, CA: Stanford University Press.

Terman, L. M. (1916). *The measurement of intelligence*. Boston, MA: Houghton Mifflin.

Terman, L. M. & Merrill, M. A. (1937). *Revised Stanford–Binet scale*. Boston, MA: Houghton Mifflin.

(1960). *Stanford–Binet intelligence scale: Manual for the third revision, form L-M*. Boston, MA: Houghton Mifflin.

Thorndike, E. L. (1904). *An introduction to the theory of mental and social measurements*. New York: Science Press.

(1920). Intelligence and its use. *Harper's Magazine, 140,* 227–235.

Thorndike, R. M. & Lohman, D. F. (1990). *A century of ability testing*. Chicago, IL: Riverside.

Thurstone, L. L. (1931). Multiple factor analysis. *Psychological Review, 38,* 175–197.

(1935). *The vectors of the mind*. Chicago, IL: University of Chicago Press.

(1938). *Primary mental abilities*. Psychometric monographs, No. 1.

Uniform Guidelines on Employee Selection Procedures. (1978). *Federal Register, 43*(166), 38296-38309.

Wechsler, D. (1939). *The measurement of adult intelligence.* Baltimore, MD: Williams & Wilkins.

Weiner, I. B. (2013). Assessment of personality and psychopathology with performance-based measures. In K. F. Geisinger (ed.), *APA handbook of testing and assessment in psychology: Vol. 2. Testing and assessment in clinical and counseling psychology* (pp. 153–170). Washington, DC: APA.

Woodworth, R. S. (1910). Racial differences in mental traits. *Science, 31*(788), 171–186.

Wright, C. V., Beattie, S. G., Galper, D. I., Sawaqdeh Church, A., Bufka, L. F., Brabender, V. M., & Smith, B. L. (2017). Assessment practices of professional psychologists: Results of a national survey. *Professional Psychology: Research and Practice, 48*(2), 73–78.

Yoakum, C. S. & Yerkes, R. M. (1920). *Army mental tests.* New York: H. Holt.

CHAPTER 19

Looking Back, Moving Forward
Assessment Futures in the Global Village

Sumaya Laher

19.1 Introduction

To move forward, it is necessary to look back and learn from the past. The Akan tribe from Ghana use the Sankofa to represent this wisdom. The Sankofa, as depicted on the front cover, is a mythical bird with its feet firmly planted forward and its head turned backward collecting an egg in its beak, which represents the future. For the Akan, it is this wisdom in learning from the past that ensures a strong future. Hence this diverse collection of histories provides an excellent opportunity to reflect on what a future assessment might look like globally.

Across the regions in this book the themes for the future of assessment were similar. These centered around the need to adapt tests, to incorporate more local or emic assessments as well as the need to use more indigenous knowledge. There was a clear narrative of a lack of training and resources in countries that would typically be described as developing or as low- to middle-income countries. This need was also evident in countries that are relatively developed but engaged with psychological assessment later in their histories in comparison to the United States, Britain, France, and Germany, for example. Typically, countries that were colonized, especially those colonized by Britain, showed more developments in the field of assessment as they had more contact with early developments in the field. Aside from highlighting the core themes, the chapters in this book have provided an excellent opportunity to look globally at what we assess, why we assess, who assesses, and how we assess. In so doing we are presented with a possible blueprint for the way forward for assessment in the global village that will be equally accessible and applicable to all.

I would like to thank Kurt Geisinger, Peter Macqueen, and Ross St. George for their feedback and constructive comments on previous drafts of this chapter.

19.2 What Is Assessment?

It is clear from the chapters in this volume that although there is some evidence of assessment being used in earlier societies, the history of assessment as we know it today or the modern history of assessment as we have referred to it in the book is dominated by the work of early psychologists in Europe namely Wundt and Galton.

Hence the way in which we understand assessment at this moment is dominated by a particular way of understanding science as espoused by the scientists working within modernist assumptions of what science should be.

There is therefore an oft assumption that psychological characteristics are largely universally represented across all groups of people, and that these can be measured using assessments for diagnostic or other decision-making purposes, for example, job selection, university entrance, and so on. The majority of assessments today are rooted in a model that differentiates people for comparative purposes. Such assessments promote the objective measurement of psychological characteristics in a linear way that allows for comparisons between groups or a comparison of an individual to a group to be made easily. Even when assessments do not compare individuals to groups, they are primarily objective, static measures based on theories founded within Euro-American contexts and developed using primarily Western, educated, industrialized, rich, and democratic (WEIRD) samples (Heinrich et al., 2010). The language of most assessments is English, thus excluding a majority of the developing world from an essential psychological service (Laher & Cockcroft, 2017). In fairness, the voice of cross-cultural psychology in particular allowed for a more critical exploration of these assumptions and methods, and the assessment field has evolved toward a more pluralistic understanding of what assessments are and how we use them.

19.3 Why We Assess

It is evident across the chapters particularly in countries where assessment has only started developing around the late twentieth century that the focus is on a particular area of assessment, that is, educational, organizational, or clinical, and so on (see Chapters 3, 14, and 17). These foci are not surprising as the modern history of assessment shows that assessment developed just before the turn of the nineteenth century in a similar way. Binet was commissioned by the French government to find something to identify those children who were not profiting from public education (see Chapter 7). In the United States there was a need to assess individuals to serve in the army among other needs (see Chapter 18). Hence the field of assessment often starts within a particular area but grows to encompass others.

Of note is how these commissioned assessments have been used. Assessments have often been commissioned by some governmental structure seeking direction in a particular field and this approach has been open to abuse. One of the worst examples of such abuse comes from South Africa with its apartheid policies. Psychological assessment provided a pseudo-scientific legitimacy to a system that has oppressed one racial group over another (see Chapter 2). This system of assessment being related to political agendas typically in oppressive regimes is evident from reports in the Eastern European, Central Asian, and United Kingdom chapters (see Chapters 9, 10, and 11). Politics also defines assessments in other ways. El Hasan and Zeinoun (Chapter 5), as well as Zaraen and Tarighat (Chapter 11), speak to the mental health of the population being affected in the region due to political instability. This context necessitated mental health assessments and as such there is a strong focus on adapting and developing clinical instruments.

Assessments have increasingly also become a very profitable enterprise with a number of chapters citing the dominance of a commercial test publishers in countries that limit access to assessment instruments particularly in low- to middle-income countries. Hence assessment is not, as with all fields of knowledge, exempt from agendas linked to power. It is necessary going forward for these to be acknowledged in a transparent manner and discussed within the context of an open science framework.

19.4 Who Assesses?

Adopting more innovative, inclusive methods of assessing also means looking at who can conduct assessments. Test users particularly in countries where assessment is still developing are few in number and training for test users and test developers is lacking. This theme has been consistent across chapters from the developing world. Hence it is necessary that we improve access to resources. In this regard the resources already offered by the International Test Commission (ITC) have been very useful. There are several guideline documents that speak to test use, test translation and adaptation, online testing, and testing in linguistically and culturally diverse populations among others.[1] Iliescu (2017) also provides useful guidance for adapting tests. The most recent online test user training

---

[1] See www.intestcom.org/page/5.

offered by the ITC at a nominal cost provides a more dynamic alternative for training and has the potential to add much value globally.[2] The ITC initiatives and lessons learned from remote working during the COVID-19 pandemic provide opportunities for demonstrating the possibilities of partnerships in the global village either regionally or internationally to improve access to training and resources. These avenues need to be further explored.

A theme across many of the chapters also referred to the legislation or other forms of control over who may administer psychological assessments (or not). In South Africa there is legislation along with guidelines from professional organizations in terms of test administration (Laher & Cockcroft, 2014; Chapter 2). Similar forms of control are evident in Australia (Chapter 15) and in Europe, the European Federation of Psychologists Associations (EFPA) have several documents guiding test use, test user certification, and training.[3] However, it was evident that in a number regions such guidelines still need to be developed (see Chapters 4, 5, 12, 14, and 16).

Many countries have a system of test review in place to also ensure the quality of assessments being used in the country. Among the more prominent systems are the Buros test reviews in the United States (see Chapter 18), the Dutch and German systems (see Chapter 7), the Nordic system (see Chapter 6), and the EFPA test review guidelines.[4] Several countries adopt the ITC guidelines largely through their professional associations but there is a strong need for a more unified and possibly uniform way to enhance knowledge around the proper forms of control (or not) required with psychological assessments.[5]

19.5 What We Assess

The politics of assessment aside, across the chapters one of two positions or a combination of both are advocated for in terms of what is assessed. Hence emic assessments that tap indigenous knowledge are encouraged as the gold standard or in some cases glocal (combination of emic and etic) approaches to assessment have been advocated (see Cheung, 2012; Daouk-Öyry et al., 2016). The difficulty with both these positions is that they undermine the value of knowledge produced in other regions and countries by restricting them with reference to emic or assessments that only

---

[2] See www.itc-learning.net.   [3] See www.efpa.eu/professional-development/assessment.
[4] See http://assessment.efpa.eu/documents-/.   [5] See www.intestcom.org/page/5.

have local utility. Just like the error of assuming that tests developed in the United Kingdom or the United States will have universal applicability, the assumption that emic or glocal approaches have only national or regional applicability must be interrogated. Oftentimes these assessments like the CPAI-2, for example, have not been widely tested in other contexts so there is no evidence to discuss the applicability of such indigenous knowledge in other contexts. The limited studies done on the CPAI-2 demonstrate good reliability and validity outside of Asian contexts (Laher, 2015; Chapter 13).

In terms of what we assess, the need to consider the applicability of knowledges outside of the mainstream is not something new. In assessment, cross-cultural psychologists have advocated for the use of emic measures and indigenous constructs, but the practices adopted in this field have chosen to voice these concerns while still subscribing to the traditional methods of conducting assessments. Hence it is necessary that the methods used for assessment be explored further going forward.

19.6 How We Assess

Galton's work in particular set forward a movement that led ultimately to the field of psychometrics – a discipline focused on the objective measurement of psychological constructs. However, this approach began within a context of Eugenics – essentially a branch of "science" focused on understanding the heritability of human traits with an underlying racist agenda of promoting the idea of the superiority of one group of people over another. As indicated by Bartram (Chapter 9), eugenics was discredited but the by-products of the psychometric science remain in the psychometric concepts we use to evaluate tests today. Methods in assessment strive to be objective, with items subscribing to specific response formats – a characteristic associated with the Zeitgeist of the time. These assessments are typically static, but Bartram also discusses the development of assessment centers in the United Kingdom that provide for more dynamic and contextual assessments of individuals (see Chapter 9).

Typically, we evaluate all forms of assessment in terms of efficacy using the traditional canons of reliability and validity. It needs to be acknowledged that the traditional canons are sound scientific principles and can be used effectively, but there is ample evidence from other disciplines in psychology as well as cognate disciplines that these traditional methods need to be discussed in safe spaces to generate dialog on methods that could be more innovative and inclusive.

An example of using a more innovative and inclusive way of assessing is presented by Laher, Cheung, and Zeinoun (2020) who argue for understanding gender within personality assessment using intersectionality as a framework. They claim that gender is not as simplistic as being male or female and that it can be understood along a continuum. Further, gender needs to be recognized alongside issues of culture, ethnicity, sexual orientation, nationality, and so on as part of the research and practice within the assessment field. They present evidence from within personality assessment research to demonstrate that more flexible and fluid methods are required that can capture the dynamics of the gender construct.

Performance-based assessments are sometimes advocated as fairer in terms of cross-cultural utility due to their open, unstructured format as well as ambiguous stimuli presented. Recent research from Zambia using the Panga Munthu Test, for example, demonstrates that Western forms of performance-based tests can be adapted successfully (see Chapter 2). In Zambia there is a strong focus on developing tests locally making use of easy to access materials. The Panga Munthu Test is one such test that is akin to the Draw-a-Person Test and was developed to tap into skills fostered in rural African settings. The researchers demonstrated that the medium of clay elicits stronger cognitive performance by African children than the media of pencil and paper, or construction blocks. They argue further that performance on the test was not related to intelligence but rather familiarity with the medium. There are a number of other tests that have been developed locally for use with children in Zambia. However, very little research has been conducted on these instruments to determine their applicability and generalizability outside of the Zambian context (see Chapter 2).

Similarly, Kekae-Moletsane (2008) describes Masikitlana, a traditional indigenous South African game in which children use two stones. Players hit the stone with the other stone several times while relating their imagined stories. This was demonstrated to be an effective performance-based technique that requires minimal resources and is familiar to children nationally. Children play similar games regionally as well. These ways of assessing offer opportunities for being more innovative and inclusive in the assessment space with methods that can be transported and tested in other countries and regions.

19.7 Going Digital in the Global Village – A Solution?

Going digital has often been cited as a means of resolving the access and inclusion challenges. It is interesting that it was only the European, North

American, and Oceania chapters that alluded to technology-based or online assessments. It is possible that other chapters may not have had much space once the history was written to reflect on future developments in this regard.

As is evident from these chapters, assessment has had no difficulty in transitioning to the online space and a number of tests developed internationally are online, but these are expensive and not readily available for use in middle- to low-income countries. Costs aside, there is a bigger question around whether assessment, which is quite dependent on face-to-face interaction, can be done efficaciously online (Chapter 10; Scott et al., 2017).

COVID-19 and the unprecedented rise in the use of technology for communication across spaces has compelled us to think of assessments more creatively in the digital space beyond what is already available. Organizations like the American Psychological Association (APA), British Psychological Society (BPS), EFPA, and the Psychological Society of South Africa among others have communicated guidelines for online assessment over and above what was available already. These were developed quickly in response to the context of the pandemic, but more research needs to be conducted. A number of practitioners are conducting assessments online but there is still much to explore in terms of the ethics of violating test materials, protecting the client from harm, and communicating test results to name just a few.

Despite the concerns, the online space can be used effectively. For example, researchers in South Africa have adapted an open-access depression screening tool for the South African context, and it is presently being tested for its efficacy as an easy to access online tool that can be used by anyone in the country.[6] The use of online tools like this works from the premise that going digital will solve numerous issues, from the lack of resources and personnel through to improved access and inclusion for the many marginalized groups in the country. This kind of innovation has much to offer toward creating a more inclusive discipline that is relevant, responsive, and impactful. However, the ethical concerns of assessing mental health without a professional also need to be considered as well as the implications for the field when the fundamental principles of assessment are changing along with enhancements in technology (see Iliescu & Grieff, 2019).

Technology also offers quick solutions to issues like literacy and language proficiency. Technology can, for example, aid with translation.

---

[6] See www.mddsa.co.za.

Websites can be translated fairly easily, quickly, and generally accurately as can be seen with something like Google Translate. Similarly, tests can also be easily translated. On the other hand, it is very clear that merely translating verbatim does not take into account cultural nuances nor does it necessarily reflect accurate translation in the same way that traditional forward and back translation techniques do. The online environment is also a standard interface offering possibilities for more culturally fair assessment or better control of response biases. However, not all countries have the resources (i.e., skills and equipment) to undertake online assessment initiatives. As yet, the actual costs as well as the moral and legal costs associated with this shift to online environments are unclear (Laher, 2020).

Going digital and online with assessment also means engaging with the fourth industrial revolution (4IR; Schwab, 2016) with its focus on enhanced technologies.

19.8   Assessment and the 4IR

The 4IR context we find ourselves in, as well as the accelerated use of technology precipitated by the pandemic, suggests that – the digital divide aside – assessment will probably need to embrace technology to progress. Among the 4IR technologies to consider are big data, augmented and virtual reality, and artificial intelligence.

Examples of potential big data in assessment could include the examination of country prevalence data from hospital records and predicting depression from Twitter feeds. Facebook messages or WhatsApp texts can be analyzed for individual statuses or per age group, gender, and so on. Already international studies have used the Five-Factor Model personality traits with big data from social sites like Facebook and Instagram to attempt to predict personality (see Harris & Bardey, 2019; Harlow & Oswald, 2016; Kosinski et al., 2015). However, the use of pre-existing data not necessarily collected for assessment purposes, whether this type of data can effectively be used for validation or norming, the reliability, criterion and predictive validity of such information, and the ethics of using this type of data are among the myriad issues that still need to be explored within this space (Iliescu & Grieff, 2019; Laher, 2020; Scott et al., 2017).

The accuracy of algorithms in predicting personality highlights the role that artificial intelligence can play (or not) in aiding assessment. The Kosinski et al. (2015) project used people's digital information to predict personality over 100 times more accurately than their friends, family, or spouses were able to. However, like the use of big data, the jury is still out on algorithms predicting personality. Algorithms that can predict so accurately have much to offer assessment in terms of tailoring assessments for individuals with minimal resource requirements. Using such a priori information makes dynamic assessment much easier, but algorithms are not as innocuous as they seem. The focus on neural networks and deep learning, for example, offers opportunities for self-assessments of mood or mental status by developing apps to monitor movement or other physical characteristics and use these to make exceptionally accurate predictions of behavior – but these raise ethical concerns around the invasion of privacy, data security, potential for harm, and so on (Iliescu & Grieff, 2019; Laher, 2020; MacQueen, 2019).

Augmented reality and virtual reality also may hold much promise for assessment in terms of getting people to simulate ways of relating and problem solving. Among this technology is the recent move toward gamification in assessment. Gamification involves adding game elements to assessments with the belief that this will increase their attractiveness and ease of use, thereby increasing the engagement and motivation of the individuals completing the assessment. Empirical evidence suggests that gamification enhances performance on tasks, and it does this by providing points, badges, leaderboards, levels, challenges, rewards, and so on. Gamified and game-based assessments offer opportunities for increased engagement, enjoyability, and motivation. They have less anxiety, faking, or social desirability associated with them, more ecological validity, better standardization in terms of administration, and less dependence on verbal input. Technology also reduces costs, but more research is needed on its reliability and validity. This type of assessment requires a certain amount of technological literacy, has the possibility of inducing computer anxiety, and may be biased in favor of those more familiar with technology. Also, human interaction is limited and hence very little observation of an individual's behavior during assessment can happen. At the same time, the individual has no one to guide them or hold the anxiety. The ethics are not clear and cybersecurity of data also needs to be considered (Akoodie, 2020; Laher, 2020; Macqueen, 2019; Scott et al., 2017).

As is evident, psychological assessment will very much be needed in all fields in the 4IR and beyond. There is the possibility of needing to assess new constructs and creating assessments for these as the world evolves. Current models will no doubt have to change to meet the technological context and the possibility exists that psychological assessment may become obsolete if it does not evolve (Iliescu & Grieff, 2019).

While parts of the world continue to move forward in the 4IR, other parts most notably in the developing world experience challenges. The digital divide still exists. The majority of people in middle- to low-income countries may own a phone and have access to the internet but is gamified assessment, for example, not still catering for the WEIRD. A class of South African postgraduate students who are proficient in English, are reasonably acculturated, and technologically accomplished struggled with a gamified test – what about the ordinary person with just a smartphone and little experience of gaming. Further, typical online test instructions explicitly instruct one to complete the test using a device and mouse but in low- and middle-income countries the majority of the population do not have access to such items. In developing contexts in particular where inequality is already high we need to be very aware that these technological advances while promising much can bypass many in society. Hence while the evolution in technology-based assessments offers opportunities for access and inclusion, it has the potential to exclude many. It is necessary that this be addressed at the onset of any discussion on the inclusive nature of technology-based assessments.

19.9 Transcending Disciplinary Boundaries

The discussion thus far has provided some direction for advancing the assessment discipline in the twenty-first century, but these have been limited to within the boundaries of psychology. The fluid and ever-changing context indicates that disciplinary boundaries are no longer rigid and interdisciplinary research and knowledge is increasingly critical. The evolution of careers such as the biomedical engineer, life coach, or behavioral economist indicates that, to remain relevant and responsive, psychological assessment will have to be able to demonstrate its value in other disciplines. Flexibility and a willingness to collaborate to find innovative solutions are increasingly becoming necessary (Laher, 2020).

If we look at developments beyond the 4IR, the fifth industrial revolution (5IR) is being touted as one that will promote the use of technologies for inclusivity and enhancing relationships (Gauri & Van Eerden, 2019). The Kondratieff waves – something often cited alongside the 4IR – suggests that we are moving into an era where health, well-being, and relationships are going to occupy a place alongside technology, innovation, and science.[7]

To fully realize the potential of assessment in such contexts, we need to look at the sustainable development goals, for example, and see how what we do in assessment can aid solutions toward achieving these worldwide

---

[7] See www.kondratieff.net/kondratieffcycles.

goals. Oftentimes it is argued that the largest contributions made by psychologists and assessment specialists are in the health sphere or with occupational or educational assessments. However, it is necessary for the discipline to evolve and export its skills to contribute in other spaces transcending disciplinary boundaries. We should be able to transfer our skills to projects working with measures or interventions for climate change or food security, for example. Other disciplines like engineering can benefit strongly from the rigorous methods used to develop instruments in psychology. Cross- and trans-disciplinary teams are the order of the day and social scientists have much to contribute to these collaborations – who better to understand context, inclusion, and indigenization than the psychologist and assessment practitioner.

19.10   Conclusion

As is evident from the book and this chapter, psychological assessment has a prominent role to play in the global village now and in the future. In order to fully realize its potential, the historical roots of modern-day assessment must be understood as a means toward developing a discipline that is more accessible and inclusive. This chapter argues that, in order to do this, it is necessary to consider what we assess, why we assess, who assesses, and how we assess with a critical eye. The chapter has provided several recommendations for an agenda for psychological assessment going forward, but these are only a few of myriad possibilities. It is the wish of the authors and editors of this book that we have inspired readers to examine their work to develop an agenda going forward that will contribute to being relevant and responsive to both the assessment discipline and society. Further, in the interests of open science and the need to share resources, assessment professionals should look to disseminating their innovations and results widely. Dissemination must extend beyond just the journals and universities and must be shared with communities if assessment is to continue and grow as a discipline. Such work must happen within countries and cultures, and it must also happen internationally. The world is shrinking, and we must redouble our efforts to build bridges and not walls.

REFERENCES

Akoodie, Y. (2020). Gamification in psychological assessment in South Africa: A narrative review. *African Journal of Psychological Assessment*, 2(0), a24. https://doi.org/10.4102/ajopa.v2i0.24.
Cheung, F. M. (2012). Mainstreaming culture in psychology. *American Psychologist*, 67(8), 721–730.

Daouk-Öyry, L., Zeinoun, P., Choueiri, L., & van de Vijver, F. (2016). Integrating global and local perspectives in psycholexical studies: A GloCal approach. *Journal of Research in Personality*, *62*, 19–28, https://doi.org/10 .1016/j.jrp.2016.02.008.

Gauri, P. & Van Eerden, J. (2019). *What the fifth industrial revolution is and why it matters*. Retrieved from https://europeansting.com/2019/05/16/what-the-fifth-industrial-revolution-is-and-why-it-matters/.

Harlow, L. L. & Oswald, F. L. (2016). Big data in psychology: Introduction to the special issue. *Psychological Methods*, *21*(4), 447–457. http://dx.doi.org/10 .1037/met0000120

Harris, E. & Bardey, A. C. (2019) Do Instagram profiles accurately portray personality? An investigation into idealized online self-presentation. *Frontiers in Psychology*, *10*, 871. http://dx.doi.org/10.3389/fpsyg.2019 .00871.

Henrich, J., Heine, S. J., & Norenzayan, A. (2010). The weirdest people in the world? *Behavioral and Brain Sciences*, *33*(2–3), 61–83. http://dx.doi.org/10 .1017/S0140525X0999152X.

Iliescu, D. (2017). *Adapting tests in linguistic and cultural situations*. Cambridge: Cambridge University Press. http://dx.doi.org/10.1017/9781316273203.

Iliescu, D. & Grieff, S. (2019). The impact of technology on psychological testing in practice and policy: What will the future bring. *European Journal of Psychological Assessment*, *35*(2), 151–155. https://doi.org/10.1027/1015-5759/a000532.

Kekae-Moletsane, M. (2008). Masekitlana: South African traditional play as a therapeutic tool in child psychotherapy. *South African Journal of Psychology*, *38*(2), 367–375. https://doi.org/10.1177/008124630803800208.

Kosinski, M., Matz, S. C., Gosling, S. D., Popov, V., & Stillwell, D. (2015). Facebook as a research tool for the social sciences: Opportunities, challenges, ethical considerations, and practical guidelines. *American Psychologist*, *70*, 543–56. https://doi.org/10.1037/a0039210.

Laher, S. (2020). *The 4I=R² framework: Advancing an agenda for psychological assessment in South Africa*. Inaugural address presented at the University of the Witwatersrand, Johannesburg, South Africa. Retrieved from: www .youtube.com/watch?v=7_E_f3Ookt8&feature=youtu.be.

(2015). Exploring the utility of the CPAI-2 in a South African sample: Implications for the FFM. *Personality and Individual Differences*, *81*, 61–75.

Laher, S., Cheung, F. & Zeinoun, P. (2020). Gender and personality research in Psychology: The need for intersectionality. In Cheung, F. & Halpern, D. (eds). *The Cambridge international handbook on psychology of women*. Cambridge: Cambridge University Press.

Laher, S. & Cockcroft, K. (2017). Moving from culturally biased to culturally responsive assessment practices in low resource, multicultural settings. *Professional Psychology: Research and Practice*, *48*(2), 115–121.

(2014). Psychological assessment in post-apartheid South Africa: the way forward. *South African Journal of Psychology*, *44*(3), 303–314.

Macqueen, P. (2019). Artificial Intelligence. *InPsych*. Retrieved from www
.compassconsulting.com.au/page/News_Articles/White_Papers/, accessed
17 January 2021.

Schwab, K. (2016). *The fourth industrial revolution: What it means and how to
respond.* Retrieved from www.weforum.org/agenda/2016/01/the-fourth-
industrial-revolution-what-it-means-and-how-to-respond/.

Scott, J. C., Bartram, D. & Reynolds, D. H. (2017). *Next generation technology-
enhanced assessment: Global perspectives on occupational and workplace testing.*
Cambridge: Cambridge University Press.

Index